4/28

WITHDRAWN
UTSA LIBRARIES

P9-DTS-109

CLINICAL DISORDERS AND STRESSFUL LIFE EVENTS

International Universities Press
Stress and Health Series

Edited by
Leo Goldberger, Ph.D.

Monograph 7

Clinical Disorders and Stressful Life Events

edited by

Thomas W. Miller, Ph.D.

International Universities Press, Inc.
Madison   Connecticut

Copyright © 1997, International Universities Press, Inc.

INTERNATIONAL UNIVERSITIES PRESS, and IUP (& design) ® are registered trademarks of International Universities Press, Inc.

Library of Congress Cataloging-in-Publication Data

Clinical disorders and stressful life events / edited by Thomas W.
   Miller.
      p.   cm. — (International Universities Press stress and health
   series ; monograph 7)
   Includes bibliographical references and index.
   ISBN 0-8236-0910-3
   1. Life change events—Psychological aspects.   2. Post-traumatic
stress disorder.   3. Psychic trauma.   4. Stress (Psychology)
5. Psychoneuroimmunology.   I. Miller, Thomas W., 1943-
II. Series: Stress and health series ; monograph 7.
   [DNLM: 1. Stress Disorders, Post-Traumatic.   2. Mental Disorders.
3. Life Change Events.   W1 ST799K monograph 7 1997 / WM 170 C641
1997]
RC455.4.L53C55   1997
616.85'21—dc21
DNLM/DLC
for Library of Congress   96-39360
                                                                                  CIP

Manufactured in the United States of America

This book is dedicated to all of humankind who have experienced the trauma of stressful life events and who have come to know, understand, and adapt to the normative and catastrophic transitions that we encounter in our lives. And it is to my wife, my children, and my family that I dedicate this compendium of clinical theory, practice, and research on stressful life events.

Contents

PART V: TREATMENT AND FUTURE CONSIDERATIONS

Contributors

Dalia M. Adams, M.A., Research Associate, Department of Psychology, Case Western Reserve University, Cleveland, Ohio.

Metin Başoğlu, M.D., Ph.D., Hon. Senior Lecturer in Psychiatry, Institute of Psychiatry, University of London, London, England; Director Istanbul Center for Behavior Research and Therapy, Istanbul, Turkey.

Paul Bebbington, M.A., Ph.D., F.R.C.P., F.R.C.Psych., Reader, MRC Social and Community Psychiatry Unit, Institute of Psychiatry, Decrespigny Park, London, England.

James K. Boehnlein, M.D., M.Sc., Associate Professor, Department of Psychiatry, Oregon Health Sciences University, Portland.

Raymond Bossé, Ph.D., Professor, Normative Aging Study, Department of Veterans Affairs, Outpatient Clinic, Boston, Massachusetts, and Hellenic College, Brookline, Massachusetts.

Patrick A. Boudewyns, Ph.D., Chief, Psychology Service, Augusta VA Medical Center, Georgia, and Professor of Psychiatry, Medical College of Georgia, Augusta.

Jo Bowen, M.B., B.S., M.R.C.Psych., Senior Registrar, Department of Psychiatry, Chelsea and Westminster Hospital, University of London, London, England.

Shirley Brown, Ph.D., Professor, Department of Psychiatry, University of California at Los Angeles.

Zack Zdenek Cernovsky, Ph.D., Assistant Professor, Department of Psychiatry, St. Thomas Psychiatric Hospital, The University of Western Ontario, St. Thomas, Ontario, Canada.

Sheldon Cohen, Ph.D., Professor, Department of Psychology, Carnegie Mellon University, Pittsburgh, Pennsylvania.

Raina E. Eberly, Ph.D., U.S. Department of Veterans Affairs Medical Center, Minneapolis, Minnesota, and Clinical Associate

xii   CONTRIBUTORS

Professor, Department of Psychology, University of Minnesota, Minneapolis.

Brian E. Engdahl, Ph.D., Clinical Associate Professor, U.S. Department of Veterans Affairs Medical Center and Department of Psychology, University of Minnesota, Minneapolis.

Carlo Faravelli, M.D., Department of Neurology and Psychiatry, Instituto Malattie Nervose, Florence, Italy.

Thomas F. Garrity, Ph.D., Professor and Chair, Department of Behavioral Science, College of Medicine, University of Kentucky, Lexington.

Goldine C. Gleser, Ph.D., Professor Emeritus, Department of Psychiatry, University of Cincinnati, Cincinnati, Ohio.

Mary C. Grace, M.S., Senior Research Associate, Department of Psychiatry, University of Cincinnati, Cincinnati, Ohio.

Bonnie L. Green, Ph.D., Professor, Department of Psychiatry, College of Medicine, Georgetown University, Washington, DC.

Laurie L. Humphries, M.D., Professor, Eating Disorders Program, Department of Psychiatry, University of Kentucky.

Leon A. Hyer, Ed.D., A.B.P.P., Clinical Psychologist, Augusta VA Medical Center, and Associate Professor of Psychiatry, Medical College of Georgia, Augusta.

Bryan M. Johnstone, Ph.D., Assistant Professor, Department of Behavioral Science, College of Medicine, University of Kentucky, Lexington.

Peter V. Kamenchenko, M.D., Director, Research Division, Department of Organizational Psychiatric Services, National Mental Health Research Center, Moscow, Russia.

J. David Kinzie, M.D., Professor, Department of Psychiatry, Oregon Health Sciences University, Portland.

Darlene S. Klein, Ph.D., Clinical Psychologist, Augusta VA Medical Center, and Clinical Assistant Professor of Psychiatry, Medical College of Georgia, Augusta.

Teresa L. Kramer, Ph.D., Assistant Professor of Clinical Psychiatry, Department of Psychiatry, University of Cincinnati, Cincinnati, Ohio.

Anthony C. Leonard, B.A., Department of Biostatistics, University of Cincinnati, Cincinnati, Ohio.

Michael R. Levenson, Ph.D., Professor, Department of Human Development and Family Studies, University of California, Davis.

Jacob D. Lindy, M.D., Associate Professor of Clinical Psychiatry, Department of Psychiatry, University of Cincinnati, and Director of Research, Cincinnati Psychoanalytic Institute, Cincinnati, Ohio.

Richard J. McNally, Ph.D., Associate Professor, Department of Psychology, Harvard University, Cambridge, Massachusetts.

Charles W. Nichols, Ph.D., Clinical Psychologist, Augusta VA Medical Center, and Clinical Assistant Professor of Psychiatry, Medical College of Georgia, Augusta.

Ann O'Leary, Ph.D., Associate Professor, Department of Psychology, Rutgers University, New Brunswick, New Jersey.

James C. Overholser, Ph.D., Professor, Department of Psychology, Case Western Reserve University, Cleveland, Ohio.

Sabrina Paterniti, M.D., Department of Psychiatry and Neurology, University of Florence, Florence, Italy.

Rajini Ramana, M.D., B.S., M.R.C.Psych., Consultant Psychiatrist, Fulbourn Hospital, Cambridge, England.

Paola Servi, M.D., Department of Psychiatry and Neurology, University of Florence, Florence, Italy.

Andrew P. Smith, Ph.D., Professor, Department of Psychology, University of Bristol, United Kingdom.

Edwin V. Sperr, Ph.D., Clinical Psychologist, Augusta VA Medical Center, and Assistant Professor of Psychiatry, Medical College of Georgia, Augusta.

Avron Spiro III, Ph.D., Research Health Scientist, Normative Aging Study, Department of Veterans Affairs, Outpatient Clinic, Boston, Massachusetts, and Assistant Professor, School of Public Health, Boston University, Boston, Massachusetts.

Mariana Suarez-Al-Adam, M.S., Research Associate, Department of Psychology, Rutgers University, New Brunswick, New Jersey.

Robert Straus, Ph.D., Emeritus Professor, Department of Behavioral Science, College of Medicine, University of Kentucky, Lexington.

A. S. Tiganov, M.D., Senior Professor, National Mental Health Research Center, Moscow, Russia.

David A. J. Tyrrell, M.D., Public Health Laboratory Service, Centre for Applied Microbiology and Research, Salisbury, England.

Marshall G. Vary, M.D., Director of Education and Research, Harding Hospital, Worthington, Ohio.

V. S. Yastrebov, M.D., Director, National Mental Health Research Center, Moscow, Russia.

Preface

This volume, *Clinical Disorders and Stressful Life Events,* is designed to inform and update the theoretician, clinician, and researcher on the latest information related to our understanding stressful life events and their impact on our lives. Theoretical formulations and hypotheses, issues, and implications related to the validity and reliability of life stress measurement and its applications to both medical and mental-health-related concerns are addressed here. Furthermore, attention is given to the individual and how that individual functions within various life settings. This book views the person as both producer of stress and reactor to stress and attempts to identify a variety of sources of stressful life experiences from within and beyond the individual's life space.

The chapters herein are directed toward the myriad of health care theoreticians, practitioners, and researchers and attempt to gather a representative sample of the authorities in each of the areas covered. Many of the individuals have pioneered extremely fruitful clinical research, and their understanding of certain ethnogenic mainstream concepts has become important in defining, analyzing, and treating stress-related disorders. There are several rich perspectives that effectively integrate the variety of generalizations about functional and dysfunctional aspects of stress.

Life-event research has become a focus of our understanding of the relationship between psychological stress and physical illness. Our purpose is to examine and summarize clinical and research evidence addressing the assessment of stressful life events, prominent measures utilized, and various issues and implications for both clinical and research application. A perspective on critical directions that might yet emerge in this significant arena of study is offered.

Traumatic experience can create anxiety, stress, and tension sufficient to impact severely on one's psychological well-being.

Identification and measurement of such stressful life events have gained considerable clinical and research interest. The medical and health-related professions have, over the past decade, begun to scrutinize the role and function of stressful life events as a contributing factor to physical illness. Examined herein are prominent theoretical and applied considerations, assessment, and methodological issues, life stress within the components of physical and behavioral medicine, life events and their impact on individuals with psychiatric disorders, and stressful life events throughout the life span.

The health profession has endeavored to address the importance of stress in life events through its inclusion of evidence as to the occurrence and severity of recent stressful life events in the *Diagnostic and Statistical Manual of Mental Disorders* (DSM). Basic to our understanding of the effects of stressful life events on health is considering illness and adaptation throughout the life span. The contributions to the first edition of *Stressful Life Events* laid the groundwork for these completely revised and updated volumes that contribute significantly to our understanding of life stress.

Introduction

Thomas W. Miller, Ph.D., A.B.P.P.

Critical issues in theory and assessment were examined in the previous volume, *Theory and Assessment of Stressful Life Events*. Since then, a growing body of information and clinical findings have expanded our theoretical understanding of the traumatization caused by stress from both a psychological context and a biopsychosocial model.

The chapters assembled in this volume, *Clinical Disorders and Stressful Life Events*, focus on the impact of psychotraumatization from the trauma itself to the symptomatology that results. Emerging is a dose–effect relationship in which the risk of developing posttraumatic stress disorder (PTSD) increases with the intensity and duration of the trauma. Examined is the interest in interactions between the central nervous system and the immune system. There is an overview of studies that investigates the psychoneuroimmunological aspects of stress. The emerging work is at the cutting edge of preclinical models that address such concepts as behavioral sensitization and electrophysiological kindling.

Adaptation to trauma is the continued focus of clinicians and researchers. A rapidly evolving science examines the multidirectional influence of life stress events and their impact on human functioning. A review of various theoretical models of stress adaptation, the impact of stress, health and the interrelationship with the immunological system, are examined. Furthermore, the focus of psychological hardiness as a critical factor in moderating the impact of traumatization on psychological or physical illness is explored within the context of a stress buffer that may help to explain why some individuals accommodate stress more effectively than others.

A conceptual overview of assessment within the construct of traumatization caused by stress reviewed both theoretical and applied concepts important to the assessment process. Current measures used in the assessment of stressful life events, and recommendations for further study are examined, as are psychophysiological measures, structured clinical interviews, and the potential for biochemical means of assessment. Chapters addressing civilian trauma, rape, torture, and refugee trauma offer the reader an opportunity to examine the unique field of study that is concerned with the impact of traumatic experiences on civilians. Finally, a quick response disaster study sampling methods and practical issues in trauma research is explored. Innovative methodological techniques for researchers conducting prospective studies are reviewed, with emphasis on the specifics to be considered in choosing a particular disaster event for study, the time of interviews, the advantages of making more than one assessment over time, access to subjects, the selection of a comparison group, and practical matters important to disaster research.

As we move into diagnosis and treatment related to stressful life events, questions emerge for further exploration: (1) How do humans process trauma? (2) Are there ethnocultural variants related to stressful life events? (3) Which treatment models are most helpful for traumatized persons? and (4) What research is needed in the 1990s to aid clinicians in their work?

OVERVIEW

Brian Engdahl, Ph.D., and Raina Eberly, Ph.D., examine the course of posttraumatic stress disorder in the first chapter of this volume. The authors present a summary of several theories of traumatic stress disorder, noting the implications for the development and course of PTSD symptoms. In gaining an understanding of the diagnostic implications of posttraumatic stress disorder, careful examination is offered by the authors of both anxiety disorders and depressive disorders within the context of the PTSD spectrum. Longitudinal studies are also considered in an effort to understand the implications of the course of chronic posttraumatic stress disorder.

Cultural perspectives on traumatization and stress are examined by Drs. James Boehnlein and J. David Kinzie, of the Oregon Health Sciences University. Reviewed are a brief cross-cultural history of traumatic stress syndromes, cultural aspects of PTSD, sociocultural studies of veteran populations, and cross-cultural studies among nonrefugee civilian populations. The authors also look at current controversies and future directions in studying traumatization and stressful life events from a cross-cultural perspective.

Metin Başoğlu, M.D., Ph.D., of the Institute of Psychiatry, University of London, addresses the impact of torture as a stressful life event and studies the consequences of torture by delineating the psychological effects and addressing the issue of whether a torture-specific syndrome exists. Also addressed are the assessment of the survivors of torture and treatment implications for survivors of torture experiences.

Traumatization of refugees is the focus of Professor Zack Cernovsky, of the St. Thomas Psychiatric Hospital, St. Thomas, Ontario, Canada. Addressed in this chapter are three important studies that consider core symptoms related to traumatization and stress in refugee victims. Its implications for refugees of Europe, Asia, the Americas, and Africa give keen insights to the impact of stressful life events associated with this population.

Professors Paul Bebbington, Jo Bowen, and Rajini Ramana, of the Social and Community Psychiatry Unit of the Institute of Psychiatry, University of London, Chelsea and Westminster Hospital, and the University of Cambridge, address the impact of life events on individuals and subsequent psychotic disorders. A review of the studies of life events and schizophrenia, together with three recent studies that address psychotic disorders and event specificity, make this chapter a unique contribution to our knowledge base in examining the psychotic components involved in victims' response to the traumatization process.

Stressful life events and the social support process in depressed psychiatric patients are examined by Professors James Overholser and Dalia Adams, of Case Western Reserve University. Clinical research, provided by the authors, suggests that among depressed psychiatric inpatients, stressful events and the availability of social support exert direct effects on the psychological, social, and personality functioning of the victims. The authors conclude that life stress is an important ingredient in understanding the etiology of clinical depression, and they encourage stress researchers to focus on a broader picture in which stress is assessed in relation to the social functioning and personality of the individual.

Within the construct of understanding anxiety disorders through the *Diagnostic and Statistical Manual of Mental Disorders* of the American Psychiatric Association, Fourth Edition, Professors Carlo Faravelli, Sabrina Paterniti, and Paola Servi, of the Department of Psychiatry and Neurology, University of Florence, Italy, examine the correlates of stressful life events and panic disorder. Life events as predisposing factors to panic disorder and the relationship between recent stressful life events and the onset of panic disorder are discussed. Causality is considered, as is the specificity of events, in aiding the clinician in understanding the course and vulnerability factors associated with the impact of stressful life events on health.

In the following chapter, Professor Richard McNally, of Harvard University, asks the question: Can panic attacks produce post-traumatic stress disorder? The author argues that an objective definition of what constitutes a traumatic stressor ought to be retained in DSM-IV criteria for PTSD and argues that convictions of impending catastrophe do not necessarily precede even the worst attacks of those with panic disorder. This is to say that during their most recent frightening attacks, panic disorder individuals may not be wholly convinced that danger is truly imminent.

Stress and immune function is the topic of Drs. Ann O'Leary and Mariana Suarez-Al-Adam of the Department of Psychology, Rutgers University and Shirley Brown of the University of California at Los Angeles. The resurgence of interest in the influence of psychosocial factors on immunologically mediated illness, including cancer, autoimmune disorders, and infectious disease, prompted these authors to provide an empirical review of the growing body of work that seeks to link life-events stress processes to immune function in human beings. Theoretical and methodological considerations of psycho-immunological research are summarized, as are directions for future research. In addressing stress in immune function, the authors argue we are now at a stage at which we must demonstrate the applicability of our knowledge to the alleviation of suffering from illness. Argued is the important role of the controlled intervention design, in which psychosocial interventions are tested for their impact on immune function and health; this argument has given promise to understanding the causal role of psychological factors in understanding the nature of psycho-immunological relationships.

In examining life stress, Medical and Behavioral Medicine Professors Sheldon Cohen, of Carnegie Mellon University, David Tyrell, of the MRC Common Cold Unit, Salisbury, United Kingdom, and Andrew P. Smith, of the Health Psychology Research Unit, University of Wales, Bristol, United Kingdom, discuss the relationship between stress and susceptibility to biologically verified clinical colds among persons experimentally exposed to respiratory viruses. They also examine the biological and behavioral pathways that may explain a relationship between stress and disease.

Drs. Peter Kamenchenko, V. S. Yastrebov, and A. S. Tiganov, of the National Mental Health Research Center, Moscow, Russia, deal with the psychiatric consequences of traumatic amputation. Measurable environmental stress and the onset of symptoms are seen as crucial in understanding psychosomatic mechanisms in psychiatric disorders. The biopsychosocial model of understanding psychosomatic disorders is viewed as the model of choice in studying the impact of trauma, including traumatic amputations. Treatment and rehabilitation procedures are discussed, as are future directions in addressing the cross-cultural implications of traumatization and stressful life experiences.

Professors Bryan Johnstone, Thomas Garrity, and Robert Straus, of the Department of Behavioral Sciences, University of Kentucky College of Medicine, discuss the relationship between alcohol and life stress. Both perceptions and evidence regarding relationships between the uses and abuses of alcohol and the experience of emotions, such as stress, tension, and anxiety, are seen in the complex fear of stressful life events. The versatility of alcohol, its paradoxes, and the variability of human response to alcohol are considered, as are initial scientific assumptions in alcohol-related research. The authors provide keen insight into our understanding and the clarification of how and in what sequence factors come into play in the relationship between stress and alcohol use and abuse.

Traumatic events over the life span, with specific emphasis on survivors of the Buffalo Creek Disaster, are examined by Professor Bonnie L. Green, of the Department of Psychiatry, Georgetown University, and her colleagues, Teresa Kramer, Mary Grace, Goldine Glesser, and Anthony Leonard, of the University of Cincinnati. This chapter focuses on a series of studies of survivors of the Buffalo Creek dam collapse and flood, which this research group had the opportunity to conduct over nearly two decades. Guided by theories of adult development and, especially, by theorists who have conceptualized the impact of trauma across the life span, the authors provide a unique longitudinal and life span assessment of traumatization. Recognized from their analysis is a noncontinuity of psychopathology over time. The authors argue that integrating the "trauma self" with the "nontrauma self" may be a challenge that continues throughout the lifetime of victims of stressful life events.

Eating disorders and their relationship to stress and stressful life events are the subject of the chapter by Dr. Laurie L. Humphries, Professor of Psychiatry, University of Kentucky College of Medicine. Developmental issues and eating disorders in stress, with specific emphasis on disordered eating and stress in adolescent populations, are emphasized. Noted with interest is the coping cycle and personality factors related to eating disorders. Referring to the most recent of diagnostic nomenclatures, the DSM-IV, the author recognizes that the field of stress research and eating disorders will make significant advances over the next decade.

Considered a stressful life event is the process of retiring from the world of work. Dr. Raymond Bossé, of the Normative Aging Study of the VA Outpatient Clinic and Hellenic College, and Drs. Avron Spiro, of the Normative Aging Study of the VA Outpatient Clinic and the School of Public Health, Boston University, and Michael Levenson, of the Human Development and Family Studies Program at the University of California, Davis, explore answers to the question of who experiences retirement as a stressful life event. Predictors of retirement state stress are examined, as is evidence from various clinical research studies. Future research needs are identified, as is the observation that retirees constitute a very heterogeneous group.

In the final chapter of this volume, Professor Patrick A. Boudewyns, of the Department of Veterans' Affairs Medical Center and the Medical College of Georgia, and his colleagues, Drs. Leon Hyer, Darlene Klein, Charles Nichols, and Edwin Sperr, explore the lessons learned in the treatment of chronic, complicated posttraumatic stress disorder. Offered are guidelines for the treatment of traumatization and stress, the importance of establishing personal control in a safe environment, and the relevance of rehabilitating the core psychological processes. The lessons to be learned about chronic posttraumatic stress disorder have not come easily. When our children are victimized, the authors ask, will we be able to recognize the potential for disability and come to their aid with treatment, education, and concern? In the same view, the authors are also concerned about women who experience abuse and domestic violence: Will we, as a society, recognize how the long-term effects of traumatization and victimization affect them and significant others?

How Do Humans Process Trauma from Life Stress?

Horowitz (1986) and others have generated paradigms for assessing the normal and pathological phases of processing trauma.

Generally recognized in these paradigms are a series of stages or phases that first recognize the traumatic event, allow for the person to decipher both the psychological and physical impact of the traumatic stress, and then lead to a stage of disorganization and denial. This may then be followed by a period of reevaluation wherein both the psychological and physical components of the disorder are revisited. This stage leads to an eventual acceptance of the trauma or a resolution of the psychopathological impact of the trauma.

Miller and Veltkamp (1989, 1993) suggest that the victim processes the trauma by moving through a series of stages. The initial stage of the Trauma Accommodation Syndrome involves the victimization, which is recognized as a stressor. Usually the person realizes he or she has suffered an acute physically and psychologically traumatic experience. The victim's response is usually one of feeling overwhelmed and intimidated. Loss of control is recognized, and it is not uncommon for the victim to think recurringly of the stressful experience and focus upon the intimidating factors of the abuse.

The acute traumatic stage is followed by a stage involving more cognitive disorganization and confusion. This stage is marked by vagueness in understanding both the concept of trauma and the expectations associated with adaptation, adjustment, or accommodation.

The next stage involves a phase of avoidance, which can take two directions and may vary in its choice. First there is a conscious inhibition: an effort is made on the part of the victim to actively inhibit the thoughts and feelings related to the trauma. This may involve revisiting the traumatic experience itself or early memories through flashbacks to a more acute physical and psychological trauma. Second there is avoidance: by means of unconscious denial, the victim remains unaware of his or her efforts to avoid the psychological trauma associated with the traumatic event. Unconscious denial can infrequently allow a revisitation to the cognitive disorganization stage as well as the stressor and stressful life event itself.

ARE THERE ETHNOCULTURAL VARIANTS RELATED TO STRESSFUL LIFE EVENTS?

Cross-cultural aspects of any disease entity are significant in understanding the etiology, processing, and adaptation of individuals to the disorder. Cross-cultural studies offer an opportunity to compare like populations who have experienced like stressors with the search for social and cultural correlates that may provide clues to the etiology of certain conditions, their onset, maintenance, and resolution.

Boehnlein and Kinzie (1994) note that the diagnosis of psychiatric disorders cross-culturally remains an area of great opportunity and controversy and that traumatization and stress must be analyzed and assessed cross-culturally. Westermeyer (1987) has noted that, cross-culturally, diagnosis can have a variety of meanings and raises the question as to whether a clinician from one culture can make a diagnosis for a patient from another culture. It becomes imperative that clinicians and researchers realize that understanding the entire sociocultural milieu in which the patient functions is a critical factor in recognizing diagnostic symptomatology consistent with traumatization and stress. Boehnlein, Kinzie, and Fleck (1992), and Boehnlein and Kinzie (1994) have carefully examined the process of traumatization and subsequent responses and have determined that this is highly cultural in nature. Culturally constituted symbols, communication patterns, and healing approaches vary considerably from culture to culture. These researchers argue that these rituals that enable individuals to address the traumatization process are culture-bound, thus spearheading answers to the many questions that have been raised within an ethnocultural perspective. The authors encourage clinical researchers to show a significant sensitivity to the individual's social structures, cultural values, and self-identity within the ethnocultural context.

The growing interest in cross-cultural and cross-national studies has helped us to unlock and recognize important interpretative aspects of accommodation and assimilation in psychiatric disorders. Research (Tsygankov and Melanin, 1991) evaluating the effects of PTSD on Russian veterans of the Afghan conflict suggested that in this study of 195 veterans, symptoms most frequently occurring included recall of painful experiences, guilt feelings, anxiety attacks, sleep disturbance, intrusive thoughts, intense conflict, emotional instability, and irritability. The researchers noted that these symptoms occurred years after the wartime experiences. Of the populations studied, 17.4 percent continue to show serious current symptomatology and 27.6 percent yield a lifetime prevalence of these symptoms. Such figures as these are quite consistent with those realized in American studies (Miller, Kraus, Kamenchenko, and Kraznianski, 1993). The researchers further noted that the prolonged stress resulting from the war had had an unfavorable long-term effect on their return to civilian life.

Likewise, American veterans who have met the same criteria for admission studies have shown persistence of depressive symptoms for long periods of time. This is suggestive that over an extended period of time, anxiety may diminish but depression may increase as a reaction to the chronicity associated with delayed stress syndrome. Furthermore, pathological scores for depression on standardized measures may not indicate either dysthymia or major affective disorder, but rather a more complex psychiatric disorder such as generalized anxiety disorder and traumatic stress. Depressive symptoms are clearly an associated feature of PTSD as well as a major affective disorder and share three diagnostic criteria with PTSD: loss of interest in activities, impaired concentration, and sleep disturbance. Other investigators, including Mollica, Wyshak, Lavelle, Truong, Tor, and Yang (1990) and Boehnlein and Kinzie (1994), have examined cross-cultural samples and realized similar findings.

Which Treatment Models Are Most Helpful to Traumatized Persons?

There is considerable interest today in understanding the impact of treatment for traumatic stress. What is being realized, however, is that data from a number of studies have shown that various stressors can adversely affect immune function. The bodily immune system is a complex surveillance apparatus that differentiates between self and nonself. An immune reaction is activated in response to exposure to foreign antigens in an effort to maintain the body's homeostasis. There is ample evidence from human and animal studies that demonstrate the downward modulation of immune function concomitant with stressful life experiences. As a consequence of this, the possible enhancement of immune function by behavioral strategies has generated considerable interest. Clinicians and researchers have used a number of diverse strategies to modulate immune functioning, including relaxation, hypnosis, exercise, classical conditioning, self-disclosure, and exposure to a phobic stress, to enhance perceived coping self-efficacy and cognitive behavioral interventions.

The treatment of traumatization must also be seen within the cultural context (Boehnlein and Sparr, 1993). The development of a biological perspective in the treatment of traumatization and PTSD must be given serious consideration in the alleviation of symptoms. Friedman (1993) and others have addressed the psychobiological and pharmacological approaches to the treatment of traumatization and PTSD. There is significant optimism with the variety of approaches that have addressed physiological alterations, neurohumoral and neuroendocrinological alterations, and the role of the immune system. It is, however, essential that the treatment of a broad spectrum of symptoms associated with traumatic stress must also be realized within the indigenous healing approaches, socialization process, and group healing context that is so readily apparent when one examines the culture-bound perspective of traumatization and stress.

Treatment efforts need to be individualized. It is imperative that as we attempt to answer the etiological question in the treatment of traumatization and stress, we must take into consideration the biopsychosocial and cultural dimensions of the individual within the societal context. There needs to be a sensitivity to gender differences, as recently realized in the diagnosis and treatment of cardiological disorders. The role of therapeutic boosters must also be considered, as well as the value of drug and various cognitive and behavioral approaches to treatment. Finally, questions related to whether concurrent or sequential treatment is better must be answered. All of these can be addressed within the context of tailormade treatment interventions for individuals who are victims of stressful life experiences.

The impact of stressful life experiences is one of the most critical clinical, societal, and research challenges facing the mental health community in the 1990s.

WHAT RESEARCH DO PRACTITIONERS NEED?

There remain numerous questions about the etiology, adaptation, and accommodation of traumatization and the effectiveness of various specific interventions for its treatment. Further models that guide clinical practice are not fully explained. The field of stressful life experiences lacks an integrative theory and requires extensive replication of promising intervention strategies. Nonetheless, the essence of research in this area has become increasingly rigorous and based on empirical findings that have been interpreted theoretically.

Attention must continually be paid to numerous methodological issues in research such as random assignment, effective use of control groups, the validity and reliability of measures used, and the attrition rate of subjects in studies. Researchers are actively considering ways to improve the quality of their research methods, and this should have beneficial effects in the future.

It is to the traumatized individuals who have suffered and survived that our efforts to further our knowledge and understanding of traumatization and its processes are dedicated. It is hoped that this work will generate the next wave of hypotheses to be tested, diagnostic issues to be considered, and treatment interventions to be offered.

REFERENCES

American Psychiatric Association (1987), *Diagnostic and Statistical Manual of Mental Disorders*, 3rd ed. rev. (DSM-III-R). Washington, DC: American Psychiatric Press.

Blake, W., Weathers, P., Nagy, R., & Friedman, M. (1993), *Clinician-Administered PTSD Scale (CAPS)*. Boston: National Center for PTSD, Behavioral Sciences Division.

Blanchard, E. B. (1990), Biofeedback treatment of essential hypertension. *Biofeed. & Self-Reg.*, 15:209–228.

———— Mold, L. C., & Pallmeyer, T. P. (1982), A psychological study of PTSD in Vietnam veterans, *Psychiat. Quart.*, 54:220–229.

Boehnlein, J. K., & Kinzie, J. D. (1994), Cross-cultural assessment of traumatization. In: *Stressful Life Events*, ed. T. W. Miller. Madison, CT: International Universities Press.

———— ———— Fleck, J. (1992), DSM diagnosis of posttraumatic stress disorder and cultural sensitivity: A response. *J. Nerv. & Ment. Dis.*, 180:597–599.

———— Sparr, L. F. (1993), Group therapy for WWII ex-POW's: Long-term posttraumatic adjustment in a geriatric population. *Amer. J. Psychother.*, 47:273–282.

Dohrenwend, B. S., Raphael, K., Schwartz, S., Stuave, A. & Skodol, A. (1993), Structured event probe and narrative rating method for measuring stressful life events. In: *Handbook of Stress*, 2nd ed., ed. L. Goldberger & S. Breznitz. New York: Free Press.

Figley, C. (1985), Introduction. In: *Trauma and Its Wake*. ed. C. Figley. New York: Brunner/Mazel, pp. xvii–xxvi.

Friedman, M. (1993), Neurological alterations associated with post-traumatic stress disorder. National Center for PTSD, Clinical Laboratory and Education Diversion, Teleconference Report, July 1991.

Green, B. (1990), Defining trauma: Terminology and generic stress dimensions. *J. Appl. Soc. Psychol.*, 20:1632–1642.

Hammerberg, J. (1992), *The PEN Inventory*. Unpublished typescript.

Horowitz, M. J. (1986), Stress response syndromes: A review of posttraumatic and adjustment disorders. *Hosp. & Commun. Psychiatry*, 37:241–249.

—— Field, N. P., & Classen, C. C. (1993), Stress response syndromes and their treatment. In: *Handbook of Stress* 2nd ed., ed. L. Goldberger & S. Breznitz. New York: Free Press.

Keane, T. M., Caddell, J. M., & Taylor, K. L. (1988), The Mississippi Scale for Combat-Related PTSD: Three studies in reliability and validity. *J. Consult. & Clin. Psychol.*, 56:85–90.

—— Malloy, P. F. & Fairbank, I. A. (1984), Empirical development of an MMPI subscale for the assessment of combat-related posttraumatic stress disorder. *J. Consult. & Clin. Psychol.*, 52:888–891.

Kulka, R. A., Schlenger, W. E., Fairbank, J. A., Hough, R. L., Jordan, B. K., Marmar, C. R., & Weiss, D. S. (1990), *Contractual Report of Findings from the National Vietnam Veterans Readjustment Society*. Research Triangle Park, NC: Research Triangle Institute.

Lyons, J. A., & Keane, T. (1992), Posttraumatic stress disorder and MMPI-2, *Develop. & Behav. Med.*, 8:349–356.

Miller, T. W., Ed. (1996), *Theory and Assessment of Stressful Life Events*, Madison, CT: International Universities Press.

—— Ed. (1989), *Stressful Life Events*. Madison, CT: International Universities Press.

—— Kraus, R. F., Kamenchenko, P., & Kraznienski, A. (1993), Posttraumatic stress disorder in U.S. and Russian veterans. *Hosp. & Commun. Psychiatry*, 44:585–587.

—— Veltkamp, L. J. (1989), The abusing family in rural America. *Internat. J. Fam. Psychiatry*, 9:259–275.

—— —— (1993), Family violence: Clinical indicators in military and post-military personnel. *Military Med.*, 86:384–395.

Mollica, R. F., Wyshak, G., Lavelle, J., Truong, T., Tor, S., & Yang, T. (1990), Assessing symptom change in Southeast Asian refugee survivors of mass violence and torture. *Amer. J. Psychiatry*, 147:83–88.

Pitman, R. K. (1988), Post-traumatic stress disorder, conditioning, and network theory. *Psychiat. Ann.*, 18:182–189.

Tsygankov, B., & Melanin, A. (1991), Mental disorders among Soviet veterans of the war in Afghanistan. *WISMIC*, 3:18–21.

Watson, D., Clark, L. A., & Tellegen, A. (1991), Development and validation of brief measures of positive and negative affect: The PANAS Scales. *J. Personal. & Soc. Psychol.*, 54:1063–1070.

Westermeyer, J. (1987), Clinical considerations in cross-cultural diagnosis. *Hosp. & Commun. Psychiatry*, 38:160–165.

Part I

Posttraumatic Stress Disorder

Chapter 1
The Course of Chronic
Posttraumatic Stress Disorder

Brian E. Engdahl, Ph.D., and Raina E. Eberly, Ph.D.

It has been suggested that DSM-III (APA, 1980) and DSM-III-R (APA, 1987) are linked to "the narrowing of the psychiatric gaze in contemporary psychiatry" (Wilson, 1993, p. 408), particularly in the sharp limits they have placed on considerations of time: "time has shrunk from a lifetime to a moment, from the extended evaluation to the 45-minute cross-sectional interview" (p. 408). Inquiries about the unfolding of an individual's life over time and the changing place of symptoms in that life are often neglected. Eitinger (1971) studied Norwegian survivors of the Nazi concentration camps for 25 years and noted a fluctuating symptom course that often was delayed in its onset. He asserted that this variability interferes with our awareness of the human toll exacted by severe trauma. Theory and research on the course of most psychiatric disorders are scarce. Even less is known about the course of posttraumatic stress disorder (PTSD).

Psychological Models of chronic PTSD

Horowitz (1993) postulated five phases of adjustment to trauma exposure: outcry, denial, oscillation between denial or numbing

3

and intrusive memories, working through, and completion of the response. These phases are variable in duration, and progression through these phases is often incomplete. In this model, symptoms can wax and wane over time, depending upon the adjustment phase a person is in, other intrapsychic factors, and environmental factors. A "residual stress model" (Grinker and Spiegel, 1945) was proposed to explain observations of PTSD-like symptoms among World War II airmen with significant combat exposure. In accord with the model, symptoms appeared to be directly proportional to the severity of the stressors to which the airmen were exposed, and symptom severity gradually diminished over time. Individual risk (or vulnerability) factors were given minimal emphasis under this residual stress model, which was restated by Figley (1978). A competing "stress evaporation" model of posttraumatic symptoms was proposed (Borus, 1973; Worthington, 1978) in which individual risk factors played a major role in producing any symptoms that persisted following an initial period of symptom decline. A fluctuating course of posttraumatic symptoms is suggested by the Horowitz model. Fluctuating symptoms also would be consistent with a residual stress model, while the stress evaporation model suggests that posttraumatic symptoms may steadily decline.

BIOLOGICAL MODELS OF CHRONIC PTSD

Beebe (1975), in his study of former prisoners of war (POWs), proposed a model of symptoms following prolonged psychic and physical trauma that involves two injury components: one is somatic and essentially short-term, caused by physical injury, illness, or other physical insult; the other component is psychological and is essentially permanent. These injury components lead to decreased feelings of well-being and self-efficacy (loss of ego strength), and lowered thresholds for both physical and psychological distress.

Kolb (1987) postulated a neuropsychological basis for PTSD. He suggested that central cortical changes occur as a consequence of prolonged and excessive sensitizing stimulation. When an individual's capacity to process traumatic life-threatening stimuli is overwhelmed, the neuronal function and perhaps structure is impaired. This leads to both hypersensitivity and impaired habituation learning, and thus impaired discriminative perception and learning, accounting for the range and persistence of symptoms observed in PTSD populations. Posttraumatic stress disorder's persistent symptoms (e.g., hyperalertness, repetitive nightmares, irritability, other conditioned emotional responses) may be explained through functional impairments in neuronal and synaptic cortical processing.

Eberly, Harkness, and Engdahl (1991) interpreted their findings among POWs within the context of evolutionary biology (McGuire, Marks, Nesse, and Troisi, 1992). They suggested that trauma can produce a *persistent* generalized increase in the experience of negative emotions, or negative emotionality (NE; Tellegen, 1985), defined as the predisposition to experience subjective distress and unpleasurable engagement with the environment. To account for increased NE, they proposed an adaptive model of trauma response in which persisting posttraumatic symptoms have adaptational value in traumatic environments. Perceiving the world as a more unpleasant and threatening place (increased NE) increases one's chances for survival (and reproduction) in dangerous environments. The tenacity of these symptoms following an individual's return to a more benign environment reflects an increase in the trait of NE. Biological hypotheses of PTSD (see Saporta and van der Kolk [1992] for a review) suggest that persistent posttraumatic symptoms stem from relatively permanent internal biological changes caused by exposure to intense levels of traumatic stimulation. Biological models suggest that symptom change may typically appear as a gradual decline, although symptom fluctuation can occur in response to individual and environmental factors.

Longitudinal Research on Depression and Anxiety

Longitudinal studies of adults suggest that stability of personality traits over time is the norm (McCrae and Costa, 1990). Less is known about the stability of psychiatric symptoms. A statistical model of stability and change in psychiatric symptoms was proposed and applied to several data sets (Duncan-Jones, Fergussen, Ormel, and Horwood, 1990). Substantial symptom stability was found, along with a high correlation between stable symptom levels and the trait of neuroticism. Angst and Vollrath (1991) demonstrated that anxiety disorders may be triggered by life events, and their course is often chronic and complicated by depression in the general population. They reported that the strongest predictors of persistent anxiety disorders were the severity and duration of symptoms, and comorbidity with depression. Additional contributing factors were used in a structural equations modeling approach in a 4-year prospective study (Holahan and Moos, 1991). Selected personality characteristics, family support, and prior depression were strongly predictive of subsequent depression.

Longitudinal Research on PTSD

McFarlane (1988) provided a series of reports on the longitudinal course of posttraumatic adjustment among victims of an Australian brushfire disaster. Delayed and chronic symptoms were more frequent than acute symptoms, and included painful memories, depressed affect, and physical complaints. McFarlane (1986) noted both the delayed emergence of PTSD and the resolution of chronic cases. In a further report of 50 randomly selected brushfire fighters at high risk for PTSD, McFarlane (1988) assessed their status at 5 points over a 42-month period. He noted that intrusion was more prominent early in the disorder and then diminished over time. At the group level, symptoms of posttraumatic morbidity declined over a 29-month period (McFarlane, 1989) but, in partial support of the stress evaporation model, the longer the symptoms persisted, the stronger became their association with several vulnerability factors. These included neuroticism, a family or personal history of psychiatric illness, and a tendency to not confront conflicts. McFarlane noted that these vulnerability factors appeared to play a lesser role in the etiology of PTSD than they do in the etiologies of other psychiatric disorders seen in nontraumatized populations.

Kilpatrick, Saunders, Veronen, Best, and Von (1987) assessed criminally victimized adult females and found a lifetime postcrime PTSD rate of 27.8 percent. With an average postcrime interval of 15 years, the observed current PTSD rate was 7.5 percent. Saigh (1988) assessed civilians attending the American University of Beirut who had experienced heavy shelling during 1983 and 1984. Structured interviews conducted one year after the shelling revealed that 9 of the 12 students experienced PTSD symptoms. One individual developed chronic PTSD, while the other 8 experienced spontaneous remission of their symptoms within one month after the shelling.

Grace, Green, Lindy, and Leonard (1993) conducted a follow-up study of 120 survivors of a 1972 flood in Buffalo Creek, West Virginia. They reported highly significant changes over the 12-year period following the flood, with symptoms decreasing in all cases. Twenty-eight percent of subjects retrospectively diagnosed with PTSD in 1974 did not meet criteria in 1986. Eleven percent experienced "delayed onset," being PTSD negative in 1974 and PTSD positive in 1986. Feinstein (1993) conducted a 6-month prospective study of 48 victims of physical trauma. Almost two-thirds of the victims were classified as psychiatric cases within the first week following their injury. This fell to about 25 percent at 6 weeks and remained at 25 percent at 6 months, although during that interval five patients deteriorated and moved into the group classified as psychiatric, and five improved and moved out of that group. Feinstein concluded that following accidental injury, the majority of cases improve spontaneously and consistently, with one small subgroup experiencing a fluctuating symptom course and another small subgroup experiencing a delayed onset of psychiatric symptoms.

CHRONIC PTSD AMONG COMBAT VETERANS

Blank (1992) and Solomon (1993) recently summarized the work conducted by Solomon and colleagues on Israeli combat soldiers, much of which sheds light on the course of PTSD. Solomon's primary findings with respect to the course of PTSD are largely consistent with other findings in the literature. As an example, soldiers who experienced an acute combat stress reaction did not necessarily later develop PTSD, and those who later developed PTSD may or may not have experienced a previous combat stress reaction (Solomon, 1989). Solomon, Kotler, Shalev, and Lin (1989) studied delayed trauma reactions among Israeli veterans. They found that those who returned from war apparently unimpaired and then later developed a disorder are only a small minority of those who apply for treatment. In most cases, it was not the disorder that was delayed but the help-seeking. Five categories were identified: delayed-onset PTSD (10%), delayed help-seeking for chronic PTSD (40%), exacerbation of subclinical PTSD (33%), reactivation of PTSD (13%), and other disorders (4%).

Op den Velde, Falger, Hovens, de Groen, Lasschuit, van Duijn, and Schouten (1993) conducted retrospective diagnostic interviews with 147 Dutch Resistance veterans from World War II, 123 of whom had PTSD symptoms. Of these, about 30 percent experienced their first symptoms within the first 5 years after World War II, 30 percent during the next 20 years, and the remainder more than 25 years later. In other words, PTSD occurred for the first time in nearly 70 percent of the cases 5 or more years after the end of World War II. Several general courses were noted: a *(sub)acute PTSD* which progressed to a chronic condition (9.7%) or remitted within 5 years (12.2%); a *delayed form of PTSD* in which the first symptoms developed between 5 and 35 years after World War II and persisted (12.2%) or remitted (20.3%); and *PTSD with remissions and exacerbations,* including both (sub)acute onset cases (13.8%) and delayed onset cases (35.8%). One group experienced *mixed conditions with PTSD complaints* for about 5 years post–World War II, symptom-free periods of 15 to 30 years, and then the recurrence of their PTSD symptoms (no percentage noted).

CHRONIC PTSD AMONG FORMER PRISONERS OF WAR

Beebe (1975) noted that most POWs experienced persisting psychiatric symptoms following release, although symptom intensity typically diminished. A smaller proportion suffered persistent, diagnosable psychiatric disorders. Posttraumatic stress disorder, other anxiety disorders, and depressive disorders were the most common (Eberly and Engdahl, 1991). Using the Center for Epidemiologic Studies Depression scale (CES-D; Radloff, 1977) in a 1984–1985 national survey of POWs, depressive symptoms were found to be elevated among the POWs relative to their combat controls 40 years after repatriation (Page, Engdahl and Eberly, 1991). In further analyses of these results, Engdahl, Harkness, Eberly, Page, and Bielinski (in press) examined the interrelationships of trauma exposure, individual resilience, and trauma responses. These responses included negative affect, positive affect, and somatic symptoms as assessed by the Cornell Medical Index in 1967 and the CES-D scale in 1985.

As shown in Figure 1.1, these responses were strongly associated with captivity trauma (as indexed by captivity weight loss, torture, and disease) and resilience (as indexed by age and education at capture). Symptoms reported in 1967 were related to symptoms reported in 1985, suggesting symptom stability. Figure 1.1 indicates that the effects of resilience (F1) and time 1 trauma response (F3) made approximately equal contributions to time 2

Figure 1.1. A Structural Equations Model of POW Trauma, Resilience, and Trauma Response Measured in 1967 and Again in 1985

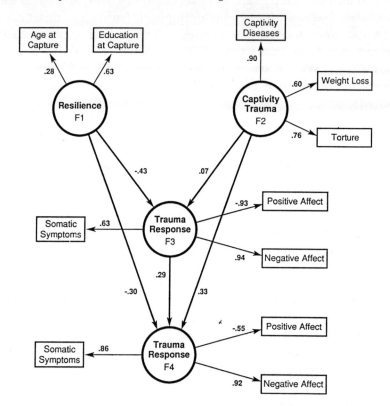

Circles designate latent constructs and squares enclose the construct indicator variables. Adapted from Engdahl et al. (in press).

trauma response (F4), with captivity trauma (F2) being a somewhat stronger contributor. Research noted earlier in this chapter suggests that symptom levels decrease over time for these men. Figure 1.1 could indicate that many POWs have experienced symptom level decreases of similar magnitude between time 1 and time 2 (i.e., they have maintained their symptom-level "rank order"). It is also likely that group-level analyses such as that presented here mask considerable individual variation in the development and course of posttraumatic symptoms. Further research is needed to directly examine these competing hypotheses.

Case histories suggest that depressive symptoms experienced upon release from captivity often were in reaction to the various losses sustained in the course of combat and captivity. Other depressive symptoms may arise over time in response to chronic anxiety symptoms. Several reports suggest that current life stress can reactivate quiescent PTSD. Zeiss and Dickman (1989) surveyed 442 POWs from World War II and found a 55.7 percent current PTSD rate, with much reported symptom fluctuation: 62.2 percent of their entire sample reported being temporarily or intermittently troubled by their PTSD symptoms over the years, but described no consistent pattern of symptom occurrence over the years. About one in seven (13.8%) reported never having been seriously troubled by their symptoms, while nearly one-fourth (23.5%) reported being continuously troubled.

TABLE 1.1
Posttraumatic Stress Disorder (PTSD) Criteria: Current and Lifetime Endorsement Percentages Using the Structured Clinical Interview for Diagnosis (SCID)

| | | PTSD Critera | | | | | | PTSD | |
| | | B | | C | | D | | Overall | |
POW GROUPS	n	curr.	life.	curr.	life.	curr.	life.	curr.	life.
WWII Pacific	42	46	76	22	33	24	48	17	29
WWII Europe	41	28	59	15	32	38	46	15	27
Korean War	74	57	65	35	45	50	57	32	41
All POWs	157	47	66	26	38	40	52	24	34

Note: Figures shown are percentages. POW = Former Prisoner of War. Curr.= currently meets criterion. Life.= has met criterion at some point during lifetime. See text for criteria definition.

Table 1.1 summarizes PTSD criteria (current and lifetime) assessed using the Structured Clinical Interview for Diagnosis (Spitzer and Williams, 1986). Data on these groups of POWs are drawn from samples reported in Page (1992). Posttraumatic stress disorder criterion A (exposure to a distressing event outside the range of usual human experience) was met for all cases. Criterion B (persistent reexperiencing of the traumatic event) requires only one symptom from a group of four symptom categories, and in this study was the most frequently met "non-A" criterion. Criterion C (persistent avoidance of trauma-associated stimuli or numbing of general responsiveness) requires three symptoms from a group of seven, making it the most difficult criterion to meet, at least from a purely numerical standpoint (several criterion C symptoms also are difficult to assay in an individual clinical interview); it was the least frequently met "non-A" criterion. Criterion D (persistent symptoms of increased arousal) requires two symptoms from a group of six, and overall, it was met less frequently than B and more frequently than C, with some subgroup exceptions. Of course, criterion E (duration of the symptoms greater than 1 month) was met for all PTSD-positive cases.

The relative prominence of intrusion, avoidance, and increased arousal may fluctuate over time. Although the varying number of symptoms required to satisfy criteria B, C, and D makes comparisons difficult, contrasting the differences between lifetime and current rates across criteria groups may tell us something about symptom change over time. Seventy-seven percent of the POWs who reported experiencing two or more symptoms of increased arousal (criterion D) at some point in their lives also reported two or more symptoms at present, while 71 percent continued to experience one or more symptoms of intrusion (criterion B), and 68 percent continued to report three or more signs of avoidance (criterion C). Consistent with these observations, Op den Velde et al. (1993) concluded that increased arousal was the most persistent symptom in their sample of World War II Dutch Resistance fighters. Among veterans who survived the attack on Pearl Harbor, Wilson, Haral, and Kahana (1989) found that PTSD symptoms declined nearly equally across the categories of intrusion, avoidance, and increased arousal between discharge from service and 1986.

Kulka, Schlenger, Fairbank, Hough, Jordan, Marmar, and Weiss (1990) reported lifetime and current PTSD prevalence rates of 30.9 percent and 15.2 percent, respectively, among Vietnam War veterans. Eberly and Engdahl (1991) reported lifetime and current PTSD rates of 70.9 percent and 34.5 percent among POWs. Op den Velde et al. (1993) reported some of the highest PTSD rates, and also noted extraordinary persistence of PTSD in their sample of Dutch Resistance veterans: lifetime and current

PTSD rates were 83.7 percent and 55.8 percent, respectively. The ratios of current to lifetime rates in these groups (.50 or greater) clearly show that PTSD is a chronic disorder for many individuals, especially those exposed to severe trauma.

PTSD-RELATED PSYCHOPATHOLOGY

Among trauma survivors, a largely unexplored area concerns the timing and development of disorders other than PTSD, or of disorders coexistent with PTSD. An overview of these associated (comorbid) conditions was provided by Rundell, Ursano, Holloway, and Silberman (1989). These conditions include depression, substance abuse, and somatic complaints. Mellman, Randolph, Brawman-Mintzer, Flores, and Milanes (1992) reported a preliminary study using a clinical sample of combat veterans and POWs. Posttraumatic stress disorder was the most common lifetime psychiatric disorder, and its onset almost always closely followed the experiences of combat and captivity. Posttraumatic stress disorder most commonly preceded the onset of phobias, major depression, and panic disorder. The phenomenology of older individuals' long-term posttraumatic adaptation is being actively studied, especially amongst war veterans, and was reviewed by Schnurr (1991). A differing symptom picture may exist among older trauma survivors. Various factors may account for this, including the survivors' age, their generation (a cohort effect), or the sheer amount of time elapsed since trauma.

Hovens, Falger, Op den Velde, Schouten, de Groen, and van Duijn (1992) reported that a differing symptom picture accounted for failures to diagnose PTSD in older Dutch Resistance veterans. Twelve percent of their sample met PTSD criteria via the SCID and yet were judged not to have PTSD upon clinical interview. They analyzed the discrepant cases and confirmed that the SCID-based PTSD-positive cases did fulfill DSM-III criteria, but that the distress level of these individuals generally was minimal, leading to a negative clinical diagnosis. Clearly, caution is needed when using diagnostic information drawn from unstructured clinical interviews. A more interesting point was raised by the authors in their suggestion that rating scales be used that weight symptom intensity (see Blake, Weathers, Nagy, Kaloupek, Klauminzer, Charney, and Keane [1990] for an example), presumably allowing certain PTSD-positive cases with low symptom intensity to be reclassified as PTSD-negative. This would in effect alter PTSD criteria, and has not, so far as the available literature would suggest, been among the proposed revisions for PTSD in DSM-IV (Davidson and Foa, 1992).

CONCLUSION

No review can be complete and current, including the present chapter. Reports that document the courses that PTSD can take are appearing with increasing frequency, and informative projects are currently in progress. Much more will be known in the near future. This review has attempted to highlight issues important to an increased understanding of PTSD's course. Such increased understanding can broaden the view of PTSD's effects on and its place in an individual's life, benefiting care providers, researchers, policymakers, and PTSD sufferers and their families.

REFERENCES

American Psychiatric Association (1980), *Diagnostic and Statistical Manual of Mental Disorders,* 3rd ed. (DSM-III). Washington, DC: American Psychiatric Press.
——— (1987), *Diagnostic and Statistical Manual of Mental Disorders,* 3rd ed., rev. (DSM-III-R). Washington, DC: American Psychiatric Press.
Angst, J., & Vollrath, M. (1991), The natural history of anxiety disorders. *Acta Psychiat. Scand.,* 84:446–452.
Beebe, G. W. (1975), Follow-up studies of World War II and Korean War prisoners, II: Morbidity, disability, and maladjustments. *Amer. J. Epidemiol.,* 101:400–422.

Blake, D. D., Weathers, F. W., Nagy, L. M., Kaloupek, D. G., Klauminzer, G., Charney, D. S., & Keane, T. M. (1990), A clinician rating scale for assessing current and lifetime PTSD: The CAPS-1. *Behav. Therap.*, 18:187–188.

Blank, A. S. (1992), The longitudinal course of posttraumatic stress disorder. In: *Posttraumatic Stress Disorder: DSM-IV and Beyond*, ed. R. T. Davidson & E. B. Foa. Washington, DC: American Psychiatric Press, pp. 3–22.

Borus, J. F. (1973), Reentry: I. Adjustment issues facing the Vietnam returnee. *Arch. Gen. Psychiatry*, 28:501–506.

Davidson, R. T., & Foa, E. B., Eds. (1992), *Posttraumatic Stress Disorder: DSM-IV and Beyond*. Washington, DC: American Psychiatric Press.

Duncan-Jones, P., Fergussen, D. M., Ormel, J., & Horwood, L. J. (1990), A model of stability and change in minor psychiatric symptoms: Results from three longitudinal studies. *Psychological Med.*, Monograph supplement No. 18.

Eberly, R. E., & Engdahl, B. E. (1991), Prevalence of somatic and psychiatric disorders among former prisoners of war. *Hosp. Comm. Psychiatry*, 42:807–813.

——— Harkness, A. R., & Engdahl, B. E. (1991), An adaptational view of trauma response as illustrated by the prisoner of war experience. *J. Traum. Stress*, 4:363–380.

Eitinger, L. (1971), Acute and chronic psychiatric reactions in concentration camp survivors. In: *Society, Stress and Disease*, ed. L. Levin. New York: Oxford University Press, pp. 219–230.

Engdahl, B. E., Harkness, A. R., Eberly, R. E., Page, W. F., & Bielinski, J. (in press), Structural models of captivity trauma, resilience, and trauma response among former prisoners of war 20 to 40 years after release. *Soc. Psychiatry Psych. Epidem.*

Feinstein, A. (1993), A prospective study of victims of physical trauma. In: *International Handbook of Traumatic Stress Syndromes*, ed. J. P. Wilson & B. Raphael. New York: Plenum Press, pp. 157–164.

Figley, C. R. (1978), Psychosocial adjustment among Vietnam veterans: An overview of the research. In: *Stress Disorders among Vietnam Veterans: Theory, Research and Treatment*, ed. C. R. Figley. New York: Brunner/Mazel, pp. 57–70.

Grace, M. C., Green, B. L., Lindy, J. D., & Leonard, A. C. (1993), The Buffalo Creek disaster: A 14-year follow-up. In: *International Handbook of Traumatic Stress Syndromes*, ed. J. P. Wilson & B. Raphael. New York: Plenum Press, pp. 441–449.

Grinker, R. R., & Spiegel, J. P. (1945), *Men Under Stress*. Philadelphia: Blakiston.

Holahan, C. J., & Moos, R. H. (1991), Life stressors, personal and social resources, depression: A 4-year structural model. *J. Abnorm. Psychol.*, 100:31–38.

Horowitz, M. J. (1993), Stress-response syndromes: A review of posttraumatic stress and adjustment disorders. In: *International Handbook of Traumatic Stress Syndromes*, ed. J. P. Wilson & B. Raphael. New York: Plenum Press, pp. 49–60.

Hovens, J. E., Falger, P. R., Op den Velde, W., Schouten, E. G., de Groen, J. H., & van Duijn, H. (1992), Occurrence of current post traumatic stress disorder among Dutch World War II resistance veterans according to the SCID. *J. Anxiety Disord.*, 6:147–157.

Kilpatrick, D. G., Saunders, B. E., Veronen, L. J., Best, C. L., & Von, J. M. (1987), Criminal victimization: Lifetime prevalence, reporting to police, and psychological impact. *Crime Delinq.*, 33:479–489.

Kolb, L. C. (1987), A neuropsychological hypothesis explaining post-traumatic stress disorders. *Amer. J. Psychiatry*, 144:989–995.

Kulka, R. A., Schlenger, W. E., Fairbank, J. A., Hough, R. L., Jordan, B. K., Marmar, C. R., & Weiss, D. S. (1990), *Trauma and the Vietnam War Generation: Report of Findings from the National Vietnam Veterans Readjustment Study.* New York: Brunner/Mazel.

McCrae, R. R., & Costa, P. T., Jr. (1990), *Personality in Adulthood.* New York: Guilford Press.

McFarlane, A. C. (1986), Long-term psychiatric morbidity after a natural disaster. *Med. J. Australia*, 145:561–563.

——— (1988), The longitudinal course of posttraumatic morbidity: The range of outcomes and their predictors. *J. Nerv. Ment. Dis.*, 176:30–39.

——— (1989), The aetiology of post-traumatic morbidity: Predisposing, precipitating and perpetuating factors. *Brit. J. Psychiatry*, 154:221–228.

McGuire, M. T., Marks, I., Nesse, R. M., & Troisi, A. (1992), Evolutionary biology: A basic science for psychiatry? *Acta Psychiat. Scand.*, 86:89–96.

Mellman, T. A., Randolph, C. A., Brawman-Mintzer, O., Flores, L. P., & Milanes, F. J. (1992), Phenomenology and course of psychiatric disorders associated with combat-related posttraumatic stress disorder. *Amer. J. Psychiatry*, 149:1569–1574.

Op den Velde, W., Falger, P. R., Hovens, J. E., de Groen, J. H., Lasschuit, L. J., van Duijn, H., & Schouten, E. G. (1993), Posttraumatic stress disorder in Dutch resistance veterans from World War II. In: *International Handbook of Traumatic Stress Syndromes*, ed. J. P. Wilson & B. Raphael. New York: Plenum Press, pp. 219–230.

Page, W. F. (1992), *The Health of Former Prisoners of War: Results from the Medical Examination Survey of Former POWs of World War II and the Korean Conflict.* Washington, DC: National Academy Press.

——— Engdahl, B. E., & Eberly, R. E. (1991), Prevalence and correlates of depressive symptoms among former prisoners of war. *J. Nerv. Ment. Dis.*, 179:670–677.

Radloff, L. S. (1977), The CES-D scale: A self-report depression scale for research in the general population. *Appl. Psychol. Meas.*, 1:385–401.

Rundell, J. R., Ursano, R. J., Holloway, H. C., & Silberman, E. K. (1989), Psychiatric responses to trauma. *Hosp. Comm. Psychiatry*, 40:68–74.

Saigh, P. A. (1988), Anxiety, depression, and assertion across alternating intervals of stress. *J. Abnorm. Psychol.*, 97:338–341.

Saporta, J. A., & van der Kolk, B. A. (1992), Psychobiological consequences of severe trauma. In: *Torture and Its Consequences: Current Treatment Approaches*, ed. M. Başoğlu. New York: Cambridge University Press, pp. 151–181.

Schnurr, P. P. (1991), PTSD and combat-related psychiatric symptoms in older veterans. *PTSD Res. Quart.*, 2:1–6.

Solomon, Z. (1989), A three year prospective study of post-traumatic stress disorder in Israeli combat veterans. *J. Traum. Stress*, 2:59–74.

———— (1993), Immediate and long-term effects of traumatic combat stress among Israeli veterans of the Lebanon War. In: *International Handbook of Traumatic Stress Syndromes*, ed. J. P. Wilson & B. Raphael. New York: Plenum Press, pp. 321–332.

———— Kotler, M., Shalev, A., & Lin, R. (1989), Delayed onset PTSD among Israeli veterans of the 1982 Lebanon War. *Psychiatry*, 52:428–436.

Spitzer, R. L., & Williams, J. B. (1986), *Structured Clinical Interview from DSM-III-R-Non-patient Version* (Modified for Vietnam veterans readjustment study 4/1/87). New York: New York State Psychiatric Institute, Biometrics Research.

Tellegen, A. (1985), Structures of mood and personality and their relevance to assessing anxiety, with an emphasis on self-report. In: *Anxiety and the Anxiety Disorders*, ed. A. H. Tuma & J. D. Maser. Hillsdale, NJ: Lawrence Erlbaum Associates, pp. 681–716.

Wilson, J. P., Haral, Z., & Kahana, B. (1989), The day of infamy: The legacy of Pearl Harbor. In: *Trauma, Transformation and Healing: An Integrative Approach to Theory, Research, and Post-Traumatic Therapy*, ed. J. P. Wilson. New York: Brunner/Mazel, pp. 129–156.

Wilson, M. (1993), DSM-III and the transformation of American psychiatry: A history. *Amer. J. Psychiatry*, 150:399–410.

Worthington, E. R. (1978), Demographic and pre-service variables as predictors of post-military service adjustment. In: *Stress Disorders Among Vietnam Veterans: Theory, Research and Treatment*, ed. C. R. Figley. New York: Brunner/Mazel, pp. 173–187.

Zeiss, R. A., & Dickman, H. R. (1989), PTSD 40 years later: Incidence and person-situation correlates in former POWs. *J. Clin. Psychol.*, 45:80–87.

Chapter 2
Cultural Perspectives on Posttraumatic Stress Disorder

James K. Boehnlein, M.D., M.Sc., and J. David Kinzie, M.D.

Posttraumatic stress disorder (PTSD) is a psychiatric syndrome that has been described in a wide variety of conditions and in a large number of populations throughout the world. Following extraordinary trauma from war, concentration camp experiences, natural disasters, rape or other assaults, or accidents, a very uniform symptom complex has been noted, including insomnia, nightmares, emotional numbing, startle reactions, memory impairment, and social isolation. The goal of this chapter is to place PTSD in a cultural context. This will be done from a number of perspectives, including an initial discussion of the development of the PTSD concept, a review of the epidemiology of PTSD across cultural groups, and a discussion of the effect of culture on diagnosis, treatment, and on the interpretation of traumatic experiences within cultural belief systems. Any discussion of PTSD cross-culturally also requires an examination of the sociocultural framework of affected populations, such as family and social structure, religious beliefs, and political environment.

The understanding of PTSD as a clinical phenomenon and a diagnostic entity within society and within the scientific community has itself been influenced by cultural factors over time. A brief historical review of the entity we now call PTSD will help initially to define the syndrome and also bring into bold relief the influences of history, culture, and politics on the developing understanding of the disorder. It should be noted that there has been a long-standing debate concerning the validity of the PTSD diagnosis; points of controversy include the definition of life event contexts and their influence on the development of this disorder, and also the influence of pretrauma personal characteristics on posttraumatic symptomatology and functioning (Horowitz, Weiss, and Marmar, 1987). As late as the mid-1980s some argued that there was little empirical research on the validity of the PTSD diagnosis or the distinctive nature of subsequent psychopathology (Breslau and Davis, 1987). The sheer volume of research that has accumulated since that time makes that argument difficult to defend today. The fact that different individuals faced with the difficulties of cognitively and emotionally processing traumatic events will behave in different ways, giving a different form to the total psychopathological picture, does not mean that a distinct core PTSD psychopathology does not exist (Lindy, Green, and Grace, 1987).

A BRIEF CROSS-CULTURAL HISTORY OF TRAUMATIC STRESS SYNDROMES

A complete review of the development of the concept of PTSD is beyond the scope of this chapter, but a brief historical review will help to place the subsequent cross-cultural discussion in proper context. Since recorded history there have been descriptions of societies' and individuals' reactions to traumatic events. Over 4000 years ago the Sumerians described profound psychological reactions to the destruction of Ur (Kramer, 1969). Similar reactions attributed to Jeremiah are told in Lamentations (Holy Bible, Newly Revised Standard Version) of the destruction of Jerusalem in the Fifth Century BC. At around the same time, Thucydides described the social breakdown of Athens in reaction to a devastating plague (Findley, 1959). In the last 150 years, a large number of terms from diverse cultures and a variety of disasters have described similar reactions.

For example, in the middle nineteenth century, Erichsen in England described the "railroad spine syndrome" (Erichsen, 1866), the symptoms of which were caused by damage to the spinal cord due to the motion of trains; the primary symptoms included anxiety, memory and concentration problems, irritability, disturbed sleep, distressing dreams, and multiple somatic symptoms that were thought to have an organic etiology (Fischer-Homberger, 1970; Trimble, 1991). The railroad spine syndrome could be considered the beginning of the scientific description of traumatic neuroses. Beard, in 1869, coined the term *neurasthenia* or nervous exhaustion (Gosling, 1987) to cover nonspecific emotional disorders such as insomnia, headaches, and melancholia that were also recognized to occur after traumatic events. Stierlin (1911) described similar reactions by survivors of different types of disasters, including earthquakes, a volcanic eruption, mine disasters, and a train accident. He noted that, after an Italian earthquake, 25 percent of survivors suffered from sleep disorders from 1 to 3 months and many had vivid dreams of the event. Mott (1919) described traumatic reactions within the context of two of the major psychiatric diagnoses of the time, hysteria (paralysis, disorders of gait, tremors) and neurasthenia (fatigue, headaches). His basic premise was that physical shock and horrifying circumstances caused emotional shock and fear, producing a lasting effect on the mind. The major symptom he described was vivid and terrifying dreams of war experiences, causing the person to awaken in a cold sweat.

Between the World Wars much was written about traumatic neurosis, but in the context of industrial and occupational medicine. During this period, a great deal of debate raged as to what constituted a trauma, what types of syndromes could follow trauma, and what posttraumatic reactions were organic and what were neurotic. Larer (1933) noted the similarities among symptoms that occurred following war experiences, railroad accidents, and automobile accidents.

Concurrent with this early to midtwentieth century research was the publication of Sigmund Freud's pioneer work on the human psyche. The basic premise of Freud's work was that symptoms of hysteria were the result of psychic trauma at an early age (Brenner, 1974). Although Freud was aware of traumatic neurosis and its symptoms (Freud, 1919), the eventual shift in his theoretical emphasis from consideration of actual trauma to emphasis on fantasies led him to minimize external events and concentrate on premorbid factors, such as intrapsychic conflict, when describing posttraumatic reactions. This fit well with early and midtwentieth century scientific thought which viewed many posttraumatic patients as having a hereditary predisposition to the development of their symptoms, or an unstable personality. This may have been useful in studying mild trauma such as industrial accidents, but it did not hold up later in attempting to conceptualize massive trauma such as occurred among World War II combatants or concentration camp survivors. Throughout the 1940s and 1950s, as Freud's theories became increasingly influential in Europe and North America, many of the posttraumatic symptoms observed in Holocaust survivors and veterans of World War II and Korea were largely explained with reference to psychoanalytic principles, and treatment approaches were reflective of this theoretical model of causality (Archibald and Tuddenham, 1965; Niederland, 1964; Grauer, 1969; Dewind, 1971).

Despite the accumulated evidence of traumatic responses to war among combatants and civilians in World Wars I and II, the American Psychiatric Association diagnostic classification in 1952 (DSM-I) only mentioned the category of gross stress reaction, classified under transient situational personality disorder. This early classification did not recognize that posttraumatic reactions could occur in normal personalities at times of extreme physical and emotional stress. Moreover, with the publication of DSM-II in 1968, the only comparable diagnosis listed was adjustment reaction of adult life.

It was not until 1980, with the publication of DSM-III (APA, 1980), that PTSD was finally recognized as a diagnostic entity. This was due to a number of social and historical factors that had occurred in the 1960s and 1970s. Primary among them was that the PTSD syndrome was again observed in Vietnam veterans returning to civilian life, and conceptualizations of the symptom complex and approaches to treatment were further modified by significant advances in neurophysiology, psychopharmacology, and cognitive psychology that had occurred in the prior decades (Boehnlein, 1989). It should also be noted that, paralleling the development of cognitive theoretical models of traumatic stress disorders, investigators were considering experimental laboratory models that focused primarily on human and animal physiological responses to generic stress. And throughout this century, research studies continued to develop a data base showing the large role that biological and physiological factors play in the phenomenology of PTSD.

A historical review does show that a comprehensive model for understanding the clinical presentation of PTSD would include physiological, cognitive, social, and cultural perspectives that have been drawn from diverse theoretical points of view (Boehnlein, 1989). Horowitz and colleagues (Horowitz and Becker, 1971; Horowitz, 1974, 1975, 1976, 1986; Horowitz, Wilner, Kaltreider, and Alvarez, 1980) have shown the important parallels that exist between human responses to traumatic war experiences and a wide variety of other stressors including bereavement, assault, and accidents. In fact, a biopsychosocial model of PTSD is currently the most valuable foundation upon which to build an understanding of PTSD. Neurochemical changes that occur during intense trauma can give rise to behavioral attempts (e.g., isolation and withdrawal from others) by the individual to minimize external environmental stimuli in order to decrease chances of an adverse emotional response (and this, in turn, reduces social interactions and opportunities for support relationships). Coexisting with this response is a cognitive set that, as a result of the trauma, looks upon the world as a hostile and dangerous place. In this unpredictable world which has been turned upside down by the experienced trauma, one's previous acculturation, social values, or religious beliefs may appear useless in guiding one's posttraumatic adjustment in the world.

CULTURAL ASPECTS OF PTSD

The development of theoretical models of PTSD has truly occurred in a cross-cultural context. Although virtually all of the scientific studies of PTSD have occurred in Europe or North America, the focus of these studies has been on a wide variety of cultural and ethnic groups in a variety of historical settings.

The study of cultural factors in PTSD began after World War II with the advent of published reports of the acute and long-term psychosocial adjustment of Jewish refugees from Nazi Germany. Follow-up studies have been done in Europe, Israel, and the Americas on the long-term adjustment of these Holocaust survivors. Concurrent with these studies has been a literature that has looked at the long-term adjustment of veterans of World War II and Korea, including prisoners of war, who predominantly came from Northern Europe and North America. The Vietnam War was another major turning point in the developing science of PTSD research, with the return of American veterans and the mass migration of refugees from Southeast Asia after the war. These studies, in turn, began to influence the study of PTSD among other refugee populations and among other veteran groups. A true cross-cultural perspective on PTSD can only be obtained from a more detailed analysis of the literature pertaining to posttraumatic responses among these major groups. Prior to a final synthesis and discussion, the remainder of this chapter will be focused upon these diverse groups who have experienced severe trauma.

EARLY REFUGEE STUDIES—JEWISH SURVIVORS OF THE NAZI HOLOCAUST

The brutal long-term effects of Nazi concentration camps began to be studied in the 1950s, and reached a critical mass of information in the 1960s. The conditions experienced by these survivors included mass executions, torture, forced labor, and starvation. Despite a wide variety of methodology used in these studies, the various countries in which these studies were conducted, and the time of follow-up, a consistent series of symptoms were described that are consistent with what we now call PTSD. Chronic effects of the trauma included fear and paranoia (Bensheim, 1960), mistrust (Mattusek, 1975), along with chronic personality changes (Venzlaff, 1967). Depression, anxiety, and multiple somatic symptoms have been described in long-term follow-up studies of concentration camp survivors (Eitinger, 1961; Ostwald and Bittner, 1968; Klein, 1974; Eaton, Sigal, and Weinfeld, 1982; Arthur, 1982). These symptoms often directly impaired survivors' social adjustment and resulted in a passive fatalistic personality style, hopelessness, and loss of previously enjoyed activities (Chodoff, 1975). Again, distrust and hostility were common sequelae (Niederland, 1964).

Much of the early debate concerning the etiology of PTSD took place in the context of studies of concentration camp survivors. During the 1950s organic factors were considered to be the major factor in the concentration camp syndrome (Hoppe, 1971). Even though Eitinger (1961) thought that organic factors such as trauma, starvation, and infection caused some brain damage at the core of the PTSD syndrome, he later modified his views (Eitinger, 1980) by describing both physical and psychological factors as being implicated in the etiology of the disorder. As early as the early 1960s, Von Bayer (1961) argued for a psychophysiological reaction as the etiology of PTSD.

In the philosophical and political climate following World War II, and in the context of political chaos, some of the first writing concerning existential factors in the etiology of PTSD occurred. Those who survived concentration camps were faced with the task of explaining to themselves or to others why the seemingly meaningless events occurred. Meaning in all cultures is influenced primarily by secular and religious values; therefore, what constitutes meaning in any society will be highly culturally determined. For example, Frankl (1969) in his work with concentration camp survivors noted that it was important to encourage survivors to realize that their lives still had meaning and the future still was expecting something from them. These early writings related to existential and moral issues as core elements of PTSD also influenced later studies of Vietnam veterans and Southeast Asian refugees. It is conceivable that certain posttraumatic symptoms (e.g., avoidance of thoughts or feelings associated with the trauma, a feeling of detachment from others, a sense of a foreshortened future) that are observed across a wide spectrum of clinical populations and cultures may represent a universal human response to the cognitive disruption of a sense of order and meaning that derive from a stable system of culturally specific beliefs and values.

LATER REFUGEE STUDIES—THE AFTERMATH OF THE VIETNAM WAR

Many Southeast Asian refugees who left their native lands after 1975 continue to carry with them memory scars from brutal war, escape, or concentration camp experiences. Cambodians have brought memories of the Khmer Rouge era between 1975 and 1979, during which over 1 million Cambodians died of disease or starvation, or were executed. Vietnamese refugees describe seeing family members killed, possessions confiscated, and their villages destroyed. The ethnic Laotians, Mien, and Hmong also had irreparable damage done to their cultures and societies. As data have accumulated on the mental health of Southeast Asian refugees, this population has been seen to be at great risk for developing psychiatric illness. Epidemiological survey data by Gong-Guy (1987) and Lin, Tazuma, and Masuda (1979) have shown high levels of distress and psychiatric needs. Initial studies of Southeast Asian refugees showed that depression was the most prevalent disorder (Kinzie, Tran, Breckenridge, and Bloom, 1980; Kinzie and Manson, 1983; Westermeyer, 1985a) and depression is still noted to be a very common diagnosis among Southeast

Asian refugees (Kroll, Habenicht, MacKenzie, Yang, Chan, Vang, Nguyen, Ly, Phammasouvanh, Nguyen, Vang, Souvannasoth, and Cabugao, 1989). Among Southeast Asian refugee groups, PTSD was first described among Cambodian concentration camp survivors (Kinzie, Frederickson, Rath, and Fleck, 1984; Boehnlein, Kinzie, Rath, and Fleck, 1985; Kinzie, 1986). Other clinical reports have continued to describe the debilitating effects of trauma on all Southeast Asian refugee groups (Kleinman, 1987; Mollica, Wyshak, and Lavelle, 1987; Goldfeld, Mollica, Pesavento, and Faraone, 1988; Mollica, 1988; Kinzie, 1989; Mollica, Wyshak, Lavelle, Truong, Tor, and Yang, 1990), along with other refugees (Cervantes, de Snyder, and Padilla, 1989). Mollica et al. (1987) reported a PTSD prevalence of 50 percent among a Southeast Asian patient population of multiple ethnic groups. In a nonpatient community sample, a PTSD prevalence of 50 percent was also found among Cambodian adolescents (Kinzie, Sack, Angell, and Manson, 1986) and a high prevalence of PTSD was found to be persistent over time among these young refugees (Kinzie, Sack, Angell, and Clarke, 1989; Sack, Clarke, Him, Dickason, Goff, Lanham, and Kinzie, 1993; Clarke, Sack, and Goff, 1993). Studies of longitudinal psychiatric and psychosocial functioning among these refugee groups have been limited, but those studies that have been done have shown psychiatric symptoms subsequent to trauma to be persistent and frequently treatment resistant. Westermeyer, Neider, and Callies (1989) found that while some psychiatric symptoms such as depression and somatization became less evident with time and acculturation, other symptoms such as anxiety, hostility, and paranoia changed little. Others have noted that among Southeast Asian refugees depression often improves with treatment, but many PTSD symptoms are persistent and debilitating (Boehnlein et al., 1985; Moore and Boehnlein, 1991a,b).

A number of factors in the host country can contribute to the reactivation of PTSD symptoms, such as accidents observed or experienced, exposure to crime, or anniversary reactions to traumatic events. Advanced age, female gender, and the comorbid diagnosis of depression have been correlated with a higher prevalence of PTSD in Southeast Asian refugee groups (Kinzie, Boehnlein, Leung, Moore, Riley, and Smith, 1990). Psychosis either as a comorbid diagnosis or as part of the posttraumatic syndrome has also been noted among Cambodian refugees (Kinzie and Boehnlein, 1989).

In summary, the literature over the past 50 years on PTSD among refugees has revealed that they are at great risk for developing psychiatric illness and, besides experiencing the same psychiatric illnesses that would occur among any ethnic group, refugees are at great risk for developing chronic PTSD that is frequently refractory to conventional psychiatric treatment. There are additional difficulties in attempting to overcome language and cultural barriers during the process of acculturation (Westermeyer, 1986). Acculturation stressors, language barriers, PTSD, and depression often interact to produce a downward spiral of illness and withdrawal.

SOCIOCULTURAL STUDIES OF VETERAN POPULATIONS

Much of the early twentieth-century literature related to traumatic stress syndromes among combatants referred to PTSD by a variety of names such as shell shock, battle fatigue, war neurosis, or irritable heart. Again, insomnia, nightmares, irritability, startle reactions, and anxiety were common findings in veterans of World Wars I and II. Kardiner (1941) further extended the work of previous authors by pointing out that this core group of symptoms greatly impaired an individual's ability to adapt to his environment, both psychological and social. He also hinted at postwar existentialism by noting that many survivors of World War I combat held the fundamental belief of wanting nothing to do with their present world, wishing instead to reestablish a relationship with a more amicable world. Grinker and Spiegel (1945) elegantly described many of the physiological and psychological stress responses of World War II veterans, but they also highlighted the sociocultural impact of PTSD by describing the impact that symptoms may have on an individual's domestic and community adjustment.

It was not until the 1970s, however, that initial attempts were made to study social and cultural factors in the etiology and maintenance of posttraumatic symptoms among Vietnam veterans. Egendorf, Kadushin, Laufer, Rothbart, and Sloan (1981) noted that veterans with supportive wives and Vietnam veteran friends had fewer PTSD symptoms than those who had a less supportive social network. They found that minority ethnic groups had a more difficult posttraumatic adjustment, and particularly they noted that black veterans had PTSD symptoms at rates twice as high as whites. Parson (1984, 1985) noted that black Vietnam combat veterans had to resolve the simultaneous effects of a bicultural identity, residual stress from the trauma, and racism both during their Vietnam tour and upon their return to the United States. It is interesting to note that the factors of residual stress from the trauma, racism, and the challenge of a bicultural identity are also factors that can contribute to the chronicity and severity of PTSD among a variety of refugee groups.

Further epidemiological studies among Vietnam veterans in the 1980s also noted poorer posttraumatic adjustment among nonwhite Vietnam veterans (Center for Disease Control Vietnam Experience Survey, 1988; Kulka, Schlenger, Fairbank, Hough, Jordan, Marmar, and Weiss, 1988). It is generally acknowledged that the degree of combat exposure is the major factor implicated in the development of significant PTSD among black combatants (Penk and Allen, 1991), but identification with Vietnamese civilians as a minority group, racism in the military, and civilian racial and social upheaval during the Vietnam War are thought to be other factors (Allen, 1986). Again, this highlights the importance of social, cultural, and political factors in the development and maintenance of PTSD.

How one deals cognitively with the trauma of wartime combat may be as important as the actual traumatic experiences themselves. Values and belief systems may be important factors in determining how one deals with intrusive or avoidant PTSD symptoms. In fact, it is possible that social and cultural variables are most important in PTSD symptoms that are partially shaped by cultural values and norms, such as shame, emotional numbing, and withdrawal from others (Boehnlein, 1989). Green, Grace, Lindy, and Leonard (1990) noted in their study that blacks not only were exposed to higher levels of grotesque death during the war and subsequently had higher lifetime and current rates of PTSD, but they also were significantly more likely to experience avoidance of thoughts and feelings about the war, even though levels of intrusive symptoms were similar to those of white veterans studied. Yager, Laufer, and Gallops (1984) noted that blacks were significantly more disturbed by atrocities committed against the Vietnamese than were whites; they speculated that blacks were less able to dehumanize the Vietnamese civilians and less able to rationalize the brutality that they witnessed. Again harkening back to sociocultural explanations for differences in observed behavior and adjustment, Green et al. (1990) hypothesized that cognitive avoidance among blacks may have become an adaptive coping strategy that had developed over prior decades to cope with racism in American society.

Even though the literature on black Vietnam veterans is quite limited, studies focusing on the adjustment of Hispanic veterans is even more so. Kulka et al. (1988), in comparing groups of white, Hispanic, and black veterans in the late 1980s, found that Hispanics evidenced greater maladjustment than black Vietnam combat veterans. They also noted that the rate of PTSD among Hispanics, as compared to whites, was twice as great (27 to 13%). Escobar, Randolph, Puente, Spiwak, Asamen, Hill, and Hough (1983) noted that highly symptomatic Hispanic veterans with PTSD reported significantly smaller social networks, fewer contacts outside the close family circle, and more negative emotionality directed toward family members than minimally symptomatic veterans. They also noted that veterans with PTSD appeared more alienated from their cultural heritage than those who did not have PTSD.

Studies of PTSD among American Indian veterans are just beginning to emerge, despite the fact that, per capita, nearly three times as many American Indians have served in the armed forces as non-Indians (Holm, 1992). No large-scale data concerning the prevalence of PTSD among American Indian populations are currently available, although a recent study among a Pacific Northwest tribal group (Kinzie, Leung, Boehnlein, Matsunaga, Johnson, Manson, Shore, Heinz, and Williams, 1992; Boehnlein, Kinzie, Leung, Matsunaga, Johnson, and Shore, 1993) showed a community prevalence of PTSD of 5 percent, with the majority of those cases being related to military combat.

American Indian groups tend to view combat reactions as a problem of the spirit as much as, or more than, a problem of the mind (Silver, 1992). Dreams and trance states are used in a social and community context for the purpose of healing; relying upon the healing traditions of both Plains and Mountain American Indian groups, healing ceremonies for returning combat veterans foster trance and self-hypnotic states (Silver, 1992). It is also acknowledged and accepted that many of the healing ceremonies are not cures, but simply a part of the ongoing healing process that occurs within a social context (Johnson and LaDue, 1992). It is also possible that neurophysiological components of PTSD may be altered by traditional healing approaches, such as the sweat lodge ritual, while at the same time effecting psychological healing in a culturally symbolic way (Wilson, 1989; Silver and Wilson, 1990).

Most of the studies of Israeli combat veterans have involved PTSD subsequent to the 1982 Lebanon War (Solomon, Weisenberg, Schwarzwald, and Mikulincer, 1987). Solomon and Mikulincer (1987) found that veterans with PTSD reported more problems related to their social, family, sexual, and work functioning than veterans not suffering from PTSD, and also compared to noncombat veterans. These results are similar to findings among Hispanic veterans of the Vietnam War (Escobar et al., 1983). Solomon and Flum (1988) also noted that negative life events preceding the Lebanon War were associated with the degree of postwar PTSD intensity.

Finally, it should be noted while interpreting all of the studies related to PTSD cross-culturally among veterans and refugee groups, that PTSD symptoms and acculturation stressors may interact continuously over time, and civilian trauma also may exacerbate war-related PTSD (Penk and Allen, 1991). Unfortunately, all currently available diagnostic tests of PTSD omit culturally specific aspects of trauma, and PTSD tests and interviews do not assess psychological and social stressors related to minority group status (Penk, Peck, Robinowitz, Bell, Black, and Dorsett, 1989; Penk and Allen, 1991).

CROSS-CULTURAL STUDIES AMONG NONREFUGEE CIVILIAN POPULATIONS

Most of the existing cross-cultural PTSD literature related to non-refugee civilian populations has come from studies of victims of natural disasters in South America. Lima, Pai, Lozano, and Santacruz (1990) studied the survivors of a volcanic eruption in Colombia, and noted a high prevalence of posttraumatic symptoms. Reinforcing the notion of a core group of PTSD symptoms that occurs cross-culturally, Lima, Chavez, Samaniego, Pompei, Pai, Santacruz, and Lozano (1989) noted that victims of different natural disasters and victims with a different degree of exposure to the same natural disaster had different prevalence rates of emotional distress but a similar pattern of symptoms and complaints. They also noted that these core group of symptoms remained stable for at least 2 years after the disasters. It has been noted (Lopez, Boccellari, and Hall, 1988) that certain Latino health behaviors such as frequent somatization and the reluctance to discuss prior traumatic events because of respect or shame, may somewhat complicate the cross-cultural diagnosis of PTSD among individuals from Central or South America.

CURRENT CONTROVERSIES AND FUTURE DIRECTIONS

The diagnosis of psychiatric disorders cross-culturally remains an area of great opportunity and great controversy. The diagnosis of

PTSD cross-culturally is no exception. As Westermeyer (1985b) has noted, diagnosis cross-culturally can have different meanings—it can refer to diagnostic schemata across cultures or it can refer to the ability of a clinician from one culture to make a diagnosis for a patient from another culture. As he also notes, not only must techniques, skills, and conceptual frameworks cross-culturally be available for evaluating a patient who may not share the same culture as the clinician, but furthermore, diagnostic classification is a key step in pursuing cross-cultural factors related to epidemiology, etiology, prognosis, and treatment. In essence, understanding the entire sociocultural milieu in which the patient functions is crucial in distinguishing psychopathology from culture bound beliefs or behavior (Westermeyer, 1987).

Although cultural belief systems influence an individual's interpretation of events and also influence cognition and behavior (Levy, 1984), after trauma the latter are also influenced by a dysphoric and pervasive neurophysiological arousal that has been observed across many cultural groups. In regard to PTSD, addressing the physiological symptoms only addresses part of the problem (Rechtman, 1992). The patient is left with other chronic and debilitating sequelae of trauma (social withdrawal, emotional numbing, nihilism) that are, in the patient's subjective experience and in the objective observation of his or her behavior both inside and outside the cultural group, strongly influenced by social and cultural variables.

Regarding the specific diagnosis of PTSD cross-culturally, Eisenbruch (1991, 1992) argues that the DSM-III PTSD criteria are often based on an ethnocentric view of health that prescribes how refugees should express this stress and how their distress should be ameliorated. He says further that the posttraumatic reaction should be termed *cultural bereavement* rather than PTSD, and this bereavement may be a normal and constructive existential response rather than a psychiatric illness. He further asserts that the PTSD diagnosis labels people as mentally ill and prescribes Western treatment for which efficacy is lacking. Others (Boehnlein, 1987a, b; Kinzie and Fleck, 1987; Boehnlein and Kinzie, 1992; Kinzie and Boehnlein, 1993) agree that reconstructing meaning and purpose in life after trauma through bereavement is highly culturally determined, but the search for meaning itself and the struggle with grief (which includes the reconstitution of self-concept and comfort in interpersonal relationships) are experienced by many other groups besides refugees. For example, American veterans of the Vietnam War with chronic PTSD, although they returned to their country of origin, also have struggled with issues that are analogous to bereavement in refugee groups—a loss of social structures, cultural values, and self-identity. Culturally constituted symbols, communication patterns, and healing approaches vary tremendously within the process of posttraumatic recovery, but cognitive disruption and existential pain remain a universal human response to traumatic events. Lifton (1967) described the culturally specific symbols and cognitive structures among survivors of Hiroshima, but also described guilt, psychic numbing, and the cognitive and emotional imprint of the death encounter that now have been described in many other cultural groups following trauma.

Any psychiatric taxonomy should allow for variations in cultural background and, in the case of PTSD, that would include sensitivity to cultural values, religious beliefs, and social structure in conceptualizing and treating symptoms and restoring the patient to health. Because the complex existential questions that center around loss and meaning are some of the major challenges for those individuals suffering from PTSD, it is imperative that the clinician understand the belief system of his or her patients, and that would include not only secular–cultural attitudes and beliefs but also religious background. The person with PTSD does not have to be religious in a formal sense; how the person was socialized to reconcile loss and deal with bereavement is what is important (Eisenbruch, 1984). The assessment of PTSD patients from this perspective, regardless of cultural background, takes into account the impact of philosophy, values, and social attitudes upon illness (Fabrega, 1975). In fact the use of ritual, which can take many forms not only in formal psychiatric treatment but also in culturally specific modes of healing, attempts to reinforce central cultural beliefs which reestablish the concept that there is some order in the universe (Wallace, 1966; Leach, 1970; Levi-Strauss, 1979).

The rituals that enable individuals or groups to deal with loss and death very often entail elements of both majority and folk religions, along with secular culture. The treatment of a broad spectrum of veterans in Vet Center treatment groups or groups for ex-POWs (Boehnlein and Sparr, 1993), the treatment of American Indian veterans with indigenous healing approaches, or the treatment of Southeast Asian refugees in socialization group settings (Kinzie, Leung, Bui, Keopraseuth, Ben, Riley, Fleck, and Ades, 1988), all have a great deal in common through their focus on group healing in a social context. These group treatment approaches enable survivors to gradually come to a realization that life must go on for them, and encourages them to reintegrate with the rest of society (Rosenblatt, Walsh, and Jackson, 1976). These group interventions with a variety of cultural groups closely follow the model of Frank (1961) by providing hope and relief from suffering, an explanatory model of healing, and therapeutic relationships to enhance healing.

As long as it is done in the proper cultural context, biomedical interventions also have the potential to diminish PTSD symptoms cross-culturally, and can enhance and compliment the sociocultural interventions previously described. For example, the treatment of insomnia and nightmares with antidepressant medication or clonidine (Kinzie and Leung, 1989) can enhance daily functioning and improve subjective well-being, thus optimizing role functioning as spouse, parent, student, or employee. Reducing intrusive PTSD symptoms can also allow the patient to benefit more fully from psychotherapy, tolerate interpersonal intimacy in their social environment, and participate in culturally sanctioned activities that enhance the grieving and recovery process.

Certain questions remain unanswered in regard to the prevalence of certain PTSD symptoms in different cultural groups. Despite the frequent mention of substance abuse, explosiveness, and antisocial behavior among American veterans of the Vietnam War, these characteristics have been found to be virtually absent in studies of Israeli veterans (Lerer, Bleich, Kotler, Garb, Hertz-berg, and Levin, 1987), in civilians with PTSD in Northern Ireland (Bell, Key, Loughrey, Roddy, and Curran, 1987), and in the refu-gee studies previously noted. These associated characteristics of PTSD among some American veteran populations may be instead reflective of the social milieu rather than specific characteristics of the core PTSD syndrome. A recent comparative study of PTSD and depression among American Vietnam War veterans and Rus-sian veterans of the Afghanistan conflict revealed a similar PTSD symptom picture between the two groups, but a significantly higher rate of depressive symptoms among the Americans (Miller, Kraus, Kamenchenko, and Krasnienski, 1993). Future research studies also need to take into account possible gender differences in posttraumatic responses, and also need to ascertain what devel-opmental, personality, or social network characteristics contrib-ute to, or prevent, the development of acute and chronic PTSD, and associated depression.

Working with individuals cross-culturally who have experienced immense trauma can greatly challenge the clinician. One must be aware of differing concepts of personal identity and meaning that are influenced by cultural values, while at the same time remaining cognizant of the sociocultural values that one has been influenced by not only in professional training but also in ongo-ing clinical practice. Regardless of culture, patients often seek treatment after having gone through years of suffering. After at-tempting to deal with the symptoms on their own they may still present nightmares, intrusive thoughts, startle reactions, depres-sion, hopelessness, fear, and demoralization. Comprehensive as-sessment and treatment of PTSD can and should occur within a true biopsychosocial context. Although the DSM PTSD criteria are severely limited in placing illness or distress in a sociocultural context, they should not be limiting to the astute and experienced clinician. The DSM taxonomy is merely a scaffolding upon which the clinician constructs a multilayered picture of the biological, psychological, and sociocultural effects of severe trauma upon the individual, family, and the culture at large. A therapeutic relationship within a biopsychosocial framework can serve as an important catalyst in assisting the patient in recovery.

REFERENCES

Allen, I. M. (1986), Posttraumatic stress disorder among black Vietnam veterans. *Hosp. Comm. Psychiatry,* 37:55–61.

American Psychiatric Association (1952), *Diagnostic and Statistical Manual of Mental Disorders,* 1st ed. (DSM-I). Washington, DC: American Psychiatric Association.

—— (1968), *Diagnostic and Statistical Manual of Mental disorders,* 2nd ed. (DSM-II). Washington, DC: American Psychiatric Press.

—— (1980), *Diagnostic and Statistical Manual of Mental Disorders,* 3rd ed. (DSM-III). Washington, DC: American Psychiatric Press.

Archibald, H. D., & Tuddenham, R. D. (1965), Persistent stress reaction after combat: A twenty year follow-up. *Arch. Gen. Psychiatry,* 12:475–481.

Arthur, R. J. (1982), Psychiatric syndromes in prisoners of war and concentration camp survivors. In: *Extraordinary Disorders of Human Behavior,* ed. C. T. Fiemann & R. A. Faguet. New York: Plenum Press.

Bell, P., Kee, M., Loughrey, G. D., Roddy, R. J., & Curran, P. S. (1988), Posttraumatic stress in Northern Ireland. *Acta Psychiat. Scand.,* 77:166–169.

Bensheim, H. (1960), Die K.Z. neurose rassische verfolger: Ein beitrag zur psychopathologie der neurosen. *Der Nervenarzt,* 31:462–469.

Boehnlein, J. K. (1987a), Clinical relevance of grief and mourning among Cambodian refugees. *Soc. Sci. Med.,* 25:765–772.

—— (1987b), Culture and society in posttraumatic stress disorder: Implications for psychotherapy. *Amer. J. Psychother.,* 41:519–530.

—— (1989), The process of research in posttraumatic stress disorder. *Persp. Bio. Med.,* 32:455–465.

—— Kinzie, J. D. (1992), DSM diagnosis of posttraumatic stress disorder and cultural sensitivity: A response. *J. Nerv. Ment. Dis.,* 180:597–599.

—— —— Leung, P. K., Matsunaga, D., Johnson, R., & Shore, J. H. (1993), The natural history of medical and psychiatric disorders in an American Indian community. *Cult. Med. Psychiatry,* 15:543–554.

—— —— Rath, B., & Fleck, J. (1985), One year follow-up study of posttraumatic stress disorder among survivors of Cambodian concentration camps. *Amer. J. Psychiatry,* 142:956–959.

—— Sparr, L. F. (1993), Group therapy for WWII ex-POW's: Long-term posttraumatic adjustment in a geriatric population. *Amer. J. Psychother.,* 47:273–282.

Brenner, C. (1974), *An Elementary Textbook of Psychoanalysis.* Garden City, NY: Anchor Press/Doubleday.

Breslau, N., & Davis, G. C. (1987), Posttraumatic stress disorder—The stressor criterion. *J. Nerv. Ment. Dis.*, 175:255–264.

Center for Disease Control Vietnam Experience Survey (1988), Health status of Vietnam veterans. *JAMA*, 259:2701–2707.

Cervantes, R. C., de Snyder, N. S., & Padilla, A. M. (1989), Posttraumatic stress in immigrants from Central America and Mexico. *Hosp. Comm. Psychiatry*, 40:615–619.

Chodoff, P. (1975), Psychiatric aspects of the Nazi persecution. In: *American Handbook of Psychiatry*, 2nd ed., ed. S. Arieti. New York: Basic Books.

Clarke, G., Sack, W. H., & Goff, B. (1993), Three forms of stress in Cambodian adolescent refugees. *J. Abnorm. Child Psychol.*, 21:65–77.

Dewind, E. (1971), Psychotherapy after traumatization caused by persecution. *Internat. Psychiatry Clin.*, 8:93–114.

Eaton, W. W., Sigal, J. J., & Weinfeld, M. (1982), Impairment in Holocaust survivors after 33 years: Data from an unbiased community sample. *Amer. J. Psychiatry*, 139:773–777.

Egendorf, A., Kadushin, C., Laufer, R. S., Rothbart, G., & Sloan, L. (1981), *Legacies of Vietnam*. Washington, DC: U.S. Government Printing Office.

Eisenbruch, M. (1984), Cross-cultural aspects of bereavement, I: A conceptual framework for comparative analysis. *Cult. Med. Psychiatry*, 8:283–309.

——— (1991), From posttraumatic stress disorder to cultural bereavement: Diagnosis of Southeast Asian refugees. *Soc. Sci. Med.*, 33:673–680.

——— (1992), Toward a culturally sensitive DSM: Cultural bereavement in Cambodian refugees and the traditional healer as taxonomist. *J. Nerv. Ment. Dis.*, 180:8–10.

Eitinger, L. (1961), Pathology of the concentration camp syndrome. *Arch. Gen. Psychiatry*, 5:371–379.

——— (1980), The concentration camp syndrome and its late sequellae. In: *Survivors, Victims and Perpetrators: Essays on the Nazi Holocaust*, ed. J. E. Dinsdale. Washington, DC: Hemisphere.

Erichsen, J. E. (1866), *On Railway Spine and Other Injuries of the Nervous System*. London: Walton & Moberly.

Escobar, J. I., Randolph, E. T., Puente, G., Spiwak, F., Asamen, J. K., Hill, M., & Hough, R. L. (1983), Post-traumatic stress disorder in Hispanic Vietnam veterans. *J. Nerv. Ment. Dis.*, 171:585–596.

Fabrega, H. (1975), The need for an ethnomedical science. *Science*, 189:969–975.

Findley, M. I., Ed. (1959), *The Portable Greek Historians: The Essence of Herodotus, Thucydides, Xenophon, and Polybius*. New York: Viking Press.

Fischer-Homberger, E. (1970), Railway spine und traumatische neurose-seele und rueckenmark. *Desnerus*, 27:96–111.

Frank, J. D. (1961), *Persuasion and Healing*. Baltimore: Johns Hopkins University Press.

Frankl, V. E. (1969), *Man's Search for Meaning*. New York: Washington Square Press.

Freud, S. (1919), Turnings in the ways of psycho-analytic therapy. *Standard Edition*, 17:392–401. London: Hogarth Press, 1955.

Goldfeld, A. E., Mollica, R. F., Pesavento, B. H., & Faraone, S. V. (1988), The physical and psychological sequelae of torture. *JAMA*, 259:2725–2729.

Gong-Guy, E. (1987), *California Southeast Asian Mental Health Needs Assessment.* Oakland: Asian Community Mental Health Services, California State Department of Mental Health.

Gosling, F. G. (1987), *Before Freud: Neurasthenia and the American Medical Community 1870–1918.* Urbana, IL: University of Chicago Press.

Grauer, H. (1969), Psychodynamics of the survivor syndrome. *Can. Psychiatry Assn. J.,* 14:617–622.

Green, B. L., Grace, M. D., Lindy, J. D., & Leonard, A. C. (1990), Race differences in response to combat stress. *J. Traum. Stress,* 3:379–393.

Grinker, R. R., & Spiegel, J. P. (1945), *Men Under Stress.* New York: McGraw-Hill.

Holm, T. (1992), Warriors all. In: *Report of the Working Group on American Indian Vietnam Veterans.* Washington, DC: Readjustment Counseling Service, Department of Veterans Affairs.

Hoppe, K. D. (1971), The aftermath of Nazi persecution reflected in recent psychiatric literature. *Internat. Psychiatry Clin.,* 8:169–204.

Horowitz, M. J. (1974), Stress response syndromes: Character style and dynamic psychotherapy. *Arch. Gen. Psychiatry,* 31:768–781.

—— (1975), Intrusive and repetitive thoughts after experimental stress. *Arch. Gen. Psychiatry,* 32:1457–1463.

—— (1976), *Stress Response Syndromes.* New York: Jason Aronson.

—— (1986), Stress response syndromes: A review of posttraumatic and adjustment disorders. *Hosp. Comm. Psychiatry,* 37:241–249.

—— Becker, S. S. (1971), Cognitive response to stressful stimuli. *Arch. Gen. Psychiatry,* 25:419–428.

—— Weiss, D. S., & Marmar, C. (1987), Diagnosis of posttraumatic-stress disorder. *J. Nerv. Ment. Dis.,* 175:267–268.

—— Wilner, N., Kaltreider, N., & Alvarez, W. (1980), Signs and symptoms of posttraumatic stress disorder. *Arch. Gen. Psychiatry,* 37:85–92.

Johnson, D., & LaDue, R. (1992), A cultural and community process. In: *Report of the Working Group on American Indian Vietnam Veterans.* Washington, DC: Readjustment Counseling Service, Department of Veterans Affairs.

Kardiner, A. (1941), *The Traumatic Neuroses of War.* Washington, DC: National Research Council.

Kinzie, J. D. (1986), Severe post-traumatic stress syndrome among Cambodian refugees: Symptoms, clinical course, and treatment. In: *Disaster Stress Studies: New Methods and Findings,* ed. J. H. Shore. Washington, DC: American Psychiatric Press.

—— (1989), Therapeutic approaches to traumatized Cambodian refugees. *J. Traum. Stress,* 2:75–91.

—— Boehnlein, J. K. (1989), Posttraumatic psychosis among Cambodian refugees. *J. Traum. Stress,* 2:185–198.

—— —— (1993), Psychotherapy of the victims of massive violence: Countertransference and ethical issues. *Amer. J. Psychother.,* 47:90–102.

—— —— Leung, P., Moore, L., Riley, C., & Smith, D. (1990), The high prevalence rate of PTSD and its clinical significance among Southeast Asian refugees. *Amer. J. Psychiatry,* 147:913–917.

—— Fleck, J. (1987), Psychotherapy with severely traumatized refugees. *Amer. J. Psychother.,* 41:82–94.

———— Fredrickson, R. H., Rath, B., & Fleck, J. (1984), Posttraumatic stress disorder among survivors of Cambodian concentration camps. *Amer. J. Psychiatry*, 141:645–650.

———— Leung, P. K. (1989), Clonidine in Cambodian patients with posttraumatic stress disorder. *J. Nerv. Ment. Dis.*, 177:546–550.

———— ———— Bui, A., Keopraseuth, K. O., Rath, B., Riley, C., Fleck, J., & Ades, M. (1988), Group therapy with Southeast Asian refugees. *Comm. Ment. Health J.*, 24:157–166.

———— ———— Boehnlein, J. K., Matsunaga, D., Johnson, R., Manson, S., Shore, J. H., Heinz, J., & Williams, M. (1992), Psychiatric epidemiology of an Indian village: A 19-year replication study. *J. Nerv. Ment. Dis.*, 180:33–39.

———— Manson, S. (1983), Five-years' experience with Indochinese refugee psychiatric patients. *J. Oper. Psychiatry*, 14:105–111.

———— Sack, W. H., Angell, R. H., & Clarke, G. (1989), A three-year follow-up of Cambodian young people traumatized as children. *J. Amer. Acad. Child Adolesc. Psychiatry*, 28:501–504.

———— ———— Manson, S. (1986), The psychiatric effects of massive trauma on Cambodian children: I. The children. *J. Amer. Acad. Child Psychiatry*, 25:370–376.

———— Tran, K. A., Breckenridge, A., & Bloom, J. D. (1980), An Indochinese refugee psychiatric clinic: Culturally accepted treatment approaches. *Amer. J. Psychiatry*, 137:1429–1432.

Klein, H. (1974), Delayed affects and after-effects of severe traumatization. *Israel Ann. Psychiatry*, 12:293–303.

Kleinman, S. (1987), Trauma and its ramifications in Vietnamese victims of piracy. *Jeff. J. Psychiatry*, 5:3–15.

Kramer, S. N. (1969), Lamentation over the destruction of Ur. In: *Ancient Near Eastern Texts Relating to the Old Testament*, 3rd ed., ed. J. B. Pritchard. Princeton: Princeton University Press.

Kroll, J., Habenicht, M., MacKenzie, T., Yang, M., Chan, S., Vang, T., Nguyen, T., Ly, M., Phammasouvanh, B., Nguyen, H., Vang, Y., Souvannasoth, L., & Cabugao, R. (1989), Depression and posttraumatic stress disorder in Southeast Asian refugees. *Amer. J. Psychiatry*, 146:1592–1597.

Kulka, R. A., Schlenger, W. E., Fairbank, J. A., Hough, R. L., Jordan, B. K., Marmar, C. R., & Weiss, D. S. (1988), *Contractual Report of Findings from the National Vietnam Veterans Readjustment Study*. Research Triangle Park, NC: Research Triangle Institute.

Larer, R. (1933), Psychic trauma. *Physiother. Rev.*, 13:229–232.

Leach, E. (1970), *Levi-Strauss*. London: Fontana-Collins.

Lerer, B., Bleich, A., Kotler, M., Garb, R., Hertzberg, M., & Levin, B. (1987), Posttraumatic stress disorder in Israeli combat veterans. *Arch. Gen. Psychiatry*, 44:976–981.

Levi-Strauss, C. (1979), *Myth and Meaning*, New York: Schocken Books.

Levy, R. I. (1984), Emotion, knowing, and culture. In: *Culture Theory*, ed. R. A. Shweder & R. A. Levine. Cambridge, U.K.: Cambridge University Press.

Lifton, R. J. (1967), *Death in Life: Survivors of Hiroshima*. New York: Basic Books.

Lima, B. R., Chavez, H., Samaniego, N., Pompei, S., Pai, S., Santacruz, H., & Lozano, J. (1989), Disaster severity and emotional responses: Implications for primary mental health care in developing countries. *Acta Psychiat. Scand.*, 79:74–82.

――― Pai, S., Lozano, J., & Santacruz, H. (1990), The stability of emotional symptoms among disaster victims in a developing country. *J. Traum. Stress*, 3:497–505.

Lin, K. M., Tazuma, L., & Masuda, M. (1979), Adaptational problems of Vietnamese refugees, Part I: Health and mental health status. *Arch. Gen. Psychiatry*, 36:955–961.

Lindy, J. D., Green, B. L., & Grace, M. C. (1987), The stressor criterion and posttraumatic stress disorder. *J. Nerv. Ment. Dis.*, 175:269–272.

Lopez, A., Boccellari, A., & Hall, K. (1988), Posttraumatic stress disorder in a Central American refugee. *Hosp. Comm. Psychiatry*, 39:1309–1311.

Mattusek, P. (1975), *Internment in Concentration Camps and Their Consequences.* New York: Springer-Verlag.

Miller, T. W., Kraus, R. F., Kamenchenko, P., & Krasnienski, A. (1993), Posttraumatic stress disorder in U.S. and Russian veterans. *Hosp. Comm. Psychiatry*, 44:585–587.

Mollica, R. F. (1988), The trauma story: The psychiatric care of refugee survivors of violence and torture. In: *Post-Traumatic Therapy and Victims of Violence.* ed. F. M. Ochberg. New York: Brunner/Mazel.

――― Wyshak, G., & Lavelle, J. (1987), The psychosocial impact of war trauma and torture on Southeast Asian refugees. *Amer. J. Psychiatry*, 144:1567–1572.

――― ――― Lavelle, J., Truong, T., Tor, S., & Yang, M. (1990), Assessing symptom change in Southeast Asian refugee survivors of mass violence and torture. *Amer. J. Psychiatry*, 147:83–88.

Moore, L. J., & Boehnlein, J. K. (1991a), Posttraumatic stress disorder, depression, and somatic symptoms in U.S. Mien patients. *J. Nerv. Ment. Dis.*, 179:728–733.

――― ――― (1991b), Treating psychiatric disorders among Mien refugees from highland Laos. *Soc. Sci. Med.*, 32:1029–1036.

Mott, F. W. (1919), *War Neurosis and Shell Shock.* London: Oxford University Press.

Niederland, W. G. (1964), Psychiatric disorders among persecution victims. *J. Nerv. Ment. Dis.*, 139:458–474.

Ostwald, P., & Bittner, E. (1968), Life adjustment after severe persecution. *Amer. J. Psychiatry*, 124:1393–1400.

Parson, E. R. (1984), Ethnicity and traumatic stress. In: *Trauma and Its Wake*, ed. C. R. Figley. New York: Brunner/Mazel.

――― (1985), The black Vietnam veteran: His representational world in posttraumatic stress disorder. In: *Post-Traumatic Stress Disorder and the War Veteran Patient*, ed. W. E. Kelly. New York: Brunner/Mazel.

Penk, W. E., & Allen, I. M. (1991), Clinical assessment of post-traumatic stress disorder (PTSD) among American minorities who served in Vietnam. *J. Traum. Stress*, 4:41–66.

――― Peck, R. F., Robinowitz, R., Bell, W. E., Black, J., & Dorsett, D. (1989), Posttraumatic stress disorder: Psychometric assessment and race. In: *Primer on Diagnosing and Treating Vietnam Combat-Related Posttraumatic Stress Disorder,* ed. T. Miller. Madison, CT: International Universities Press.

Rechtman, R. (1992), The appearance of ancestors and the deceased in traumatic experiences: Introduction of clinical ethnography in Cambodian refugees in Paris. *Cahiers d'anthropologie et de biometrie humaine,* 10:1–19.

Rosenblatt, P. C., Walsh, R. P., & Jackson, D. A. (1976), *Grief and Mourning in Cross-Cultural Perspective.* New Haven, CT: HRAF Press.

Sack, W. H., Clarke, G., Him, C., Dickason, D., Goff, B., Lanham, K., & Kinzie, J. D. (1993), A 6-year follow-up study of Cambodian refugee adolescents traumatized as children. *J. Amer. Acad. Child Adolesc. Psychiatry,* 32:431–437.

Silver, S. M. (1992), Lessons from child of water. In: *Report of the Working Group on American Indian Vietnam Veterans.* Washington, DC: Readjustment Counseling Service, Department of Veterans Affairs.

———— Wilson, J. P. (1990), Native American healing and purification rituals for war stress. In: *Human Adaption to Stress: From the Holocaust to Vietnam,* ed. J. P. Wilson, Z. Harel, & B. Kahara. New York: Plenum Press.

Solomon, Z., & Flum, H. (1988), Life events, combat stress reaction and posttraumatic stress disorder. *Soc. Sci. Med.,* 26:319–325.

———— Mikulincer, M. (1987), Combat stress reactions, posttraumatic stress disorder, and social adjustment—A study of Israeli veterans. *J. Nerv. Ment. Dis.,* 175:277–285.

———— Weisenberg, M., Schwarzwald, J., & Mikulincer, M. (1987), Post-traumatic stress disorder among soldiers with combat stress reation: The 1982 Israeli experience. *Amer. J. Psychiatry,* 144:448–454.

Stierlin, E. (1911), Nervoese und psychische stroerungen nach katastrophen. *Deutsche Medizinische Wochenschrift,* 37:2028–2035.

Trimble, M. R. (1991), *Post-Traumatic Neurosis from Railway Spine to Whiplash.* New York: John Wiley.

Venzlaff, U. (1967), *Die Psychoreaktiven Stoerungen nach Entschaedigungspflichtigen Ereignissen* (Die Sogenarnten Unfallneurosen). Berlin: Springer-Verlag.

Von Bayer, W. (1961), Erlebnisbedingte verfolgungsschaeden. *Der Nervenarzt,* 32:534–538.

Wallace, A. (1966), *Religion: An Anthropological View.* New York: Random House.

Westermeyer, J. (1985a), Mental health of Southeast Asian refugees: Observations over two decades from Laos and the United States. In: *Southeast Asian Mental Health: Treatment, Prevention, Services, Training and Research,* ed. T. C. Owan. Washington, DC: National Institute of Mental Health.

———— (1985b), Psychiatric diagnosis across cultural boundaries. *Amer. J. Psychiatry,* 142:798–805.

———— (1986), Migration and psychopathology. In: *Refugee Mental Health Issues in Resettlement Countries,* ed. C. Williams & J. Westermeyer. New York: Hemisphere.

———— (1987), Clinical considerations in cross-cultural diagnosis. *Hosp. Comm. Psychiatry,* 38:160–165.

———— Neider, J., & Callies, A. (1989), Psychosocial adjustment of Hmong refugees during their first decade in the United States—A longitudinal study. *J. Nerv. Ment. Dis.,* 177:132–139.

Wilson, J. P. (1989), *Trauma, Transformation, and Healing.* New York: Brunner/ Mazel.

Yager, T., Laufer, R., & Gallops, M. (1984), Some problems associated with war experience in the men of the Vietnam generation. *Arch. Gen. Psychiatry,* 41:327–333.

Chapter 3
Torture as a Stressful Life Event: A Review of the Current Status of Knowledge

METIN BAŞOĞLU, M.D., Ph.D.

Since the inclusion of Posttraumatic Stress Disorder (PTSD) as a diagnostic category in the DSM-III classification of anxiety disorders (APA, 1980), there has been a proliferation of literature on psychological trauma. Much of this work has concerned traumas such as war violence, natural disasters, accidents, and rape. Despite its prevalence throughout the world and serious mental health implications, torture as a stressful life event has received relatively little attention. It is interesting to note that little can be found on torture in the vast literature on life events and trauma research.

In the last two decades growing awareness of and interest in the problem of torture has led to numerous studies of torture and its effects on individuals. Although these studies have been extremely useful in promoting awareness of the problem, they have not dealt sufficiently with many of the important scientific issues that are essential to an understanding of the processes of traumatization by torture and possible ways of preventing them. As will be reviewed later, these studies have methodological problems which preclude definitive conclusions on important issues.

45

Much work was done on combat trauma throughout the 1980s, particularly after the recognition of combat-related psychological problems in U.S. veterans of the Vietnam War. Since then, significant progress has been made in the diagnosis, assessment, and treatment of combat-related PTSD. Although torture has important similarities with combat trauma (Keane, Albano, and Blake, 1992), the knowledge gained with combat veterans has not been sufficiently utilized in work with survivors of torture.

The Importance of Studying Torture

There are several important reasons why more scientific attention should be given to the problem of torture. Most importantly, it is a serious human rights problem the aftereffects of which can at least be alleviated by concerted efforts on the part of all those who are concerned about it. Scientists have an important role to play in turning media attention to this human rights issue and in bringing about the political will necessary to combat the problem. They are also in a unique position to contribute to the human rights struggle by providing reliable and valid data on the nature and extent of human rights abuses in the world.

Human rights abuses may seem like a problem which concerns mainly totalitarian regimes or dictatorships and less so the democratic societies in which we live. This impression is not entirely realistic. In its 1993 annual report, Amnesty International listed 161 countries, including some in Western Europe and North America, about which there had been allegations of human rights abuses in the previous year (Amnesty International Report, 1993). These abuses include torture and ill-treatment while in police custody or in prison. Although it is true that torture is more widespread in certain parts of the world, no society or ideological system appears to enjoy complete freedom from this human rights problem.

The Western countries today face a serious refugee problem. The mental health implications of torture can be better appreciated when one considers that 5 to 35 percent of the world's 14 million refugee population (700,000 to 4.9 million refugees) are estimated to have had at least one experience of torture (Baker, 1992). These figures do not reflect the current extent of the problem after the recent developments in Eastern Europe, the former Yugoslavia, the Middle East, and other parts of the world torn by political turmoil, nationalist movements, and regional wars. Traumatized refugees pose a serious challenge to Western health care providers concerned with human rights. Much research is needed to understand the psychological effects of torture in different social, cultural, and political settings, and possible ways of treating them.

Study of torture can also contribute to our understanding of the mechanisms involved in psychological trauma since there are striking parallels between experimental models in animals and human experience under torture (Başoğlu and Mineka, 1992). Indeed, no other trauma seems to come closer to the experimental paradigms used to explore the processes of traumatization in animals and humans. Survivors' accounts of their experience under torture often provide valuable insights into the effects of unpredictable and uncontrollable traumatic stress and effective ways of coping with extreme trauma (Başoğlu and Mineka, 1992). Study of torture may therefore have much to offer to trauma and stress research in general.

This chapter will review some of the current issues in the diagnosis, assessment, classification, and treatment of torture-related psychological problems. A comprehensive review of the literature will not be attempted as such reviews are available elsewhere (Goldfeld, Mollica, Pesavento, and Faraone, 1988; Somnier, Vesti, Kastrup, and Genefke, 1992). The chapter will focus on the psychological consequences of torture. A detailed review of the most commonly observed physical sequelae in torture survivors can be found elsewhere (Skylv, 1992).

DEFINITION OF TORTURE

The difficulties in defining torture have been widely recognized. *Torture* is a moral–sentimental term which is often used to designate any form of ill-treatment with or without any purpose (Peters, 1985). Scientific study of this problem requires a more precise definition. A widely accepted definition of torture has been provided by the United Nations Convention Against Torture and Other Cruel, Inhuman or Degrading Treatment or Punishment (United Nations, 1987):

Torture, the most readily recognized of the human rights violations described here as traumatic human rights abuses, has occurred for millennia. Legally torture is defined as: [A] any act by which severe pain or suffering, whether physical or mental, is intentionally inflicted on a person for such purposes as obtaining from him or a third person information or a confession, punishing him for an act he or a third person has committed or is suspected of having committed, or intimidating or coercing him or a third person, or for any reason based on discrimination of any kind, when such pain or suffering is inflicted by or at the instigation of or with the consent or acquiescence of a public official or other person acting in an official capacity.

This definition primarily emphasizes torture for political purposes. Much of the work reviewed in this chapter concerns this form of torture.

PSYCHOLOGICAL EFFECTS OF TORTURE

In eight studies (Cathcart, Berger, and Knazan, 1979; Rasmussen and Lunde, 1980; Berger, 1980; Warmenhoven, van Slooten, Lachinsky, de Hoog, and Smeulers, 1981; Allodi and Cowgill, 1982; Lunde, 1982; Wallach and Rasmussen, 1983; Domovitch, Berger, Waver, Etlin, and Marshall, 1984) reviewed by Goldfeld et al. (1988), the most common problems in torture survivors were psychological symptoms (anxiety, depression, irritability/aggressiveness, emotional lability, self-isolation/social withdrawal), cognitive symptoms (confusion/disorientation, memory and concentration impairment, impaired reading ability), and neurovegetative symptoms (lack of energy, insomnia, nightmares, sexual dysfunction). Other studies (Rasmussen, Dam, and Nielsen, 1977; Kjaersgaard and Genefke, 1977; Lunde, Rasmussen, Lindholm, and Wagner, 1980; Abildgaard, Daugaard, Marcussen, Jess, Petersen, and Wallach, 1984; Petersen, Abildgaard, Daugaard, Jess, Marcussen, and Wallach, 1985; Petersen and Jacobsen, 1985; Somnier and Genefke, 1986; Hougen, Kelstrup, Petersen, and Rasmussen, 1988) have reported similar findings.

Other specific findings reported in torture survivors include cerebral atrophy (Jensen, Genefke, Hyldebrandt, Pedersen, Petersen, and Weile, 1982; Somnier, Jensen, Pedersen, Bruhn, Salinas, and Genefke, 1982), abnormal sleep patterns (Åstrom, Lunde, Ortmann, and Boysen, 1989), somatization (Mollica, Wyshak, and Lavelle, 1987), and personality changes (Somnier and Genefke, 1986; Ortmann and Lunde, 1988). The finding of cerebral atrophy was not confirmed, however, in another study using computerized tomography of the brain (Somnier et al., unpublished data, cited in Somnier et al., 1992). In addition, other studies found no evidence of progressive cognitive impairment in torture survivors (Somnier and Genefke, 1986).

A more recent review of the literature (Somnier et al., 1992) involving 46 studies published up until February 1991 found that the most commonly reported symptoms in torture survivors were anxiety, cognitive, memory, and attention problems, mood disturbance, sleeping difficulty, sexual dysfunctions, personality changes, lack of energy, and behavioral disturbances. Some studies (Lunde et al., 1980; Wallach and Rasmussen, 1983; Abildgaard et al., 1984; Foster, 1987; Pagaduan-Lopez, 1987; Kordon, Edelman, Nicoletti, Lagos, Bozzolo, and Kandel, 1988; Lunde and Ortmann, 1990; Jadresic, 1990) noted that these problems were equally common in nonrefugee torture survivors.

Recent reviews (Goldfeld et al., 1988; Somnier et al., 1992; Başoğlu, 1993) have drawn attention to the methodological problems in these studies. These include insufficient description of the
interview procedures, assessment instruments, diagnostic criteria,
and medical diagnoses. Medical historical data and physical findings were often not reported; such information would be helpful
in examining the associations between physical symptoms and
types of torture. Inadequate reporting of neurological and neuropsychological findings made it difficult to rule out head trauma
as a possible etiological factor. The length of time between the
torture and assessment was often not reported. Few studies examined the relationship between the symptoms and the diagnosis of
PTSD. Often it was not clear how factors such as gender, age,
education, cultural traits, and personality factors related to post-
torture symptoms.

An important shortcoming of most studies is their uncontrolled
design. Most of them have been carried out on refugees so the
additional effects of refugee trauma are not controlled for. Similarly, studies of nonrefugee survivors have not controlled for
other potentially traumatic life events that did not involve torture.
Torture is only one of the many traumatic stressors in an environment characterized by political repression (van Willigen, 1992;
Başoğlu, 1993) and such stressors are associated with increased
psychiatric morbidity (Venzlaff, 1964). These include other forms
of political repression such as harassment and persecution by
the authorities, unlawful detentions, unfair trials, imprisonment,
exposure to mass violence and life-threatening situations, threats
of death to self and family, and having to go into hiding. Furthermore, many survivors experience other related stressful life events
such as loss of employment or educational opportunities, bereavement, loss of social ties, uprooting, displacement, forced exile,
seeking asylum, and problems in settling in a new country. It is
yet unclear how these additional stressors interact with the trauma
of torture. It is therefore difficult to draw definitive conclusions
concerning the effects of torture alone without controlling for
these variables.

Although some studies used controlled designs to examine this issue, they had many of the above-mentioned methodological problems as well as others which may have affected the results. These are reviewed below.

Controlled Studies

A controlled Danish study (Hougen et al., 1988) compared 14 tortured refugees with 14 controls who were neither imprisoned nor tortured. The torture survivors had more psychological symptoms than did controls. The sample size, however, was too small, and matching of controls was not adequate. Stressful life events other than torture were not systematically measured in either group so a between-group comparison on additional stressors was not possible. The measurement of symptoms was not sufficiently detailed. Furthermore, more controls than torture survivors had refugee status at assessment, a factor which was found to be related to better psychological health.

Another controlled study (Thorvaldsen [1986], cited in Somnier et al. [1992]) of 105 Latin American refugees in Denmark found that the tortured refugees (n = 44), compared with controls, had significantly more symptoms of headaches, fatigue, sleep disturbance, nightmares, and difficulty with concentration. The differences were significant despite several controls having been imprisoned and ill-treated (but not tortured) in their countries.

A prospective controlled study (Petersen and Jacobsen, 1985) of Spanish torture survivors found that tortured individuals, relative to controls, had more symptoms of depression, anxiety, emotional lability, sleep disturbance, nightmares, and memory and concentration difficulties. The measures were not sufficiently detailed; standardized assessments of anxiety, depression, and post-traumatic stress symptoms were not used, and the symptoms were not compared with established diagnostic criteria. In addition, the controls were not adequately matched and the sample size (n = 10) was too small for statistical analysis.

A more recent study (Paker, Paker, and Yüksel, 1992) involved 246 nonpolitical prisoners in Turkey, 208 of whom were tortured. At assessment the subjects were inmates of the same prison, so the sample had some homogeneity with respect to nontorture stressors. In addition, the study involved the entire prison population so the sample was not biased by referral factors. The study did not use matching procedures but multiple regression analyses were used to control for some of the confounding variables on which data were available. In addition, the DSM-III-R criteria for PTSD were used to assess the symptoms (APA, 1987). The study showed that tortured compared with nontortured prisoners had significantly more PTSD-related symptoms. Torture predicted higher scores on the Symptoms Checklist-90 (SCL-90). The study, however, did not take into account the length of time since the last torture. Furthermore, a more stringent control for nontorture stressors during imprisonment would be desirable, but a detailed assessment of other stressful life events had not been possible due to the difficult circumstances in which the study was conducted.

STUDIES OF FORMER PRISONERS OF WAR

In his recent review of the literature, Miller (1992) has concluded that studies of former POWs, despite methodological limitations in some of them (e.g., small sample size and imprecise sampling procedures) have provided sufficient evidence to support the following conclusions: (1) POW experience involves multiple traumatic stressors, including physical deprivation and psychological stress; (2) torture is an important component of captivity experience; (3) 40 years postcaptivity, former POWs continue to have anxiety, depression, and PTSD symptoms; and (4) torture during captivity is related to more severe psychological problems in the long term.

Miller (1992) also studied two groups of former POWs held captive by the Japanese and by the Germans. Japanese-held POWs, compared with German-held POWs, reported more severe torture and had significantly more chest pain, rapid heartbeat, numbness in the extremities, weakness, and emotional distress at assessment. The Japanese-held POWs were more often captured individually (as opposed to being with an intact group) and spent significantly longer time in captivity than did German-held POWs (35.9 vs. 8.8 months). The latter variables were not statistically controlled for in between-group comparisons and within-group torture effects were not reported.

STUDIES OF CONCENTRATION CAMP SURVIVORS

Solkoff (1992), in his review of the literature on concentration camp survivors, pointed to various methodological problems which characterize the research from which the "survivor' syndrome" evolved. These included lack of statistical testing, insufficient description of assessments, problems of validity and reliability in the interviewing methods and other assessment instruments used, insufficient attention to the reliability of observations and diagnoses, sampling biases, and lack of controls. The author concluded that the effects of Holocaust-related trauma on survivors and the second generation have not been adequately investigated.

In conclusion, there is some evidence from these studies that torture has short- and long-term consequences. This conclusion, however, needs to be confirmed by further studies avoiding the methodological problems reviewed earlier. Controlled studies of torture survivors are, however, particularly difficult to carry out, due to problems in sample selection, referral biases, definitional problems concerning torture, a wide array of confounding factors, and problems in assessment (Petersen, 1989). Furthermore, the politically sensitive nature of the issue poses serious difficulties for research, particularly in countries where there is continuing political repression.

IS THERE A TORTURE SPECIFIC SYNDROME?

Two earlier studies (Allodi and Cowgill, 1982; Abildgaard et al., 1984) claimed to have found evidence for a "torture syndrome."

Abildgaard et al. (1984), in a study of 22 Greek torture survivors, reported a "chronic organic psychosyndrome" (COP) character- ized by four groups of symptoms: (1) impaired memory and con- centration; (2) sleep disturbance and nightmares; (3) psycholability, anxiety, and depression; and (4) vegetative symp- toms, including gastrointestinal symptoms, cardiopulmonary symptoms, and sudden attacks of sweating without demonstrable organic cause. Eight survivors having three or more of these symp- toms were diagnosed as having COP.

This study was retrospective, uncontrolled, and based on a fairly small sample. The possible effects of head trauma were not ruled out. The three-symptom criterion was not validated; the syndrome was not related to age, sex, neurological signs, frequency of head trauma, or history of loss of consciousness during torture or fol- lowing head trauma. It was, however, related to longer duration of torture, suggesting that COP might have reflected more severe symptoms due to more severe trauma. Furthermore, the symp- toms did not appear to be different from PTSD.

The second study (Allodi and Cowgill, 1982) examined 41 survi- vors with a history of torture occurring a few months to six years prior to the assessment. The symptoms reported in this study were similar to those of other studies reviewed earlier. The authors claimed that these symptoms constituted a torture syndrome. The study was uncontrolled and involved asylum seekers. In addition, the symptoms were not compared with PTSD criteria.

None of the studies reviewed so far examined whether the symptoms observed in torture survivors formed a coherent cluster so as to constitute a syndrome. Demonstration of a torture syn- drome would require (1) evidence of a causal connection be- tween the trauma and subsequent symptoms; (2) a meaningful clustering of symptoms, validated across samples and cultures; and (3) comparison of symptoms with established diagnoses such as PTSD. These requirements have not yet been adequately ad- dressed. Definitive conclusions on the issue of a torture specific syndrome therefore appear premature.

A RECENT CONTROLLED STUDY OF TORTURE

A recent study in Turkey (Başoğlu, Paker, Paker, Özmen, Marks, Incesu, Sahin, and Sarimurat, 1994) attempted to avoid some of the methodological problems in earlier studies. This study compared tortured political activists with closely matched controls, using semistructured interviews based on DSM-III-R and other standardized assessor- and self-rated instruments. The study included three groups, 55 study participants in each: (1) tortured political activists; (2) nontortured political activists; and (3) nontortured individuals with no political activity or involvement. All groups were closely matched for age, sex, marital, and sociocultural status. The first two groups were also matched for political orientation (left-wing), and level of political involvement. The following discussion concerns only the first two groups since analysis of the data on the third group is not yet completed.

The study attempted to control for a number of confounding variables. Nontorture stressors before, during, and after the detention–imprisonment period were measured using the DSM-III-R Severity of Psychosocial Stressors Scale for adults (0 = none, 5 = catastrophic). This measure enabled a check on the success of the matching procedures which had aimed at selecting two groups similar in all life experiences except torture. The two groups were indeed similar in the number and severity of nontorture stressors during all life stages. Second, the groups turned out to be almost identical in all matching variables and remarkably similar in others such as ethnic status, past psychiatric history, family history of psychiatric illness, and history of alcohol and drug abuse. Finally, the study involved nonrefugee survivors of torture, thereby avoiding the issue of refugee status.

The study used an Exposure to Torture Scale to assess the severity of the torture experience. This scale yielded two objective measures of torture severity (number of forms of torture exposed to and total number of exposures to all forms of torture) and two subjective measures of torture severity (sum of perceived stress ratings relating to each torture event and a global rating of overall stressfulness of torture experience). The study therefore allowed examination of both between- and within-group effects of torture.

The survivors had been detained or imprisoned and tortured during the late 1970s and throughout the 1980s (mean 61 months before assessment). The survivors reported mean 23 (range 9–41) different torture events, including verbal abuse, beating, blind-folding, stripping naked, falaqa (beating of the soles of the feet), hanging by the wrists, electrical torture, exposure to extreme heat or cold, witnessing torture, solitary confinement, threats of death, further torture, rape, or harm to family, prevention of urination or defecation, sleep deprivation, and restriction of movement. Overall, the survivors had mean 291 (range 24–822) exposures to various forms of torture during 47 months (range 1 day to 166 months) of captivity (detention + imprisonment).

Despite the severity of their trauma, only 33 percent of the survivors had PTSD at some stage compared with 11 percent of the controls. Only 18 percent of the survivors had current PTSD compared with 4 percent of the controls. These differences were statistically significant. No survivor had severe current PTSD. The tortured group had higher anxiety and depression but the scores in both groups were within normal range. More remarkable be-tween-group differences were observed on the PTSD symptoms; torture survivors had significantly more PTSD symptoms at some stage after the trauma.

The relatively low prevalence of PTSD and absence of anxiety and depression in the tortured group possibly reflected the select nature of the individuals involved. Referral biases might have led to less severely traumatized survivors being overrepresented in the study. In their discussion of the factors which may have pro-tected the survivors against traumatic stress (Başoğlu, Paker, Taş-demir, Özmen, and Şahin, 1994), the investigators pointed to the possible role of a strong belief system, commitment to a cause, prior knowledge and expectation of torture, and prior immuniza-tion to traumatic stress. A longer stay in prison also appeared to be a protective factor, possibly due to greater opportunities for emotional support from comrades who were kept in the same prison.

An examination of the association between severity of torture and subsequent symptoms (Başoğlu and Paker, in press) revealed that only perceived stressfulness of torture related to PTSD. Objective measures of torture did not correlate with posttorture symptoms, suggesting that, beyond a certain "threshold," repeated exposures to torture did not have an additional impact. Multiple regression analyses allowed study of the independent effects of torture and postcaptivity (nontorture) stressful life events. Severity of torture predicted PTSD while postcaptivity stressors related to both PTSD and anxiety-depression. The independent contributions of torture and nontorture stressors to subsequent PTSD supported the hypotheses that both types of stressors are associated with psychological problems observed in torture survivors. The results also pointed out the sequential nature of traumatization in torture survivors.

Within the confines of the available measures, no evidence of a syndrome different from PTSD was found (Başoğlu, 1992a). The most common symptoms were (in descending order of frequency) memory–concentration impairment, nightmares, distress in response to reminders of trauma, recollections of trauma, startle reactions, psychogenic amnesia, reexperiencing of the trauma, sleep disturbance, irritability, avoidance of reminders of trauma, physiological arousal, restricted expectations for the future, detachment from others, hypervigilance, restricted affect, diminished interest in activities, and avoidance of trauma thoughts. A principal components analysis of all anxiety and depression measures and PTSD symptom ratings was carried out to examine the clustering of symptoms. The analysis yielded seven components representing depression/anxiety, social withdrawal/estrangement, autonomic reactivity/avoidance of trauma stimuli, problems of impulse control, reexperiencing phenomena, emotional numbing/amnesia, and nightmares or memory/concentration impairment (bipolar). The clustering of symptoms made clinical and theoretical sense. Interestingly, depression and PTSD, which are often overlapping features in posttrauma symptomatology, were independent in this group.

IMPLICATIONS FOR THEORY

Başoğlu and Mineka (1992) provided a detailed review of the evidence on the role of unpredictable and uncontrollable traumatic stressors in subsequent anxiety, depression, and posttraumatic stress. They also analyzed data from interviews with survivors about their torture experience and concluded that the element of unpredictability and uncontrollability in torture is an important mediator of traumatic stress. This study provided some support for their conclusion. The survivors' accounts in the study leave no doubt as to the massive nature of the trauma they endured. Yet, the traumatic effects of torture were not associated with its objective severity. The majority of the survivors had prior knowledge of and were psychologically prepared for torture. Most did not experience it as an unpredictable event. Many survivors also use elaborate coping strategies, thus avoiding total loss of control during torture (Başoğlu and Mineka, 1992).

On the other hand, the survivors did experience moderately severe PTSD symptoms. In the absence of other confounding factors such as previous psychiatric history or concomitant anxiety and depression, the connection between torture and PTSD symptoms was fairly clear. Nightmares, intrusive thoughts, reexperiencing phenomena, and avoidance of trauma-related cues clearly related to the torture experience. These symptoms seemed to reflect the direct conditioning effects of trauma while anxiety and depression were related to helplessness and hopelessness induced by subsequent stressors and lack of social support. It appears that uncontrollable stressors during torture were severe enough to produce fear and anxiety responses, but not sufficiently severe for this group of survivors to induce helplessness, hopelessness, and depression.

CONCLUDING REMARKS

This study may have important implications for human rights, theory, assessment, classification, treatment of trauma responses, and legal issues concerning torture survivors. It has provided evidence that systematic torture can have long-term psychological effects even in individuals highly resilient to traumatic stress. The possibly biased nature of the sample may have led to an underestimation of the traumatic effects of torture. Future research, therefore, will need to include survivors of torture with no political commitment and less preparedness for torture. Examples of such survivors are nonpolitical detainees or prisoners, individuals who are accidentally involved in political events, and "ordinary" civilians who suffer torture as a result of wars, invading armies, and so on.

In this study it was possible to study the effects of trauma independent of other confounding factors such as previous psychiatric history, premorbid personality, and concomitant depression. Such factors have plagued trauma research in other groups (e.g., in combat survivors). In certain instances (e.g., Vietnam, concentration camp, and POW experience), the length of time since the trauma is too long to allow a reliable study of the effects of trauma per se. In addition, premorbid personality may confound the issue, as is the case in studies of Vietnam veterans. In natural disasters or accidents, the trauma may not be sufficiently prolonged and, again, personality factors may interfere with a study. In less extreme life events, definition of the stressor as being "out of the ordinary" may be problematic. These issues are less of a problem in survivors of torture, particularly in those tortured for their political involvement. These individuals appear to have certain personal history and personality characteristics which make them less vulnerable to traumatic stress. Traumatic stress symptoms in such individuals are therefore more likely to reflect the independent effects of trauma.

ASSESSMENT OF SURVIVORS OF TORTURE

The problems in obtaining valid and reliable information from survivors of torture have recently been reviewed (Mollica and

Caspi-Yavin, 1992). These include definitional problems sur-rounding torture, variability in trauma responses across cultures, inaccurate reporting due to cultural, emotional, psychiatric, and memory factors, and cultural and language barriers in thera-pist–patient interactions. Furthermore, correlations between vari-ous types of torture and physical sequelae are difficult to establish, due to overlapping physical injuries arising from more than one form of torture (Skylv, 1992).

Many concerns have been raised regarding the usefulness and validity of the DSM-III-R diagnosis of PTSD in survivors of torture. Mollica and Caspi-Yavin (1992) have argued that culture-specific symptoms equivalent to PTSD have not yet been demonstrated. Whether there are torture-induced "core" PTSD symptoms across cultures is not known. Other authors (e.g., van Willigen, 1992) have questioned the validity of the term *post*traumatic stress disorder given the *ongoing* nature of trauma experienced by tor-ture survivors. Recent evidence (Başoğlu, Paker, Taşdemir, sub-mitted) has indeed shown that repeated traumatization following the torture experience is an important factor in determining sub-sequent PTSD.

Other issues in assessment concern ethical problems in as-signing diagnostic labels to torture-related psychological prob-lems (Turner and Gorst-Unsworth, 1990). Some authors view torture as a primarily political event and argue that psychiatric terminology may reflect a reductionist approach which "medi-calizes" the problem. Current views in the field on this issue are varied and often conflicting (Başoğlu, 1992b; Mollica, 1992).

Attempts to measure torture events and their physical and psychological effects began in the early 1970s. The Danish Medi-cal Group within Amnesty International initiated systematic medi-cal and psychiatric assessment procedures. While initially using open-ended questions about the torture experience, they later adopted the standardized methods developed by Allodi (1985). A review of their methods can be found in Rasmussen (1990).

The Allodi Trauma Scale

The Allodi Trauma Scale (Allodi, 1985) is a 41-item questionnaire designed to assess the various trauma experiences of torture survivors. These include nonviolent persecution, history of arrest, torture, deprivation during imprisonment, sensory manipulation, psychological forms of torture, and violence to family members. The scale yields subtotal scores for each of these events as well as a total score (range 0–40) reflecting the overall trauma experience.

The Harvard Trauma Questionnaire

The Harvard Trauma Questionnaire (Mollica, Caspi-Yavin, Bollini, Truong, Tor, and Lavelle, 1991) was designed to assess the trauma events and symptoms reported by Indochinese refugees. The instrument, available in three Indochinese languages, consists of three sections: (1) 17 trauma events relating to Indochinese refugee experience; (2) open-ended questions relating to the most traumatic events experienced by the refugees; and (3) 30 symptoms relating to the torture and trauma experience. Sixteen of the 30 symptoms in the third section were derived from the DSM-III-R criteria for PTSD and 14 were derived from clinical studies of Indochinese survivors of torture. The questionnaire was designed as a screening instrument to identify Indochinese refugees with PTSD and has been shown to have discriminative validity.

The Semi-Structured Interview for Survivors of Torture

The Semi-Structured Interview for Survivors of Torture (SIST) (Başoğlu, Paker, Paker et al., 1994) is a new questionnaire designed for mainly research purposes. Certain parts of it are based on the Jackson Interview Form (Keane, Scott, Chavoya, Lamparski, and Fairbank, 1985) which was designed for Vietnam veterans. The interview consists of two parts:

1. Demographic details, personal history, forensic history (political), history of political activity, nontorture stress factors before, during, and after detention-imprisonment, posttrauma adjustment.

The impact of nontorture stressors is measured using the DSM-III-R Severity of Psychosocial Stressors Scale for adults (0 = none, 5 = catastrophic). By separating life stressors as "nonpolitical" (e.g., natural death of a loved one, accidents, disasters) and "political" (e.g., killing of a loved one in political events such a torture or execution by the authorities), the scale allows examination of the effects of various forms of political repression other than torture.

2. Exposure to Torture Scale includes an assessor-rated checklist of forms of torture endured, number and duration of exposures, and subjective distress ratings related to each form of torture (1 no/minimal distress, 4 extremely distressing). This checklist includes commonly used forms of torture throughout the world. The scale yields two *objective* and two *subjective* measures of torture severity; (a) total number of forms of torture reported by the survivor; (b) total number of exposures to all forms of torture; (c) Total Distress score (sum of all distress ratings); and (d) Global Stress Rating ("How stressful was your torture experience overall?" [1 = not at all/minimally stressful, 4 = extremely stressful]).

The SIST includes certain items designed to test various hypotheses concerning factors related to posttrauma symptoms in torture survivors. These items were based on learning theory formulations of anxiety, depression, and PTSD responses following psychological trauma (reviewed in Başoğlu and Mineka, 1992). Examples are items relating to prior expectations and knowledge of torture (predictability of stressor), psychological preparedness for torture, threat of torture prior to arrest, commitment to a cause, level of political activity, nature of political activity (group vs. individual), social and emotional support during captivity, contact with other prisoners, coping behaviors during torture, perceived loss of control (uncontrollability of stressors), posttrauma political and nonpolitical stressors, impact of trauma on various aspects of life, posttrauma social support and adjustment, current legal status, and threats of further arrest and torture. Most of these items are rated on a scale ranging from 0 to 4 with well-defined anchor points.

This interview form has been piloted in the controlled study (Başoğlu, Paker, Paker et al., 1994) described earlier. Data analyses to study its validity and reliability are currently underway. It has yielded an interrater reliability of over 90 percent. The severity of torture trauma defined by the Exposure to Torture Scale has both between- and within-group predictive validity with respect to subsequent PTSD symptoms (Başoğlu, Paker, Taşdemir et al., 1994; Başoğlu and Paker, 1995). Further study to examine its validity in other countries is in planning.

Other commonly used questionnaires to measure trauma symptoms include The Mississippi Scale for Combat Related PTSD (Keane, Caddell, and Taylor, 1988), The Impact of Event Scale (Horowitz, Wilner, and Alvarez, 1979), Beck Depression Inventory (Beck, Ward, Mendelson, Mock, and Erbaugh, 1961), State-Trait Anxiety Inventory (Spielberger, Gorsuch, and Lushene, 1970), and General Health Questionnaire (Goldberg and Hillier, 1979). The usefulness of these questionnaires in torture survivors has not yet been established.

Treatment of Survivors of Torture

Rehabilitation of Torture Survivors

Torture survivors often present with physical, psychological, economic, social, and legal problems. The multiplicity of their problems has necessitated a multidisciplinary approach addressing various needs. Accordingly, rehabilitation centers for torture survivors have been set up in various parts of the world, run by teams consisting of medical and mental health professionals, social workers, and legal advisors. These centers, in addition to their rehabilitation services, also participate in human rights work against torture (see van Willigen [1992] for a review of rehabilitation models).

Psychotherapy. A variety of psychotherapies are available to torture survivors. The choice of psychological treatment often depends on the theoretical orientation of professionals involved in work with survivors. Psychodynamic psychotherapy is widely used, particularly in Latin American countries. Alternative methods include various forms of individual and group psychotherapy, "insight therapy" (Vesti and Kastrup, 1992), the "testimony" method (Cienfuegos and Monelli, 1983; Agger and Jensen, 1990), cognitive treatment (Somnier and Genefke, 1986), and the cognitive–behavioral approach (Başoğlu, 1992c). Evidence concerning the efficacy of these treatments is scarce. No controlled treatment studies are available. Most reports of effective treatment are insufficiently detailed and appear to lack a theoretical basis. Furthermore, most outcome evaluations are not based on careful measurement of problem areas and do not include long-term follow-up.

It has been suggested that behavioral treatments may be effective in treating torture-related stress symptoms (Başoğlu, 1992c). The psychotherapies commonly used in torture survivors appear to have an important common element: imaginal reconstruction of the trauma and consequent extinction of anxiety–fear responses. There is considerable evidence on the efficacy of behavioral treatments in anxiety disorders (Marks, 1987) and similar evidence is becoming increasingly available for PTSD (Keane et al., 1992). There is some preliminary evidence from a case study (Başoğlu, in press) that the cognitive–behavioral approach may also be effective in treating torture-related PTSD. Further research in this area seems worthwhile.

The therapeutic ingredients of cognitive–behavioral treatment are still unclear. There is as yet no evidence on the efficacy of cognitive treatment alone in PTSD (Keane et al., 1992). Cognitive therapy in torture survivors often involves cognitive interventions to help the survivor to leave the "victim role" induced by the traumatic experience. This may be effective through helping the survivor regain a sense of control over the trauma as well as current environmental stressors. Certain techniques seem to achieve this effect. For example, getting the survivor to document his or her experience in detail to be used in the future as evidence against the perpetrators ("testimony method") appears to alter torture-induced cognitions of "helplessness" by turning the traumatic experience into an effective instrument of political struggle against torture and/or particular torturers. On the other hand, such alterations in cognitions may be achieved by the imaginal exposure element rather than the cognitive interventions in a cognitive–behavioral treatment program. Helplessness cognitions may be sustained by fear and anxiety responses evoked by intrusive recollections of the trauma and other trauma-related cues. Habituation through imaginal exposure to such cues may help regain perceptions of control, thereby reducing feelings of helplessness and depression. The relative efficacy of cognitive and behavioral treatments in PTSD remains to be investigated.

CONCLUSION

It should be obvious from this review that torture, as a major stressful life event concerning millions of people throughout the world, has not received the scientific attention that it has deserved for a long time. The field of psychological trauma is itself at an early stage of development but it has nevertheless gained considerable momentum after the recognition of mental health implications of various trauma experiences. The problem of torture has not yet gained similar recognition in the scientific world. Perhaps torture is too disturbing a life event, for sufferers and witnesses alike, the mere awareness of which may necessitate a painful revision in one's own basic assumptions about the goodness and trustworthiness of fellow human beings. As Solkoff (1992) has pointed out in his review of Holocaust survivors and their children, torture is a complex topic, fraught with emotion, but we need a better understanding of this problem before we can take effective action against it and its effects on individuals, communities, and societies. In our eagerness to voice our protest against this abhorrent act and its perpetrators, we should not lose sight of the fact that, until torture is completely eradicated from our world, there will be sufferers in need of our attention.

REFERENCES

Abildgaard, U., Daugaard, G., Marcussen, H., Jess, P., Petersen, H. D., & Wallach, M. (1984), Chronic organic psycho-syndrome in Greek torture victims. *Dan. Med. Bull.*, 31:239–241.

Agger, I., & Jensen, S. B. (1990), Testimony as ritual and evidence in psychotherapy for political refugees. *J. Traum. Stress*, 3:115–130.

Allodi, F. (1985), Physical and psychiatric effects of torture: Canadian study. In: *The Breaking of Bodies and Minds*, ed. E. Stover & E. O. Nightingale. New York: W. H. Freeman, pp. 66–78.

—— Cowgill, G. (1982), Ethical and psychiatric aspects of torture: A Canadian study. *Can. J. Psychiatry*, 27:98–102.

American Psychiatric Association (1980), *Diagnostic and Statistical Manual of Mental Disorders*, 3rd ed. (DSM-III). Washington, DC: American Psychiatric Press.

—— (1987), *Diagnostic and Statistical Manual of Mental Disorders*, 3rd ed. rev. (DSM-III-R). Washington, DC: American Psychiatric Press.

Amnesty International (1993), *Amnesty International Report*. London: Amnesty International Publications.

Åstrom, C., Lunde, I., Ortmann, J., & Boysen, G. (1989), Sleep disturbances in torture survivors. *Acta Neurol. Scand.*, 79:150–154.

Baker, R. (1992), Psychosocial consequences for tortured refugees seeking asylum and refugee status in Europe. In: *Torture and Its Consequences: Current Treatment Approaches*, ed. M. Başoğlu. Cambridge, U.K.: Cambridge University Press.

Başoğlu, M. (1992a), The impact of torture experience on psychological adaptation: Approaches to research. Paper presented at the conference on Science on Refugee Mental Health: New Concepts and Methods. Harvard University Faculty Club, Cambridge, Massachusetts, September 29–October 1.

—— (1992b), Introduction. In: *Torture and Its Consequences: Current Treatment Approaches*, ed. M. Başoğlu. Cambridge, U.K.: Cambridge University Press.

—— (1992c), Cognitive-behavioural approach in the treatment of torture-related psychological problems. In: *Torture and Its Consequences: Current*

Treatment Approaches, ed. M. Başoğlu. Cambridge, U.K.: Cambridge University Press.

——— (1993), Prevention of torture and care of survivors: An integrated approach. *JAMA*, 270:606–611.

——— (1996), Behavioral and cognitive treatment of survivors of torture. In: *The Role of Psychiatrists and Other Physicians in Caring for Victims of Torture*, ed. J. M. Jaranson & M. K. Popkin. Washington, DC: American Psychiatric Press.

——— Mineka, S. (1992), The role of uncontrollability and unpredictability of stress in the development of post-torture stress symptoms. In: *Torture and Its Consequences: Current Treatment Approaches*, ed. M. Başoğlu. Cambridge, U.K.: Cambridge University Press.

——— Paker, M. Paker, Ö., Özmen, E., Marks, I. M., Incesu, C., Sahin, D., & Sarimurat, N. (1994), Psychological effects of torture: A comparison of tortured with non-tortured political activists in Turkey. *Amer. J. Psychiatry*, 151:76–81.

——— ——— Taşdemir, Ş. (1995), Severity of trauma as predictor of long-term psychological status in survivors of torture. Unpublished manuscript. Institute of Psychiatry, University of London, England.

——— ——— ——— Özmen, E. Şahin, D. (1994), Factors related to long-term traumatic stress responses in survivors of torture. *JAMA*, 272:357–363.

Beck, A. T., Ward, C. H., Mendelson, M., Mock, J., & Erbaugh, J. (1961), An inventory for measuring depression. *Arch. Gen. Psychiatry*, 4:561–571.

Berger, P. (1980), Documentation of physical sequelae. *Dan. Med. Bull.*, 27:215–217.

Cathcart, L. M., Berger, P., & Knazan, B. (1979), Medical examination of torture victims applying for refugee status. *Can. Med. Assn. J.*, 121:179–184.

Cienfuegos, J., & Monelli, C. (1983), The testimony of political repression as a therapeutic instrument. *Amer. J. Orthopsychiatry*, 53:43–51.

Domovitch, E., Berger, P. B., Waver, M. J., Etlin, D. D., & Marshall, J. C. (1984), Human torture: Description and sequelae of 104 cases. *Can. J. Fam. Physician*, 30:827–830.

Foster, D. (1987), *Detention and Torture in South Africa. Psychological, Legal, and Historical Aspects*. Cape Town & Johannesburg: David Phillip.

Goldberg, D. P., & Hillier, V. F. (1979), A scaled version of the General Health Questionnaire. *Psychol. Med.*, 9:139–145.

Goldfeld, A. E., Mollica, R. F., Pesavento, B. H., & Faraone, S. V. (1988), The physical and psychological sequelae of torture: Symptomatology and diagnosis. *JAMA*, 259:2725–2729.

Horowitz, M., Wilner, N., & Alvarez, W. (1979), Impact of Event Scale: A measure of subjective stress. *Psychosom. Med.*, 41:209–218.

Hougen, H. P., Kelstrup, J., Petersen, H. D., & Rasmussen, O. V. (1988), Sequelae to torture. A controlled study of torture victims living in exile. *Foren. Sci. Internat.*, 36:153–160.

Jadresic, D. (1990), Medical, psychological and social aspects of torture: Prevention and treatment. *Med. & War*, 6:197–203.

Jensen, T. S., Genefke, I. K., Hyldebrandt, N., Pedersen, H., Petersen, H. D., & Weile, B. (1982), Cerebral atrophy in young torture victims. *New Eng. J. Med.*, 307:1341.

Keane, T. M., Albano, A. M., & Blake, D. D. (1992), Current trends in the treatment of post-traumatic stress symptoms. In: *Torture and Its Consequences: Current Treatment Approaches*, ed. M. Başoğlu. Cambridge, U.K.: Cambridge University Press.

———— Caddell, J. M., & Taylor, K. L. (1988), The Mississippi Scale for Combat-Related PTSD: Three studies in reliability and validity. *J. Consult. Clin. Psychol.*, 56:85–90.

———— Scott, W. O., Chavoya, G. A., Lamparski, D. M., & Fairbank, J. A. (1985), Social support in Vietnam veterans with posttraumatic stress disorder: A comparative analysis. *J. Consult. Clin. Psychol.*, 53:95–102.

Kjaersgaard, A. R., & Genefke, I. K. (1977), Victims of torture in Uruguay and Argentina: Case studies. In: *Evidence of Torture: Studies of the Amnesty International Danish Medical Group*. London: Amnesty International Publications.

Kordon, D., Edelman, L. I., Nicoletti, E., Lagos, D. M., Bozzolo, R. C., & Kandel, E. (1988), Torture in Argentina. In: *Psychological Effects of Political Repression*, ed. Group of Psychological Assistance to Mothers of 'Plaza de Mayo.' Buenos Aires, Argentina: Sudamericana/Planeta Publishing Company.

Lunde, I. (1982), Mental sequelae of torture (Psykiske folger has torturofet). *Manedsskr. Prakt. Laegegern.*, 60:476–488.

———— Ortmann, J. (1990), Prevalence and sequelae of sexual torture. *Lancet*, 336:289–291.

———— Rasmussen, O. V., Lindholm, J., & Wagner, G. (1980), Gonadal and sexual functions in tortured Greek men. *Dan. Med. Bull.*, 27:243–245.

Marks, I. M. (1987), *Fears, Phobias and Rituals*. Oxford: Oxford University Press.

Miller, T. W. (1992), Long-term effects of torture in former prisoners of war. In: *Torture and Its Consequences: Current Treatment Approaches*, ed. M. Başoğlu. Cambridge, U.K.: Cambridge University Press.

Mollica, R. F. (1992), The prevention of torture and the clinical care of survivors: A field in need of science. In: *Torture and Its Consequences: Current Treatment Approaches*, ed. M. Başoğlu. Cambridge, U.K.: Cambridge University Press.

———— Caspi-Yavin, Y. (1992), Overview: The assessment and diagnosis of torture events and symptoms. In: *Torture and Its Consequences: Current Treatment Approaches*, ed. M. Başoğlu. Cambridge, U.K.: Cambridge University Press.

———— ———— Bollini, P., Truong, T., Tor, S., & Lavelle, J. (1991), The Harvard trauma questionnaire: Validating a cross-cultural instrument for measuring torture, trauma and posttraumatic stress disorder in Indochinese refugees. *J. Nerv. Ment. Dis.*, 180:111–116.

———— Wyshak, G., & Lavelle, J. (1987), The psychosocial impact of war trauma and torture on Southeast Asian refugees. *Amer. J. Psychiatry*, 144:1567–1572.

Ortmann, J., & Lunde, I. (1988), Changed identity, low self-esteem, depression, and anxiety in 148 torture victims treated at the RCT. Relation to sexual torture. Paper presented at World Health Organization workshop on health situation of refugees and victims of organized violence. Gothenburg, Sweden, August 26–27.

Pagaduan-Lopez, J. C. (1987), *Torture Survivors. What Can We Do for Them?* Manila, Philippines: Medical Action Group, Inc.

Paker, M., Paker, Ö., & Yüksel, Ş. (1992), Psychological effects of torture: An empirical study of tortured and non-tortured non-political prisoners. In: *Torture and Its Consequences: Current Treatment Approaches*, ed. M. Başoğlu. Cambridge, U.K.: Cambridge University Press.

Peters, E. (1985), *Torture*. Oxford: Basil Blackwell.

Petersen, H. D. (1989), The controlled study of torture victims. *Scand. J. Soc. Med.*, 17:13–20.

———— Abildgaard, U., Daugaard, G., Jess, P., Marcussen, H., & Wallach, M. (1985), Psychological and physical long-term effects of torture. A follow-up examination of 22 Greek persons exposed to torture 1967–1974. *Scand. J. Soc. Med.*, 13:89–93.

———— Jacobsen, P. (1985), Psychical and physical symptoms after torture. A prospective controlled study. *Foren. Sci. Internat.*, 29:179–189.

Rasmussen, O. V. (1990), Medical aspects of torture. *Dan. Med. Bull.*, 37:1–88.

———— Dam, A. M., & Nielsen, I. L. (1977), Torture: A study of Chilean and Greek victims. In: *Evidence of Torture: Studies by the Amnesty International Danish Medical Group*. London: Amnesty International Publications.

———— Lunde, I. (1980), Evaluation of investigation of 200 torture victims. *Dan. Med. Bull.*, 27:241–243.

Skylv, G. (1992), The physical sequelae of torture. In: *Torture and Its Consequences: Current Treatment Approaches*, ed. M. Başoğlu. Cambridge, U.K.: Cambridge University Press.

Solkoff, N. (1992), The Holocaust: Survivors and their children. In: *Torture and Its Consequences: Current Treatment Approaches*, ed. M. Başoğlu. Cambridge, U.K.: Cambridge University Press.

Somnier, F. E., & Genefke, I. K. (1986), Psychotherapy for victims of torture. *Brit. J. Psychiatry*, 149:323–329.

———— Jensen, T. S., Pedersen, H., Bruhn, P., Salinas, P., & Genefke, I. K. (1982), Cerebral atrophy in young torture victims. *Acta Neurol. Scand.*, 65:321–322.

———— Vesti, P., Kastrup, M., & Genefke, I. K. (1992), Psycho-social consequences of torture: Current knowledge and evidence. In: *Torture and Its Consequences: Current Treatment Approaches*, ed. M. Başoğlu. Cambridge, U.K.: Cambridge University Press.

Spielberger, C. D., Gorsuch, R. L., & Lushene, R. E. (1970), *Manual for the STAI*. Palo Alto, CA: Consulting Psychologists Press.

Thorvaldsen, P. (1986), *Torturfølger blandt latinamerikanske flygtninge i Danmark* (Torture sequelae among Latin American refugees in Denmark). Copenhagen, Denmark: Laegeforeningens Forlag.

Turner, S., & Gorst-Unsworth, C. (1990), Psychological sequelae of torture: A descriptive model. *Brit. J. Psychiatry*, 157:475–480.

United Nations Convention Against Torture and Other Cruel, Inhuman or Degrading Treatment or Punishment (1987), GA Res. 39/46,39 GAOR Supp. (No. 51) at 197, U.N. Doc. A/39/51, opened for signature February 4, 1985, entered into force, June 26.

van Willigen, L. H. M. (1992), Organisation of care and rehabilitation services for victims of torture and other forms of organised violence: A review of current issues. In: *Torture and Its Consequences: Current Treatment Approaches*, ed. M. Başoğlu. Cambridge, U.K.: Cambridge University Press.

Venzlaff, U. (1964), Mental disorders resulting from social persecution outside concentration camps. *Internat. J. Soc. Psychiatry*, 10:177–183.

Vesti, P., & Kastrup, M. (1992), Psychotherapy for torture survivors. In: *Torture and Its Consequences: Current Treatment Approaches*, ed. M. Başoğlu. Cambridge, U.K.: Cambridge University Press.

Wallach. M., & Rasmussen, O. V. (1983), An investigation in their own country of Chilean nationals submitted to torture (Tortur i Chile 1980–1982: En undersogelese of torturede chilenere i deres hjemland). *Ugeskr. Laeger*, 145:2349–2352.

Warmenhoven, C., van Slooten, H., Lachinsky, N., de Hoog, M. I., & Smeulers, J. (1981), Medical consequences of torture (Medische gevolgen van martelingen; een onderzoek bij uluchtelingen in Nederland). *Nederlands Tijdschrift voor Geneeskunde*, 125:104–108.

Chapter 4
Traumatization in Refugees

Zack Zdenek Cernovsky, Ph.D.

Recurring nightmares are an important diagnostic marker in the assessment of posttraumatic stress disorder (PTSD). Their incidence in victims of traumatic events such as natural disasters (Lifton and Olson, 1976), concentration camp activity (Trautman, 1964), or military combat (Hastings, Wright, and Glueck, 1944) is documented in numerous clinical reports. However, the research on nightmares in large groups exposed to intensive prolonged stress has only rarely been carried out with modern statistical tools. This paper reviews statistical research on Czechoslovak refugees from the part of Europe once controlled by the former Soviet Union. The studies were carried out in the period before the collapse of the Soviet Union. In their nightmares, East European refugees found themselves back to their former homeland, met old friends or family, were in familiar places such as their parents' house or apartment, and feared that the police might apprehend them or prevent them from leaving the country again. With distress or panic, they searched for means of reescaping that country. They frequently woke up frightened, exhausted, or depressed. Some of the more dramatic scenes included escaping over extensive minefields and several rows of electrically charged barbed wire fences, under the threat of fire from the

---

This chapter is based in part on a paper presented at the World Psychiatric Association Regional Symposium, October 13–16, 1988, Washington, DC.

71

machine-gun towers on the border, and with fear of the military patrols. Some nightmares focused on the highly bureaucratic system that made it almost impossible to obtain the passports and permits necessary for any trips abroad. These nightmares have been briefly mentioned in sociopsychiatric studies of Hungarian refugees (Bene, 1961; Pinter, 1969). No statistical data were available.

STUDY 1

Initially, a pilot investigation of these nightmare dreams was carried out on 100 Czechoslovak refugees. This group consisted of 82 men and 18 women residing in Switzerland. All were interviewed there, in the Czech language, between 1970 and 1972. They had escaped from Czechoslovakia after that country's invasion in August 1968 by the Warsaw Pact armies. Their age ranged from 17 to 47 years, with the average of 24.8 (SD = 5.3). Most of them were university students (54.0%) or white collar professionals (26.0%). The rest consisted of blue collar workers (17.0%), and housewives or unemployed persons (3.0%).

All underwent structured interviews with questions about the content and emotional aspects of the nightmare. The interviews included an assessment, via brief rating scales, of the knowledge of the language of the host country, the extent of previous experiences with living outside the homeland, and questions about depressive feelings. Further details of the sample and procedures were published elsewhere (Cernovsky, 1988a).

Nightmares on the theme of being again in their native country, attempting or wanting to escape, and experiencing a fear that the escape could fail, were reported by 56.0 percent of the refugees. Five of the 100 refugees indicated that they had this nightmare only once, 46 reported that this was more frequent, and 5 were uncertain or gave an ambiguous response.

Persons with a previous experience of life abroad (29% of the sample) reported the nightmares slightly less often than their inexperienced counterparts (41.4% vs. 62.0%, chi-square = 3.5, $p < .05$). The nightmare was also less frequently reported by white collar than blue collar workers (42.3% vs. 70.6%, corrected chi-square = 3.3, $p < .05$). Although statistically significant, these relationships are of a rather weak magnitude (phi correlation coefficients derived from the chi-square values are low: .19 for previous experiences outside of the native land and .28 for occupation). A weak but statistically significant relationship was also found with respect to age: The nightmare reports were somewhat more frequent in younger than in older persons (point biserial correlation coefficient = .24, $p < .02$). No significant differences (chi-square tests, $p > .05$) were found between reporters and nonreporters with respect to gender, the refugees' knowledge of the language of the host country, and with respect to self-reports of depression (67% of the refugees admitted to having experienced at least mild feelings of depression at some time within the first years following their escape).

There was a large interindividual variation in the initial, central, and concluding section of the nightmare. With respect to the onset of the dream, many nightmare reports failed to clarify why or how the person, in the dream, happened to be in their homeland again. Some persons described their trip as intentional (e.g., as a planned visit to their family). Some of the others reported arriving there by a mistake; for example, after boarding a wrong train, or as a result of an airplane hijacking. A 24-year-old machinist briefly described his nightmare about being tricked into reentering his homeland by the police: "They promised that nothing would happen to me. Then, however, they locked me up in a room. I became aware I would not be allowed to leave anymore and wanted to run away through the garden or by jumping on the car of a railroad train."

Some of the nightmare reports included neither escape plans nor escape scenes: The person only wanted to leave but felt too discouraged to attempt it for fear of being killed on the border or arrested and tortured by the police. While no dramatic physical action was present, the emotions were intense and strenuous.

Some felt exhausted upon awakening. A 22-year-old student reported: "I suddenly somehow came there. It was very nice—I met old friends. Suddenly, I realized I did not want to live there—I could not mentally take it. However, I would not be allowed to leave. The situation became very tense for me. I woke up feeling exhausted. I was sitting up for about 10 minutes in my bed, trying to realize where I was now."

Over half (57.1%) of those who recalled the escape nightmares described them as having no solution or end. Some refugees suggested that the nightmare ended with their awakening, often at the peak of anxiety. A clear-cut failure to escape was reported by seven, and an unknown, unclear, or poorly recalled ending by eight refugees.

Many reports were excessively concise (and, if taken out of their situational context, also ambiguous); for example, a 20-year-old electrician reported: "I was there and was not allowed to leave. They were getting ready to arrest me. I woke up." It became clear from our interviews that many refugees would probably recall more details if asked specific questions about all major aspects of the nightmares. This possibility was examined in the next study (Cernovsky, 1990a).

Study 2

The study was carried out between 1973 and 1975. The reports of nightmares were quantified via a 79-item questionnaire, written in the Czech language, and dealing with various aspects of the nightmare. The item content (for the full English text see Cernovsky [1990a]) was developed on the basis of interview transcripts from the previous study on the 100 refugees. The items are classified as follows: The first five deal with the *arrival*, in the dream, in the homeland (e.g., "I went there intentionally" or "I arrived there due to some mistake such as boarding a wrong train or airplane while traveling, etc."). Subsequent items deal with the *scenery in the homeland or meetings with friends or family* (e.g., "I saw my parents there" or "I met there former colleagues from work, former classmates, or those who grew up in the same place with me"). The next group of items deal with *travel documents and problems with the police or with reescaping, and with the dream anxiety* (e.g., "I had a fake travel document"; "They shot at me"; "I was afraid of being arrested and mistreated"; "I was escaping over the border in an illegal manner"; "I wanted to escape and thought about the problems at the border"; "I was very afraid in that dream"; "I felt mostly relaxed in that dream"; or "I came to the free world without any difficulty"). The last group describes the *mood upon awakening* and includes items such as "I felt insecure after that dream" or "I felt depressed upon awakening." The items were responded to by means of three categories. "True," "False," and "Neither/Nor (or Unknown)." Acceptable responses were available from 83 Czechoslovak refugees (59 men, 24 women) recruited in the same settings in Switzerland as in the previous study. Their age ranged from 21 to 68 years with the average at 36.6 years (SD = 11.3). The majority were university trained professionals (32.5%), students (28.9%), or various office workers (21.7%). Only persons who experienced and recalled at least one "escape nightmare" were included in this sample.

The proportions of responses (i.e., the percentage of "True," "False," and of "Neither/Nor [or Unknown]"), by the 83 refugees to the 79 items are published in Cernovsky (1990a). In summary, about one-third (33.7%) dreamt that they had arrived intentionally in their homeland. Only a minority recalled arriving there against their will (15.9%). Many met their parents (67.5%), other relatives (43.9%), close friends or companions (57.8%), or were again in their former homes (53.1%). Most of the dreamers suddenly wanted to leave the country but were afraid that they would not be allowed to (90.4%). Some were afraid of being recognized (65.1%) or arrested (75.6%). They reported feeling afraid (80.7%) or very afraid (54.9%). Often, they had to hide (50.0%). They frequently reported feeling very depressed toward the end of the dream (61%). Most of the refugees attempted to reescape (76.3%) and have never succeeded in leaving that country (59.8%). Only a few successfully returned to the free world (12.5%). The majority indicated that they woke up due to the suspense or tension (65.1%).

The key features of the nightmare (i.e., the anxiety level, attempts to cross the border, and success or failure of escape), as represented in the questionnaire items, were not related significantly ($p > .01$, 2-tailed) to the refugees' age (Pearson r), or to educational level, occupation, and gender (Kendall's tau). This suggests that the clinically most important aspects of the "refugee nightmare" were *independent* of the basic demographic characteristics.

STUDY 3

The data discussed in the following paragraphs were gathered in a questionnaire study of 38 Czechoslovak refugees (29 men, 9 women) who resided in Switzerland in 1978. Some of the members of this group also participated in the previous two studies. The extent of the sample overlap is unknown because the questionnaires were completed on an *anonymous* basis. The participation in this research involved, at least implicitly, an acknowledgment of the various physical or bureaucratic obstacles created by the Czechoslovak government to prevent persons from leaving their country at that time. Some refugees wished to remain anonymous to avoid retaliatory harassment by the Czechoslovak police against their relatives who still lived in Czechoslovakia.

The age of our 38 refugees ranged from 24 to 71 with the average at 37.5 years (SD = 12.1). The group consisted only of those who completed a lengthy questionnaire that included several scales (their text is published in Cernovsky, 1988b, 1990b, c) to assess the following variables: stressful events during and after escape from the homeland, frequencies of sleep disorders during the postescape years, and the level of assimilation in or satisfaction with the host country.

One of the series of data analyses focused on the changes in nightmare frequency over time. The refugees were to rate, on a set of questionnaire items, the frequencies of escape nightmares within each of five 2-year intervals following their escape (i.e., from about 1968 to 1978—this 10-year period was divided into five sections). Their estimates are summarized in Table 4.1 (based on Cernovsky, 1987). The response categories for ratings of nightmare frequencies are listed in the left-hand column. A visual inspection of the *mode* values over the five periods suggests that the

TABLE 4.1

Reported Frequency of Escape Nightmares Within 10 Years After Escape: Percent Responding (based on Cernovsky, 1987)

Frequency:	Year 1–2	Year 3–4	Year 5–6	Year 7–8	Year 9–10
Once Weekly or More Often	10.3	12.9	3.4	3.3	3.6
At Least Once a Month	34.5**	19.4	17.2	3.3	3.6
At Least Every 3 Months	10.3	19.4**	13.8	13.3	0.0
At Least Every 6 Months	6.9	19.4	27.6**	16.7	10.7
At Least Once a Year	20.7	16.1	20.7	30.0**	28.6
Only Once	6.9	6.4	10.3	6.7	14.3
Never	10.3	6.4	6.9	26.7	39.3**
N of Refugees	29	31	29	30	28

**Denotes the *mode* for each column. The N is listed for each time interval because some refugees were unable to estimate the nightmare frequency for some of the periods.

escape nightmare frequency gradually dropped from the original "at least once a month" to "never" toward the end of the 10-year span. This decrease was assessed statistically by means of the Wilcoxon matched-pairs, signed-ranks test. All comparisons of the frequency data from the neighboring time intervals (i.e., of the first with the second, then the second with the third, then the third with the fourth, and finally the fourth with the fifth) were significant ($p < .01$, 2-tailed) except the comparison of the data from the first with those from the second time interval ($p > .05$, 2-tailed). This indicates that a significant decrease in the reported incidence of escape nightmares occurred about 4 years after the escape and that the decline continued over the subsequent years.

It should be noted that some of those who failed to experience (or recall and report) the escape nightmares in the first years after escape did so at a later time. From this perspective, the cumulative data indicated that at the end of 10 years following escape, 84.2 percent of the refugees in this sample reported having had at least one escape nightmare within the 10-year span (see Cernovsky, 1987). The "cumulative data" are not those from Table 4.1, they were derived from responses to another item within the questionnaire because some refugees recalled having had "escape nightmares" without feeling able to estimate in which years they had occurred. While they provided no data for some or all of the time intervals of Table 4.1 (see the low Ns in Table 4.1), their data were suitable for the cumulative estimate on the other item of our questionnaire.

The refugees in this group were also asked to compare their escape nightmares as they experienced them the first few times with how they were toward the end of the 10-year period. With respect to *intensity*, 70.8 percent indicated their nightmares were now "less intensive than before," 25.0 percent "the same," and 4.2 percent "more intensive" than before. With respect to *anxiety* in their escape nightmares, 68.2 percent of the respondents indicated they now experienced "less anxiety than before," 27.3 percent "the same," and 4.5 percent "more anxiety." When asked to rate how important (or salient) the *problems with escape* were in their nightmare, 43.8 percent of the refugees replied "less important than before," 43.8 percent "the same," and only 12.5 percent "more important." Similarly, *emotional ties* to people in Czechoslovakia as experienced in these dreams were described by 56.5 percent as "less intense than before," by 39.1 percent as "the same," and by 4.3 percent as "more intense." Their ratings suggest that over years, the escape nightmares often lost at least some of their intensity, produced lower levels of anxiety, were now less focused on problems with reescaping the homeland, and showed less emotional investment in persons living in their homeland (Cernovsky, 1987).

It is occasionally assumed by clinicians that PTSD symptoms can be triggered, exacerbated, or intensified by various new, unrelated, and sometimes minor stressful events (e.g., stress at work settings, financial problems, or difficulties in close relationships). To evaluate whether the escape nightmares are more frequent among refugees who experienced more stress during their postescape life in the host country, the 38 refugees were given a list including the following stressful events: (1) serious illness or accident; (2) death, serious illness, or accident of a significant other; (3) marked conflicts with close friends, acquaintances, or family members; (4) difficulties or overload in employment settings; (5) marked financial problems; (6) serious difficulties associated with change of residence; (7) birth of first child; (8) marked problems with examinations at university or other schools; (9) other marked problems.

On the questionnaire, the refugees were to indicate in which of the 10 years following escape each of the nine types of stress occurred. The most stressful year, as shown by the *mode* value, was the second year, and the data also indicated that this year fell within the most frequent period for escape nightmare. However, the overall statistical relationships between the escape nightmare and postescape stressful events were too weak to be statistically significant (Pearson rs, $p > .05$, 1-tailed). Refugees who experienced more postescape stress reported somewhat higher incidence of nightmares on themes *other* than escape ($r = .34$) and also tended to obtain lower scores on a 25-item scale (see Cernovsky [1990b]) measuring their assimilation in or their satisfaction with the host country ($r = .38$) than those experiencing less post-escape stress. These data suggest that concurrent stressful events in the postescape years had, at best, only a minimal impact on the frequency of escape nightmares but were associated with slightly higher frequencies of *other* nightmares, and also with lower levels of reported assimilation in the host country (Cernovsky, 1988b, 1990b).

A high level of assimilation in the host country is often clinically presumed to lessen PTSD symptoms in refugee groups. More rigid refugees are sometimes assumed to be more prone to being traumatized by the separation from their homeland. However, neither the scores of the 38 Czechoslovak refugees on the 25-item scale measuring their reported assimilation (or their satisfaction with the life) in Switzerland (the proportions of their responses to each item are reported in Cernovsky [1990b]) nor their scores on a translated version of the Flexibility/Rigidity Scale of the California Psychological Inventory, were related to the reported frequency of escape nightmares (Pearson r, $p > .05$, 1-tailed). The incidence of escape nightmares might be unrelated to the assimilation level and to personality characteristics involving the rigidity–flexibility dimension (Cernovsky, 1990c).

Another potentially powerful correlate of escape nightmares could be the extent of the original stress, that is, of the fear experienced during the actual escape from the homeland or also during the preparations for the escape. Unfortunately, it is difficult to accurately assess the extent of the original stress in retrospective field studies. In the study on 38 Czechoslovak refugees, an 18-item questionnaire dealing with the details of the real-life escape from Czechoslovakia (Cernovsky, 1990c) was used to quantify our refugees' reports about that event. The items assessed the refugees' perceptions about how difficult, risky, or dangerous the escape was (e.g., "I was afraid someone would denounce me to the authorities for planning an escape"; "When approaching the border control station, I was worried whether I would succeed in crossing the border"; "I felt tense while escaping"; and "I knew from the beginning that everything would go well during my escape"). According to their responses to the questionnaire, 47.1

percent in this sample of refugees were afraid of the Czechoslovak border police, 86.1 percent were tense when escaping, and 62.1 percent felt afraid while at the border. While only 18.4 percent reported escaping in "dangerous circumstances," the majority (83.3% of refugees) indicated in their response to another item that they felt their escape was risky because, even if leaving as a "tourist" with valid documents and all necessary permits, they could not know in advance whether the police had suddenly introduced new measures against escape.

The total scores on this escape stress questionnaire were significantly related to the incidence of escape nightmares within the 4 years following escape (Pearson $r = .46$ to escape nightmare frequency within the first 2 years and .36 to the one in the two subsequent years). Those who described their escape as more frightening or risky were more likely to report escape nightmares in the 4 postescape years. The relationships between the two variables were no longer significant for the reported frequency of escape nightmares after the first 4 postescape years (see details in Cernovsky [1990c]).

While the focus of the studies reviewed in this paper is on escape nightmares, it is noteworthy that the reported level of escape stress was also significantly correlated to scores on a scale assessing the incidence of sleep disorders other than nightmares, for example, to reports of *restless sleep within the first 2 years following escape.* Those who described their escape as more frightening reported more restless sleep ($r = .55$).

A related clinical issue is the extent of change, in the quality of sleep, associated with the refugees' escape from their home country. All 38 refugees were asked to compare, on a set of questionnaire items, the quality of their sleep in the host country in the 2 postescape years with the quality of their sleep in the homeland. With respect to *difficulties falling asleep,* 37.5 percent indicated that they were more frequent than in their homeland, 56.3 percent of the same frequency, and 6.3 percent less frequent. Ratings of *waking up at night with difficulties falling asleep again* indicated that this was more frequent in 36.7 percent, of the same frequency in 63.3 percent, and as less frequent by 0 percent of the refugees. *Restless sleep* was reported as more frequent by 40.6 percent, of the same frequency by 50.0 percent, and less frequent by 9.4 percent of the refugees (Cernovsky, 1990c). The overall trend on these three sleep variables indicates that more than half of the refugees rated their sleep as unchanged, at least one-third as deteriorated, and only a small number ($< 10\%$) as improved.

DISCUSSION

The focus of the present review was on descriptive and correlational statistics. The data suggested the following overall patterns. The escape nightmares were reported slightly more frequently by younger blue collar workers without past experience of life outside their homeland than by older white collar professionals; however, while statistically significant, these relationships were only weak. There were no significant relationships of frequencies of these nightmares to the following variables: gender, knowledge of the language used in the host country, level of assimilation in the host country, and self-reports of depressive feelings following the escape. The key features of escape nightmares (i.e., reported level of anxiety, attempts to cross the border, and success or failure of escape) were unrelated to the refugees' demographic data (age, gender, educational level, and occupation). Within the first four years following escape, the escape nightmares were somewhat more frequent in refugees who described their actual real-life escape as more frightening or risky. The frequencies of escape nightmares were unrelated to reports of various stressful events (e.g., "financial problems" or "difficulties or overload at employment settings") during the years following escape. The escape nightmares were most frequent during the first 4 years following escape and their frequency showed a statistically significant decline in the subsequent years. The ratings by the refugees also suggested that, over years, their escape nightmares were frequently associated with less anxiety, less focused on problems with escape, and less intensive. With respect to symptoms of sleep disorders other than nightmares, more than half of our sample rated the quality of their sleep as unchanged. More than 80 percent of those reporting a change rated the difficulties falling asleep, problems with waking up at night, and problems with restless sleep as more frequent in the first years in the host country than previously in their homeland.

The contribution of this research lies in quantifying the information that is readily available in assessment interviews with refugees in clinical settings and in statistically analyzing the trends and relationships in these data. This is one of the first steps on the path from clinical speculations toward extensive and precise statistical analyses. The weakness of these studies lies in the small sample size and in the reliance on retrospective self-reports, with respect to many key variables (descriptions of the nightmares, estimates of their frequencies, descriptions of the real life escape, etc.). Similar problems are not unique to the research on refugees. Any information about dream content is obtained only indirectly and retrospectively, after the fact, in the form of the person's subjectively slanted or distorted verbal reports.

It could also be suggested that dreams are easily forgotten and only rarely recalled. It is possible that our refugees underestimated the real frequencies of escape nightmares or that their estimates are inadequate approximations. While this is at least partly true, the escape nightmares differ from regular dreams in several important clinical respects. They tend to be more persistently repetitive, unusually intensive, uniquely unpleasant, and emotionally painful. These characteristics render them remarkably salient and more difficult to forget. To some extent, they are comparable to the highly repetitive and notorious "camp nightmares" reported by concentration camp survivors (Trautman, 1964) or to the recurrent "battle dreams" experienced by war veterans (Hastings, Wright, and Glueck, 1944). Since our retrospective estimates of escape nightmare frequency might differ considerably from the real underlying incidence of these nightmares, they cannot be interpreted as adequate indicators of the true underlying frequencies. In the extreme, these subjective estimates might differ from the real phenomenon as much as the EEG recordings on the scalp differ from the underlying biochemical processes within the cranium. Similarly, the value of our retrospective estimates lies more at the pragmatic clinical level as a source of *quantifiable* data, that might systematically correlate with some other sets of clinical data, and eventually produce clinically valuable insights and an empirical basis for treatment decisions and prognostic evaluations.

It could be suggested that persons habitually prone to complaining about aversive experience (e.g., in an attention-seeking style) would obtain high scores both on self-report measures of escape stress and on those of sleep disorders without actually experiencing more stress in the two areas. The observed relationships would be spurious. This hypothesis, however, could not explain why high escape stress scores were statistically unrelated to reports of a wide variety of stressful events other than escape (e.g., financial problems, conflicts with friends or family members, and difficulties at employment settings).

In summary, in these studies on refugees, within the first 2 years after escape, more than 50 percent reported escape nightmares. After 10 years in the host country, more than 80 percent reported having experienced the escape nightmare at least once. The peak incidence was within the first 4 years following escape, with a subsequent gradual decrease to very low levels. The relationships of frequencies of these escape nightmares to demographic data were mostly not significant. The few significant relationships were only of weak or moderate magnitude. It is of much interest to obtain similar statistical data on other groups of refugees or on survivors of unusually stressful events.

REFERENCES

Bene, E. (1961), Anxiety and emotional impoverishment in men under stress. *Brit. J. Med. Psychol.*, 30:281–289.

Cernovsky, Z. Z. (1987), Repetitive escape nightmares of refugees. *Percept. & Motor Skills*, 65:895–898.

——— (1988a), Refugees' repetitive nightmares. *J. Clin. Psychol.*, 44:702–707.

——— (1988b), Escape nightmares and postescape stressful events. *Percept. & Motor Skills*, 66:551–555.

——— (1990a), Group nightmares about escape from ex-homeland. *J. Clin. Psychol.*, 46:581–588.

——— (1990b), Stressful events and assimilation level of refugees. *Soc. Behav. & Personal.*, 18:27–34.

——— (1990c), Escape stress, sleep disorders, and assimilation of refugees. *Soc. Behav. & Personal.*, 18:287–298.

Hastings, D. W., Wright, D. G., & Glueck, E. G. (1944), *Psychiatric Experiences of the Eighth Air Forces.* New York: Josiah Macy Jr. Fund.

Lifton, R. J., & Olson, E. (1976), The human meaning of total disaster: The Buffalo Creek Experience. *Psychiatry*, 39:1–18.

Pinter, E. (1969), *Wohlstandsfluechtlinge. Eine sozial-psychiatrische Studie an ungarischen Fluechtlingen in der Schweiz.* Basel & New York: Karger Verlag.

Trautman, E. C. (1964), Fear and panic in Nazi concentration camps. *Internat. J. Soc. Psychiatry*, 10:134–141.

Part II

Life Events and Mental Illness

Chapter 5
Life Events and Psychotic Disorders

PAUL BEBBINGTON, M.A., Ph.D., F.R.C.P., F.R.C.Psych., JO BOWEN, M.B., B.S., M.R.C.Psych., AND RAJINI RAMANA, M.B., B.S., M.R.C.Psych.

Over the last 30 years or so, the idea that psychoses are influenced by the social environment has become widely accepted. Nevertheless, there has been more difficulty in demonstrating the impact of life events on psychotic disorders than many clinicians realize.

Serious research into the effects of life events in schizophrenia dates back to Brown and Birley's classic paper (1968), although Kraepelin (1913) claimed that remission was frequently brought to an end by major changes in patients' lives.

In this chapter, we shall concentrate on reviewing the life event literature relating to psychotic conditions. Because the findings are not robust we must pay some attention to the methodological issues of life event research.

METHODOLOGICAL ISSUES

THE MEASUREMENT OF LIFE EVENTS

A few studies have examined responses to a single type of event. Thus, Steinberg and Durell (1968) studied the effects of recruitment into the army, following which they plotted the frequency

89

of schizophrenic breakdown. They were able to demonstrate that the rate of breakdown was significantly higher in the few months immediately after recruitment than later in the period of military service.

Most studies, however, have attempted to evaluate the response of sufferers to a wide range of life events. This inevitably brings up issues of measurement, since, once life event stress is considered as a whole, it becomes clear that events are not equivalent. There must therefore be some way of assessing the likely impact of a given event on a subject. This depends on a large number of variables, relating both to the nature of the event and to the subject's prior experiences. Inevitably, each person's experience of events is unique and is responsible for a unique susceptibility.

We can, nevertheless, attempt general statements about relative impact. The death of a child will always vastly outweigh a child moving out of the home to go to college or to get married. Most events, however, are like the last examples rather than the first, and distinguishing their relative severity is difficult and heavily dependent on context. It might seem an obvious strategy to ask subjects how events did indeed affect them, but this leads to two types of potential bias. On the one hand, subjects unfortunately share their research hypotheses with the researcher: it is characteristic of human beings that they seek to impose meaning to their lives in terms of their experiences. The second bias is that the effects of mental illness itself may distort subjects' assessments of their experiences. Yet, if we decline to accept a respondent's own judgments, we are faced with the difficulty of arriving at our own.

There have been two basic attempts to deal with this problem. One was to define events by constructing a list of event types. This is the "inventory" approach, associated with the names of Holmes and Rahe (1967). A history is then elicited from respondents by presenting them with the list, either on paper or verbally, and asking them to identify events experienced within a given period. The disadvantage of this method is that it largely delegates to the respondent the decision as to whether an experience matches up with an event category, leading to what Dohrenwend,

Stueve, Skodol, and Link (1993) call the problem of *intracategory variability*. The authors of this approach dealt with the problem of the differential impact of events by using a rating sample to ascribe values to each event category. The scores of the rating sample were then averaged to give a stress rating for the event. The effect of this was to give a crude rating completely divorced from the specific circumstances that might surround given events in the individual case. It was certainly one way of discounting the subjective evaluation of individual experience.

Event inventories are still used in psychiatric research, although the method is an insensitive one. The alternative technique, of a semistructured interview based around role areas, in our view offers a considerable improvement (Brown, 1974; Brown and Harris, 1978). People using this approach have relied heavily on the development of the Life Events and Difficulty Schedule (LEDS) of Brown and his colleagues, although it is sometimes modified to suit local circumstances (e.g., Ambelas, 1979, 1987; Kennedy, Thompson, Stancer, Roy, and Persad, 1983; Al Khani, Bebbington, Watson, and House, 1986). Potential life events are identified by the interviewer and then presented to a rating panel, which ascribes a severity rating to the elicited events. As the interviewer is able to provide a considerable amount of context, so the individual circumstances of the event can be taken into account, in a way which is not feasible using an inventory approach. Thus, some degree of individuality of response is retained, while the subjects' evaluation is removed from consideration. This represents a reasonable compromise between pure subjectivity and the crudeness of evaluating events merely by categorizing them.

The LEDS procedure has encouraged others to increase the validity of history taking in similar ways. The Structure Event Probe and Narrative Rating Scale (SEPRATE) procedure of Dohrenwend and his colleagues (1993) deliberately separates context and disposition from event assessment, but an interviewer collects descriptions of individual events after they have been endorsed from an inventory by the respondent. The argument is that the context of the event can be determined objectively from sociodemographic data. Events are then rated by two or more independent judges, rather in the manner of the LEDS procedure.

A further problem concerns the choice of dimensions along which to rate impact. There was dispute between those who thought impact was best denoted by the amount of change following an event, and those who felt that the degree of stress was a more crucial attribute. Empirically, it would seem that the most predictive dimension is indeed stressfulness (Mueller, Edwards, and Yarvis, 1977), although this raises more conceptual difficulties than the measurement of mere change. The LEDS relies on measures of *threat*, although events can also be rated according to the degree of loss they connote.

Other important issues apart from the dimensions of impact must be considered in evaluating the causal relationship between events and any kind of psychiatric disorder. Thus, it is not always possible to be absolutely sure that the temporal requirements for a causal inference have been made. Plainly, for an event to be held to cause a relapse into psychosis, it must precede the relapse. Relapse itself can be difficult to define, however, and, indeed, date. As a result, we are very often not quite sure that the identified event does in fact precede relapse. Though it might not at first sight appear to do so, the event may itself have come about because of changes in the subject's behavior that were themselves occasioned by impending relapse.

In response to this problem, Brown and his colleagues have developed the concept of *independence* (Brown and Harris, 1978). This is a measure of the extent to which events are independent of illness-related behavior on the part of the subject. This rating has become increasingly complex over the years since it was introduced. However, most of the existing life event research using the LEDS depends on a threefold division of events into independent, possibly independent, and dependent. Independent events are basically those that are in logical terms very unlikely to have been brought about by impending breakdown. Possibly independent events are those where such a relationship cannot be ruled out, but where there is no actual evidence that the event in question was brought about by changed behavior. In most cases, people either use the independent category, or combine it with the possibly independent category, to define the events to be considered in analyses.

The SEPRATE procedure of Dohrenwend and his colleagues (1993) includes measures of change and threat: violence; independence; fatefulness; magnitude of change; life threatening quality. This procedure, by firming up the definition of events, increases the odds ratio by a factor of 2. Interrater reliability was good (Shrout, Link, Dohrenwend, Skodol, Stueve, and Mirotznik, 1989).

Eliciting a history of life events from subjects inevitably requires that they are able to recall the events in question. This assumption is often misplaced. Everyone has a tendency to forget things that have happened to them, and powers of recall obviously differ between individuals. Mental illness is particularly likely to impair recall, especially when the patient is still acutely disturbed. Some authors have attempted to get around this by delaying the interview until the patient has considerably recovered, but this does mean that patients are being asked to remember events that are consequently more remote in time. Recall is obviously best when the period recalled is not very remote, and where the interviewers are well trained (Wittchen, Essau, and Hecht, 1989). There is also evidence that, for events of moderate and marked threat at any rate, the dangers of recall are minimized by using the LEDS. These difficulties are particularly significant for case control studies where life events are usually elicited over a longer period than in prospective studies.

RESEARCH DESIGN AND THE INFERENCE OF CAUSALITY

There are several different ways in which the association between life events and the onset or relapse of psychosis might be tested. In retrospective within-patient designs, the experience of life events is compared between a defined period immediately prior to the onset of illness and a more distant period. This approach can be combined with a classic, retrospective case-control design in which the life event experience of the cases prior to onset is compared with an equivalent period in normal controls, usually the period immediately preceding interview. The problem with both of these approaches is that the length of recall differs between the period where the events are expected to be elevated and the period in which they are not. In the within-case comparison, this operates in favor of the hypothesis of an excess of events preceding onset, while in the case-control design, it works against it.

The difficulties of the retrospective case control design have been discussed at length elsewhere (Day, 1981, 1989; Brown and Harris, 1989; Creed, 1990; Hirsch, Cramer, and Bowen, 1992). Together, they contribute to the inconsistencies in research findings and make comparison difficult.

There is a further difficulty. What is the appropriate control group for a group of people with psychotic disorders? Such people may have attributes that affect their life event rate. One would, perhaps, expect the rate to be lowered, as their illness, and indeed their premorbid adjustment, might lead them to withdraw from certain areas of life that may be a source of events; for example, intense emotional relationships or employment. If anything, however, event rates in schizophrenia may be higher than would be expected in a normal control group (Schwarz and Myers, 1977; Bebbington, Wilkins, Jones, Foerster, Murray, Toone, and Lewis, 1993). Both Kennedy and his colleagues (1983) and Sclare and Creed (1990) found that subjects who had many previous episodes of manic-depression had a restricted social network and fewer confidants. While Sclare and Creed (1990) reported that this group, as might be expected, was less likely to experience adverse life events, Kennedy and his colleagues (1983) found the reverse to be true. It is of interest that Wicki and Angst (1991) provide evidence, in subjects who became hypomanic during the course of a prospective community study in Zurich, of raised life events rates up to 7 years before onset. As a consequence, the most secure evidence in support of a triggering role for life events in psychotic relapse may be the finding of a within-patient peaking of events before the episode.

A further problem with using the case-control design is that people with psychosis may be abnormally sensitive to the impact of stress. Because of this, they may respond adversely to relatively minor disturbances in their social world. In consequence, their experience of more major life events may be no more than would be expected. This is another reason why the within-case comparison may be the most appropriate.

It is possible to investigate the life event hypotheses using a prospective design; that is, prospective in the sense that the life event history is established prior to an episode of recurrence. Thus, patients may be interviewed, say, every 2 months, at which time life events and symptom status are evaluated for the intervening period. The actual evaluations have to be inevitably retrospective. The researcher is left, however, with a continuous series of periods in which life events or exacerbations, or both, may have occurred. It is then possible to look at the experience of life events in the period *immediately preceding* that in which an exacerbation occurred. Once more, it is possible to compare such periods with dissimilar periods in the same subject, or in other subjects who did not experience exacerbations. This is a powerful design, but depends crucially on evaluating patients sufficiently frequently for events in one period not to be too distant in time from an exacerbation in the next. It also requires diligent evaluation of life events and the careful definition of exacerbation or relapse. The studies of this type carried out on bipolar subjects have had evaluation periods determined by the timing of clinic visits and which thus varied considerably both within and between patients.

In general, little attention has been devoted to the differences in sampling procedures between studies of life events and psychosis. This is partly because the condition is a serious one that usually leads to specialist psychiatric contact. The sampling of patient groups has varied, but retrospective studies have generally been of hospitalized patients with first onsets or relapse. Prospective designs inevitably require that the patient has already experienced an episode of disorder. Cohorts of such patients can then be followed in remission. Studying relapses rather than first onsets necessarily defines groups of patients at particularly high risk.

In addition to these administrative aspects, the phenomenological characteristics of patients have varied. Recent studies have used operationalized diagnostic criteria to determine the entry of patients, but in many studies the sample has been of mixed clinical profile. In several studies, particularly of schizophrenia, some of the so-called relapses have merely been increases in the level of psychotic symptoms, in other words exacerbations. Because most studies are actually of small numbers, the effect of these case differences cannot be satisfactorily examined. A lack of difference between subgroups may indicate the true state of affairs, or merely be a type-2 error.

A final methodological issue concerns the length of the causal period in which life events are thought to operate. It is important that the antecedent period chosen for canvasing a life event history should be at least as long as the causal period. Events would be seen as having a triggering role in this sense if they occurred in close proximity to the onset of relapse of disorder. It has generally been held that a 6-month period of study should be sufficient to cover all events that might have a role in engendering relapse, although this has recently been queried (Bebbington et al., 1993).

A REVIEW OF STUDIES OF LIFE EVENTS AND SCHIZOPHRENIA

In early 1993, there were 16 published studies specifically examining the effect of life events on the etiology or course of schizophrenia. The inaugural and still seminal study in this area is that of Brown and Birley (1968). They used careful methods, and a retrospective case-control and within-patient design. They found a significantly raised rate of life events, limited to the 3 weeks before the onset or relapse of schizophrenia. Forty-six percent of cases had at least one independent event in the 3 weeks before relapse compared with 12 percent in more distant periods. This finding was later interpreted to indicate an effect of life events in precipitating, or "triggering," the onset of illness which would have happened anyway, albeit a few weeks later (Brown, Harris, and Peto, 1973).

Studies from a wide range of cultural settings have followed, but offer only inconsistent support for these initial findings (see Table 5.1). Some found that independent events were significantly more frequent in the 3 or 4 weeks before relapse compared with control periods. In a retrospective multicenter World Health Organization (WHO) study, Day, Neilsen, Korten, Ernberg, Dube, Gebhart, Jablensky, Leon, Marsella, Olatawura, Sartorius, Strömgren, Takahashi, Wig, and Wynne (1987) used loglinear methods to demonstrate similar results to Brown and Birley (1968) in five of six centers. Ventura, Nuechterlein, Lukoff, and Hardisty (1989), investigating patients on regular neuroleptic medication, found support for a triggering hypothesis.

Other studies, based on widely varying methods, have found significant increases in independent events over longer periods, up to 6 months or even a year preceding relapse or illness onset (Dohrenwend, Levav, and Shrout, 1987; Bebbington et al., 1993; Hirsch, Bowen, Emami, Cramer, Jolley, Haw, and Dickinson, submitted). Yet others failed to detect a significant excess of independent life events in variously defined prerelapse periods compared with control periods (e.g., Jacobs and Myers, 1976; Malzacher, Merz, and Ebnother, 1981; Al Khani et al., 1986; Chung, Langeluddecke, and Tennant, 1986; Gureje and Adewumni, 1988; Malla, Cortese, Shaw, and Ginsberg, 1990). A study from Saudi Arabia (Al Khani et al., 1986) obtained no overall effect, but did find a significant difference for a married female subgroup. Other studies have found elevations of life event rates preceding illness onset (e.g., for Japan, and for two of the three developing countries in the WHO study [Day et al., 1987]), but methodological problems limit the weight that can be placed on these trends as support for the earlier findings.

Prospective life event studies of schizophrenia are increasing in number and avoid many of the important methodological problems affecting retrospective studies. So far, however, they too have offered inconsistent support for the triggering hypothesis. One study which followed up patients who had been well for 2

TABLE 5.1
Studies of Independent Life Events in Schizophrenic Illness

Study	Country	Period/Method	Patient Sample	Number	Significant Results for Time Period 3–5 weeks	Significant Results for Time Period >3/12
Retrospective						
Brown and Birley (1968)	U.K.	12/52	Broad group: 30% 1st onset	50	Yes, for 3 weeks	Not addressed
Jacobs and Myers (1976)	U.K.	1 year: not LEDS	Narrow definition: all 1st onset	62	Not addressed	NS
Malzacher et al. (1981)	Germany	6/12	1st onset	90	Not addressed	NS
Canton and Fraccon (1985)	Italy	6/12: not LEDS	24 1st onset	54	Not addressed	Possible support
Chung et al. (1986)	U.S.	6/12	Narrow definition: some 1st onset	15	NS	NS
Al Khani et al. (1986)	Saudi Arabia	1 year	Narrow definition: recent onset	48	Small sub-groups only	NS
Day et al. (1987) WHO	10 centres worldwide	12/52	Broad definition: some 1st onset	13-67	Yes for 5 of 6 analyzed fully	Not addressed
Dohrenwend et al. (1987)	U.S.	6/12: not LEDS	21 1st onset	66	NS	Yes, for 'non-fateful' events
Gureje and Adewumni (1988)	Nigeria	6/12: not LEDS	All 1st onset: RDC definition	42	NS	NS
Bebbington et al. (1993)	U.K.	6/12	Narrow definition	52	Not addressed	Yes, for up to 6 months

Prospective

Leff et al. (1973)	U.K.	Clinical Trial	9 on medication relapsed	116	For medicated only (5 weeks)	NS
Hardesty et al. (1985)	U.S.	1 year	2–3 years in remission	36	NS (morbidity 3/52 post LE)	Not addressed
Ventura et al. (1989)	U.S.	1 year on medication (see 1992*)	Recent onset: 11/30 relapsers	22	Yes for 4 weeks	NS
Malla et al. (1990)	Canada	1 year	7 relapsed	22	Not addressed	NS unless trivial events included
Ventura et al. (1992)	U.S.	1 year of medication status (see 1989*)	Recent onset: off medication	13	NS for those off medication status	NS
Hirsch et al. (1993)	U.K.	1 year on/off medication status	Narrow. Relapses: off medication 21/35; on medication 5/36	71	NS for both on and off medication groups	Yes, for up to 1 year

Recent onset: illness history < 2 years

or 3 years in the community found no increase in morbidity in the 3 weeks following major independent events (Hardesty, Falloon, and Shirin, 1985). This was the first study to use a prospective design, but it was limited by the small numbers of cases and of major independent events. Two subsequent prospective studies have found no increase in independent major events in the 4 weeks preceding relapse (Malla et al., 1990; Hirsch et al., submitted) and another found a significant excess of events preceding illness only for patients on regular neuroleptic medication (Ventura et al., 1989; Ventura, Nuechterlein, Hardisty, and Gitlin, 1992).

THREE RECENT STUDIES

Three recent studies, two British and one American, merit further discussion. They have used a range of designs to investigate the relationship between life events and psychotic disorders. The first of these is the Camberwell Collaborative Psychosis Study (Jones, Bebbington, Foerster, Lewis, Murray, Russell, Sham, Toone, and Wilkins, 1993; Bebbington et al., 1993). This involved the collection of a range of biological and social data on a large sample of people suffering from psychosis, broadly defined. In the course of the study, 51 subjects were identified as having experienced a datable episode of schizophrenic relapse within the past year. Life event histories were taken for the 6-month period immediately preceding the relapse, using the LEDS (Brown and Harris, 1978). These were compared with equivalent histories from a psychiatrically healthy sample obtained from a community survey carried out in the same area. There was a significant excess of life events, particularly in the 3 months before relapse.

Figure 5.1 shows the results from this study relating to schizophrenia: there is a significantly elevated rate of events in cases throughout the period of assessment. This might arise because events throughout the period are of etiological significance, but could equally be the result of a persistent tendency for cases to experience more events. The authors excluded from analysis dependent events (those that clearly arose from psychotic behavior) and indeed the findings stood even when they analyzed only those events that were logically independent of the patients' disorders.

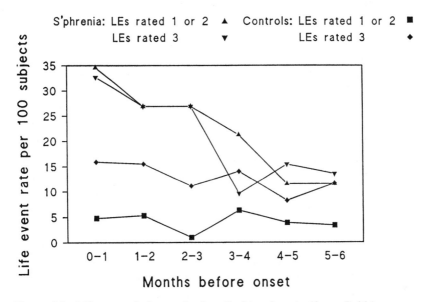

Figure 5.1. Life events before episodes of schizophrenia (from: Bebbington et al., 1993)

However, it remains possible that the mere fact of having been ill once, or of having the sort of personality associated with an increased likelihood of psychotic breakdown, might lead to a lifestyle that renders the experience of *apparently independent* events more likely.

There are thus a number of explanations for the pattern of the results from this study. One is that there is a general tendency for psychotic patients to experience a large number of events that do not actually have any etiological significance. In other words, something about the way they live increases the chance of random events. Under this proposition, it remains necessary to explain the *increase* over the period of assessment as the time of onset is approached. This could be due to an etiological role, albeit much more limited, or to the impaired recall of more remote events. Recall effects were unremarkable in the normal control group, but the presence of psychosis might well lead to difficulties in this area. In anticipation of this, cases were interviewed some time after admission, when they seemed able to cooperate effectively. While it is impossible to know exactly how successful this strategy was in overcoming problems of recall, cases certainly remembered a lot of events.

A second possibility is the one the LEDS and the Contextual Rating of Threat are intended to obviate; both patients and researchers may have worked harder to identify life events because they shared the belief that events were of causal significance. Most events elicited by overdiligence are trivial, however, and connote little or no threat. Many will thus be eliminated completely from the analyses given here. It is possible that the identification of events rated was more zealous in cases than in controls, but it seems an unlikely explanation for the excess of more severe events.

The authors' favored explanation, however, is that events do tend to increase before onset, that this increase is of etiological significance, and that it begins quite far back in time. In other words, events can exert an etiological effect across a sizeable interval.

The excess of events in this study was not restricted to the more severe events, being evident also in events rated 3 (mild) on the contextual rating of threat. The connection of disorders with minor events is less understandable in a Jasperian sense (Jaspers, 1963), but might yet be genuine.

Whatever the arguments about these findings, most can be applied equally to other studies of life events and psychosis. They therefore offer no explanation of the discrepancies with the results of other researchers. It may be possible to elucidate these through further analysis.

A further recent British study is that of Hirsch et al. (submitted). Only this study and that of Ventura et al. (1992) have so far examined the effects of medication and of life events together in a prospective design. This study was of 71 patients fulfilling criteria for DSM-III-R schizophrenia (APA, 1987), half of whom were receiving regular neuroleptic medication. A subgroup of the cohort were randomized on a double-blind basis to medication and placebo groups. Patients were followed up for 1 year with morbidity and life event ratings being made every 2 months by trained raters. Life events were elicited and rated with the LEDS.

During the study, 21 of the patients without medication relapsed, in contrast to only 5 of the medicated group. The experience of life events in the 4 weeks before relapse was not found to be significantly different to that of the same patients in earlier 4-week periods. This was true whether or not patients were receiving active medication, although as we have seen the treated group had very few relapses. Using a proportional hazards regression analysis, the cumulative experience of events for the whole period of assessment before relapse was found to be significantly related to the risk of relapse.

The relative risk and population attributable risk were calculated. The relative risk of relapse during the study was decreased by 80 percent if patients were on active medication. When this medication effect was controlled, an increase in life event exposure from zero to the mean rate only increased risk by about 23 percent. Another way of looking at this is to calculate the population attributable risk, the percentage reduction in relapse to be expected if it were possible to eliminate event exposure. For a reduction in event exposure from an average rate to zero, it was calculated that around 8 percent of relapses would be saved. The paper concluded that the size of the protective effect of regular neuroleptic medication considerably overshadowed the effect of events on relapse.

Dohrenwend and his colleagues (1993) have recently provided initial results from the New York Risk Factor Study, part of which involved a comparison of 65 subjects suffering from recent episodes on nonaffective psychosis with 404 general population controls; 21 of the 65 were first episode cases. The majority (30 out of 44) of the repeat-episode cases met DSM-III criteria for schizophrenia: 18 paranoid, 5 residual, and 7 undifferentiated. The remaining 14 repeat episode cases consisted of 2 schizophreni-form disorder, 6 schizoaffective disorder, 3 atypical psychosis, 2 paranoia, and 1 acute paranoid disorder. Probably because of the 6-month duration criterion for symptoms, only a minority, 6 out of 21, of the first-episode cases were diagnosed as DSM-III schizo-phrenia; of the remaining 15, 7 were schizophreniform disorder, 3 atypical psychosis, 2 paranoia, and 3 acute paranoid disorder.

Events were evaluated with the SEPRATE technique described above. A history of events was established for the year before onset for cases and before interview for controls. Most of the analyses were based on the 3 months prior to episode-interview, in order to be consistent with the work of Brown and Birley (1968). Some analyses did focus on the year period, especially for major fateful events. These were quite rare and produced unexpected results, their rate being highest in the repeat episode cases of psychosis. Otherwise, there were no differences between first and repeat episode cases.

Overall, the odds ratios offered somewhat unimpressive sup-port for a role of life events in precipitating episodes of psychosis, being greatest (3.42, $p < 0.1$) for nonfateful negative events.

What can be made of these findings? If the life event results could be taken on their own, the lack of robustness in the findings might justify the conclusion that social factors were relatively un-important in schizophrenic relapse. This must be set against the Expressed Emotion (EE) studies, however, which suggest a large and robust effect for another sort of social factor. It is not tenable to argue on this basis that social factors are unimportant. Why is it that the life event research does not corroborate the EE re-search in a more convincing manner? One possibility is that the relatively abrupt changes represented by life events may not be so important in producing relapse as the continuing, albeit perhaps relatively low, level of stress occasioned by living with a high EE family member. Another explanation is that the rating of life events is essentially derived from research concerned mainly with depressive disorders. In consequence, the ratings may be set at the wrong threshold for picking up the life events important in schizophrenia. If people with schizophrenia are unnaturally sensitive to life events, it is possible that the relapse is brought about by events that on the surface would seem incapable of provoking an emotional response. One study (Malla et al., 1990) only obtained a significant effect of events in causing relapse by including trivial events or "hassles." The Camberwell Collaborative Psychosis study described above also suggested that events of mild threat were in excess in schizophrenia, as in other psychoses (Bebbington et al., 1993). This would certainly tie in with the experience of many clinicians, who in managing people with long-standing schizophrenia, are very concerned to protect them from even minor changes in their daily routines.

Life Events Preceding Bipolar Illness

There is a large literature on the relationship between stressful life events and the development of depression (Dohrenwend and Dohrenwend, 1974; Brown and Harris, 1978), but the effects of life events on episodes of bipolar illness have not been studied so exhaustively. In the past this was probably due to the assumption that in this condition biological factors play a more important role than psychosocial factors. Nevertheless, from the time of Kraepelin there were voices insisting that mania might be precipitated by stress. The French were aware that widowhood might be followed by an irreverent manic reaction (Bonnafais-Serieux and Ey, 1938), and there were many anecdotal accounts of mania following a variety of upsetting events. Studies of events affecting the whole community (a hurricane, the fall of the Berlin wall) have not reported consistent findings (Aronson and Shukla, 1987; Bohlken and Priebe, 1991).

Table 5.2 lists investigations of the role of life events in bipolar illness. It is quite clear from this that strict comparison is impossible because of varying methodology. The earlier studies depend predominantly on the retrospective evaluation of ordinary clinical records not designed to establish links between life events and disorder. In some, the period of retrospective recall is very long, leading to a strong likelihood of significant distortion (e.g.,

Dunner, Patrick, and Fieve, 1979; Glassner and Haldipur, 1983). Few of the specifically designed studies have attempted to date the onset of mania precisely, with some using the date of admission as the point of onset. For example, Ambelas in both his studies (1979, 1987) investigated the 4 weeks prior to admission, with the underlying assumption that the date of admission would coincide with the date of onset. While the onset of mania does tend to be rapid, this design risks the inclusion of events that may actually be the result of behavioral disturbance in the prodromal period.

TABLE 5.2
Life Events Preceding Episodes of Bipolar Disorder

STUDY	N	Patients with Antecedent Event	Controls with Events
Hudgens et al. (1970)[1]	6	17	
Clancy et al. (1973)[2,3]	100	27	
Leff et al. (1976)[2,4]	63	29	
Dunner et al. (1979)[3,6]	79	57	
Ambelas (1979)[4,6]	67	28	6
Kennedy et al. (1983)[5,6,8]	20	85	70
Glassner and Haldipur (1983)[6,7]	48	Early onset 23 Late onset 64	
Chung et al. (1986)[1]	14	14	
Ambelas (1987)[4,5]	90	66	8
Sclare and Creed (1990)[1]	30	40	
Bebbington et al. (1992)[3]	31	45	10

[1]26-week antecedent period
[2]Case note study
[3]13-week antecedent period
[4]4-week antecedent period
[5]Surgical patients as controls
[6]Very long recall period in some cases
[7]1 year antecedent period
[8]Antecedent period 4 months before admission

The prospective studies of Hall, Dunner, Zeller, and Fieve (1977) and Ellicott, Hammen, Gitlin, Brown, and Jamison (1990) are discussed in the text.

The study by Ambelas (1979) was one of the first to examine manic patients specifically and to compare their event rate with a control group, actually of surgical patients. The manic patients were initially assessed by perusal of case notes. Events included in a predetermined list were identified in the notes, the event definition following the principles set out by Brown and Birley (1968). If patients appeared to have experienced events in the 4-week period before admission, the author confirmed the fact at interview. Compared with controls, there was a notable excess of events judged independent of disorder in this period. Events after onset were apparently excluded, although as we have indicated the anchor date was admission, not onset.

Each of the studies using the LEDS also attempted to date the onset of mania accurately. Two of the three found no significant relationship between life events and the onset of mania (Chung et al., 1986; Sclare and Creed, 1990). Chung and his colleagues (1986) studied 38 cases of psychosis, of which 14 had mania. The treating psychiatrist used ordinary clinical assessment to provide a diagnosis according to DSM-III (APA, 1980). Cases were identified by perusal of case notes over a 4-week period. All were then interviewed. "Onset" was carefully dated, and in all the manic subjects took the form of a transition from normality to psychotic symptoms. Events were elicited using the LEDs, and independent and possibly independent events were analyzed over the 26 weeks before onset. The control group was not wholly satisfactory, being made up partly of subjects randomly chosen from the general population and partly of patients with positive organic pathology undergoing surgery. Although the rate of threatening events in manic patients was twice that in controls, this was not significant, due perhaps to a remarkably low event rate in both groups.

Sclare and Creed (1990) used essentially the same methods as Brown and Birley (1968) in their classic study of life events in schizophrenia. The event rate in their manic patients (n = 30) was not elevated, resembling that in the controls in the earlier study. It was notably different from the rate in Brown and Birley's schizophrenic group. The study concentrated on events of any degree of threat, but in a subset of 24 cases the proportion who had experienced threatening events that appeared independent or possibly independent was 12.5 percent. The comparable figure obtained by Bebbington and his colleagues (1993) was four times greater.

Figure 5.2 illustrates findings from the Camberwell Collaborative Psychosis Study relating to mania (Bebbington et al., 1993).
The increase in life events rated as of marked or moderate severity
of threat before the onset of mania (n = 31) was highly significant
in comparison with the community controls. The increase in life
events occurred over a considerable period before onset, somewhat at odds with the authors' expectations and with other positive results in the literature. The samples in all three of these
studies were fairly small, in the Australian study particularly so,
making definitive conclusions difficult in the fact of the contrasting results.

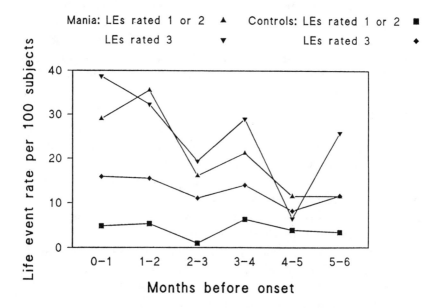

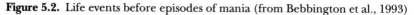

Figure 5.2. Life events before episodes of mania (from Bebbington et al., 1993)

There have now been two *prospective* studies of life events in
mania. Hall, Dunner, Zeller, and Fieve (1977) assessed 38 patients
attending a lithium clinic at every visit for a year. The interval
between visits varied from 1 week to 3 months. If subjects reported
that they had experienced any of a list of 86 events presented to
them, they were interviewed to confirm it. Seventeen subjects

relapsed in the period but their recent event rate did not distinguish them from those who remained well. It is possible, as with schizophrenia, that the provocation of relapse differs between patients on prophylactic medication and those not so protected. In some ways this study was a lost opportunity, as the authors might have had access to more powerful analyses by dating events into periods that could have been related more precisely to relapse.

Ellicott, Hammen, Gitlin, Brown, and Jamison (1990) have reported a similar prospective study. They examined the impact of life events on the course of 61 outpatients with bipolar disorder over a 2-year period. All subjects had either been free of affective symptoms for 2 months or had achieved a "best clinical state" for at least 6 months. Regular assessments were made of life stress, symptoms, and medication. Current symptoms were evaluated at each visit, at intervals from 3 days to 3 months. Life stress interviews were conducted by telephone at 3-monthly intervals, and were based on the methods of Brown and Harris (1978). The actual definition of life events was based on guidelines from Paykel and Mangen (1982). Events were then rated using a technique essentially similar to that of Brown and Harris (1978). The authors summed the total level of objective threat in the 3 months before illness episodes and for the final 3 months of assessment in those who did not relapse. Total objective stress levels were divided into quartiles. The highest quartile had a risk of relapse 4.53 times higher than patients without stress. This association was independent of levels of medication and compliance. Lower levels of stress were not significantly related to relapse.

Although direct attempts to demonstrate an association between life events and the onset of bipolar disorder do not permit clear conclusions, some corroboration can be gleaned from more tangential studies.

Beck (1983) has suggested that people who develop affective disorders can be divided into two broad types in terms of their vulnerability to specific stresses. *Sociotropic* individuals are particularly susceptible to interpersonal events, whereas *autonomous* persons are self-contained in a social sense, but invest emotionally in projects, and are thus vulnerable to events that reflect badly on their sense of achievement. Hammen, Ellicott, Gitlin, and Jamison (1989) have investigated this distinction in a 6-month followup study of patients with unipolar and bipolar disorder. As predicted, onsets or exacerbations of symptoms in sociotropic patients were indeed more likely to follow negative interpersonal events than achievement events, while the reverse was true for autonomous patients. These findings applied only to unipolar patients, but for bipolar patients, the particular personal meaning of events seemed less relevant. Ambelas and George (1988) approached the problem of specificity from a different angle: they looked for patterns of similarity of events in sequential relapses, and concluded that persistent themes could be identified in individuals, although these might differ considerably between patients.

Some studies have suggested that susceptibility to relapse following psychosocial stress may be greater in certain subgroups. Thus, Aronson and Shukla (1987) studied patients attending a lithium clinic soon after a catastrophic hurricane. They found that, despite adequate lithium levels, the relapse rate was considerably raised in the aftermath of what was effectively a major independent event affecting the entire population. The patients who relapsed were more unstable in terms of recent prodromal symptoms and other complaints, and had shorter periods of previous stability than those who did not relapse. It remains to be seen whether there is any difference between patients for whom psychosocial events seem to play a causative or contributory role and those for whom they are insignificant.

Stern (1944) was the first to suggest that events are more important in the initial provocation of mania, and that subsequent episodes, following the activation of the "manic mechanism," required less in the way of stress. This is consistent with much clinical experience, and there is also support from specific life event studies (Leff, Roach, and Bunney, 1970; Dunner et al., 1979; Perris, 1984; Ambelas, 1987). Ambelas (1987) found that before initial episodes more subjects experienced events and that the mean stress score from summed events was greater. Sclare and

Creed (1990) found a notably higher event rate preceding episodes close to the beginning of the illness. Only Glassner and Haldipur (1983) failed to observe this pattern.

If it is genuinely the case that events have a greater role in precipitating first episodes, this might account for the difficulties of demonstrating an overall association between mania and events, since most studies are not solely of first episodes. However, this finding would then itself require explanation. Does it come about because sufferers develop some kind of internal rhythm of relapse, such that they no longer require the provocation of events? Patients experiencing subsequent relapses may be on prophylactic medication, and this may have the effect of protecting them from external precipitants and thus revealing underlying rhythms. Or does it mean that subjects are so sensitized, for biological or for social reasons, that they require only the slightest stimulus to precipitate relapse, a stimulus so trifling that it is not often picked up by life event technologies? In this context, Ambelas and George (1986) noted that manic patients whose initial episode was precipitated by minor rather than major stress were significantly more vulnerable to subsequent relapse.

The tendency for episodes of bipolar disorder to become more frequent and autonomous has led some authors to suggest that the process involves some kind of equivalent to *kindling*, whereby the repetitive application of subthreshold electrical stimuli to nerve cells results in the development of an autonomous epileptic focus. This idea comes partly from the apparent efficacy in bipolar disorder and the known mode of action of carbamazepine, essentially a kindling blocker (Post, 1990).

While many studies have focused only on attacks of mania, some have examined both depressive and manic episodes in the course of bipolar disorder. Hall et al. (1977) and Ambelas (1987) found that events were commoner before episodes of mania than of depression, while Dunner et al. (1979) found a gender difference that is hard to interpret: in women events were commoner before depression, in men before mania.

It is reasonable to suppose that where bipolar illness is precipitated by social factors, the biological predisposition is correspondingly smaller. Indeed, the study by Glassner and Haldipur (1983) appears to have been motivated by exactly this consideration. They divided their cases into "early" and "late onset" groups, late onset being a relative term for those with no evidence of illness before the age of 20. As others have suggested that a family history of bipolar disorder is commoner in patients whose illness emerges relatively early (e.g., Rice, Reich, Andreasen, Endicott, Van Eerdewegh, Fishman, Hirschfeld, and Klerman, 1987), they argued that life events would be less important precipitants of illness in this group. Their results confirmed this, but others have found that, in terms of the proportion experiencing events before onset, subjects with bipolar family history are no different from those without (Dunner et al., 1979; Ambelas, 1987).

The overall conclusion from this literature of variable quality is that stressful life events probably do operate as precipitating factors in some subjects with bipolar affective disorders, particularly in first episodes. It remains to be seen whether there is any difference between those patients for whom psychosocial events contribute to onset and those for whom they appear to have no significant role.

Psychotic Disorders and Event Specificity

Does the relationship with preceding life events differ, either in degree or in kind, in different psychiatric conditions? Clancy, Crowe, Winokur, and Morrison (1973) compared the occurrence of life events in three groups of mentally ill people, those with unipolar and bipolar affective disorder and those with schizophrenia. They found that patients with unipolar depression were most likely to have significant life events preceding episodes (39%), those with schizophrenia least likely (11%), with bipolar patients in between (27%). However, if unipolar depressions related to the puerperium and menopause were excluded, the difference between bipolar and unipolar disorder was no longer significant. Perris (1984) also found no difference in the event rate preceding episodes of unipolar and bipolar illness.

In their study described above, Chung and his colleagues (1986) compared manic patients with those with schizophrenia and with schizophreniform psychosis. In the 26 weeks before onset, only 14 percent of manic patients had experienced an event, in contrast with 33 percent of the schizophrenia group and 66 percent of those with schizophreniform psychosis. Bebbington and his colleagues (1993) found virtually no difference in the excess life event rate apparent before the onset of schizophrenia, mania, or psychotic depression, and the rate was elevated to the sorts of level seen in equivalent studies of unipolar depression (e.g., Bebbington, Brugha, MacCarthy, Potter, Sturt, Wykes, Katz, and McGuffin, 1988). Contrasting results come from the New York Risk Factor study (Dohrenwend et al., 1993). In addition to the psychotic subjects described above, this also included 96 patients with major (nonpsychotic) depression, of whom 48 were experiencing a first episode, and thus it was possible to compare the odds ratios for depression and psychosis. It was clear that the relationship with life events was far stronger in the depressed patients, particularly for major events. The position therefore remains uncertain.

It is possible that the *type* of event associated with onset may vary in different psychiatric disorders. In particular, it has been suggested that the events preceding depression are of types that might be expected—losses, humiliations, and the like—while those associated with nondepressive psychotic disorders are specified more by a general requirement to adapt. However, the evidence for this distinction is limited. Although some clinicians have felt that mania is as likely to be associated with positive as with negative events, most studies have found that the life events preceding bipolar episodes tend to be unpleasant. They are usually related to work, interpersonal relationships, and marriage. In these respects, they cannot be distinguished from the sorts of events preceding depression.

The Interaction of Stress, Medication, and Relapse in Schizophrenia

Medication is important in protecting patients from the deleterious effects of living with high EE relatives (Bebbington and Kuipers, 1994). What is the evidence for a similar role in protecting people with schizophrenia from the effects of life event stress? A number of studies have addressed this issue. Birley and Brown (1970) found the strength of the relationship between life events and relapse was weakest in those patients who had been off medication for less than one year. The relationship was stronger both in patients who had not taken medication for more than one year and for those who remained on medication. This might be interpreted as meaning that groups either inherently resilient or made so by medication were more resistant to the impact of everyday hassles, and required actual events to precipitate relapse.

The findings of Leff, Hirsch, Gaind, Rohde, and Stevens (1973) can be understood in a similar manner. They used data from a double-blind placebo-control trial to examine the effect of medication on the life event/relapse relationship. Life events appeared to precede relapse in patients on active medication but not those on placebo. Bartko, Maylath, and Herczeg (1987) report similar findings from a nonrandomized design.

There are also links with the EE research. Leff and Vaughn (1980) found that there was a much stronger event/relapse relationship in schizophrenic patients who came from low EE families than those who came from high EE families. These patients were largely off medication, but even so can be seen as protected by their family situation. In contrast, people living with a high EE relative may be so vulnerable in consequence that very small perturbations in the social environment can precipitate relapse. Leff, Kuipers, Berkowitz, Vaughn, and Sturgeon (1983) used results from their family intervention study to explore this issue further. They concluded that for patients off medication, relapse can be provoked either by life event or contact with a high EE relative. However, for patients on medication relapse appeared to require the presence of the two factors in combination.

There is also information from recent prospective studies about the interaction between medication and events. Ventura and his colleagues (1992), in a study of patients with short histories of illness, found an excess of events in patients on regular medication compared with those not receiving any. Hirsch and his colleagues (1993) studied a population with more long-standing illness. However, they failed to find any differences in the experience of events prerelapse in medicated and unmedicated groups. This is possibly a Type 2 error, as only 5 of 36 patients on medication relapsed during the one-year follow-up.

CONCLUSION

The clearest thing about the literature on the effects of life events relapse in psychosis is that it is inconsistent. Overall, it looks as though there is something in the association, but it does not admit of assertive claims. Usually when findings lack robustness across different studies, this is an indication that the relationship is not a strong one. There is support for this view from the medication studies. So, for instance, the study of Hirsch and his colleagues (submitted) compares the relative size of the effect of medication with that of the cumulative event rate and found that the former was much the greater. This provides an interesting contrast with the results from the aggregate analysis of EE studies conducted by Bebbington and Kuipers (1994), which indicates that the social environment measured by EE is more important than the effects of medication.

Thus the life events studies cannot be held to indicate that the course of psychosis is relatively independent of social influences, but rather that this particular measure does not pick up the relationship very strongly. This in turn offers support for our argument for an increased vulnerability to circumstances in people suffering from psychosis.

REFERENCES

Al Khani, M. A. F., Bebbington, P. E., Watson, J., & House, F. (1986), Life events and schizophrenia: A Saudi Arabian study. *Brit. J. Psychiatry*, 148:12–22.

Ambelas, A. (1979), Psychologically stressful events in the precipitation of manic episodes. *Brit. J. Psychiatry*, 35:15–21.

————— (1987), Life events and mania: A special relationship? *Brit. J. Psychiatry*, 150:235–240.

————— George, M. (1986), Predictability of course of illness in manic patients positive for life events. *J. Nerv. Ment. Dis.*, 174:693–695.

————— ————— (1988), Individualized stress vulnerabilities in manic depressive patients with repeated episodes. *J. Roy. Soc. Med.*, 18:448–449.

American Psychiatric Association (1980), *Diagnostic and Statistical Manual of Mental Disorders*, 3rd ed. (DSM-III). Washington, DC: American Psychiatric Press.

————— (1987), *Diagnostic and Statistical Manual of Mental Disorders*, 3rd ed. rev. (DSM-III-R). Washington, DC: American Psychiatric Press.

Aronson, T. A., & Shukla, S. (1987), Life events and relapse in bipolar disorder: The impact of a catastrophic event. *Acta Psychiatr. Scand.*, 75:571–576.

Bartko, G., Maylath, E., & Herczeg, I. (1987), Comparative study of schizophrenia patients relapsed on and off medication. *Psychiat. Res.*, 22:221–227.

Bebbington, P. E., Brugha, T., MacCarthy, B., Potter, J., Sturt, E., Wykes, T., Katz, R., & McGuffin, P. (1988), The Camberwell Collaborative Depression Study. I. Depressed probands: Adversity and the form of depression. *Brit. J. Psychiatry*, 152:754–765.

————— Kuipers, L. (1994), The predictive value of Expressed Emotion in schizophrenia: An aggregate analysis. *Psycholog. Med.*, 24:707–718.

————— Ramana, R. (submitted), Epidemiology of bipolar affective disorder.

————— Wilkins, S., Jones, P., Foerster, A., Murray, R., Toone, B., & Lewis, S. (1993), Life events and psychosis: Initial results from the Camberwell Collaborative Psychosis study. *Brit. J. Psychiatry*, 162:72–79.

Beck, A. T. (1983), Cognitive therapy of depression: New perspectives. In: *Treatment of Depression: Old Controversies and New Approaches*, ed. P. J. Clayton & J. E. Barrett. New York: Raven Press, pp. 265–290.

Birley, J. L. T., & Brown, G. W. (1970), Crises and life changes preceding the onset or relapse of acute schizophrenia: Clinical aspects. *Brit. J. Psychiatry*, 116:327–333.

Bohlken, J., & Priebe, S. (1991), Political change and course of affective psychoses: Berlin 1989–90. *Psychiat. Res.*, 37:1–4.

Bonnafais-Serieux, H., & Ey, H. (1938), Manies de veuvage. *Medico-Psychologiques*, 96:225–232.

Brown, G. W. (1974), Meaning, measurement and stress of life events. In: *Stressful Life Events: Their Nature and Effects*, ed. B. S. Dohrenwend & B. P. Dohrenwend. New York: John Wiley.

————— Birley, J. L. T. (1968), Crises and life changes and the onset of schizophrenia. *J. Health Soc. Behav.*, 9:203–214.

————— Harris, T. O. (1978), *Social Origins of Depression: A Study of Psychiatric Disorder in Women*. London: Tavistock.

————— ————— (1989), *Life Events and Illness*. London: Unwin Hyman.

————— ————— Peto, J. (1973), Life events and psychiatric disorders. Part 2: Nature of causal link. *Psycholog. Med.*, 3:159–176.

Canton, G., & Fraccon, I. G. (1985), Life events and schizophrenia: A replication. *Acta Psychiat. Scand.*, 71:211–216.

Chung, R. K., Langeluddecke, P., & Tennant, C. (1986), Threatening life events in the onset of schizophrenia, schizophreniform psychosis and hypomania. *Brit. J. Psychiatry*, 148:680–686.

Clancy, J., Crowe, R., Winokur, G., & Morrison, J. (1973), The Iowa 500: Precipitating factors in schizophrenia and primary affective disorder. *Comprehen. Psychiatry*, 14:197–202.

Creed, F. (1990), Life events and disorder. *Curr. Op. in Psychiatry*, 3:259–263.

Day, R. (1981), Life events and schizophrenia: The triggering hypothesis. *Acta Psychiat. Scand.*, 64:97–122.

―――― (1989), Schizophrenia. In: *Life Events and Illness*, ed. G. W. Brown & T. O. Harris. London: Unwin Hyman.

―――― Neilsen, J. A., Korten, A., Ernberg, G., Dube, K. C., Gebhart, J., Jablensky, A., Leon, C., Marsella, A., Olatawura, M., Sartorius, N., Stromgren, E., Takahashi, R., Wig, N., & Wynne, L. C. (1987), Stressful life events preceding the acute onset of schizophrenia: A cross-national study from the World Health Organization. *Cult. Med. & Psychiatry*, 11:123–206.

Dohrenwend, B. P., Levav, I., & Shrout, P. E. (1987), Life stress and psychopathology: Progress and research begun with Barbara Snell Dohrenwend. *Amer. J. Commun. Psychol.*, 15:677–713.

―――― Stueve, A., Skodol, A. E., & Link, B. (1993), Life events vulnerability and schizophrenia episodes: A case-control study. Paper presented at WPA Section of Epidemiology and Community Psychiatry Symposium, Groningen, Netherlands, September 1–3.

Dohrenwend, B. S., & Dohrenwend, B. P. (1974), Overview and prospects for research on stressful life events. In: *Stressful Life Events: Their Nature and Effects*, ed. B. S. Dohrenwend & B. P. Dohrenwend. New York: John Wiley.

Dunner, D. L., Patrick, V., & Fieve, R. R. (1979), Life events at the onset of bipolar affective illness. *Amer. J. Psychiatry*, 136:508–511.

Ellicott, A., Hammen, C., Gitlin, M., Brown, G., & Jamison, K. (1990), Life events and the course of bipolar disorder. *Amer. J. Psychiatry*, 147:1194–1198.

Glassner, B., & Haldipur, C. V. (1983), Life events and early and late onset of bipolar disorder. *Amer. J. Psychiatry*, 140:215–217.

Gureje, O., & Adewumni, A. (1988), Life events in schizophrenia in Nigerians. A controlled investigation. *Brit. J. Psychiatry*, 153:367–375.

Hall, K. S., Dunner, D. L., Zeller, G., & Fieve, R. R. (1977), Bipolar illness: A prospective study of life events. *Comprehen. Psychiatry*, 18:497–502.

Hammen, C., Ellicott, A., Gitlin, M., & Jamison, K. R. (1989), Sociotropy/autonomy and vulnerability to specific life events in patients with unipolar depression and bipolar disorders. *J. Abnorm. Psychol.*, 98:154–160.

Hardesty, J., Falloon, I. R. H., & Shirin, K. (1985), The impact of life events, stress and coping on the morbidity of schizophrenia. In: *Family Management of Schizophrenia*, ed. I. R. Falloon. Baltimore: Johns Hopkins University Press.

Hirsch, S., Cramer, P., & Bowen, J. (1992), The triggering hypothesis of the role of life events in schizophrenia. *Brit. J. Psychiatry*, 161:84–87.

—— Bowen, J., Emami, J., Cramer, P., Jolley, A., Haw, C., & Dickinson, M. (submitted), A one year prospective study of the effect of life events and medication in the aetiology of schizophrenic relapse.

Holmes, T. H., & Rahe, R. H. (1967), The Social Readjustment Rating Scale. *J. Psychosom. Res.*, 11:213–218.

Hudgens, R. W., Robins, E., & DeLong, W. B. (1970), The reporting of recent stress in the lives of psychiatric patients. *Brit. J. Psychiatry*, 117:635–643.

Jacobs, S., & Myers, J. (1976), Recent life events and acute schizophrenia psychosis: A controlled study. *J. Nerv. Ment. Dis.*, 162:75–87.

Jaspers, K. (1963), *General Psychopathology*, tr. J. Hoenig & M. W. Hamilton. Manchester, U.K.: Manchester University Press.

Jones, P. B., Bebbington, P. E., Foerster, A., Lewis, S. W., Murray, R. M., Russell, A., Sham, P. C., Toone, B. K., & Wilkins, S. (1993), Premorbid social underachievement in schizophrenia: Results from the Camberwell Collaborative Psychosis Study. *Brit. J. Psychiatry*, 163:65–71.

Kennedy, S., Thompson, R., Stancer, H. C., Roy, A., & Persad, E. (1983), Life events precipitating mania. *Brit. J. Psychiatry*, 142:398–403.

Kraepelin, E. (1913), *Clinical Psychiatry*. New York: William Wood.

Leff, J. P., Hirsch, S., Gaind, R., Rohde, P., & Stevens, B. (1973), Life events and maintenance therapy in schizophrenic relapse. *Brit. J. Psychiatry*, 123:659–660.

—— Kuipers, L., Berkowitz, R., Vaughn, C. E., & Sturgeon, D. (1983), Life events, relatives' Expressed Emotion and maintenance neuroleptics in schizophrenic relapse. *Psycholog. Med.*, 13:799–806.

—— Vaughn, C. E. (1980), The interaction of life events and relative's Expressed Emotion in schizophrenia and depressive neurosis. *Brit. J. Psychiatry*, 136:146–153.

Leff, M. H., Roach, J. F., & Bunney, W. E. (1970), Environmental factors preceding the onsets of severe depressions. *Psychiatry*, 33:293–311.

Malla, A. K., Cortese, L., Shaw, T. S., & Ginsberg, B. (1990), Life events and relapse in schizophrenia: A one year prospective study. *Soc. Psychiatry Psychiatric Epidem.*, 25:221–224.

Malzacher, M., Merz, J., & Ebnother, D. (1981), Einschneidende Lebensereignisse im Vorfeld akuter schizophrener Episoden: Erstmals erkrankte Patienten im Vergleich mit einer Normalstichprobe. *Archiv für Psychiatrie u. Nervenkrankheiten*, 230:227–242.

Mueller, D. P., Edwards, D. W., & Yarvis, R. M. (1977), Stressful life events and psychiatric symptomatology: Change or undesirability. *J. Health & Soc. Behav.*, 18:307–317.

Paykel, E. S., & Mangen, S. P. (1982), Life events and social stress in neurotic patients. *British Journal of Psychiatry*, 140(4):573–581.

Perris, H. (1984), Life events and depression. Part 2. Results in diagnostic subgroups, and in relation to the recurrence of depression. *J. Affect. Dis.*, 7:25–36.

Post, R. M. (1990), Sensitization and kindling perspectives for the course of affective illness: Toward a new treatment with the anticonvulsant carbamazepine. *Pharmacopsychiatry*, 23:3–17.

Rice, J., Reich, T., Andreasen, N. C., Endicott, J., Van-Eerdewegh, M., Fishman, R., Hirschfeld, R. M., & Klerman, G. L. (1987), The familial transmission of bipolar illness. *Arch. Gen. Psychiatry*, 44:441–447.

Schwarz, C., & Myers, J. (1977), Life events and schizophrenia. Parts I and II. *Arch. Gen. Psychiatry*, 34:1238–1248.

Sclare, P., & Creed, F. (1990), Life events and the onset of mania. *Brit. J. Psychiatry*, 156:508–514.

Shrout, P. E., Link, B. G., Dohrenwend, B. P., Skodol, A. E., Stueve, A., & Mirotznik, J. (1989), Characterising life events as risk factors for depression. The role of fateful loss events. *J. Abnorm. Psychol.*, 98:460–467.

Steinberg, H., & Durell, J. (1968), A stressful situation as a precipitant of schizophrenic symptoms: An epidemiological study. *Brit. J. Psychiatry*, 114:1097–1105.

Stern, E. S. (1944), The psychopathology of manic-depressive disorder and involutional melancholia. *Brit. J. Med. Psychol.*, 20:20–32.

Ventura, J., Nuechterlein, K. H., Lukoff, D., & Hardisty, J. P. (1989), A prospective study of stressful life events and schizophrenic relapse. *J. Abnorm. Psychol.*, 98:407–411.

———— ———— Hardisty, J. P., & Gitlin, M. (1992), Life events and schizophrenic relapse after medication withdrawal: A prospective study. *Brit. J. Psychiatry*, 161:615–620.

Wicki, W., & Angst, J. (1991), The Zurich Study. X. Hypomania in a 28- to 30-year-old cohort. *Eur. Arch. Psychiatry Clin. Neurosci.*, 240:339–348.

Wittchen, H. U., Essau, C. A., & Hecht, H. (1989), Reliability of life event assessments test retest reliability and fall off effects of the Munich Interview for the assessment of life events. *J. Affect. Disord.*, 16:77–92.

Chapter 6
Stressful Life Events and Social Support in Depressed Psychiatric Inpatients

JAMES C. OVERHOLSER, Ph.D., AND DALIA M. ADAMS, M.A.

Stressful life events often precede a major depressive episode. Negative life events may involve a loss of status, power, friendship, self-esteem, or security. Such stressful events can serve as "provoking agents" (Brown and Bifulco, 1985) precipitating depressive episodes. Furthermore, stress affects the course and treatment of depression. In depressed patients, high levels of stressful events are associated with relatively prompt seeking of professional treatment (Monroe, Simons, and Thase, 1991). Unfortunately, stress is also related to reduced responsiveness to treatment (Monroe, Kupfer, and Frank, 1992), and poor long-term outcomes (Swindle, Cronkite, and Moos, 1989). Despite evidence that stress is implicated in the onset and course of clinical levels of depression, most studies examining the relationship between stress and depression have focused on community samples. Therefore, research examining stress and severe depression in psychiatric inpatients can play an important role in helping us understand the course and treatment of depression.

In addition to depression, stress is associated with other psychological symptoms. Elevated levels of stress are related to hopelessness (Dixon, Heppner, and Anderson, 1991), suicidal behavior (DeVanna, Paterniti, Milievich, Rigamonti, Sulich, and Faravelli, 1990; Rich, Warsradt, Nemiroff, Fowler, and Young, 1991), anxiety (Nezu, 1986; Long, 1988), and problematic personality styles (Holahan and Moos, 1986; Perris, 1989). Thus, depressed patients who report numerous stressful events may be experiencing a variety of psychological problems which could affect the course of treatment. Unfortunately, the relationship between stressful events and overall psychological functioning of persons suffering from clinical levels of depression has not been examined. As a result, the impact of stressful events on the symptomatology of depressed psychiatric inpatients remains unclear.

During stressful times, individuals who have well-established social networks typically report fewer psychological problems than those who lack social supports (Myers, Lindenthal, and Pepper, 1975). Adequate social support is related to a reduced risk of anxiety (Hart and Hittner, 1991), depression (Duer, Schwenk, and Coyne, 1988), and suicidal behavior (D'Attilio, Campbell, Lubold, and Jacobsen, 1992). The presence of adequate social support can reduce the risk of depression onset (Brown, Andrews, Harris, Adler, and Bridge, 1986; Monroe, Bromet, Connell, and Steiner, 1986) and the risk of relapse following recovery from a major depressive episode (Surtees, 1980). Social supports help a person by providing tangible assistance, emotional support, and directive guidance. Thus, the presence and availability of social support is associated with a reduced frequency and reduced intensity of psychological problems.

The mechanism through which social support has its beneficial effect on psychological well-being has not been clarified. The effects of social support may be direct or indirect. Direct effects theory posits that social support has a direct positive influence on psychological well-being (Andrews, Tennant, Hewson, and Vaillant, 1978; Williams, Ware, and Donald, 1981; Aneshensel and Frerichs, 1982). Thus, the presence of social support should be associated with reduced symptomatology regardless of the degree of life stress the person happens to be experiencing.

The stress buffering theory argues that social support provides an important contribution to a person's well-being by helping to reduce the negative impact of life stress (Cohen and Wills, 1985). Individuals lacking in social support are more likely to experience physical and psychological problems during stressful times. Therefore, social support is most helpful during highly stressful periods.

Methodological issues have influenced stress research. Because both stress and social support are broad and overlapping constructs, measurement redundancy often results when stress and support are assessed (Monroe and Steiner, 1986). Furthermore, the relationships between stress, support and psychological symptoms among psychiatric patients remains unclear because research on stress and social support has focused primarily on community samples (Cohen and Wills, 1985).

The overlap between life stress and social support has often been neglected. Many aspects of life stress have a social basis. For example, common stressors include divorce, death of a spouse, frequent arguments with family members, conflict with a supervisor or coworker, and relocation away from an established network of friends. These stressors can be conceptualized as a loss of support. Conversely, many aspects of social support are related to life stress. Often, stress brings people together. Many friendships are established during stressful times (e.g., wartime battles, medical school) and are later maintained over long intervals with little ongoing contact needed to keep the relationship alive. Thus, it is necessary for research to clearly separate the concepts of life stress and social support.

Many studies have shown a relationship between stress and psychological problems. A relationship between social support and psychological well-being has also been demonstrated. However, research examining the interaction between life stress and social support has primarily used college student or community samples (Cohen and Wills, 1985). Research on college student or community samples is limited by a restricted range on most measures. It is unlikely that severe levels of depression, high amounts of life stress, or extremely low levels of social support would be reported by adults who are functioning well enough to remain in the community or attend college. This may restrict our ability to generalize from community to clinical samples. One study found results supporting the stress buffering theory when using nondepressed college students, but an interaction between life stress and social support was not found in a clinical sample (Wise and Barnes, 1986).

Many studies have shown that life stress is associated with depression in psychiatric patients (Paykel, 1976; Robins, Block, and Peselow, 1990; Hammen, 1991; Monroe et al., 1991). However, few studies with psychiatric patients have examined the direct or mediating role that social support plays in the stress process. Thus, the relationship between stress, social support, and symptomatology in depressed psychiatric inpatients remains unclear.

RESEARCH METHOD

In our study (Overholser, Norman, and Miller, 1990), 84 depressed inpatients were assessed in terms of recent life stress, degree of social support, and various psychiatric symptoms. All patients had been hospitalized for a major depressive episode and were classified as depressed using the NIMH Diagnostic Interview Schedule (DIS; Robins, Helzer, Croughan, and Ratcliff, 1981). Because this was a highly focused clinical sample, the overall sample size was lower than that often seen in community-based studies.

The sample included 18 males and 66 females. The average age of patients was 35.63 (SD = 11.79). The majority of patients were married. Twenty-seven percent of the patients had less than 12 years of education, 27 percent had their high school diploma, and 45 percent had some schooling beyond high school. Most patients (83%) reported at least one previous episode of depression, and many patients (42%) admitted to having attempted suicide at some point in their lives.

Patients were assessed using both self-report questionnaires and structured clinical interviews. Stressful events were rated using the Life Experience Survey (LES; Sarason, Johnson, and Siegel, 1978), which contains a listing of 60 stressful events. Subjects were asked to rate each event for its presence or absence during the previous 6 months. If any events occurred during the previous 6 months, subjects were asked to rate its subjective impact on a 7-point scale ranging from extremely negative to extremely positive. Several items were dropped from the LES to avoid methodological bias. Only negative events were used. Also, events were omitted if they seemed related to depressive symptomatology (e.g., major change in sleeping habits; sexual difficulties) or were not often seen in psychiatric inpatients (e.g., failing an important exam).

In order to follow a cognitive model of stress, our assessment focused on the subjective impact of the stressors reported by the patients. The cognitive model of stress (Lazarus and Folkman, 1986) argues that the objective occurrence of life events plays a minor role in the stress process. The person's subjective appraisal determines what is stressful. According to the cognitive model, appraisal is a two-step process. First, primary appraisal evaluates the danger involved in the situation. If the situation is not seen as posing any risk of harm, no stress occurs. Then, secondary appraisal evaluates the individual's resources that are available for coping with the life changes. If the person feels unable to cope, then stress reactions will occur. Recent research has shown that the individual's perception of live events can be more important than the events themselves (Robins et al., 1990).

Social supports were rated using the Social Supports Inventory (SSI; Habif, 1981). The SSI is a greatly expanded and modified version of the Social Supports Scale (Habif and Lahey, 1980). The SSI includes 27 statements decribing the availability of people perceived as helpful and supportive in the patient's life. Statements are phrased in general terms (e.g., "I often feel encouragement or approval from others for the things that I do"; "There are few subjects that I don't feel free to talk about with my close friends"). Patients were asked to rate each statement from 1 (strongly agree) to 5 (strongly disagree).

Depression severity was measured using both questionnaires and structured interview measures. The Beck Depression Inventory (BDI; Beck, Ward, Mendelson, Mock, and Erbaugh, 1961) is a self-report measure that includes 21 symptoms of depression rated from absent to severe using a multiple-choice format. The BDI is a well-established and widely used measure of depression severity. The Hamilton Rating Scale for Depression (HRSD; Hamilton, 1960) provides scoring guidelines for 17 different symptoms of depression. The HRSD is administered in a structured interview and provides a measure of depression severity.

Suicidal tendencies were assessed using both questionnaire and structured interview formats. The Hopelessness Scale (HS; Beck, Weissman, Lester, and Trexler, 1974) includes 20 statements regarding expectations for the future. Patients were asked to score each statement as true or false according to their own expectations. The HS provides a well-established measure of pessimism and negative expectations. High levels of hopelessness have been found related to suicidal tendencies in cross-sectional (Beck, Kovacs, and Weissman, 1975) and follow-up studies (Beck, Steer, Kovacs, and Garrison, 1985). The Scale for Suicidal Ideation (SSI) was used to rate the severity of suicidal thoughts. The SSI was originally developed by Beck, Kovacs, and Weissman (1979) but has been expanded and modified by Miller, Norman, Bishop, and Dow (1986). The Modified SSI includes 19 items to be scored after a structured clinical interview. Items evaluate the frequency, intensity, and duration of suicidal thoughts, the presence and detail of a suicidal plan, and the individual's reasons for living versus reasons for dying.

The presence and severity of other psychiatric symptoms were assessed with the SCL-90-R (Derogatis, Lipman, and Covi, 1973). The SCL-90-R is a 90-item self-report inventory designed to measure the symptom patterns in persons from community and clinical populations. It is scored for nine symptom dimensions:

somatization, obsessive–compulsive, interpersonal sensitivity, depression, anxiety, hostility, phobic anxiety, paranoid ideation, and psychoticism. The SCL-90-R also yields a Global Severity Index indicating overall levels of distress. Numerous studies have demonstrated adequate reliability and validity for the SCL-90-R (Derogatis, 1983).

Additional variables potentially related to stress and social support include social adjustment and personality style. Social adjustment was measured with the Social Adjustment Scale–Self-Report Version (SAS-SR: Weissman, Prusoff, Thompson, Harding, and Myers, 1978). The SAS-SR is a 54-item self-report instrument that yields an overall adjustment score and subscale scores measuring functioning within specific roles (e.g., work, social situations, marriage, family). Personality style was measured with the Eysenck Personality Inventory (EPI; Eysenck and Eysenck, 1968). The EPI includes 57 items designed to measure two primary personality dimensions: neuroticism and introversion-extroversion.

STATISTICAL ANALYSES

Before proceeding into categorical analysis, a Pearson correlation coefficient was used to examine the degree of overlap between the measures of life stress and social support. The two measures were not correlated to any meaningful degree ($r = -.06$). The lack of overlap between the measures indicate that they represented separate dimensions.

Subjects were classified into four subgroups of depressed patients using the Life Experiences Survey and the Social Supports Inventory. Median splits on these two measures were used to determine high and low classification. Twenty-three patients reported high stress and high social support. Twenty-two patients reported high stress and low social support. Twenty-two patients reported low stress and high social support. Seventeen patients reported low stress and low social support.

Preliminary group analyses examined demographic and clinical variables across the four groups of depressed patients. No significant differences were observed across groups in terms of patient age, race, sex, marital status, level of education attained, length of stay in the hospital, likelihood of having suffered from previous episodes of depression or suicidal feelings, and likelihood of suffering from chronic or endogenous depression. Thus, in many important ways, the four groups of depressed inpatients appeared similar in terms of their previous psychological problems and background variables.

Four categories of variables (depressive symptoms, anxiety, social adjustment, and personality variables) were analyzed with a series of Multivariate Analyses of Variance (MANOVA) in order to examine differences across groups based on levels of perceived stress and social support. Significant MANOVA's were followed with Analyses of Variance (ANOVA's) to determine main and interaction effects for stress and social support on specific measures within each category (see Table 6.1). Significant main effects were observed for stress and social support on measures of depression, anxiety, social adjustment and personality variables. No significant interaction effects were observed. When significant effects were found, analyses were repeated with an Analysis of Covariance (ANCOVA) in order to control for the effects of depression level.

When the measures of depression and suicidal tendencies were examined, significant differences were found across the groups. A MANOVA revealed a significant main effect for social support on the measures of depression and suicidality, Wilks' Lambda $(4.77) = 4.50$, $p < .003$. The main effect for life stress and for the interaction term were nonsignificant.

The degree of life stress did not influence the severity of depression observed across the four groups. Perceived availability of social support did influence depression severity across the four groups. The two groups reporting low levels of social support were found to display higher levels of depression on the questionnaire (DBI: $F(1,80) = 8.49$, $p < .01$) and the structured interview measure (HRSD: $F(1,80) = 4.47$, $p < .02$). Thus, among psychiatric

TABLE 6.1

Effects of Stress and Social Support on Psychological Symptoms, Social Adjustment, and Personality Variables (without controlling for depression/with depression levels statistically controlled)

		Stress (main effect)	Support (main effect)	Stress X Support (interaction)
Depressive Symptoms				
Depression	(BDI)	ns	**	ns
Depression	(HRSD)	ns	*	ns
Suicidal Ideation	(MSSI)	ns/ns	*/ns	ns/ns
Hopelessness	(HS)	ns/ns	***/***	ns/ns
Anxiety				
General Anxiety	(SCL-90)	*/*	ns/ns	ns/ns
Phobic Anxiety	(SCL-90)	***/ns	*/ns	ns/ns
Social Adjustment				
Social Functioning	(SAS-SR)	ns/ns	***/**	ns/ns
Family Functioning	(SAS-SR)	**/*	**/ns	ns/ns
Marital Adjustment	(SAS-SR)	ns/ns	**/*	ns/ns
Economic Adjustment	(SAS-SR)	**/**	ns/ns	ns/ns
Personality Variables				
Neuroticism	(EPI)	***/***	ns/ns	ns/ns
Introversion	(EPI)	*/ns	ns/ns	ns/ns

ns = effect statistically not significant

* = $p < .05$; ** = $p < .01$; *** = $p < .001$

BDI = Beck Depression Inventory; HRSD = Hamilton Rating Scale for Depression; MSSI = Modified Scale for Suicidal Ideation; HS = Hopelessness Scale; SAS-SR = Social Adjustment Scale; EPI = Eysenck Personality

inpatients, perceived lack of social support is related to increased severity of depression (see Figure 6.1).

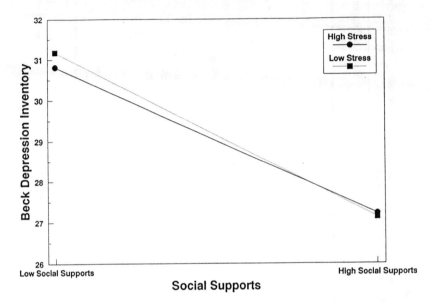

Figure 6.1. Effects of life stress and social supports on depression severity.

The availability of social support was related to suicidal tendencies, but stressful events were not. Patients with few social supports displayed stronger suicidal tendencies on the Hopelessness Scale, $F(1,81) = 18.31$, $p < .001$, and on the Modified Scale for Suicidal Ideation, $F(1,80) = 6.52$, $p < .01$. Furthermore, the effects of social support on hopelessness remained significant even after using an ANCOVA to control for patients' different levels of depression (see Figure 6.2).

When using a MANOVA to examine symptoms of anxiety, significant main effects were found for life stress, Wilks' Lambda $(3,77) = 2.87$, $p < .05$, and for social support, Wilks' Lambda $(3,77) = 2.75$, $p < .05$. The interaction term was nonsignificant. Patients low in social support reported higher levels of phobic anxiety, $F(1,80) = 4.47$, $p < .05$. Patients reporting high levels of stress reported higher levels of general anxiety, $F(1,80) = 4.46$,

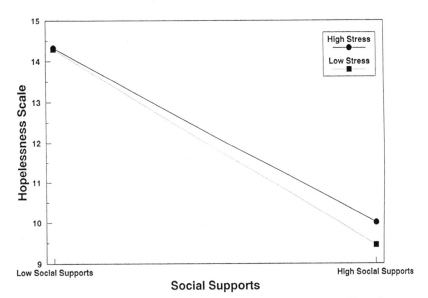

Figure 6.2.   Effects of life stress and social supports on feelings of hopelessness.

$p < .05$, and phobic anxiety, $F(1,80) = 13.40$, $p < .001$. Despite significant main effects for each grouping variable, no significant interactions between life stress and social support were observed. After using an ANCOVA to control for the effects of depression severity, significant effects were maintained only for stress on general anxiety (see Figure 6.3).

When a MANOVA was used to examine the social adjustment of the depressed patients, significant main effects were found for both life stress, Wilks' Lambda $(4,65) = 2.71$, and social support, Wilks' Lambda $(4,65) = 3.16$, $p < .01$. The interaction between life stress and social support was nonsignificant. Social functioning was related to social support, $F(1,71) = 14.75$, $p < .001$. Economic adjustment was related to life stress, $F(1,68) = 8.39$, $p < .005$. Family functioning was related to life stress, $F(1,71) = 8.03$, $p < .01$, and to social support, $F(1,71) = 7.16$, $p < .01$. For married patients, marital adjustment was related to the availability of social support, $F(1,42) = 8.32$, $p < .01$. All of these effects remained significant even after using an ANCOVA to control for depression

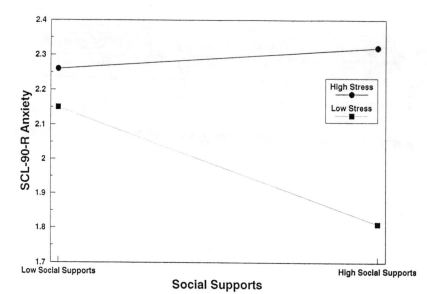

Figure 6.3.   Effects of life stress and social supports on feelings of anxiety.

severity, except for the effect of social support on family function-ing, which was reduced to a nonsignificant trend, $F(1,71) = 2.99$, $p < .08$. Thus, among psychiatric inpatients, social adjustment is related to levels of perceived stress and to levels of perceived social support (see Figure 6.4).

When a MANOVA was used to examine personality styles across the four groups, significant effects were found for life stress, Wilks' Lambda $(3,57) = 3.29$, $p < .03$. The main effect for social support and for the interaction term were nonsignificant. De-pressed patients high in life stress scored significantly higher on EPI scales for neuroticism, $F(1,59) = 14.68$, $p < .001$, and intro-version, $F(1,59) = 3.79$, $p < .05$. Even after using an ANCOVA to control for depression severity, the effects of life stress on neu-roticism scores remained significant (see Figure 6.5). Although it is unlikely that these reflect stress-induced personality changes, these findings may show the importance of personality styles in stress research. The relationship between personality and stress

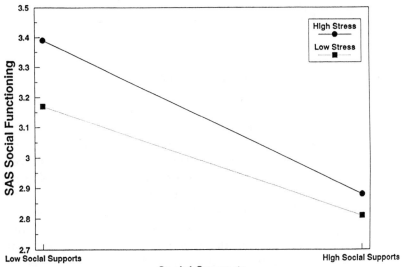

Figure 6.4. Effects of life stress and social supports on general social functioning.

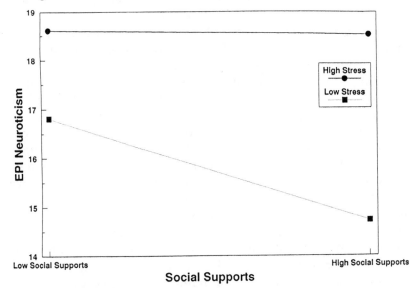

Figure 6.5. Effects of life stress and social supports on neuroticism.

may influence the effect that stressful events have on psychological functioning.

IMPLICATIONS

Among depressed psychiatric inpatients, stressful events and availability of social support exert direct effects on psychological, social, and personality functioning. In the present study, low levels of support and high levels of stress were related to psychological problems. The interaction between these two variables never attained statistical significance, suggesting that negative events and availability of social support exert their effects independently rather than interactively within a psychiatric inpatient population. These results have both theoretical and clinical implications.

The results of the present study support the direct effects theory and contribute to the understanding of the mechanisms through which stress and social support are related to depression and psychological functioning. Given clinical levels of dysfunction and nonoverlapping measures of social support and stress, social support does not buffer the effects of stress. This contradicts numerous studies with community populations indicating a stress buffering effect for social support (see Cohen and Wills [1985] for review). The contradictions may be due to the level of pathology, type of stress, or the nature of support considered.

The interaction between stress and support that has been observed in groups displaying subclinical levels of depression may not generalize to clinical populations. A threshold level of stressful events may be necessary to trigger the onset of a depressive episode, and beyond this stress threshold, increased stress no longer impacts severity of depressive symptoms (Veiel, 1987). Thus, beyond the stress threshold, an interaction between stress and support would also not be observed. In the present study, levels of stress were not related to depression severity.

Stress and support have been defined and assessed in a variety of ways. It is possible that not all types of support interact with all forms of stress. For example, buffering effects have been found when the quality of intimacy in supportive relationships was assessed (Brown and Bifulco, 1985). Interactions between stress and support have been found when chronic stress has been considered (Kessler and Essex, 1982). The present study focused on perceived availability of support and discrete stressful events. Each of these directly influences psychological functioning in depressed patients, but the availability of social support does not buffer the effects of stressful events.

The clinical implications of the present findings emphasize the need to help depressed patients manage stress and increase their available social support. Reducing stress and increasing social support may help alleviate a broad spectrum of psychological and social problems experienced by these patients. As a result, responsiveness to treatment and prognosis may be improved for depressed patients.

Although the present sample was limited to depressed inpatients, significant variability in depression severity was observed across subjects. Patients reporting low levels of social support displayed more severe levels of depression and hopelessness. These results are in agreement with other studies showing increased depression and suicide potential when social alienation is present (Bock and Webber, 1972; Trout, 1980; Magne-Ingvar, Ojehagen, and Traskman-Bendz, 1992). Hopelessness predicts the persistence of depression among depressed patients (McCranie and Riley, 1992). Furthermore, among depressed patients, hopelessness may persist beyond the remission of depressive symptoms (Overholser, Miller, and Norman, 1987), possibly increasing the risk of relapse. Because perceived availability of social support is directly related to levels of hopelessness in depressed patients, improving social support may be necessary for effective treatment and positive long-term outcomes.

In the present study, patients with low levels of social support noted problems related to their marriages and to general social functioning. Lack of support within the marital relationship is related to depression onset, remission, and relapse (Brown and Bifulco, 1985; Hooley and Teasdale, 1989). Thus, social support deficits experienced by depressed patients may stem from a poor marital relationship as well as an inadequate social network. Because social support deficits had direct effects on depression severity and levels of hopelessness, improving a patient's available social support can have beneficial effects regardless of the degree of life stress that is present in the patient's life.

The assessment of social support should become a regular part of clinical assessment and discharge planning for depressed patients. Treatment should address the interpersonal aspects of depression. Many patients may benefit from social skills training, assertiveness training, marital therapy, group therapy, or encouragement to become actively involved in community-based group programs (e.g., AA, church groups). By enhancing the client's social support system, depression severity may be reduced and future episodes of depression may be prevented.

Stress was not related to depression severity among the psychiatric inpatients. However, results showed that depressed inpatients undergoing high levels of life stress reported increased levels of anxiety. This is in agreement with other studies showing a relationship between negative life events and feelings of anxiety (Nezu, 1986). Although events involving loss are often related to depression, events representing a severe danger are more closely related to anxiety (Finlay-Jones, 1989). Thus, life stress may cause anxiety in depressed patients complicating both assessment and treatment issues.

Depressed patients reporting high levels of stressful events reported problematic family functioning and poor economic adjustment. Because of the cross-sectional nature of the data, the causal directions in these relationships remain unclear. However, in clinical settings, these may represent areas to target for stress management and skills training components of treatment. Thus, when depressed patients report high levels of stressful events, social adjustment issues may need to be addressed in treatment.

Personality factors can play an important role in the stress process. Certain individuals are at risk for experiencing negative emotional states in response to even minor life stressors (Watson and Clark, 1984). Our study found higher levels of neuroticism in the high stress patients even when levels of depression severity were statistically controlled. Although stress may cause emotional lability, it seems more likely that adult personality styles precede the onset of stressful events. Thus, the negative affect and emotional lability that characterize neuroticism may serve to increase the patient's perceived level of stress. Because our study focused on the subjective impact of life events, the patients high in neuroticism may have tended to overperceive, focus on, and amplify the threat involved in many life events. Thus, patients with tendencies for neuroticism may be more vulnerable to depression and other symptomatology because they exacerbate the level of perceived stress in their lives. Future research could benefit by expanding the assessment of personality styles as related to life stress.

Research on interpersonal dependency has shed light on personality factors related to stress. In one study (Overholser, 1990), the assessment of life stress focused on social loss, or exit events whereby a person important in the patient's life has left them through death, divorce, or relocation. Psychiatric inpatients reporting high levels of interpersonal dependency following a recent social loss displayed less severe depression than did those patients who were reporting high dependency in the absence of any social loss. Thus, at low levels of interpersonal dependency, social loss had no effect on depressive symptoms. Therefore, exit events do not necessarily produce depressive reactions, but are filtered through the personality style and dependency needs of the patient.

Further evidence for the role of personality styles in life stress reactions comes from longitudinal studies. Levels of life stress are often stable over time (Billings and Moos, 1982; Lin, 1986). Thus, individuals may partially determine the amount of stress in their lives. Chronic problems can set in motion a complex network of effects, potentially causing stressful life events and a loss of social support (Depue and Monroe, 1986). For example, a person with a borderline personality disorder may engage in a variety of dangerous behaviors, including promiscuous sexual behavior, driving while intoxicated, intense arguments, and assaultive behavior. These behaviors may increase the likelihood that stressful events (e.g., trouble with the law, unwanted pregnancy) will occur. Furthermore, the same behaviors may increase the likelihood of rejection by family and friends, thus decreasing available social support.

In summary, stressful events and perceived available social supports are independently related to psychological problems and social adjustment among depressed psychiatric inpatients. Social support is related to depression severity regardless of the levels of reported stress. Poor marital adjustment and inadequate social functioning may account for the low levels of perceived support reported by severely depressed patients. Among depressed patients, stressful events are not related to depression severity. However, among depressed inpatients, stressful events were related to increased levels of anxiety, poor social adjustment, and to maladaptive personality styles.

Life stress may be viewed as important in the etiology of clinical depression. However, a person's social and psychological vulnerability must be taken into consideration in order to understand how stressful events impact the etiology and course of clinical depression. Thus, it becomes essential that stress researchers focus on a broader picture in which stress is assessed in relationship to the social functioning and personality of an individual. Without taking into account the person variables, stress research loses much of its potential benefits. Research on the effects of life stress must continue to expand its focus to a person's internal and external adaptive resources.

REFERENCES

Andrews, G., Tennant, C., Hewson, D., & Vaillant, G. (1978), Life event stress, social support, coping style, and risk of psychological impairment. *J. Nerv. Ment. Dis.*, 166:307–316.

Aneshensel, C., & Frerichs, R. (1982), Stress, support, and depression: A longitudinal causal model. *J. Commun. Psychol.*, 10:363–376.

Beck, A., Kovacs, M., & Weissman, A. (1975), Hopelessness and suicidal intention: An overview. *AMA*, 234:1146–1149.

—— —— —— (1979), Assessment of suicidal intention: The Scale for Suicidal Ideation. *J. Consult. & Clin. Psychol.*, 47:343–352.

—— Steer, R. A., Kovacs, M., & Garrison, B. (1985), Hopelessness and eventual suicide: A 10-year prospective study of patients hospitalized with suicidal ideation. *Amer. J. Psychiatry*, 142:559–563.

—— Ward, C., Mendelson, M., Mock, J., & Erbaugh, J. (1961), An inventory for measuring depression. *Arch. Gen. Psychiatry*, 4:561–571.

—— Weissman, A., Lester, D., & Trexler, L. (1974), The measurement of pessimism: The Hopelessness Scale. *J. Consult. & Clin. Psychol.*, 42:861–865.

Billings, A., & Moos, R. (1982), Stressful life events and symptoms: A longitudinal model. *Health Psychol.*, 1:99–117.

Bock, E., & Webber, I. (1972), Suicide among the elderly: Isolating widowhood and mitigating alternatives. *J. Marr. & Fam.*, 34:24–31.

Brown, G. W., Andrews, B., Harris, T., Adler, Z., & Bridge, L. (1986), Social support, self-esteem and depression. *Psycholog. Med.*, 16:813–831.

—— Bifulco, A. (1985), Social support, life events and depression. In: *Social Support: Theory, Research and Applications*, ed. I. Sarason & B. Sarason. Boston: Martins Nijhoff, pp. 349–370.

Cohen, S., & Wills, T. (1985), Stress, social support, and the buffering hypothesis. *Psycholog. Bull.*, 98:310–357.

D'Attilio, J. P., Campbell, B. M., Lubold, P., & Jacobsen, P. (1992), Social support and suicide potential: Preliminary findings for adolescent populations. *Psycholog. Reports*, 70:76–78.

Depue, R. A., & Monroe, R. A. (1986), Conceptualization and measurement of human disorder in life stress research: The problem of chronic disturbance. *Psycholog. Bull.*, 99:36–51.

Derogatis, L. (1983), *SCL-90-R: Administration, Scoring and Procedures Manual—II.* Towson, MD: Clinical Psychometric Research.

—— Lipman, R., & Covi, L. (1973), SCL-90: An outpatient psychiatric rating scale: Preliminary report. *Psychopharmacol. Bull.*, 9:13–28.

DeVanna, M., Paterniti, S., Milievich, C., Rigamonti, R., Sulich, A., & Faravelli, C. (1990), Recent life events and attempted suicide. *J. Affect. Disord.*, 18:51–58.

Dixon, W. A., Heppner, P. P., & Anderson, W. P. (1991), Problem-solving appraisal, stress, hopelessness, and suicide ideation in a college population. *J. Counsel. Psychol.*, 38:51–56.

Duer, S., Schwenk, T. L., & Coyne, J. C. (1988), Medical and psychosocial correlates of self-reported depressive symptoms in family practice. *J. Fam. Pract.*, 27:609–614.

Eysenck, H., & Eysenck, S. (1968), *Eysenck Personality Inventory.* San Diego, CA: Educational Testing Service.

—— —— (1975), *Manual: Eysenck Personality Questionnaire.* San Diego, CA: Education & Industrial Testing Service.

Finlay-Jones, R. (1989), Anxiety. In: *Life Events and Illness*, ed. G. Brown & T. Harris. New York: Guilford, pp. 95–112.

Habif, V. (1981), *Development of a Scale to Measure Social Support and Its Role as a Moderator of Life Stress.* Unpublished Master's Thesis, University of Georgia.

———— Lahey, B. (1980), Assessment of the life stress-depression relationship: The use of social support as a moderator variable. *J. Behav. Assess.*, 2:167–173.

Hamilton, M. (1960), A rating scale for depression. *J. Neurol., Neurosurg., & Psychiatry*, 12:56–62.

Hammen, C. (1991), Generation of stress in the course of unipolar depression. *J. Abnorm. Psychol.*, 100:555–561.

Hart, K. E., & Hittner, J. B. (1991), Irrational beliefs, perceived availability of social support, and anxiety. *J. Clin. Psychol.*, 47:582–587.

Holahan, C., & Moos, R. (1986), Personality, coping, and family resources in stress resistance: A longitudinal analysis. *J. Person. & Soc. Psychol.*, 51:389–395.

Hooley, J. M., & Teasdale, J. D. (1989), Predictors of relapse in unipolar depressives: Expressed emotion, marital distress, and perceived criticism. *J. Abnorm. Psychol.*, 98:229–235.

Kessler, R. C., & Essex, M. (1982), Marital status and depression: The role of coping resources. *Soc. Forces*, 61:484–507.

Lauer, R. (1973), The Social Readjustment Scale and anxiety: A cross-cultural study. *J. Psychosom. Res.*, 17:171–174.

Lazarus, R. S., & Folkman, S. (1986), Cognitive theories of stress and the issue of circularity. In: *Dynamics of Stress: Physiological, Psychological, and Social Perspectives*, ed. M. H. Appley & R. Trumbull. New York: Plenum Press, pp. 63–80.

Lin, K. M. (1986), Modeling the effects of social support. In: *Social Supports, Life Events, and Depression*, ed. N. Lin, A. Dean, & W. Ensel. New York: Academic Press, pp. 173–209.

Long, G. T. (1988), The relationship of voice stress, anxiety, and depression to life events and personal style variables. *Soc. Behav. & Personal.*, 16:133–145.

Magne-Ingvar, U., Ojehagen, A., & Traskman-Bendz, L. (1992), The social network of people who attempt suicide. *Acta Psychiat. Scand.*, 86:153–158.

McCranie, E. W., & Riley, W. T. (1992), Hopelessness and persistence of depression in an inpatient sample. *Cog. Ther. & Res.*, 16:699–710.

Miller, I., Norman, W., Bishop, S., & Dow, M. (1986), The Modified Scale for Suicidal Ideation: Reliability and validity. *J. Consult. & Clin. Psychol.*, 54:724–725.

Monroe, S., Bromet, E., Connell, M., & Steiner, S. (1986), Social support, life events, and depressive symptoms: A 1-year prospective study. *J. Consult. & Clin. Psychol.*, 54:424–431.

———— Kupfer, D., & Frank, E. (1992), Life stress and treatment course of recurrent depression: 1. Response during index episode. *J. Consult. & Clin. Psychol.*, 60:718–724.

———— Simons, A., & Thase, M. (1991), Onset of depression and time to treatment entry: Roles of life stress. *J. Consult. & Clin. Psychol.*, 59:566–573.

———— Steiner, S. (1986), Social support and psychopathology: Interrelations with preexisting disorder, stress, and personality. *J. Abnorm. Psychol.*, 95:29–39.

Myers, J., Lindenthal, J., & Pepper, M. (1975), Life events, social integration, and psychiatric symptomatology. *J. Health & Soc. Behav.*, 16:421–427.

Nezu, A. (1986), Negative life stress and anxiety: Problem solving as a moderator variable. *Psycholog. Rep.*, 58:279–283.

Overholser, J. C. (1990), Emotional reliance and social loss: Effects on depressive symptomatology. *J. Personal. Assess.*, 55:618–629.

—— Miller, I., & Norman, W. (1987), The course of depressive symptoms in suicidal vs. nonsuicidal depressed inpatients. *J. Nerv. Ment. Dis.*, 175:450–456.

—— Norman, W., & Miller, I. (1990), Life stress and social supports in depressed inpatients. *Behav. Med.*, 16:125–132.

Paykel, E. S. (1976), Life stress, depression and attempted suicide. *J. Hum. Stress*, 2:3–12.

Perris, H. (1989), Life events and personality characteristics in depression. In: *Stressful Life Events*, ed. T. W. Miller. Madison, CT: International Universities Press, pp. 485–499.

Reno, R., & Halaris, A. (1990), The relationship between life stress and depression in an endogenous sample. *Comprehen. Psychiatry*, 31:25–33.

Rich, C., Warsradt, G. Nemiroff, R., Fowler, R., & Young, D. (1991), Suicide, stressors, and the life cycle. *Amer. J. Psychiatry*, 148:524–527.

Robins, C., Block, P., & Peselow, E. (1990), Cognition and life events in major depression: A test of the mediation and interaction hypotheses. *Cog. Ther. & Res.*, 14:299–313.

Robins, L., Helzer, J., Croughan, J., & Ratcliff, K. (1981), National Institute of Mental Health Diagnostic Interview Schedule: Its history, characteristics, and validity. *Arch. Gen. Psychiatry*, 38:381–389.

Sarason, I., Johnson, J., & Siegel, J. (1978), Assessing the impact of life changes: Development of the Life Experiences Survey. *J. Consult. & Clin. Psychol.*, 46:932–946.

Surtees, P. (1980), Social support, residual adversity and depressive outcome. *Soc. Psychiatry*, 15:71–80.

Swindle, R. W., Cronkite, R. C., & Moos, R. H. (1989), Life stressors, social resources, coping, and the 4-year course of unipolar depression. *J. Abnorm. Psychol.*, 98:468–477.

Trout, D. (1980), The role of social isolation in suicide. *Suicide & Life-Threat. Behav.*, 19:10–23.

Veiel, H. O. (1987), Buffer effects and threshold effects: An alternative interpretation of nonlinearities in the relationship between social support, stress, and depression. *Amer. J. Commun. Psychol.*, 15:717–740.

Watson, D., & Clark, L. (1984), Negative affectivity: The disposition to experience aversive emotional states. *Psycholog. Bull.*, 96:465–490.

Weissman, M., Prusoff, B., Thompson, D., Harding, P., & Myers, J. (1978), Social adjustment by self-report in a community sample and in psychiatric outpatients. *J. Nerv. Ment. Dis.*, 166:317–326.

Williams, A., Ware, J., & Donald, C. (1981), A model of mental health, life events, and social supports applicable to general populations. *J. Health & Soc. Behav.*, 22:324–336.

Wise, E., & Barnes, D. (1986), The relationship among life events, dysfunctional attitudes, and depression. *Cog. Ther. & Res.*, 10:257–266.

Chapter 7
Stressful Life Events and Panic Disorder

Carlo Faravelli, M.D., Sabrina Paterniti, M.D., and Paola Servi, M.D.

According to the classical Freudian theory of neurosis, an early traumatic event might condition the whole of an individual's psychic development. The subject would show a peculiar vulnerability toward later events that could remind him or her, either directly or symbolically, of the initial trauma. According to this theory, the significance of the stressing event in adulthood would be that of unmasking a predisposition. In particular, Freud (1892) referred to panic attacks with agoraphobia as "anxiety hysteria," and explained the symptoms in the case of Katharina. The Freudian hypothesis of an early trauma as a predisposing factor, and of a recent trauma as a trigger for pathological conditions, is still part of most psychological and psychopathological theories, even in fields other than psychoanalysis. Behavioral models, for instance, are in line with this position, although expressing it in other terms. According to this theory, an excess of early negative reinforcements (punishments) could lead the subject to cope with later obstacles with less determination and less self-confidence, thus predisposing an anxious reaction.

Although the various theoretical models of anxiety assign different weights to the role of life events, it is possible to separate

143

the environmental determinants into two groups: (1) life events as factors which modulate the development of personal psychological features that render the subject vulnerable to anxiety (called personality, cognitive pattern, or other, according to the particular theoretical frame); (2) life events as factors which can induce, precipitate, or exacerbate a pathological anxiety state.

LIFE EVENTS AS PREDISPOSING FACTORS

Events which occurred during childhood and adolescence are commonly referred to as early events. Basically the relationship of early traumas to psychiatric disorders in adult life may be studied via prospective or retrospective studies. In the first instance the independent variable is the occurrence of an early trauma, whereas the dependent variable is whether a subsequent illness occurred. The opposite position applies to retrospective studies (i.e., the presence of an illness being the independent variable) in which researchers look for the presence of early traumas. Both methods are difficult to carry out in practice because of serious methodological limitations. Prospective studies are almost impossible for humans, because of the length of the observation period, whereas retrospective studies are seriously biased because events have to be recalled at a distance of several decades. In this case the researcher is caught between the lack of sensitivity of the methods which consider only those events that may be reliably recalled (e.g., death events), and the lack of reliability of the methods that take into account finer, but less objective events (e.g., the quality of the upbringing patterns).

In man the prospective procedure has been followed in Sweden by studying the prevalence of psychiatric illness among adoptees. In this case the cohort of adoptee subjects showed an overrepresentation of psychiatric disorders compared to normal population, whereas no relationship with any specific disorder was established (von Knorring, Bohman, and Sigvardsson, 1982).

On the other hand, the more common retrospective investigation of events which occurred at a distance of several years can only deal with rough (major) events, in order to achieve a certain reliability. In this context the only possibility of avoiding distorted recall or personal elaboration of past experiences is to evaluate only the number of previously defined events. The majority of retrospective studies have therefore used this method. This is a misrepresentation if we consider that these stressful life events could be due not so much to their occurrence per se as to their psychological and emotional impact on the subject (Tennant and Andrews, 1978).

Some empirical studies have investigated the hypothesis of separation from parental figures as a vulnerability factor in the genesis of agoraphobia. The first studies on this subject (Solyom, Beck, Solyom, and Hugel, 1974; Buglass, Clarke, Henderson, Kreitman, and Presley, 1977) did not find an increase in the rate of death of parents prior to 15 years of age for agoraphobic patients compared to normal subjects. Other studies based on population survey (Tennant et al., 1981, 1982), though failing in finding a clear definition of the problem, claimed a general tendency toward the separation from parents in the early history of anxiety states. All these studies however were carried out without using operational critera.

Raskin, Peeke, Dickman, and Pinkster (1982) using DSM III criteria found out that 33 percent of Panic Disorder (PD) patients had undergone separation from parents during childhood, a rate that was significantly higher than that found for other anxiety disorders.

In a preliminary study on a small cohort of agoraphobic patients with panic attacks we found a significant excess of early events, namely separation from mothers and divorce between parents, compared to normal controls, in a period ranging from the fourth to the fifteenth year of age of the patient (Faravelli et al., 1985).

Finlay Jones (1986), who did not use operational diagnostic criteria, suggested that the anamnestic finding of parents' divorce is especially frequent in patients defined as "cases of anxiety."

This would differentiate this cohort of patients from those suffering from depression, where loss of the mother was more frequent. Separation from the father after the parents' divorce, probably after a period of increased family conflicts, would be a specific marker for anxious patients.

Other studies comparing panic patients with depressed ones (Coryell et al., 1983) and with patients affected by Generalized Anxiety Disorder (Torgersen, 1986) point out a higher prevalence of loss events, linked either to death of parents or to divorce.

We compared 22 subjects with PD with 42 cases suffering from agoraphobia with panic attack (DSM-III), in order to evaluate whether these aspects were common to both disorders or if they were in some way specific of either group (Faravelli et al., 1988). Agoraphobics experienced a significantly higher frequence in events of death and separation during childhood or adolescence, compared to nonagoraphobic subjects: two thirds of agoraphobics underwent at least one traumatic event compared to 22 percent of panic patients without agoraphobia. Child pathology, namely separation anxiety, was also more frequent in agoraphobics, although the rates did not reach the statistical significance.

A study based on a community survey (Tweed, Schoenbach, George, and Blazer, 1989), also showed a significant relationship between death of the mother and panic disorder with agoraphobia and between separation/divorce of the parents and panic disorder with and without agoraphobia.

Analogous results are reported in a recent study investigating parental loss prior to the age of 7 years and psychopathology in 1018 pairs of female twins (Kendler et al., 1991). In partial contrast with Finlay-Jones (1986) this study revealed a higher rate of parental death and maternal, but not paternal, separation amongst panic patients. According to these findings, separation from the mother seems to be a stronger predictor of risk than separation from the father.

In a subsequent, enlarged study we compared a population of 73 outpatients affected by Panic Disorder with Agoraphobia with 27 outpatients suffering from Panic Disorder (PD) according to

TABLE 7.1

Traumatic Early Life Events Experienced by 73 Patients with Agoraphobia (AGO) and/or Panic Disorder (PD), 27 Panic Disorder Patients and 76 Control Subjects

Event	Number of Subjects Reporting at Least One Event			Chi-Square	Prob
	Controls (n = 76)	PD + AGO (n = 73)	PD (n = 27)		
Death of Mother	0	3	1	3.125	0.2096
Death of Father	2	7	2	3.149	0.2071
Death of Parent	2	9	3	5.216	0.0737
Separation from Mother	4	21	3	15.925	<0.001
Separation from Father	8	29	5	17.975	<0.001
Separation from Parents	8	30	6	18.689	<0.001
Parents' Divorce	4	19	3	13.091	<0.001
Other	15	27	7	5.573	0.0616
Any Event	21	48	13	21.777	<0.001

DSM-III diagnostic criteria (APA, 1980). The patients were also compared with a control group of healthy subjects, homogeneous for age, sex, social class and education (Faravelli and Pallanti, 1992). Among the results, shown in Table 7.1, we must emphasize the higher frequency of traumatic events generally experienced by agoraphobic patients compared both to healthy controls and to PD patients. In fact 65 percent of agoraphobic patients reported a traumatic early event in the first 15 years of their life, compared to 27 percent of healthy subjects and to 48 percent of PD patients. The single event "Separation from parents," due to any cause, was found in 41 percent of agoraphobic patients, compared to 22 percent of PD patients and 10 percent of healthy subjects (chi-square = 18.68, df = 2, $p < 0.001$). These results should be considered the most typical finding for agoraphobic patients.

In general, the results obtained demonstrated an increased number of stressful experiences for the patients compared to normals, but what is more striking is the difference between patients affected by PD without agoraphobia and patients with PD and agoraphobia, as well as the peculiarity of the events where the differences are more noteworthy.

The occurrence of an early trauma, and particularly separation from the parents, seems to represent a marker in the biography of agoraphobic patients. Such a marker clearly distinguishes the agoraphobics not only from normal controls but even from PD patients. This result must be emphasized because it appears that early separation may have a pathoplastic role in conditioning the development of agoraphobic symptoms. Our data would indirectly support the hypothesis of a preeminent role of environmental determinants in agoraphobia, compared to PD without phobic features. This last disorder is considered by many authors mainly as a biological phenomenon (Klein, 1964, 1987).

These results could be in line with some cognitive interpretations of agoraphobia. Intuitively we can understand how early events of separation can lead to a more difficult personal individuation, together with a halt in the normal explorative behavior in a world that is perceived as precarious and frightening (Guidano and Liotti, 1983). Beside the feelings of rage and desperation, which involve a continuous state of alertness of the vegetative system, the need for autonomy can even be increased in these patients, thus determining dysfunctional attachment patterns (Guidano, 1987). Early events of separation and loss seem to push the subject toward developing an avoidant behavior after experiencing the first panic attacks. The onset of acute anxiety, together with the conscious or unconscious memory of the early, painful experiences of separation, will determine an increased feeling of insecurity in the subject. The patient will try by any means to avoid all situations where the feeling of loneliness, dispersion, and loss might remind him or her of the early experiences of abandonment and breakdown.

The psychic compensation of these subjects, which is hardly maintained by the systematic control over themselves and their environment, is destined to break down after the first unforesee-able and uncontrollable panic experiences. Agoraphobia is thus born.

Studies, which took into account the "stability" of agoraphobic patients' families, showed contrasting findings. In fact, while some authors found normal stability in these families (Roth, 1959; Ter-hune, 1961; Marks and Gelder, 1965), others (Webster, 1953) pointed out that fathers were more often absent or the families were more unstable (Snaith, 1968) amongst the agoraphobic sub-jects, in respect to the norm. The bias in the interpretation of these data is mostly linked to the variability in the definition of "stability."

EARLY EVENTS AND PARENTAL REARING

As it has been mentioned above, reliable studies about early events can only deal with major events; their main limitation is linked to a lack of sensitivity in exploring the real quality of the childhood environment of the future patients. Despite the em-phasis given to parent–child relationships as predisposing factors for agoraphobia (Bowlby, 1973; Beck, 1976; Guidano and Liotti, 1983), only few controlled studies on this subject have been car-ried out.

Using the Maternal Overprotection Questionnaire, Solyom, Silberfeld, and Solyom (1976) found that the mothers of agora-phobics were more protective than those of normal controls, whereas Buglass et al. (1977) could not distinguish their 30 agora-phobic housewives from controls on the scale measuring the feel-ings toward parents. Parker (1981), using the Parental Bonding Instrument (PBI), a 25-item self-report questionnaire devised to evaluate parental child-rearing practices, reported that patients suffering from anxiety neurosis scored both their parents as sig-nificantly less caring and more overprotective than matched nor-mal controls did. Another study by Parker (1979), however, found that agoraphobics differed from controls only on the scale measuring maternal care, which was reduced among patients.

Using operational diagnostic criteria Arrindel, Emmelkamp, Monsma, and Brilman (1983) and Arrindell, Kwee, Methorst, van der Ende, Pol, and Moritz, (1989) found that agoraphobics reported their mothers as giving less emotional warmth and being more rejecting, but did not score differently on the Egna Minnen Betraffande (EMBU) Scale measuring overprotection. Stravynski, Elie, and Franche (1989) administered the Parental Bonding Instrument (PBI) to patients with avoidant personality disorder and found significantly lower scores in the dimension of care than in normal controls, although failing to show differences in overprotection. In our study (Faravelli, Panichi, Pallanti, Paterniti, Grecu, and Rivelli, 1991) we administered the PBI to 32 patients with a DSM-III-R diagnosis of PD and 32 matched healthy controls (APA, 1987). Panic Disorder patients scored both their parents as being significantly less caring and more overprotective. Moreover, the consistency of parental attitudes between the two parents was significantly lower, indicating lesser uniformity in the rearing patterns.

Silove, Parker, Hadzi-Pavolovic, Manicavasagar, and Blaszczynski (1991) found that only mother's overprotection characterized the parents of panic patients (without major phobic avoidance) when compared to healthy controls. The authors hypothesized that "panic disorder, and its earlier manifestations as separation anxiety in childhood and adolescence may elicit overprotective parenting, while the manner of coping with symptoms of panic—whether or not the sufferer succumbs to agoraphobic avoidance—may be shaped by more pathogenic parental behaviour such a deficiences in parental care" (p. 840).

Although PBI has been shown to be an acceptable measure of actual and not merely perceived parental characteristics (Parker, 1981), two types of considerations may reduce the validity of these kinds of instruments. It is possible that certain temperamental traits associated with panic could make these patients more sensitive to negative interpersonal interactions. Recall of events could be influenced by the patient's pathological condition. More generally, subjects with emotional pathology might search for the causes of their problems in the past, and especially in their earlier interactions with parents, attributing a more negative value to such relationships than they actually warrant. This systematic distortion could become a vicious circle, in which what is believed to be the cause is, in fact, the effect of pathology.

On the other hand, as a family concentration of anxiety disorders has repeatedly been reported (Cohen, Badal, Kilpatrick, Reed, and White, 1951; Crowe, Noyes, Pauls, and Stymen, 1989; Noyes, Crowe, Harris, Hamra, McChesney, and Chaudhry, 1986; GIDA, 1989), it is reasonable to conceive that parents with an anxious or phobic condition might have a reduced capacity to care for children and might overprotect the child as they protect themselves from feared situations. In order to verify these two last hypotheses, we decided to study both the mothers of PD patients and PD patients who were mothers by means of Parental Attitude Research Instrument (PARI; Schaefer and Bell, 1958), which is made up of 23 different scales investigating the mothers' opinions about chld raising. Preliminary results show that patients' mothers scored significantly higher on the scales Fostering Dependency and Intrusiveness compared to a matched control group of healthy subjects' mothers. No differences were found between PD patients who are mothers and healthy controls.

The first findings confirm an actual overprotective attitude on the part of patients' mothers, in agreement with the results obtained with PBI, suggesting that the anxiety disorder per se is not responsible for distorting parental attitudes.

RECENT STRESSFUL LIFE EVENTS AND ONSET OF PANIC DISORDER

Most clinical descriptions report that the initial symptoms of panic disorder are often preceded by a stressful life event (Klein,

1964; Raskin, Peeke, Dickman, and Pinkster, 1982; Gittelman and Klein, 1984). This observation can be easily verified in the case of panic disorder, because of the sudden and often dramatic onset of this disease. Several studies have investigated this problem and dealt with disorder categories that are quite similar to panic (Solyom et al., 1974; Buglass et al., 1977; Raskin et al., 1982; Last, Barlow, and Obrieu, 1984; Torgersen, 1985). Only a few papers have employed standardized methods for data collection, however, as well as a comparison with a control group (Finlay-Jones and Brown, 1981; Roy-Byrne, Geraci, and Uhde, 1986a; Faravelli and Pallanti, 1989; Rapee, Litwin, and Barlow, 1990; Servant, Bailly, Allard, and Parquet, 1991).

In reviewing these studies, we will take into account some particularly interesting aspects of the relationship between recent events and the onset of the disorder:

1. Is there a real increase in life stress before the onset of panic disorder, and if so, to what extent?
2. How long can life events exert their influence as risk factors?
3. Is the number of events or their severity more relevant? In other words, is there an additive factor, by which several repeated minor events may induce a pathological reaction, or, rather, an all-or-nothing effect, with a threshold of minimum severity?
4. Is the excess of life stress causally linked to panic disorder, or could panic disorder be the result of particular pathological states (e.g., latent, subclinical symptoms or stress-prone personality)?
5. Is there a specific kind of life event or, rather, a particular meaning attached to specific events, by which certain experiences are more likely than others to induce panic disorder?

Life Stress Preceding the Onset of Panic Disorder

Table 7.2 summarizes the controlled studies carried out on this subject. Most of the studies on this topic reveal an excess of

TABLE 7.2

Controlled Studies of Life Events and Panic Disorder

Author	Diagnosis	N	Methodology	Results (events associated with the onset of Panic Disorder)
Finlay-Jones and Brown (1981)	Anxiety cases	13[a] 119[b]	Semistructured interview Contextual Assessment: loss and danger events	Severe danger
Roy-Byrne et al. (1986a)	Panic disorder (RDC)	44[a] 44[b]	PERI-M Life. Events Inventory Normative and Subjective Assessment	Personal events; Subjective distress (uncontrollable, undesirable, causing extreme lowering of self-esteem events); Objective distress
Faravelli and Pallanti (1989)	Panic disorder, Agoraphobia with panic attacks (DSM-III)	64[a] 78[b]	Semistructured interview Normative and Contextual Assessment: loss, threat, and adjustment events	Greater number of events; Higher weighted normative scores; Higher contextual scores; More independent events
Rapee et al. (1990)	Panic disorder with agoraphobia (DSM-III-R)	64[a] 34[b]	Questionnaire Subjective assessment: Life Experience Survey	Events rated as having a negative impact
Servant et al. (1991)	Panic disorder (DSM-III-R)	53[a] (with dep.) 47[a] (without dep.) 50[b]	Semistructured interview Normative and Contextual Assessment	Severe Life Events

[a] = cases of anxiety or panic disorder
[b] = healthy controls

stressful life events in the period preceding the onset of panic disorder compared with control groups.

This result was evident in the Finlay-Jones and Brown study (1981), which took into account the number of subjects who experienced a severe event. "Severe" events were defined by the authors on the basis of the focus of the event (the subject or other persons), and the degree of unpleasantness associated with the event after 1 day or 1 week (short- or long-term threat, respectively). Severe events were defined as any event rated as high on the contextual measure of long-term threat plus those rated as "moderate" but focused on the respondent alone or jointly with someone else. These authors, however, studied "cases of anxiety" (which corresponded to DSM-III diagnoses of Generalized Anxiety Disorder, Panic Disorder, Agoraphobia, and Social Phobia [Finlay-Jones, 1989]), rather than PD.

Faravelli (1985) used DSM-III criteria to select a sample of 23 cases with PD and compared them with 23 healthy subjects matched for age, sex, social, and educational level. There was a significant excess of life events experienced in the 12 months prior to the first panic attack among the patients as compared to controls, however life events were assessed. Panic patients in fact scored higher on the number of events, the weighted scores (according to Paykel's scale), and the number of subjects who underwent a major life event (death or severe illness, either personal or of a cohabiting relative) in the 2 months preceding the onset of symptoms.

Roy-Byrne et al. (1986a) found that the number of personal events, but not the total number of events, were higher for panic patients compared to healthy controls. These authors, however, studied 44 outpatients affected by PD, the onset of which occurred up to 16 years prior to the time of the interview. This fact may imply a marked methodological bias. In fact it has been shown that time conditions recall of events (Monroe, 1982).

Faravelli and Pallanti (1989), in an enlarged study, compared 64 patients affected by PD with a control group of 78 healthy subjects. In this study an excess of events preceding the onset of the pathology was pointed out, taking into account the total number of events, and the normative and contextual assessment. In the normative assessment, using Paykel's method, those events which scored higher than the cut-off point of 20 in a list of 60 events were considered as "severe." The study shows that patients experienced a significantly higher rate of life stress considering the normative assessment of all events as well as the chronic ones, that is, which lasted more than 3 months (see Table 7.3).

TABLE 7.3
Life Events of Patients with Panic Disorder and Control Subjects During the Year Before the Onset of Panic Disorder

Item	Panic Disorder Patients (N = 64)		Control Subjects (N = 78)		t(a)
	Mean	SD	Mean	SD	
Normative Assessment (Paykel scale)					
Events	2.57	1.58	1.58	1.38	3.96b
Total Score (all events)	31.00	18.01	18.36	18.03	4.16b
Chronic Events Score	5.86	10.08	2.96	7.12	2.19b
Single Highest Event Score	13.39	5.58	10.05	6.19	3.34b
Independent Event Score	17.46	14.22	10.43	12.54	3.12b
Single Highest Independent Event Score	11.56	6.77	6.97	7.02	3.93
Contextual Assessment					
Events	3.66	3.63	2.78	2.04	2.08c
Loss Score	4.18	3.37	1.90	1.84	5.12b
Threat Score	4.90	3.31	2.83	2.71	4.10b
Adjustment Score	4.93	3.60	3.40	2.68	2.88d

a) $df = 140$
b) $p < 0.001$
c) $p < 0.05$
d) $p < 0.01$

Moreover, 41 patients (64.1%) had experienced at least one severe event, compared to 27 control subjects (34.6%): thus the difference was significant (chi-square = 12.21, df = 1, $p < 0.001$). Severe events seem to be less influenced by distorted recall. Events such as death of a person are in fact barely subjected to this mechanism. The use of semistructured interviews, investigating the whole field of possible events, the short interval between the onset of the disorder and the interview, which was given in a period of remission, and the use of a normative assessment of events, are all factors that contribute to excluding this bias.

Rapee et al.'s results (1990) are not in agreement with these findings. The authors did not find any difference in the number of major life events which occurred before the onset of the pathology or the administration of the Life Experiences Survey (Sarason, Johnson, and Seigel, 1978) in a group of 64 PD patients with agoraphobia, when compared with 33 patients with other anxiety disorders and with 34 healthy controls. This discrepancy might be explained by the fact that they employed only a subjective criterion for collecting data, that is, the least reliable, as we will discuss later. Moreover, a questionnaire was used, and not a semistructured interview as in the other studies, and finally, the average duration of the panic disorder and of the other anxiety disorders was 21.7 months and 48.0 months, respectively: these long durations are subject to the criticisms above. On the other hand, when the number of subjects was taken into account, the number of those with panic disorder who reported at least one major life event was higher when compared with the number of subjects with other anxiety disorders; the difference between the panic patients and the healthy controls was high too, even if not significant (chi-square $= 2.93$, df $= 1$, $p < 0.10$).

The results of Rapee's study also show that anxious subjects tend to perceive the impact of the life stressors that they have experienced as more negative than nonanxious subjects do. This result may be explained by the "effort of meaning," that is, that patients tend to exaggerate the negative impact of the events so as to find an explanation for the onset of their pathology. Finally, Servant et al. (1991) found a higher proportion of subjects affected by PD experiencing at least one severe event when compared with control subjects.

TIME OF THE EVENT

Finlay-Jones and Brown (1981) showed that during the 3 months preceding the onset, 62 percent of women reported at least one event of danger; this percentage only slightly increased when taking into consideration the whole year (77%).

The time course of events shown in the Faravelli and Pallanti study (1989) also suggests that the greater number of events experienced by the patients was due almost entirely to the more frequent occurrence of life stress in the month before the onset of PD, while in the control group the occurrence of events was evenly distributed throughout the whole period under study (Figure 7.1). Such an accumulation of life events in the period immediately before the onset of the illness is also shown by the fact

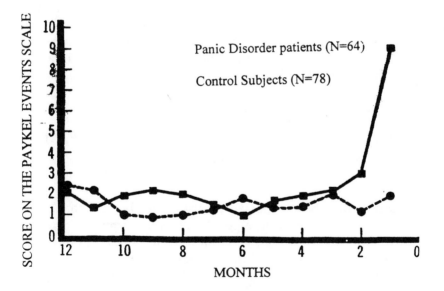

Figure 7.1. Paykel Life Events Scale. Scores of patients with panic disorder and control subjects.

that of the 41 patients who experienced a severe event, 21 did so within a month of the onset of panic disorder, 8 between 1 and 2 months, 5 during the third month, 2 between 4 and 6 months, and 5 between 7 and 12 months (chi-square $= 116.31$, df $= 3$, $p < 0.0001$).

SINGLE SEVERE EVENTS VS. REPETITIVE MINOR EVENTS

This subject has been addressed by Faravelli and Pallanti (1989) by considering only the single event with the highest score for each subject. The difference between the cohort of cases and the control group remained comparable to the difference obtained by the two groups when the total number of events was considered. This result, together with the observation that the difference was higher, considering the weighted scores, rather than their actual number, would suggest that the crucial difference lies in the severity of a particular event more than in the number of events. These data seem compatible with the hypothesis of an all or nothing effect.

CAUSAL RELATIONSHIP BETWEEN EVENT AND PANIC DISORDER

In light of the above reported results, it can be said that panic patients seem to have undergone a greater amount of real life stress before the onset of PD. However, the causal nature of the link between life stress and disease deserves close attention. For other psychiatric disorders (e.g., schizophrenia) it has been shown that the greater number of life events could be the consequence of the illness rather than its cause and could result from an insidious onset or be related to particular premorbid personality features. In the case of panic disorder, even if the onset is generally dramatic and sudden (panic attack), recent studies have pointed out the existence of prodromic symptoms preceding the onset (Fava, Grandi, and Canestrari, 1988), which might explain the events (hypochondriac symptoms, etc.)

This issue can be clarified by analyzing the events judged to be independent (i.e., beyond the subject's control). Finlay-Jones and Brown (1981), taking into consideration only independent events, obtained results comparable to those which considered the total number of events.

Also Faravelli and Pallanti (1989) found that even when only independent events were taken into account, there was still evidence of an excess of events among patients (Table 7.3). The same result was revealed considering only severe, independent events: 40 patients (62.5%) and 25 controls (32%) reported at least one severe, independent event (chi-square = 15.17, df = 1, $p < 0.001$). In line with such an assumption is also the accumulation of events in the month preceding the onset of panic, suggesting a causal relationship.

SPECIFICITY OF EVENTS

The classical psychological authors suggest that anxiety is the subject's reaction to the danger of losing the object, while the pain of mourning represents the reaction to the real loss of the object. The search for a precise relationship between event and type of pathology has characterized the studies on this subject, but it has also given rise to contrasting results. Finlay-Jones and Brown's study (1981) seems to support clinical observation. They defined as events of loss all those that concerned loss of a valued person by death or separation, loss of the respondent's physical health, loss of job, career opportunities, and material possession, or the loss of a cherished idea (i.e., the discovery of a husband's infidelity). Dangerous events were defined as "the degree of unpleasantness of a specific future crisis that might occur as a result of the event" (Finlay-Jones and Brown, 1981). Sixty-five percent of women at the onset of their depressive disorder had experienced a severe loss event, compared to 15 percent of healthy subjects. On the other hand, women at the onset of anxiety disorders reported at least one severe danger event in 37 percent of the cases, compared to 47 percent of depressed subjects and 12 percent of healthy controls.

This finding was not confirmed either in Roy-Byrne et al.'s investigation (1986a), nor by Faravelli and Pallanti (1989). In the first case, in fact, taking into account the different kinds of events (Roy-Byrne et al. 1986a), a difference between cases and control subjects was noted only for those events concerning health. Events most frequently reported by panic patients involved moving to a better or comparable home or neighborhood or to another city, and likely involving loss or separation.

Faravelli and Pallanti (1989) employed a contextual assessment procedure, using an interview derived from the Brown and Harris model (1978). Events were evaluated by their dimension of loss, threat, and adjustment, on a scale of 5. Loss was defined as the amount of personal (material or psychic) irreversible loss or sense of being diminished that was connected with the event. Threat was defined as the degree of danger, uncertainty, or risk (psychic or material) that the event bore for the future of the subject. Adjustment was defined as the amount of life change necessary to cope with the modifications consequent to the event. In this study, the entire contextual assessment of loss, threat, and adjustment revealed differences between patients and controls, and a multiple logistic regression showed that loss had the heaviest loading on the logistic function.

Concerning this aspect, Jacobs, Hansen, Kasl, Ostfeld, Berkman, and Kim (1990) reported that in the 6 months following the loss, the bereaved spouses experienced a 6-month prevalence rate of PD and generalized anxiety disorder, which was higher than the community prevalence rate for the same metropolitan area. The reported association with depression raises questions about whether anxiety disorders of bereavement are prodromal, concomitant, or residual with respect to major depression. The relationship between these two pathologies will also be discussed later.

The lack of concordance between these last studies (Roy-Byrne et al., 1986a; Faravelli and Pallanti, 1989) and the London investigation (Finlay-Jones and Brown, 1981) may be due to various factors. First of all, we have seen that the London sample is made up of a limited sample of women seen in general practice. Only 13 patients were examined, and only the most severe events were considered. Finally, a broader range of anxiety disorders was considered, so that the specificity of PD in respect to other anxiety disorders, pointed out by Crowe et al. (1983), Torgersen (1983), and Klein (1987), might be lost. On the other hand, other studies also suggest that PD might be in many aspects more similar to depression (Leckman, Weissman, Merikangas, Pauls, and Prusoff, 1983; Breier, Charney, and Heninger, 1985). It would not be unexpected, therefore, that the kind of events experienced in the two disorders might be of the same type. This subject, however, deserves further study in order to clarify the relationship.

Finally, both studies (Roy-Byrne et al., 1986a; Faravelli and Pallanti, 1989) underline the major importance that distress plays in the event, compared to the life change implied. In fact, in the first study, the normative measure of the event, assessed by methods measuring the life change (Holmes and Rahe, 1967; Tennant and Andrews, 1978), showed no differences between cases and controls, while these differences appeared when the degree of distress induced by the event was considered. Distress was rated both with a subjective method, assessing the degree of uncontrollability, undesirability and lowering of self-esteem of the event, and with a normative method (Paykel, Prusoff, and Uhlenhuth, 1971; Tennant and Andrews, 1978).

In the study by Faravelli and Pallanti (1989) the contextual rating of adjustment showed minor differences, compared to those of loss or threat (see Table 7.3). Therefore, these data also seem to confirm that the implication of distress, more than its crude occurrence, plays an important role in determining the disorder, as it was suggested in previous studies about "neurotic impairment" (Tennant and Andrews, 1978).

Vulnerability Factors

It has been shown that the divorce of parents can be considered a vulnerability factor toward later danger events, in subjects with anxiety. This would mean that the presence of the parents' divorce in the anamnesis of a subject would increase the probability that the danger event would be followed by an anxiety disorder (Finlay-Jones, 1989).

Events and Course

Life events seem to be relevant in mixed depression anxiety syndromes. In fact, PD patients who underwent loss or separation events during the year preceding the first panic attack had a greater probability of developing a major depressive episode in the follow-up period (Roy-Byrne, Geraci, and Uhde, 1986b; Servant et al., 1991).

These findings emphasize the relationship between PD and depression, a problem that needs further clarification. Finlay-Jones and Brown (1981) brought up the relevance of life events to mixed forms of depression-anxiety when they found that patients with combined depression-anxiety reported a greater number of loss and danger events than patients affected by pure anxiety or depressive disorder. Also Torgersen (1985) found that recent life events play an important role in mixed forms of depression-anxiety and a minor role in pure forms of depression and anxiety, where childhood–environmental factors and hereditary factors play more important roles, respectively. He also found that pregnancy and birth were more frequent events prior to the onset of pure anxiety, while loss or danger events characterized the period before the onset of mixed forms.

Alnaes and Torgersen (1988) found that subjects suffering from mixed forms of depression-anxiety had more frequent conflicts with their partner prior to the onset of the disorder in comparison to cases of pure anxiety. In this last study events dealing with other areas, gathered by Holmes and Rahe's Social Readjustment Rating Scale (1967), did not show differences in occurrence in either the group of pure anxiety or in the mixed forms. Finally, a recent study considered the role played by the life events in recovery and improvement in anxiety disorders, compared to the role played in depressive disorders (Brown, Lemyre, and Bifulco, 1992). The definition of "anxiety disorder" is the same as the definition used in the preceding study (Finlay-Jones and Brown, 1981).

The results show that events preceding recovery or improvement in anxiety specifically involve increased security ("anchoring events"), and those preceding changes in depression imply increased hope ("fresh start events"). These results seem to confirm the specific role of different kinds of events in anxiety and depression. Namely, "fresh start" events may be seen as the mirror image of the loss and disappointment often involved in the onset of depressive disorder; and "anchoring" events as the mirror image of the danger events, which were found by Finlay-Jones and Brown (1981) preceding the onset of anxiety disorders. As Brown et al.'s (1992) research is the unique controlled study showing such a specificity of events in anxiety and depression, the work needs further replication.

LIFE EVENTS AND PANIC DISORDER: A BIOLOGICAL LINK?

Recent data have shown that the corticotropin-releasing hormone (CRH) and the locus coeruleus–norepinephrine system participate in a mutually reinforcing feedback loop to produce the generalized stress response. Furthermore, patients with PD have been found to show a blunted adrenocorticotropic hormone (ACTH) response to CRH in association with basal hypercortisolism. This suggests that the pituitary corticotroph hormone responds appropriately to cortisol negative feedback, and that hypercortisolism in PD reflects a defect at or above the hypothalamus, resulting in the hypersecretion of endogenous CRH (Roy-Byrne, Uhde et al., 1986; Altemus and Gold, 1990). The anomalies in levels of hyperthalamic CRH could therefore explain the anomalous response to the stress of panic patients.

METHODOLOGICAL CONSIDERATIONS

The partial discordance in the results of the above mentioned studies could be explained by several methodological problems connected with requirements to avoid the most likely biases. First of all, the evaluation of life events differs according to the assessment method. Normative methods (Paykel et al., 1971) accounts for the "objectiveness" of life events, regardless of other factors, such as context, succession of facts, or personality of individuals. On the other hand, the contextual method (Brown and Harris, 1978) may be considered "semi-individualized." It incorporated the biographical factors surrounding the events, their succession and consequences, but only in terms of objective measures, and it is not influenced by personal reactions to the event.

Subjective assessment includes many other variables, not only the crude event and its objective context, but also its consequences, and the subject's emotional reactions contribute to the evaluation. The "search for meaning" would make the patients attach greater importance to the event than do healthy subjects (Brown and Harris, 1978; Dohrenwend, 1979). Moreover, it seems probable that even the subject's personality would play a role in this kind of assessment.

The difference among the three methods indicates that the subjective method yields a better relationship to symptoms than do normative scores (Vinokur and Selzer, 1973) and shows the lowest sensitivity (Grant, Sweetwood, Gerst, and Yager, 1978; Faravelli and Ambonetti, 1983). Studying a sample of depressive patients and healthy controls, Faravelli and Ambonetti (1983) found that the subjective method was the only one in which no statistical difference was demonstrable between depressives and controls.

The fact that self-reports are less discriminating could be due to a greater number of variance sources in the method compared with other methods. Relevant to this point, for instance, is the finding that some people, both affected and control subjects, tend to maximize the magnitude of self-reports, giving very high scores to each event that happened to them. In other words, some subjects do not seem to be able to discriminate the relative severity of various events in which they were involved, which results in abnormally high scores that, in turn, contribute to lowering the discriminate power of self-reports. This consideration could explain the negative finding reported by Rapee et al. (1990).

Second, it is necessary to establish how representative the sample is of the whole population of subjects affected by the pathology. For example, in Faravelli and Pallanti's study, the characteristics of the patients were compared with those of the people found to be affected by PD in a community epidemiological survey carried out in the same catchment area (Faravelli, Guerrini Degl'Innocenti, and Giardinelli, 1989). The original patients did not differ from the epidemiological sample in terms of age, sex, education, marital status, or age of onset; only the degree of agoraphobia was higher in the patients. Such a procedure allows for the studied sample to be truly representative of the population affected by the disorder.

Moreover, one must consider that the presence of a stressful life event might selectively affect the probability that an individual would seek medical help. In cases in which the onset of illness shortly followed a severe stressor, subjects could more easily consider their condition as a normal psychological reaction rather than a medical disorder, and therefore be less likely to consult a physician. If this were the case, the number of life events should be smaller in psychiatric samples than in community cases. Such a possibility might, therefore, help explain the results of the studies which did not find differences in the number of life events in the panic patients group and healthy controls group. In fact, psychiatric cases with no connection to life events might have been selected. On the other hand, different recruitment criteria and different treatment settings could explain the differences as well. It is possible, in fact, that highly regarded institutions, which often receive patients with prior poor response to treatment, treat patients in whom the biological component of the disorder is greater than average. This could be one of the reasons for the differences found in the extent of the effect of life stress on PD among the patients in Faravelli and Pallanti's study (university and private patients), those of Roy-Byrne et al. (patients at the National Institute of Mental Health), and those of Finlay-Jones and Brown (general practice patients).

CONCLUSIONS

The above reported findings lead us to the conclusion that recent life events play a role in triggering the onset of panic disorder. The degree of association between events and panic is not so high, however: Faravelli and Pallanti's study (1989) reveals a Population Attributable Risk ranging from 30 to 39. These values emphasize the importance of stress, but lead to the proposal of a multifactorial model: in order to clarify the pathogenesis of PD other variables must be taken into account. Moreover, retrospective studies may answer the question of a subject's probability of having experienced an event before the onset of the pathology, but not the probability that a subject who experienced an event will develop a disorder. For this purpose prospective studies (i.e., among first degree relatives of panic patients) need to be carried out.

REFERENCES

Alnaes, R., & Torgersen, S. (1988), Major depression, anxiety disorders and mixed conditions. Childhood and precipitating events. *Acta Psychiat. Scand.*, 78:632–638.

Altemus, M., & Gold, P. (1990), Neuroendocrinology and psychiatric illness. *Frontiers in Neuroendocrinol.*, 11:238–265.

American Psychiatric Association (1980), *Diagnostic and Statistical Manual of Mental Disorders*, 3rd ed. (DSM-III). Washington, DC: American Psychiatric Press.

——— (1987), *Diagnostic and Statistical Manual of Mental Disorders*, 3rd ed. rev. (DSM-III-R). Washington, DC: American Psychiatric Press.

Arrindell, W. A., Emmelkamp, P. M. G., Monsma, A., & Brilman, E. (1983), The role of perceived parental rearing practices in the aetiology of phobic disorders: A controlled study. *Brit. J. Psychiatry*, 143:183–187.

——— Kwee, M. G. T., Methorst, G. J., van der Ende, J., Pol, E., & Moritz, B. J. M. (1989), Perceived parental rearing styles of agoraphobic and socially phobic in-patients. *Brit. J. Psychiatry*, 155:526–535.

Beck, A. T. (1976), *Cognitive Therapy and the Emotional Disorders.* New York: International Universities Press.

Bowlby, J. (1973), *Attachment and Loss*, Vol. 2. London: Hogarth Press.

Breier, A., Charney, D. S., & Heninger, G. R. (1984), Major depression in patients with agoraphobia and panic disorder. *Arch. Gen. Psychiatry*, 41:1129–1135.

Brown, G. W., & Harris, T. (1978), *Social Origins of Depression: A Study of Psychiatric Disorder in Women.* New York: Free Press.

——— Lemyre, L., & Bifulco, A. (1992), Social factors and recovery from anxiety and depressive disorders. A test of specificity. *Brit. J. Psychiatry*, 161:44–54.

Buglass, D., Clarke, J., Henderson, A. S., Kreitman, N., & Presley, A. S. (1977), A study of agoraphobic housewives. *Psychol. Med.*, 7:73–86.

Cohen, M. E., Badal, D., Kilpatrick, A., Reed, A., & White, P. D. (1951), The high familial prevalence of neurocirculatory asthenia (anxiety neurosis, effort syndrome). *Amer. J. Hum. Gen.*, 16:126–158.

Coryell, W., Noyes, R., & Clancy, J. (1983), Panic disorder and primary unipolar depression: A comparison of background and outcome. *J. Affective Disord.*, 5:311–317.

Crowe, R. R., Noyes, R., Pauls, D. L., & Stymen, L. (1989), A family study of panic disorder. *Arch. Gen. Psychiatry*, 40:1065–1069.

Dohrenwend, B. P. (1979), Stressful life events and psychopathology: Some issues of theory and method. In: *Stress and Mental Disorder*, ed. J. E. Barrett. New York: Raven Press.

Faravelli, C. (1985), Life events preceding the onset of panic disorder. *J. Affect. Dis.*, 9:103–105.

——— Ambonetti, A. (1983), Assessment of life events in depressive disorders. A comparison of three methods. *Soc. Psychiatry*, 18:51–56.

——— Guerrini Degl'Innocenti, B., & Giardinelli, L. (1989), Epidemiology of anxiety disorders in Florence. *Acta Psychiat. Scand.*, 79:308–812.

——— Pallanti, S. (1989), Recent life events and panic disorder. *Amer. J. Psychiatry*, 146:622–626.

——— ——— (1992), Panic disorder: Epidemiology and life events. In: *Panic and Related Disorders: Current Knowledge and Perspectives*, ed. E. Sacchetti & G. B. Cassano. Lugano: Giardini Ed.

———— ———— Frassine, R., Albanesi, G., & Guerrini Degl'Innocenti, B. (1988), Panic attacks with and without agoraphobia: A comparison. *Psychopathol.*, 21:51–56.

———— Panichi, C., Pallanti, S., Paterniti, S., Grecu, L. M., & Rivelli, S. (1991), Perception of early parenting in panic and agoraphobia. *Acta Psychiat. Scand.*, 84:6–8.

———— Sacchetti, E., Ambonetti, A., Conte, G., Pallanti, S., & Vita, A. (1986), Early life events and affective disorder revisited. *Brit. J. Psychiatry*, 148:288–295.

———— Webb, T., Ambonetti, A., Fonnesu, F., & Sessarego, A. (1985), Prevalence of traumatic early events in 31 agoraphobic patients with panic attacks. *Amer. J. Psychiatry*, 142:1493–1494.

Fava, G. A., Grandi, S., & Canestrari, R. (1988), Prodromal symptoms in panic disorder with agoraphobia. *Amer. J. Psychiatry*, 145:1564–1567.

Finlay-Jones, R. (1986), Anxiety. In: *Life Events and Illness*, ed. G. W. Brown & T. O. Harris. New York: Guilford.

———— (1989), Anxiety. In: *Life Events and Illness*, ed. G. W. Brown & T. O. Harris. New York: Guilford. London: Unwin & Hyman.

———— Brown, G. W. (1981), Types of stressful events and the onset of anxiety and depressive disorders. *Psychol. Med.*, 11:803–815.

Freud, S. (1892), Studies on Hysteria. *Standard Edition*, 2. London: Hogarth Press, 1955.

GIDA (Gruppo Italiano Disturbi d'Ansia) (1989), Familial analysis of panic disorder and agoraphobia. *J. Affective Disord.*, 17:1–817.25.

Gittelman, R., & Klein, D. (1984), Relationship between separation anxiety and panic and agoraphobic disorders. *Psychopathology*, 17:137–143.

Grant, I., Sweetwood, H., Gerst, M. S., & Yager, J. (1978), Scaling procedures in life events research. *J. Psychosom. Res.*, 22:525–530.

Guidano, V. F. (1987), *Complexity of the Self.* New York: Guilford.

———— Liotti, G. (1983), *Cognitive Process and Emotional Disorder.* New York: Guilford.

Holmes, T. H., & Rahe, R. H. (1967), The Social Readjustment Rating Scale. *J. Psychosom. Res.*, 11:213–218.

Jacobs, S., Hansen, F., Kasl, S., Ostfeld, A., Berkman, L., & Kim, K. (1990), Anxiety disorder during acute bereavement: Risk and risk factors. *J. Clin. Psychiat.*, 51:269–274.

Kendler, K. S., MacLean, C., Neale, M., Kessler, R., Heath, A., & Evans, L. (1991), The genetic epidemiology of bulimia nervosa. *Amer. J. Psychiatry*, 148:1627–1636.

Klein, D. F. (1964), Delineation of two drug-responsive anxiety syndromes. *Psychopathologia*, 5:397–408.

———— (1987), Anxiety reconceptualized. In: *Anxiety*, ed. D. F. Klein. Basel: Karger.

Last, C., Barlow, D. H., & Obrieu, G. T. (1984), Precipitants of agoraphobia: Role of stressful life events. *Psychol. Rep.*, 54:567–570.

Leckman, J. S., Weissman, M. M., Merikangas, K. R., Pauls, D. L., & Prusoff, B. A. (1983), Panic disorder and major depression: Increased risk of major depression, alcoholism and phobic disorders in families of depressed probands. *Arch. Gen. Psychiatry*, 40:1055–1060.

Marks, I., & Gelder, I. (1965), A controlled retrospective study of behaviour therapy in phobic patients. *Brit. J. Psychiatry*, 111:561–573.

Monroe, S. M. (1982), Assessment of life events. Retrospective vs. concurrent strategies. *Arch. Gen. Psychiatry*, 39:606–610.

Noyes, R. J., Crowe, R. R., Harris, E. L., Hamra, B. J., McChesney, C. M., & Chaudhry, D. R. (1986), Relationship between panic disorder and agoraphobia. A family study. *Arch. Gen. Psychiatry*, 43:227–232.

Parker, G. (1979), Reported parental characteristics of agoraphobics and social phobics. *Brit. J. Psychiatry*, 135:555–560.

———— (1981), Parental representations of patients with anxiety neurosis. *Acta Psychiat. Scand.*, 63:33–36.

Paykel, E. S., Prusoff, B. A., & Uhlenhuth, E. H. (1971), Scaling of life events. *Arch. Gen. Psychiatry*, 25:340–347.

Rapee, R. M., Litwin, E. M., & Barlow, D. H. (1990), Impact of life events on subjects with panic disorder and on comparison subjects. *Amer. J. Psychiatry*, 147:640–644.

Raskin, M., Peeke, H. V. S., Dickman, W., & Pinkster, H. (1982), Panic and generalized anxiety disorders: Developmental antecedents and precipitants. *Arch. Gen. Psychiatry*, 39:687–689.

Roth, M. (1959), The phobic anxiety depersonalization syndrome. *Proc. Royal Soc. Med.*, 52:587–595.

Roy-Byrne, P. P., Geraci, M., & Uhde, T. W. (1986a), Life events and the onset of panic disorder. *Amer. J. Psychiatry*, 143:1424–1427.

———— ———— ———— (1986b), Life events and course of illness in patients with panic disorder. *Amer. J. Psychiatry*, 143:1033–1035.

———— Uhde, T. W., Post, R. M., Gallucci, W., Chrousos, G. P., & Gold, P. W. (1986), The corticotropin-releasing hormone stimulation test in patients with panic disorder. *Amer. J. Psychiatry*, 143:896–899.

Sarason, I. G., Johnson, J. H., & Seigel, J. M. (1978), Assessing the impact of life experience. *J. Consult. Clin. Psychol.*, 46:932–946.

Schaefer, E. S., & Bell, R. Q. (1958), Development of a parental attitude research instrument. *Child Dev.*, 29:339–361.

Servant, D., Bailly, D., Allard, C., & Parquet, P. J. (1991), Major depression in panic disorder: Role of recent life events. *J. Affect. Disord.*, 22:79–82.

Silove, D., Parker, G., Hadzi-Pavolovic, D., Manicavasagar, V., & Blaszczynski, A. (1991), Parental representations of patients with panic disorder and generalised anxiety disorder. *Brit. J. Psychiatry*, 159:835–841.

Snaith, R. P. (1968), A clinical investigation of phobias. *Brit. J. Psychiatry*, 114:673–697.

Solyom, L., Beck, P., Solyom, C., & Hugel, P. (1974), Some aetiological factors in phobic neurosis. *Can. Psychiatric Assn. J.*, 19:69–77.

———— Silberfeld, M., & Solyom, C. (1976), Maternal overprotection in the etiology of agoraphobia. *Can. Psychiatric Assn. J.*, 21:109–113.

Stravynski, A., Elie, R., & Franche, R. L. (1989), Perception of early parenting by patients diagnosed avoidant personality disorder: A test of the overprotection hypothesis. *Acta Psychiat. Scand.*, 80:415–420.

Tennant, C., & Andrews, G. (1978), The pathogenic quality of life event stress in neurotic impairment. *Arch. Gen. Psychiatry,* 35:859–863.

———— Hurry, J., & Bebbington, P. (1982), The relationship of childhood separation experiences to adult depressive and anxiety states. *Brit. J. Psychiatry,* 141:474–482.

———— Smith, A., Bebbington, P., & Hurry, J. (1981), Parental loss in childhood: Relationship to adult psychiatric impairment and contact with psychiatric service. *Arch. Gen. Psychiatry,* 38:309–314.

Terhune, W. B. (1961), The phobic syndrome: Its nature and treatment. *J. Arkan. Med. Soc.,* 58:236–239.

Torgersen, S. (1983), Genetic factors in anxiety disorders. *Arch. Gen. Psychiatry,* 40:1085–1089.

———— (1985), Developmental differentiation of anxiety and affective neurosis. *Acta Psychiat. Scand.,* 71:304–310.

———— (1986), Childhod and family characteristics in panic and generalized anxiety disorders. *Amer. J. Psychiatry,* 143:630–632.

Tweed, J. L., Schoenbach, V. J., George, L. K., & Blazer, D. J. (1989), The effects of childhood parental death and divorce on six months history of anxiety disorders. *Brit. J. Psychiatry,* 154:823–828.

Vinokur, A., & Selzer, M. I. (1973), Life events, stress and mental distress. *Proc. 81st Annual Convention APA,* pp. 329–330.

von Knorring, A. I., Bohman, M., & Sigvardsson, S. (1982), Reactivity to initial stimuli and the experiencing of stressful life events. *Acta Psychiat. Scand.,* 65:283–291.

Webster, A. S. (1953), The development of phobias in married women. *Psychol. Mon.,* 67:1–18.

Chapter 8
Can Panic Attacks Produce Posttraumatic Stress Disorder?

RICHARD J. McNALLY, Ph.D.

A common cause of posttraumatic stress disorder (PTSD) is exposure to a sudden, unpredictable, life-threatening event, such as violent rape or gunfire. Although the individual may emerge physically unharmed from the trauma, the *perception* of a narrow escape from death is often sufficient to produce the syndrome (Terr, 1979). Indeed, most studies have revealed a dose–response effect whereby the severity of PTSD symptoms varies as a function of perceived threat (Pynoos, Frederick, Nader, Arroyo, Steinberg, Eth, Nunez, and Fairbanks, 1987; March, 1990). Although perceived threat is usually highly correlated with genuine threat, psychopathologists have speculated whether perceived threat is sufficient to produce PTSD (March, 1993).

Spontaneous panic attacks are sudden, unpredictable events that are often perceived as life threatening. Indeed, according to some cognitive theorists (Clark, 1986), panic cannot occur unless people believe that they are in imminent danger (e.g., of dying from a heart attack). If the perception of danger is essential for panic to occur, and if such perceptions are sufficient to produce

PTSD, persons with panic disorder should commonly develop PTSD.

In this chapter, the author describes a study conducted to determine whether panic can produce PTSD (McNally and Lukach, 1992). In this study, we assessed for PTSD symptoms in subjects with panic disorder (PD), and compared their symptom profile to that of subjects with either combat-related or rape-related PTSD.

METHOD

SUBJECTS

Panic Disorder Group. The PD group included 25 women and 5 men who qualified for a current DSM-III-R diagnosis of PD (American Psychiatric Association [APA], 1987) according to the Structured Clinical Interview for DSM-III-R (SCID-R; Spitzer, Williams, Gibbon, and First, 1990). They ranged in age from 17 to 47 years ($M = 33.5$), and their years of education ranged from 10 to 19 ($M = 13.3$). Subjects were recruited from the Anxiety Disorders Clinic at the University of Health Sciences/The Chicago Medical School, the Agoraphobia Treatment Center in Arlington Heights, Illinois, and Agoraphobics in Motion, a support group in suburban Chicago. All were unpaid volunteers who agreed to participate in an interview study concerning panic. Clinic subjects were consecutive referrals who sought behavioral treatment for panic disorder. The remaining subjects were randomly selected from among active support group members.

Posttraumatic Stress Disorder (PTSD) Group. The PTSD group included 17 male Vietnam veterans with combat-related PTSD who were inpatients on the Stress Disorder Treatment Unit at the North Chicago Veterans Affairs Medical Center, and 13 community volunteers (1 male) with rape-related PTSD. The diagnosis of PTSD was established by SCID-R interviews in two unrelated studies in which these subjects participated (Cassiday, McNally, and Zeitlin, 1991; Kaspi, McNally, and Amir, in press). The subjects ranged in age from 22 to 53 years ($M = 37.6$), and their years of education ranged from 9 to 18 ($M = 14$).

To assess for PTSD symptoms in the subjects with panic disorder, we used the SCID-R PTSD module developed by Kulka, Schlenger, Fairbank, Hough, Jordan, Marmar, and Weiss (1990), in collaboration with Spitzer et al., for the Vietnam Veterans Readjustment Study. After ruling out a history of DSM-III-R traumatic stressors that might produce PTSD symptoms, we asked subjects with panic disorder to recall "the most frightening panic attack you ever experienced, perhaps one in which you thought you were about to die." Once they specified an attack, we asked them to estimate, on a zero to 100-point scale, the likelihood that they thought they were about to die during the attack. Using the SCID-R, we assessed for PTSD symptoms in reference to this attack. Subjects then completed the Impact of Events Scale—Revised (IES-R; Horowitz, Wilner, and Alvarez, 1979) in reference to the same attack. We compared their scores to those of the 12 PTSD rape victims for whom we had IES-R data.

RESULTS

Five (17%) of the subjects with panic disorder qualified for a lifetime SCID-R diagnosis of PTSD, and two (7%) of these subjects qualified for a current diagnosis of PTSD. The mean subjective likelihood of dying during the worst attack was 72 percent (range: 0–100%) for PTSD-positive panic disorder subjects, and 56 percent (range: 0–100%) for PTSD-negative panic disorder subjects, $t(28) < 1$, ns.

Chi-square tests (Yates-corrected) revealed that PTSD subjects endorsed all 17 PTSD SCID-R symptoms with greater frequency than did panic disorder subjects ($ps < .05$), and endorsed flash-backs, nightmares, loss of interest, psychogenic amnesia, concentration problems, and physiological reactivity to reminders of the trauma more often than did PTSD-positive panic disorder subjects (see Table 8.1).

TABLE 8.1

Percentage of DSM-III-R PTSD Symptom Endorsement in PTSD, Panic Disorder (PD), and in Panic Disorder with PTSD (PD-PTSD)

Symptom	Group		
	PTSD (n = 30)	PD[a] (n = 30)	PD-PTSD (n = 5)
Intrusive Thoughts	100	33	80
Nightmares[b]	93	10	20
Flashbacks[b]	90	0	0
Psychological Distress	93	37	80
Avoid Thinking/Feeling	93	33	80
Avoid Reminders	77	17	60
Amnesia[b]	60	0	0
Loss of Interest[b]	87	7	20
Cut Off from Others	87	30	80
Numbness	87	7	40
Foreshortened Future	90	33	100
Sleep Problems	97	27	60
Irritability	83	40	60
Concentration Problems[b]	87	23	20
Hypervigilance	97	57	80
Startle	97	50	100
Physiological Reactivity[b]	93	20	40

[a] = Includes subjects who met lifetime PTSD criteria.
[b] = Endorsed more often ($p < .05$) by PTSD subjects than by PD patients who also met lifetime PTSD criteria.

Two-tailed $t(39)$ tests revealed that PTSD subjects scored significantly higher than PD subjects on the IES-R total score ($M = 46.3$, $SD = 7.1$ versus $M = 33.0$, $SD = 15.4$; $p < .001$), the avoidance subscale ($M = 21.9$, $SD = 3.0$ versus $M = 17.9$, $SD = 9.0$; $p < .05$), and the intrusion subscale ($M = 24.2$, $SD = 7.2$ versus $M = 14.9$, $SD = 8.2$; $p < .001$). PTSD subjects did not score significantly higher ($ps > .10$) than PD subjects with PTSD on the IES-R total score ($M = 41.8$, $SD = 6.6$), avoidance subscale score ($M = 21.8$,

$SD = 4.6$), or intrusion subscale score ($M = 20.0$, $SD = 4.0$). Thus, the IES-R was sensitive to the presence of PTSD as diagnosed by the SCID-R.

DISCUSSION

Although panic attacks are sudden, unpredictable events that panickers often perceive as life threatening, they produce PTSD far less often than do prototypical traumatic stressors (e.g., exposure to gunfire; Pynoos et al., 1987). Certain characteristics of panic may attenuate its traumatogenic potential. For example, panic attacks are often misperceived as heart attacks, and heart attacks are more in the range of everyday experience than prototypical traumatic stressors. Indeed, DSM-III-R (APA, 1987) states that PTSD-inducing events must be "outside the range of usual human experience" (p. 250). This stipulation was influenced by the work of Horowitz (1986) whose experience with trauma victims persuaded him that PTSD symptoms arose when horrifying events could not be assimilated into the victim's current schemata concerning the world. However, many PTSD-inducing events are unfortunately all too common to meet this stipulation. Witnessing homicide is a common cause of PTSD (Malmquist, 1986), and of the approximately 19,000 murders committed in the United States in 1985, as many as 20 percent were witnessed by children (Pynoos, 1990). Accordingly, the DSM-IV PTSD criteria set is unlikely to retain the requirement that a traumatic event must lie outside the range of usual human experience (APA, 1993). But even if this stipulation were retained, one might argue that heart attacks rarely strike young adults, and young adults are those most at risk for PD. For them, heart attacks lie well outside the range of everyday experience.

Perhaps the "internal" locus of panic makes it less traumatogenic than prototypical "external" traumatic stressors. However, two case reports (Shaner and Eth, 1989; Lundy, 1992) and two studies suggest that internal stressors may produce PTSD (Kutz, Garb, and David, 1988; McGorry, Chanen, McCarthy, van Riel, McKenzie, and Singh, 1991). Posttraumatic stress disorder has been reported in as many as 25 percent of those who survive a heart attack (Kutz et al., 1988), and in as many as 46 percent of those who experience a psychotic episode (McGorry et al., 1991). Unfortunately, in neither study did the investigators use structured diagnostic interviews, nor did they rule out a history of exposure to other traumatic events. Moreover, McGorry et al. noted that reexperiencing phenomena reported by postpsychotic patients primarily concerned "external" events surrounding involuntary hospitalization (e.g., forced sedation) rather than "internal" psychotic symptoms per se (e.g., terrifying auditory hallucinations; but see Lundy, 1992). Nevertheless, these studies suggest that structured interviews to assess for PTSD are warranted, especially in heart attack survivors. In an ongoing project, Green and her colleagues are evaluating PTSD symptoms in women who have received diagnoses of breast cancer (Green, Rowland, Krupnick, and Epstein, 1993). This study ought to clarify how often "internal" life-threatening events produce the disorder.

In response to our original report (McNally and Lukach, 1992), two authors suggested that internal events might produce PTSD far more often than suggested by our data (Burstein, 1993; Lundy, 1993). Citing primarily pre-DSM-III (APA, 1980) reports, Lundy (1993) argued that psychosis can be an exceptionally terrifying experience that can produce PTSD. He noted that clinicians might miss PTSD in many postpsychotic patients because some PTSD symptoms (e.g., emotional numbing) bear similarity to certain hallmarks of schizophrenia (e.g., emotional blunting). In his commentary, Burstein (1993) noted that he recently diagnosed PTSD in 100 percent of 21 consecutive outpatients presenting with PD, and concluded that panic commonly precipitates PTSD symptoms. Unfortunately, he did not state whether he screened his patients for exposure to known PTSD-inducing events or whether PTSD symptoms were directly linked to panic per se (e.g., whether intrusive thoughts were about a *past* panic attack or whether they concerned fears about *future* attacks).

Burstein's (1993) startling data notwithstanding, panic does not appear to be a common cause of PTSD even though many panic patients report fears of dying during the attack. Most plausibly, people with PD may entertain multiple, shifting interpretations of their symptoms during a panic attack. That is, they may *fear* that they are having a heart attack without being certain of it. In contrast, most external traumatic stressors, such as gunfire, are not susceptible to such varied and potentially noncatastrophic interpretations. Thus, the inherent ambiguity of panic may reduce its capacity to produce PTSD.

In summary, our findings have etiological implications for both PTSD and PD. They are consistent with the view that an objective definition of what constitutes a traumatic stressor ought to be retained in the DSM-IV criteria for PTSD. That is, threats may need to be genuine as well as perceived for PTSD to occur. Our findings also suggest that convictions of impending catastrophe do not necessarily precede even the worst attacks of those with panic disorder (McNally, 1990). That is, even during their most frightening attack, panickers may not be wholly convinced that danger is truly imminent.

REFERENCES

American Psychiatric Association (1980), *Diagnostic and Statistical Manual of Mental Disorders* 3rd ed. (DSM-III). Washington, DC: American Psychiatric Press.
———— (1987), *Diagnostic and Statistical Manual of Mental Disorders*, 3rd ed. rev. (DSM-III-R). Washington, DC: American Psychiatric Press.
———— (1993), *DSM-IV Draft Criteria*. Washington, DC: American Psychiatric Press.
Burstein, A. (1993), Panic as a posttraumatic stressor. *Amer. J. Psychiat.*, 150:842.
Cassiday, K. L., McNally, R. J., & Zeitlin, S. B. (1992), Cognitive processing in trauma cues in rape victims with post-traumatic stress disorder. *Cog. Ther. Res.*, 16:283–295.
Clark, D. M. (1986), A cognitive approach to panic. *Behav. Res. Ther.*, 24:461–470.

Green, B. L., Rowland, J., Krupnick, J., & Epstein, S. (1993), PTSD in life-threatening illness: Phenomenology and risk. Paper presented at the Lake George Research Conference on Posttraumatic Stress Disorder, Bolton Landing, NY.

Horowitz, M. J. (1986), *Stress Response Syndromes*, 2nd ed. Northvale, NJ: Jason Aronson.

────── Wilner, N., & Alvarez, W. (1979), Impact of Event Scale: A measure of subjective stress. *Psychosom. Med.*, 41:209–218.

Kaspi, S. P., McNally, R. J., & Amir, N. (1995), Cognitive processing of emotional information in posttraumatic stress disorder. *Cog. Ther. Res.*, 19:433–444.

Kulka, R. A., Schlenger, W. E., Fairbank, J. A., Hough, R. L., Jordan, B. K., Marmar, C. R., & Weiss, D. S. (1990), *Trauma and the Vietnam Generation: Report of Findings from the National Vietnam Veterans Readjustment Study*. New York: Brunner/Mazel.

Kutz, I., Garb, R., & David, D. (1988), Post-traumatic stress disorder following myocardial infarction. *Gen. Hosp. Psychiat.*, 10:169–176.

Lundy, M. S. (1992), Psychosis-induced posttraumatic stress disorder. *Amer. J. Psychother.*, 46:485–491.

────── (1993), Panic as a posttraumatic stressor. *Amer. J. Psychiatry*, 150:841–842.

Malmquist, C. P. (1986), Children who witness parental murder. *J. Amer. Acad. Child Adoles. Psychiatry*, 25:320–325.

March, J. S. (1990), The nosology of posttraumatic stress disorder. *J. Anxiety Dis.*, 4:61–82.

────── (1993), What constitutes a stressor? The "Criterion A" issue. In: *Posttraumatic Stress Disorder: DSM-IV and Beyond*, ed. J. R. T. Davidson & E. B. Foa. Washington, DC: American Psychiatric Press, pp. 37–54.

McGorry, P. D., Chanen, A., McCarthy, E., van Riel, R., McKenzie, B., & Singh, B. S. (1991), Posttraumatic stress disorder following recent-onset psychosis: An unrecognized postpsychotic syndrome. *J. Nerv. Ment. Dis.*, 179:253–258.

McNally, R. J. (1990), Psychological approaches to panic disorder: A review. *Psychol. Bull.*, 108:403–419.

────── Lukach, B. M. (1992), Are panic attacks traumatic stressors? *Amer. J. Psychiatry*, 149:824–826.

Pynoos, R. S. (1990), Post-traumatic stress disorder in children and adolescents. In: *Psychiatric Disorders in Children and Adolescents*, ed. B. D. Garfinkel, G. A. Carlson, & E. B. Weller. Philadelphia: Saunders, pp. 48–63.

────── Frederick, C., Nader, K., Arroyo, W., Steinberg, A., Eth, S., Nunez, F., & Fairbanks, L. (1987), Life threat and posttraumatic stress in school-age children. *Arch. Gen. Psychiatry*, 44:1057–1063.

Shaner, A., & Eth, S. (1989), Can schizophrenia cause posttraumatic stress disorder? *Amer. J. Psychother.*, 43:588–597.

Spitzer, R. L., Williams, J. B., Gibbon, M., & First, M. B. (1990), *Structured Clinical Interview for DSM-III-R (SCID-R)*. Washington, DC: American Psychiatric Press.

Terr, L. C. (1979), Children of Chowchilla: A study of psychic trauma. *The Psychoanalytic Study of the Child*, 34:547–623. New Haven, CT: Yale University Press.

Part III

Life Stress, Medical, and Behavioral Medicine

Chapter 9
Stress and Immune Function

ANN O'LEARY, Ph.D., SHIRLEY BROWN, Ph.D., AND
MARIANA SUAREZ-AL-ADAM, M.S.

That psychological stress has many physiological correlates is now well established. Further, for centuries a variety of health effects have been noted in connection with psychosocial stress. When pathogens were discovered a century ago as the causes of infectious disease, biomedical research shifted focus to the control and elimination of these agents. While the developments of antibiotics and vaccines proved useful in the control of some infectious agents, we continue to be plagued by viruses for which we have no effective vaccine, most notably in recent years Human Immunodeficiency Virus (HIV). We are similarly stymied in our efforts to control some other immune-related conditions such as cancer, autoimmune disease, and allergy.

Thus, recent years have seen a resurgence of interest in the influence of psychosocial factors on immunologically mediated illness, including cancer and autoimmune disorders as well as infectious disease (Cohen and Williamson, 1991; O'Leary, 1990; Ader, Felten, and Cohen, 1991). While earlier research had provided evidence of associations between psychological processes and illness, that these associations might be immunologically mediated could not be determined without advances in the assessment of immune functioning. Major developments in the field of

Acknowledgments. This work was supported by grants MH48013 from the National Institute of Mental Health and CA8999 from the National Cancer Institute.

immunology in recent years have substantially boosted the drive to elucidate the process by which psychosocial factors can influence health outcomes.

This chapter provides an empirical review of the growing body of work that seeks to link life event stress processes to immune function in humans. A brief overview of the immune system and the neuroendocrine pathways likely to mediate psychoimmunologic relationships is followed by a review of research into the influences of psychosocial stress on basic immune function in healthy subjects. In addition to studies exploring effects of acute and chronic stressors on immune regulation, psychoimmunologic relationships in several disease models, including cancer, acquired immune deficiency syndrome (AIDS), and autoimmune disease, are reviewed. Theoretical and methodological considerations in psychoimmunological research are summarized, and directions for future research suggested. It should be noted that this review will not cover immune conditioning (reviewed in Ader and Cohen [1991]) nor immunologic effects of psychological depression (reviewed in Stein, Miller, and Trestman [1991]; Weisse [1992]; Herbert and Cohen [1993a]), but will focus rather on stress per se.

THE IMMUNE SYSTEM

The immune system is the body's means of destroying any foreign substances that contact or enter it, be they foreign antigens, such as viruses, bacteria, other microbes, or transplanted organs, or cancerous or precancerous cells. The human immune system consists of two major divisions: the humoral and the cellular arms.

The cells of the humoral immune system are the B-lymphocytes, produced in the bone marrow and responsible for the production of antigen-specific molecules known as antibodies, which include the immunoglobulins IgG, IgA, IgE, and IgM. When a cell encounters its target antigen, it develops into an antibody-producing *plasma* cell, and also "proliferates" so that the infection can be managed rapidly. This process is referred to a *blastogenesis*. Immunoglobulins comprise the predominant response to bacterial infection, and also provide specific defense against many viruses. Antibody titers can be measured by the process of immunofluorescence.

The cellular branch of the immune system is composed of cells which mature in the thymus gland and are known as T-lymphocytes. T-cells can be one of three general functional varieties (although it is possible to identify many more specific types within and between these categories). Cytotoxic T-cells kill specific cells by releasing lytic proteins, or lysozymes, and by attracting other phagocytic cells known as macrophages. Activated helper T-cells enhance the activities of many other immune cells via the release of *cytokines* such as interferon and a variety of other "interleukins," and suppressor T-cells suppress these processes. Another lymphocyte-like cell, the natural killer (NK) cell, also destroys virally infected cells, as well as certain types of tumor cells and micrometastases.

The strength of the immune response can be assessed by an array of measures within two broad categories: enumeration measures and functional assays. Enumeration measures quantify lymphocytes, yielding values of *absolute numbers* of cells within a given volume of blood, or *percentages* of cellular subtypes. Enumeration of lymphocyte subsets provides an indication of the availability of immune-competent cells necessary to eliminate neoplastic and infectious agents. Since changes in these measures may simply reflect redistribution of lymphocyte populations between lymphoid organs and the bloodstream, rather than cell destruction or proliferation, it is difficult to infer actual immune alterations and increased disease susceptibility unless relevant health outcomes are also assessed.

One of the oldest approaches to the functional assessment of the immune system measures the lymphocytes' ability to proliferate after contacting an antigen (blastogenesis). The response of lymphocytes to stimulation by relatively non-specific antigens called *mitogens* is believed to be an in vitro model of the body's response to challenge by infectious agents. These assays tend to yield variable results, being easily affected by inaccuracy in the baseline cell count and other factors. Natural killer cell function has been evaluated through assays of lytic activity.

NEUROENDOCRINE MEDIATION OF PSYCHOIMMUNOLOGIC EFFECTS

Stress has been known for some time to have a considerable impact on physiology, including activation of the sympathetic adrenal-medullary (SAM) and hypothalamic-pituitary-adrenocortical (HPAC) and other endocrine systems (Cannon and De La Paz, 1911; Henry and Stephens, 1977; Frankenhauser, 1983; Asterita, 1985). In turn, the two major stress systems have known effects on various aspects of immune function.

The two systems, SAM and HPAC, have been described in psychological terms as the "effort" and "distress" systems, respectively (Frankenhauser, 1983), or as the "fight-or-flight" and "conservation-withdrawal" systems (Henry and Stephens, 1977). The sympathetic nervous system is most involved in acute emotional states, such as fear, anger, and excitement. The hormones that are released into the bloodstream during SAM activation include epinephrine, norepinephrine, and other catecholamines. Activation of the pituitary adrenal-cortical system appears to occur in response to threats that have been appraised as more overwhelming and less readily coped with (Henry and Stephens, 1977). It has been observed with chronic stress, as well as clinical depression. HPAC activation stimulates release of adrenocorticotropic hormone (ACTH) and corticosteroids (cortisol in humans and other primates). While it is useful to discuss these two systems separately, it should be noted that, in actuality, both stress systems are often engaged during stressful encounters.

Members of a third category of substances, the endogenous opioids, have more recently been found to be released in response to psychological stress, particularly but not exclusively in the presence of pain. Endogenous opioids, morphinelike peptides found in the brain and periphery, produce stress-induced analgesia (reviewed in Kelley, 1986).

Research has demonstrated several mechanisms of sympathetic influence on immune function. One is the release of catecholamines. Direct sympathetic innervation of lymphoid organs has been demonstrated (Williams, Peterson, Shea, Schmeltje, Baue, and Felten, 1981; Felten et al. 1985). SAM activity causes a redistribution of lymphocytes out of areas of storage and into circulation while reducing their functional efficacy (Crary, Borysenko, Sutherland, Kutz, Borysenko, and Benson, 1983; Crary, Hauser, Borysenko, Kutz, Hoban, Ault, Weiner, and Benson, 1983; Felten, Felten, Carlson, Olschawka, and Livnat, 1985). In addition, injection of norepinephrine has been shown to increase NK activity (Locke, Kraus, Kutz, Edbril, Phillips, and Benson, 1984; Toennesen, Toennesen, and Christensen, 1984; Buske-Kirschbaum, Kirschbaum, Stierle, Lehnert, and Hellhammer, 1992).

By contrast, cortisol and pharmacological glucocorticoids are primarily immunosuppressive (reviewed in Cupps and Fauci [1982]; Meuleman and Katz [1985]). There is also evidence that cortisol and pharmacologic corticosteroids exert a suppressive effect on NK activity (Onsrud and Thorsby, 1981; Gatti, Cavallo, Sartori, del Ponte, Masera, Salvadori, Carignola, and Angeli, 1987).

Opioids appear to have both suppressive and enhancing effects, depending on the specific immune factor studied. Animal studies, for example, have demonstrated suppressive effects of electric shock-induced opioid activation on lymphocyte response to mitogens and NK cell activity. Addition of opioid peptides to immunologic assays in vitro has caused enhanced NK activity (Kay, Allen, and Morley, 1984; Mandler, Biddison, Mandler, and Serrate, 1986).

While the foregoing discussion has focused on hormones that traditionally have been most closely linked to stress processes, most hormones have in fact been shown both to be responsive to stress (Asterita, 1985) and to influence the immune system (Blalock, 1984, 1989; Grossman, 1985). An array of neuropeptides, proteins that regulate neural activity, have been shown to influence immune function. It is particularly interesting that receptors for most hormones and neurotransmitters have been located on the surfaces of lymphocytes, which themselves secrete neuroendocrine precursors. These discoveries suggest potential pathways for bidirectional communication between the neuroendocrine and immune systems (Blalock, 1984, 1989; Felten, 1991; Reichlin, 1993).

Thus numerous pathways and mechanisms by which psychological processes may influence immune function have been identified. Given the known complexities of the immune system and neuroendocrine dynamics, a great deal undoubtedly remains to be delineated. In the future, a comprehensive view of psychoimmunologic phenomena will include specification of the associations among specific stress states, neuroendocrine processes, and immune function.

PSYCHOSOCIAL FACTORS AND IMMUNE FUNCTION

Evidence that psychological stress can alter basic immune processes is mounting steadily. Much of the research involves assessing the effects of naturally occurring, or systematically induced, stressors on immune function in healthy people. Below we review this research, considering the role of acute naturalistic stress, acute laboratory stress, chronic and social stress.

ACUTE STRESSORS

Most psychoimmunology studies have explored the effects of acute, short-term stress on immunity. The stress associated with splashdown during manned spaceflight was one of the earliest of the research paradigms that demonstrated stress-related immune alterations, although it is important to consider that this paradigm may confound psychological and physiological stress. In a study of Apollo astronauts, higher lymphocyte counts were observed, but there was no change in response to the mitogen phytohemaglutinin (PHA) following splashdown (Fischer, Daniels, Levin, Kimzey, Cobb, and Ritzman, 1972). A later study of Skylab astronauts following splashdown disclosed an increase in numbers of polymorphonuclear leukocytes, with a concomitant decrease in percentages of T-lymphocytes, and reduced response to PHA (Kimsey, 1975; Kimsey, Johnson, Ritzman, and Mengel, 1976). These are among the few reported studies that have shown elevations in numbers of immune cells. Since the high level of fear associated with splashdown is most likely associated with epinephrine release (i.e., SAM activation), which has been shown to increase the numbers of lymphocytes in circulation, this may be the mechanism that accounts for these effects. Indeed, levels of catecholamines and glucocorticoids were elevated during spaceflight and splashdown, although associations between these neuroendocrine mediators and the immune changes were not reported.

Sleep deprivation stress was another early paradigm, utilized by Palmblad and colleagues. Subjects who were kept awake for 48 to 77 hours displayed reduced response of lymphocytes to mitogens (Palmblad, Bjorn, Wasserman, and Akerstedt, 1979).

Academic examination stress has been studied for its potential impact on immunity. Dorian, Keystone, Garfinkel, and Brown (1982) reported higher counts of B and T cells, reduced in vitro antibody synthesis, and diminished response to mitogens in psychiatry residents undergoing an oral fellowship exam, compared with 16 psychiatrists and psychiatry residents not taking the exam. Unexpectedly, cortisol levels were higher in the nonstressed group, while catecholamines were not measured.

Kiecolt-Glaser, Glaser, and colleagues have made extensive use of the examination stress paradigm in medical students to investigate a variety of immune changes. In their usual design, students are assessed immunologically during a lower-stress "baseline" period, when no exams are given and they are relatively nondistressed, and again a month later during an examination period. A number of immunologic changes have been observed in connection with this stressor, including higher antibody titers to three herpes viruses at exam time, interpreted to indicate poorer control of the latent herpes viruses by the cellular immune system (Glaser, Kiecolt-Glaser, Speicher, and Holliday, 1985; Glaser, Rice, Sheridan, Fertel, Stout, Speicher, Pinsky, Kotur, Post, Beck, and Kiecolt-Glaser, 1987; Glaser, Pearson, Jones, Hillhouse, Kennedy, Mao, and Kiecolt, 1991), relatedly, poor T-cell proliferative response to EBV peptides (Glaser, Pearson, Bonneau, Esterling, Atkinson, and Kiecolt-Glaser, 1993); reductions in the percentages of helper T-cells and suppressor/cytotoxic T-cells, and diminished responses to mitogens (Glaser, Kiecolt-Glaser, Stout, et al., 1985), lowered lytic activity of natural killer cells but increased plasma levels of IgA (Kiecolt-Glaser, Garner, Speicher, Penn, and Glaser, 1984), and extremely suppressed lymphocyte production of interferon (Glaser, Rice, Speicher, Stout, and Kiecolt-Glaser, 1986).

This series of studies is strengthened by the inclusion of sleep and nutrition assessments in their design, the common omission of which is a frequent criticism of psychoimmunologic research. This is because observed relationships between psychological stress and immune function may be mediated by alterations in diet or sleep patterns secondary to the stress, the stress itself being neither a necessary nor a sufficient cause of the immune changes. Although the nutritional assessments are not comprehensive, results from these studies generally suggest that changes in stress-related behaviors do not account for the immune changes that occur in response to the stressor.

Another acute stress paradigm for observing psychoneuroimmunologic relationships has utilized the fear experienced by phobics when exposed to the feared object. In one study (Wiedenfeld, O'Leary, Bandura, Brown, Levine, and Raska, 1990), snake phobics were assessed for lymphocyte enumeration, heart rate and

salivary cortisol levels at three time points: during an initial baseline visit on the first week, a two-day treatment period the second
week, and a posttreatment follow-up when the snake was handled
with confidence in the third week. Treatment consisted of guided
mastery, a highly effective approach to simple phobias in which
the client observes the therapist interacting comfortably with the
snake and is encouraged to do so also in a gradual, stepwise fashion. Subjects have been found to consistently experience significant fear, but also a sense of growing mastery and control, during
the treatment process.

Among the results obtained in this study was an increase during
the high-stress treatment phase in numbers of total lymphocytes
and in several lymphocyte subsets. This finding is consonant with
those from in vitro epinephrine injection studies, since this type
of acute, fear-eliciting stressor is known to induce catecholamine
release. In a small number of subjects in the Wiedenfeld et al.
study, however, lymphocytes were *reduced* on the day of the stressor; these were the same subjects whose levels of salivary cortisol
were elevated at the end of the treatment session and who also
demonstrated a slower growth of self-efficacy, or confidence in
their abilities to cope with the snake. These results draw attention
to the potential specificity of the effects of stressful emotional
stimuli on immune function, and of the usefulness of identifying
neuroendocrine mediators of psychoimmunological effects.

Recently a number of studies have examined effects of brief
laboratory stressors, such as doing mental arithmetic, on immune
parameters, and both negative and positive changes have been
reported (Bachen, Manuck, Marsland, Cohen, Malkoff, Muldoon,
and Rabin, 1992; Brosschot, Benschop, Godaert, De Smet, Olff,
Heijen, and Ballieux, 1992; Landmann, Mueller, Perini, Wesp,
Erne, and Buehler, 1984; Manuck, Cohen, Rabin, Muldoon, and
Bachen, 1991; Naliboff, Benton, Solomon, Morley, Fahey, Bloom,
Makinodan, and Gilmore, 1991; Sieber, Rodin, Larson, Ortega,
and Cummings, 1992; Sgoutas-Emch, Cacioppo, Uchino, Malar-
key, Pearl, Kiecolt-Glaser, and Glaser, in press; Weisse, Pato,
McAllister, Littman, Breier, Paul, and Baum, 1990; Zakowski,
McAllister, Deal, and Baum, 1992). Examination of these studies

reveals that lymphocyte response to mitogens is generally reduced across studies, while in those investigations that used more severe stressors such as uncontrollable electric shock or loud noise and gruesome surgery films, enumeration measures yield results that were null (Sieber et al., 1992; Zakowski et al., 1992) or mixed (Weisse et al., 1990), and decreases in NK cell activity (Sieber et al., 1992). On the other hand, studies using lower-intensity stressors such as mental arithmetic and the stroop color-word test often demonstrated increases in leukocyte numbers (Landmann et al., 1984; Manuck et al., 1991; Naliboff et al., 1991; Bachen et al., 1992; Brosschot et al., 1992; Sgoutas-Emch et al., in press), particularly NK and CD8 cell numbers; and increases in NK cell activity (Naliboff et al., 1991; Sgoutas-Emch et al., in press). These results are consonant with the notion that stressors inducing primarily SAM activity (as lower-intensity stressors should) produce immunologic effects similar to those from epinephrine injection. The consistent finding for decreased lymphocyte response to mitogens would appear to be due to the down-regulating effects of both SAM and HPAC activity for this measure. However, at seeming odds with this analysis are studies finding heart rate reactivity to be associated with less immune upregulation, or more immune down-regulation (Wiedenfeld et al., 1990; Manuck et al., 1991; Sgoutas-Emch et al., in press) as heart rate is an index of SAM activity. This apparent paradox may be explained by findings in two of these studies of positive associations between heart rate and cortisol (Wiedenfeld et al., 1990; Sgoutas-Emch et al., in press), indicating that very high levels of SAM activity are generally produced in conjunction with HPAC activity.

In summary, research with acute stressors has demonstrated mixed effects: in some studies, lymphocyte numbers have increased while in others they have decreased. When measured, the functional capacity of immune cells has tended to be reduced. Acute stressors appear to activate both the sympathetic and adrenal-cortical stress systems, and it may be that the differing effects of these systems on immune function account for some of the diverse findings. A recent meta-analytic review (Herbert and Cohen, 1993b) indicated that while acute stress has been conclusively shown to be associated with suppression of some immune indices, none of the studies reviewed in that paper utilized stressors that would be expected to create such "pure" activation of the SAM system, and only the earlier of the laboratory stress studies cited above (studies that utilized more severe stressors) were included. Another meta-analysis appearing at about the same time (Van Rood, Bogaards, Goulmy, and van Houwelingen, 1993) did include such studies and demonstrated more mixed results, with few enumeration measures showing reliable shifts across studies in either direction. Another recent review of the brief laboratory stressor studies reflected the mixed effects that they have yielded (Kiecolt-Glaser, Cacioppo, Malarkey, and Glaser, 1992). Neither of these latter two reviews distinguished between high- and low-intensity stressors.

CHRONIC STRESS

Research utilizing animal models suggests that effects of stress on immunity may change over time (Monjan and Collector, 1977). Among the relatively few studies of the effects of chronic stress on human immune function is the work of Andrew Baum and associates, investigations of stress effects upon residents of the area surrounding the Three Mile Island (TMI) nuclear power plant since the serious accident there in 1979 (Baum, Schaeffer, Lake, Fleming, and Collins, 1985). Stress levels are chronically high in this area (Baum et al., 1985) because radioactive gas and water remained trapped inside the containment building for some time following the accident, and fears of future deleterious health consequences of the accident and concerns about the possible reopening of the reactor persist. McKinnon, Weisse, Reynolds, Bowles, and Baum (1989) reported a variety of immunologic changes in TMI residents, compared to demographically matched control subjects living in another area. Subjects had considerably more neurophils, fewer B-cells, suppressor/cytotoxic T-cells, and NK cells, as well as higher antibody titers to HSV and CMV. The amount of neutrophil increase was positively related to urinary catecholamine levels, while numbers of lymphocytes and NK cells tended to be negatively related to catecholamines.

Epidemiologic studies have shown that prolonged unemployment is a chronic stressor that affects morbidity and mortality. A study conducted in Sweden examined effects of unemployment on immune function (Arnetz, Wasserman, Petrini, Brenner, Levi, Eneroth, Salovaara, Hjelm, Salovaara, Theorell, and Petterson, 1987). Subjects were women who had lost their jobs several months before the study began. Since all received unemployment benefits from the state amounting to 90 percent of their previous pay, it was possible to attribute their stress to strictly psychological origins rather than to physical effects of income loss, such as nutritional deficiencies or inadequate housing. After 9 months of unemployment, subjects showed reduced lymphocyte response to the mitogen PHA and a tuberculin antigen when compared with a matched group of controls who were not unemployed. No differences were observed in enumeration of lymphocyte subsets, in serum cortisol, or in reported health status.

Kiecolt-Glaser and colleagues (Kiecolt-Glaser, Glaser, Shuttleworth, Dyer, Ogrocki, and Speicher, 1987) examined the effects on immunity of chronic stress among the caregivers of relatives with Alzheimer's disease (also considered an interpersonal stressor, as will be discussed in the following section). In this study, caregivers had higher antibody titers to EBV (again, presumably indicating impaired cellular immunocompetence), lower percentages of total T lymphocytes and helper T-cells, and lower helper:suppressor T-cell ratios compared to sociodemographically matched control subjects. There were no differences in percentages of NK cells. In a subsequent longitudinal study of spousal caregivers (Kiecolt-Glaser, Dura, Speicher, Trask, and Glaser, 1991), caregivers showed decreases over time (average period = 13 months) in mitogen response and control of herpes virus, but not in quantitative measures, relative to controls. They also reported more infectious illnesses during the time period.

The few available reports of effects of chronic stress do not demonstrate adaptation or compensation on the part of the immune system over time. Hence prolonged stress may result in

similarly prolonged immunosuppression, the health consequences of which could be quite severe. Further research in this
area is clearly needed, and should focus on other common pro-
tracted stressors, such as occupational stress and economic hard-
ship, and on developing interventions to allay adverse effects of
chronic stress on health.

SOCIAL STRESSORS

Disruption of the social environment can be extremely stressful,
as attachment to others and the resultant "social support" are
fundamental human needs. In some instances, social disruption
is an acute stressor, such as bereavement; and in others, it is
chronic, as in the case of marital distress. However, it is here
categorized separately because the neuroendocrine effects of disrupted attachment may be unique, involving, for example, repro-
ductive hormones (e.g., Winslow, Hastings, Carter, Harbaugh,
and Insel, 1993), and endogenous opioids (Panksepp, Siviy, and
Normansell, 1985).

   Among the most severe interpersonal stressors is bereavement
following the death of a spouse or other close relative. Widows
and widowers have been shown to experience an increased likelihood of illness and mortality during the year following the death
of the spouse. A number of studies have examined the hypothesis
that at least some of this increased risk is immunologically mediated. The classic work of Bartrop, Lazarus, Luckhurst, Kiloh, and
Penny (1977) documented reduced lymphocyte response to the
mitogens PHA and Concanavalin A in bereaved subjects 6 weeks
after the spouses' death, relative to a control group. Enumeration
measures and serum concentrations of cortisol showed no differences.

   In a later study, Schleifer, Keller, Camerino, Thornton, and
Stein (1983) assessed immune function prospectively in a group
of men whose wives had terminal breast cancer. In the first 2
months following bereavement, lymphocyte response to PHA,
ConA, and PWM was lower than prebereavement values; interme-
diate responsiveness was observed 4 to 14 months after bereavement. No differences in total lymphocyte, T-cell, or B-cell

numbers were observed. Irwin, Daniels, Smith, Bloom, and Weiner (1987) reported a 50 percent reduction in NK cell activity among women who were recently bereaved, compared with an age-matched control group.

Another important and more common social stressor is marital distress and separation, which has been studied by Kiecolt-Glaser and colleagues (Kiecolt-Glaser, Fisher, Ogrocki, Stout, Speicher, and Glaser, 1987). In this study, women who had divorced or separated from their husbands showed reduced immunocompetence relative to a control group of married women, as evidenced by reduced responsiveness to PHA, higher EBV antibody titers, and lower percentages of CD4 and NK cells. Compared with a group of married women, subjects who had been separated or divorced for one year or less had significantly lower percentages of NK cells and higher EBV titers. A particularly interesting finding was that among separated–divorced women, those scoring higher on a measure of attachment to the lost spouse and who had been separated for a greater length of time had lowered percentages of NK cells and helper T-cells and higher percentages of suppressor T-cells. In the married group, higher EBV titers and lower mitogen response were associated with poorer marriage quality. In this study, the divorced–separated group did not smoke more cigarettes, but did consume more alcohol and demonstrated poorer nutritional status than the married group, leaving open the possibility of behavioral rather than emotional mediation of observed effects on immunity.

A subsequent study by this group examined effects of marital separation on immunity in men (Kiecolt-Glaser, Kennedy, Malkoff, Fisher, Speicher, and Glaser, 1988), and obtained results both consistent and inconsistent with their study of women. Compared to sociodemographically and age-matched married men, the divorced or separated men had higher antibody titers for both HSV-1 and EBV as well as more self-reported illness. Higher ratings of marital quality among married men were associated with *higher* numbers of suppressor T-cells and lower EBV titers. Further, those divorced–separated men who had been the initiators of the separation had lower EBV titers than noninitiators, suggesting that the partner who does not initiate the separation may experience greater stress. In this study, observed immune changes were more readily attributable to emotional factors than in the investigation of divorced–separated women, since health behaviors did not differ between the divorced–separated men and their married counterparts.

Marital conflict has also been studied as an immune-relevant stressor. In one study newlyweds were requested to discuss marital problems for 30 minutes (Kiecolt-Glaser, Malarkey, Chee, Newton, Cacioppo, Mao, and Glaser, 1993). Those subjects who displayed more hostile behaviors during the discussion showed greater declines in NK cell activity and lymphocyte proliferative response, and greater increases in numbers of T-cells. Women showed greater immune decrements than men. In a similar but smaller study involving married couples seeking marital therapy (Mayne, O'Leary, McCrady, Contrada, and Labouvie, 1994), a similar discussion of marital problems yielded a significant sex by time interaction, indicating a tendency for men to increase, and women to decrease, in lymphocyte response to mitogens during the course of the fight.

Less severe forms of social disruption have also been associated with immune impairment. In several studies, individuals who reported more loneliness, a measure of social support, had alterations in some of their immune measures. This was true of medical students scoring above the median on a measure of loneliness, who were found to have lower NK activity and higher antibody titers to HSV than those reporting less loneliness (Kiecolt-Glaser, Garner, Speicher, Penn, and Glaser, 1984; Glaser, Kiecolt-Glaser, Speicher, and Holliday, 1985), and of a group of psychiatric inpatients, where those who reported more loneliness had higher levels of urinary cortisol, lower NK activity, and poorer T-cell response to the mitogen PHA (Kiecolt-Glaser, Ricker, et al., 1984).

In general, social disruption and loneliness appear to be associated with impaired immune function, as would be predicted by their associations with HPAC activity. It follows, then, that interventions to enhance social support in healthy as well as in vulnerable populations may produce health-enhancing outcomes by improving immunologic functioning.

ENHANCED IMMUNOCOMPETENCE THROUGH PSYCHOSOCIAL INTERVENTION

A number of investigators have attempted to develop psychosocial interventions with the aim of enhancing immunocompetence, both in populations with particular diseases, which will be described in later sections, and in healthy populations. One example of the latter was reported by Kiecolt-Glaser and colleagues (Kiecolt-Glaser, Glaser, Williger, Stout, Messick, Sheppard, Ricker, Romisher, Briner, Bonnell, and Donnerberg, 1985), in which both a relaxation and a social contact intervention were administered to two samples within a geriatric population, with a third sample receiving no intervention. All three groups demonstrated enhanced blastogenic response to mitogens at the end of the study, and the group that had received relaxation training had significantly enhanced NK lysis activity and reduced HSV antibody levels following treatment. It is possible that the social support intervention might have been more potent with a lonelier, less socially intact geriatric group. Kiecolt-Glaser, Glaser, Strain, Stout, Tarr, Holliday, and Speicher (1986) were also able to demonstrate a positive association between percentage of T4 cells and amount of relaxation practice in medical students who had been taught relaxation techniques to manage examination stress.

In a different study, an intervention based on a model of psychotherapy that emphasizes the salutory effects of disclosure and cognitive processing of negative thoughts and feelings was tested for its potential impact on immunologic and health outcomes (Pennebaker, Kiecolt-Glaser, and Glaser, 1988a). Undergraduate subjects were asked to write essays about either a traumatic or a neutral experience on each of four consecutive days, and then underwent assessment of subsequent immunologic and health outcomes. Those who had written about traumatic events showed a greater enhancement of blastogenic response to mitogens at the end of the intervention than those who had written about neutral subjects, and the former also made significantly fewer subsequent visits to the health center than did controls. Interpretation of these results has been questioned (Neale, Cox, Valdimarsdottir, and Stone, 1988; Pennebaker, Kiecolt-Glaser, and Glaser, 1988b); however, the results are fascinating and are deserving of replication.

In summary, while the regular practice of relaxation techniques appears to be a promising approach to immunoenhancement, the data on disclosure of trauma as an intervention, which have profound implications for psychotherapy and health, await replication.

PSYCHOSOCIAL FACTORS IN DISEASE

Not all people who are exposed to pathogens become ill. Realizing this, many researchers have attempted to identify "host resistance factors," which have included psychosocial and behavioral phenomena. Some well-known early studies examined the effect of life event stress on susceptibility to disease. In a large number of these case control studies, patients generally reported having experienced a greater number of stressful life events during the preceding year or several years before disease onset than did healthy control subjects. While the sheer volume of supportive evidence for the impact of life event stress is impressive, it is also true that, as with exposure to pathogens, many people experience stressful life events and do not become ill. In the years that have ensued since the early life event studies were conducted, researchers have increasingly turned their attention to additional factors in the stress and illness equation, including immunocompetence. The following review of stress and human illness will be restricted to studies in which immune parameters have been examined directly.

INFECTIOUS DISEASE

While some of the studies described above reported effects of psychosocial factors on infectious illness symptomatology (Glaser, Rice, et al., 1987; Kiecolt-Glaser, Dura, et al., 1991), demonstrating a role for psychoimmune processes in infectious disease has generally been difficult because it is not generally possible to know whether or not someone has been exposed to infectious pathogens during any particular time period. Recently several studies have employed the approach of manipulating the exposure variable directly, by introducing pathogens in the form of viral nasal drops or vaccines. Cohen and his colleagues administered nasal drops containing either a respiratory virus or saline to patients in a controlled hospital environment (Cohen, Tyrrell, and Smith, 1991). They found that rates of infection and clinical illness were greater in subjects who reported more recent life stress (an index comprised both of objective and subjective indicators), and this relationship was independent of a number of health practices. Neither prechallenge white cell counts nor immunoglobulin levels accounted for this relationship; a postchallenge measure of immunoglobulins (which would reflect immune response to the challenge) might have been more revealing.

Another recent study evaluated effects of stress on lymphocyte proliferation to a novel antigen at several time points following immunization with this antigen (Snyder, Roghmann, and Sigal, 1993). Subjects reporting more negative recent life events displayed reduced proliferation to the antigen at 3 weeks, but enhanced response at 8 weeks. Another study measured antibody production in response to a hepatitis B vaccine (Jabaaij, Grosheide, Heijtink, Duivenvoorden, Ballieux, and Vingerhoets, 1993) and found antibody levels to be reduced in those subjects who reported more psychological distress (an index that included coping and loneliness measures and some health behaviors, as well) prior to the challenge. While neither of these latter two studies demonstrated effects on illness outcome, as the novel antigen does not produce disease and hepatitis vaccination is generally preventive of illness, they lend additional support to the role of stress on infectious illness.

CANCER

Much of the research concerning psychosocial factors in cancer incidence and progression has focused on establishing linkages between psychosocial factors and disease outcome, without examining immunologic mediation. Nevertheless, this body of literature has yielded evidence that a set of traits and coping styles may be associated with the development of cancer, more rapid progression and worse prognosis (reviewed in Contrada, Leventhal, and O'Leary [1990]). People who are depressed or hopeless, or who report being "fatigued," "less distressed," "less hostile," "helpless," and who fail to express negative affect, seem to be at greater risk. It should be noted that all of the studies involving NK cell activity described above, as well as many regarding depression (not included here; see Stein, Miller, and Trestman [1991]; Weisse [1992]; Herbert and Cohen [1993a] for reviews) are relevant to this issue, as NK cell activity is thought to protect against cancer (Gorelik and Herberman, 1986). (DNA repair, also a critical factor in guarding against cancer, has also been shown to be affected by psychological distress: Kiecolt-Glaser, Stephens, Lipetz, Speicher, and Glaser, 1985).

One study that examined immunologic parameters in a cancer model was an examination of psychological factors influencing breast cancer outcomes conducted by Sandra Levy (Levy, Herberman, Maluish, Schlien, and Lippman, 1985). She found that patients who reported less distress and who seemed better adjusted to their illness, who reported high levels of fatigue, and who perceived less social support in their environment, showed lower NK cell activity. Lower NK activity was in turn related to a higher number of positive lymph nodes at diagnosis. Three months later, after cancer treatment had begun, fatigue and low social support remained marginally significant predictors of low NK activity (Levy, Herberman, Lippman, and D'Angelo, 1987). Another study (Levy et al., 1990) found perceptions of greater social support from spouses and physicians to be significantly associated with enhanced NK cell activity in women with recently treated breast cancer when entered into a regression analysis with other significant correlates such as estrogen receptor status and surgical treatment type. In another report (Levy, Herberman, Lippman, D'Angelo, and Lee, 1991), NK cell activity was found to be related to likelihood of disease recurrence. In a 7-year follow-up of 36 patients with recurrent disease (Levy, Lee, Bagley, and Lippman, 1988) longer survival time was predicted by one psychological factor: the expression of more joy at baseline testing. These results, while inconsistent, are unusual in their attempts to examine multiple factors within a single cohort.

Results such as these led researchers to wonder whether psychological intervention could affect medical outcome from cancer. An intervention study by Spiegel and colleagues (Spiegel, Bloom, Kraemer, and Gottheil, 1989), in which breast cancer patients were randomly assigned to either a support group condition or a no-treatment comparison condition, demonstrated significantly longer survival in subjects who had received the intervention. However, immune function was not assessed as a potential mediator, and it is difficult to rule out alternative interpretations of effect mediation, such as increased assertiveness in obtaining medical treatment, and the suggestion has been made that assignment to the comparison group following informed consent may have had a *negative* effect on survival (LeShan, 1991; Fox, 1992).

To our knowledge, only one study to date has both randomized subjects to treatment conditions and assessed immunologic mediation of treatment effects (Fawzy, Cousins, Fawzy, Kemeny, Elashoff, and Morton, 1990; Fawzy, Kemeny, Fawzy, Elashoff, Morton, Cousins, and Fahey, 1990). In this study, 35 patients with malignant melanoma were randomized to receive training in problem solving and coping with personal problems related to cancer diagnosis, as well as relaxation and other aspects of stress management. The intervention was conducted in supportive group format. These subjects were compared with 26 others who received no intervention. The treatment reduced depression and produced more active coping strategies in the participants. Further, 6 weeks after the intervention, these patients also exhibited greater increases in the percent of NK cells, and these changes were maintained at 6 months. At the 6-month follow-up point, NK cell activity augmented by interferon alpha was significantly higher in the experimental than the control group. These indices of immune function were correlated with levels of depression and mood state. While this study provides some initial encouragement for the theory of immunologic mediation of psychological intervention effectiveness, the study suffers from a significant flaw. Twenty-five percent of patients randomized to the no-intervention condition dropped out of the study at that point, precisely because they were not to receive the intervention (incidentally, also lending credence to the control-group detriment criticism of the Spiegel study described above). These subjects may have differed from the others in psychological or biological ways (and given the descriptions of the "cancer-prone personality," these more assertive patients might be expected to have gained the best outcomes without intervention).

Another recent study of cancer patients is of note here. Breast cancer patients were evaluated at home and just before receiving chemotherapy, and were compared with hospital staff controls (Fredrikson, Fuerst, Lekander, Rotstein, and Blomgren, 1993). Immune measures were cell counts and NK cell activity. Patients showed higher levels of total white blood cells, accounted for by increased granulocytes but not lymphocytes, in the hospital as compared with the home; no such differences were demonstrated in controls. Patients also exhibited higher NK cell activity, averaged across home and hospital visits, than controls. Higher trait anxiety (state anxiety was not measured) was associated with reductions in monocyte numbers. The results are discussed as possibly resulting from catecholamine release prior to chemotherapy, and also to cortisol release, which is associated with increases in neutrophils, a type of granulocyte. It should be noted that these immune effects of the chemotherapy stressor may not have been of sufficient duration or impact to affect cancer outcome.

GENITAL HERPES

Since, as we have seen, cellular control over latent herpes viruses can become impaired under conditions of stress, it is reasonable to expect that this effect, if large enough, could result in an actual outbreak of herpetic lesions in infected individuals. Effects of stress and coping on immune function and genital herpes have been investigated by Kemeny, Cohen, Zegans, and Conant (1989). Subjects with recurrent HSV were followed for 6 months, undergoing assessment of psychological stress, mood, health behaviors, other possible HSV triggers, HSV recurrences and (in half of the subjects) proportion of CD4 and CD8 T-cells. Results yielded support for the hypothesized role of psychological processes in immune aspects of herpes recurrence, in that an aggregate stress index was significantly negatively related to proportions of both CD4 and CD8 cells, and a positive relationship was found between stress levels and recurrence of lesions. While further research in this area is clearly needed, this study is an important first effort to explicate the complex relationships in the disease course of herpes infections.

AUTOIMMUNE DISEASE

The immune mechanisms that operate in autoimmune disease differ substantially from those in infectious diseases in that they are characterized by *enhanced* activity in some components of immunity, and the targets of activity are the host's own cells or other "self" agents, rather than foreign ones. A further difference, consequently, is that prognosis is improved in autoimmune disease when the immune response against "self" components is *reduced*. It follows that if psychological stress and negative affective states are related to worse disease outcome (and the existing evidence indicates that this is generally the case), then stress and negative affect should be associated with elevated response in the relevant immunologic parameters, and psychological improvement with reduced response. In fact, for the two diseases described below, there is evidence that the suppressor T-cell system, which acts to keep autoimmune processes in check, is in a state of *underresponse.* Further, markers of lymphocyte activation, as well as inflammation, are associated with increased disease activity and symptomatology.

Rheumatoid Arthritis (RA) is an autoimmune disorder whose precise etiology is not yet clearly understood. Its primary symptoms are joint pain and inflammation. Evidence exists that psychosocial factors have a role in RA. Research has shown, for example, that stressful life events frequently precede the onset of RA (reviewed in Anderson, Bradley, Young, McDaniel, and Wise, 1985), and improvement in a variety of relevant outcomes has been reported in RA patients who received a cognitive-behavioral intervention (reviewed in McCracken [1991]).

Several studies have also assessed the impact of psychosocial factors on immune function in RA patients. For example, Zautra, Okun, Robinson, Lee, Roth, and Emmanual (1989) studied stress and coping in female RA patients, and reported that greater psychological distress was related to lower proportions of T-cells, and major life events with lower helper to suppressor cell ratios. Both of these results are in the unexpected direction in RA; however, subjects with greater numbers of more minor stressors had higher percentages of B-cells (which are elevated during inflammatory phases in the disease). There was no relationship in this study between immune indices and disease activity. Another study assessed cellular immune function in RA patients in conjunction with a cognitive-behavioral intervention focusing on stress and pain management (O'Leary, Shoor, Lorig, and Holman, 1988). While treated subjects demonstrated reduced pain and improved joint condition ("joint counts"), no changes in numbers of T-cell subsets or lymphocyte response to mitogens were observed. Perceived self-efficacy to cope with RA-induced stressors, including pain, poor physical functioning, and general arthritis symptoms, correlated positively with improved disease outcomes, as well as with numbers of suppressor cells, and negatively with helper to suppressor cell ratios at the end of treatment. It is difficult to interpret these associations, however, in the absence of treatment effects on cellular immunity.

Parker and his colleagues have explored relationships among psychological states such as helplessness and depressive reactions to illness, lymphocyte percentages and activation markers, and symptomatology (joint counts) (Parker, Smarr, Walker, Hagglund, Anderson, Hewett, and Caldwell, 1991; Parker, Smarr, Angelone, Mothersead, Lee, Walker, Bridges, and Caldwell, 1992). These papers report associations between psychological factors and joint count, and between immune parameters and joint count (controlling for psychological factors), although the link between psychological factors and immune function is of secondary interest to these investigators, and a model tested using path analysis failed to demonstrate immunologic mediation of psychological-disease links (Parker et al., 1992).

The psychoimmunologic processes involved in autoimmune disease remain somewhat obscure. This may in part be because the immunologic bases for many of them (including RA) remain poorly understood.

AIDS

Human Immunodeficiency Virus (HIV) is the etiologic agent of Acquired Immune Deficiency Syndrome (AIDS). Infection with this virus suppresses immune function by destroying the T-helper class of lymphocytes. Researchers have recently begun to explore the possibility that psychosocial factors influence the progression of HIV infection, both in terms of whether psychological factors might influence the rate of T-cell decline and also in terms of other immunologic processes that might affect clinical course or may mediate the T-cell decline.

Another ongoing project is following HIV-infected gay men and a control group of uninfected gay men, to evaluate the role of psychosocial factors in HIV progression (Kemeny, Fahey, Schneider, Taylor, Weiner, and Visscher, 1989). A group of subjects who had lost one or more close friends to AIDS during the preceding year were compared to a serostatus-matched group of nonbereaved men. While bereavement status itself was not found to be systematically related to any of the immune parameters studied, *depressed mood* following bereavement was associated with lower levels of NK cells in uninfected men; and in nonbereaved seropositive subjects, depressed mood again was associated with several signs of immune dysfunction, including lower responses to PHA, CD4 T-cells, and more CD8 T-cells. Another preliminary study of 11 asymptomatic HIV-infected men indicated that those who were more distressed by recent life stressors and who were using more passive coping methods had lower lymphocyte counts (Goodkin, Fuchs, Feaster, Leeka, and Rischel, 1992). On the other hand, one report of negative findings regarding the relationships between life event stress and depression on CD4 counts has also appeared (Rabkin, Williams, Remien, Goetz, Kertzner, and Gorman, 1991).

Another study examined the stress of receiving antibody testing and results among gay men, some of whom were, and some of whom were not, infected (Antoni, August, LaPerriere, Baggett, Klimas, Ironson, Schneiderman, and Fletcher, 1990; Ironson, LaPerriere, Antoni, O'Hearn, Schneiderman, Klimas, and Fletcher, 1990). Immune parameters were also assessed in a healthy nonantibody tested control group. Among seronegatives, proliferative responses to mitogens and NK cell activity were both depressed, and numbers of CD4 cells reduced, prior to receiving test results (although levels were higher immediately pre-notification than they had been at baseline). Normalization of immune response was observed 5 weeks later. HIV-infected men, however, showed no immune changes following notification despite significant increases in anxiety (although more anxious subjects tended to have lower NK activity). The investigators suggested that HIV infection reduces the immune system's ability to respond to psychological stressors. Analyses of neuroendocrine function that were carried out on the serum from the uninfected subjects (Antoni, Schneiderman, Fletcher, Goldstein, Ironson, and LaPerriere, 1990) suggested that cortisol mediated the effect of anticipation of notification on proliferative response. Interestingly, frequency of intrusive thoughts following notification were positively associated with cortisol levels. Beta-endorphin levels showed no relationships with psychological or immune measures.

Another report from this group tested an exercise intervention as a buffer for possible immune effects of antibody test result notification (LaPerriere, Antoni, Schneiderman, Ironson, Klimas, Caralis, and Fletcher, 1990). Subjects were fifty asymptomatic gay men, half of whom received an aerobic training program for five weeks prior to notification. A comparison group received no intervention. Results indicated that, while infected controls showed reductions in NK cell numbers following notification, infected exercisers did not. The exercise intervention also buffered effects of serostatus notification on psychological distress.

Another intervention study obtained less encouraging results. Coates, McKusick, Kuno, and Stites (1989) failed to find an influence on lymphocyte subset enumeration, NK activity, or mitogen response in a group of men trained in relaxation and other stress management skills.

In summary, evidence does exist for the influence of psychosocial factors on immune function in HIV-spectrum illness, although relationships may differ or be less reliable in this population. The immunologic concomitants of HIV infection and of each of a host of opportunistic conditions may introduce variability that can mask psychoimmunologic relationships (or relationships may depend on the illness and immune profiles of subjects). Furthermore, different psychoimmunologic processes may prevail at different disease stages. The continued exploration of factors influencing outcome in this illness, as well as the development of effective interventions for the HIV-infected population or subpopulations, are particularly important tasks for PNI researchers, as medical advances continue to be made. Jointly, medical and psychological intervention may come to contribute substantially to the prolongation of life of those affected.

CONCLUSIONS AND FUTURE DIRECTIONS

This chapter has reviewed the evidence for life stress influences on a variety of aspects of immune function and on several disease processes. The common perception that negative affect is associated with suppressed or less effective immune function and positive affect with enhanced function, is not uniformly accurate. One exception is the increase in circulating lymphocytes observed in the presence of catecholamines and in connection with acute fearful and laboratory stress. Another exception to this pattern is found for natural killer cell activity, which is enhanced in subjects who are excreting more urinary catecholamines, and in connection with catecholamine injection, as well as during brief laboratory stress. In cancer, there is evidence that emotionality and a "fighting spirit" are prognostically beneficial, and stoicism, fatigue, and emotional inexpressiveness harmful. Evidence for deleterious effects of depression, helplessness-hopelessness, and social loss exist as well (Contrada, Leventhal, and O'Leary, 1990). These effects may be mediated, at least in part, by beneficial effects of catecholamines or harmful effects of cortisol, on natural killer cell function, and in fact, the possible independence of these two pathways may account for the confusing and contradictory findings in the psychosocial oncology literature (Contrada et al., 1990; O'Leary, 1989). As we have argued elsewhere (O'Leary, 1990), it makes evolutionary sense that lymphocytes move to the peripheral blood in the face of fight-flight (SAM-activating) situations where injury is possible. Similar evolutionary processes might account for the enhancing effect of catecholamines (again, reflecting SAM activity) on NK cell cytotoxicity. However, it is puzzling indeed that depression and HPAC activity should be associated with immune down-regulation.

It will be important in future research to examine as many stages as possible in the process by which specific psychological factors (including specific emotional states) influence neuroendocrine activity, which in turn affects immune function and, ultimately, medical outcome. A model that includes these multiple factors in a longitudinal study of women infected with Human Papillomavirus (HPV), the virus that causes cervical cancer, is being tested by our team (O'Leary, Miller, Mills, Brown, and Grey, 1994).

It is important for investigators in the PNI area always to appreciate the possible confounding role of behavioral factors in the mediation of apparent psychosocial influences on immunity. Poor eating habits, sleep deprivation, reduced exercise, and increased use of psychotropic substances are all behaviors that may increase during stressful periods, and may produce direct effects on the immune system. It is critically important to assess these as objectively as possible in research, in addition to the neuroendocrine pathways for psychoimmunologic mediation.

As a discipline, PNI has won widespread recognition as a biologically important area of basic research. We are now at a stage at which we must demonstrate the applicability of our knowledge to the alleviation of suffering from illness. The controlled intervention design, in which psychosocial interventions are tested for their impact on immune function and health, has the additional advantage over correlational research of supporting a causal role for the psychological factors, a great need given the bidirectional nature of psychoimmunologic relationships.

REFERENCES

Ader, R., & Cohen, N. (1991), The influence of conditioning on immune responses. In: *Psychoneuroimmunology*, 2nd ed., ed. R. Ader, D. L. Felten, & N. Cohen. New York: Academic Press, pp. 611–645.
—— Felten, D. L., & Cohen, N. (1991), *Psychoneuroimmunology*, 2nd ed. New York: Academic Press.
Anderson, K. O., Bradley, L. A., Young, L. D., McDaniel, L. K., & Wise, C. (1985), Rheumatoid arthritis: Review of psychological factors related to etiology, effects, and treatment. *Psycholog. Bull.*, 98:358–387.
Antoni, M. H., August, S., LaPerriere, A., Baggett, H. L., Klimas, N., Ironson, G., Schneiderman, N., & Fletcher, M. A. (1990), Psychological and neuroendocrine measures related to functional immune changes in anticipation of HIV-1 serostatus notification. *Psychosom. Med.*, 52:496–510.
—— Schneiderman, N., Fletcher, M. A., Goldstein, D. A., Ironson, G., & LaPerriere, A. (1990), Psychoneuroimmunology and HIV-1. *J. Consult. & Clin. Psychol.*, 58:38–49.
Arnetz, B. B., Wasserman, J., Petrini, B., Brenner, S. O., Levi, L., Eneroth, P., Salovaara, H., Hjelm, R. Salovaara, L., Theorell, T., & Petterson, I. L.

(1987), Immune function in unemployed women. *Psychosom. Med.*, 49:3–12.

Asterita, M. F. (1985), *The Physiology of Stress*. New York: Human Sciences Press.

Bachen, E. A., Manuck, S. B., Marsland, A. L., Cohen, S., Malkoff, S. B., Muldoon, M. F., & Rabin, B. S. (1992), Lymphocyte subset and cellular immune responses to a brief experimental stressor. *Psychosom. Med.*, 54:673–679.

Bartrop, R., Lazarus, L., Luckhurst, E., Kiloh, L. G., & Penny, R. (1977), Depressed lymphocyte function after bereavement. *Lancet*, 1:834–836.

Baum, A., Schaeffer, M. A., Lake, C. R., Fleming, R., & Collins, D. L. (1985), Psychological and endocrinological correlates of chronic stress at Three Mile Island. In: *Perspectives on Behavioral Medicine*, Vol. 2, ed. R. Williams. New York: Academic Press.

Blalock, J. E. (1984), The immune system as a sensory organ. *J. Immunol.*, 132:1067–1070.

——— (1989), A molecular basis for bidirectional communication between the immune and neuroendocrine systems. *Physiolog. Rev.*, 69:1–32.

Brahmi, Z., Thomas, J. E., Park, M., & Dowdeswell, J. R. G. (1985), The effect of acute exercise on natural killer cell activity of trained and sedentary human subjects. *J. Clin. Immunol.*, 5:321–328.

Brosschot, J. F., Benschop, R. J., Godaert, G. L. R., De Smet, M. B. M., Olff, M., Heijnen, C. J., & Ballieux, R. E. (1992), Effects of experimental psychological stress on distribution and function of peripheral blood cells. *Psychosom. Med.*, 54:394–406.

Buske-Kirschbaum, A., Kirschbaum, C., Stierle, H., Lehnert, H., & Hellhammer, D. (1992), Conditioned increase of natural killer cell activity (NKCA) in humans. *Psychosom. Med.*, 54:123–132.

Cannon, W. B., & De La Paz, D. (1911), Emotional stimulation of adrenal secretion. *Amer. J. Physiol.*, 28:64–70.

Coates, T. J., McKusick, L., Kuno, R., & Stites, D. P. (1989), Stress reduction training changed number of sexual partners but not immune function in men with HIV. *Amer. J. Pub. Health*, 79:885–887.

Cohen, S., Tyrrell, D. A. J., & Smith, A. P. (1991), Psychological stress and susceptibility to the common cold. *New Eng. J. Med.*, 325:606–612.

——— Williamson, G. M. (1991), Stress and infectious disease in humans. *Psycholog. Bull.*, 109:5–24.

Contrada, R. J., Leventhal, H., & O'Leary, A. (1990), Personality and health. In: *Handbook of Personality: Theory and Research*, ed. L. A. Pervin. New York: Guilford Press, pp. 638–669.

Crary, B., Borysenko, M., Sutherland, D. C., Kutz, I., Borysenko, J. Z., & Benson, H. (1983), Decrease in mitogen responsiveness of mononuclear cells from peripheral blood after epinephrine administration in humans. *J. Immunol.*, 130:694–697.

——— Hauser, S. L., Borysenko, M., Kutz, I., Hoban, C., Ault, K. A., Weiner, H. L., & Benson, H. (1983), Epinephrine-induced changes in the distribution of lymphocyte subsets in the peripheral blood of humans. *J. Immunol.*, 131:1178–1181.

Cupps, T. R., & Fauci, A. S. (1982), Corticosteroid-mediated immunoregulation in man. *Immunolog. Rev.*, 65:133–155.

Dorian, B. J., Keystone, E., Garfinkel, P. E., & Brown, G. M. (1982), Aberrations in lymphocyte subpopulations and functions during psychological stress. *Clin. & Experiment. Immunol.*, 50:132–138.

Fawzy, F. J., Cousins, N., Fawzy, N. W., Kemeny, M. E., Elashoff, R., & Morton, D. (1990), A structured psychiatric intervention for cancer patients. I. Changes over time in methods of coping and affective disturbance. *Arch. Gen. Psychiatry*, 47:720–725.

—— Kemeny, M. E., Fawzy, N. W., Elashoff, R., Morton, D., Cousins, N., & Fahey, J. L. (1990), A structured psychiatric intervention for cancer patients. II. Changes over time in immunological measures. *Arch. Gen. Psychiatry*, 47:729–735.

Felten, D. (1991), Neurotransmitter signaling of cells of the immune system: Important progress, major gaps. *Brain, Behav., & Immunity*, 5:2–8.

—— Felten, S., Carlson, S., Olschawka, J., & Livnat, S. (1985), Noradrenergic and peptidergic innervation of lymphoid tissue. *J. Immunol.*, 135(2 Suppl.):755s–765s.

Fischer, C. L., Daniels, J. C., Levin, S. L., Kimzey, S. L., Cobb, E. K., & Ritzman, W. E. (1972), Effects of the spaceflight environment on man's immune system: II. Lymphocyte counts and reactivity. *Aerospace Med.*, 43:1122–1125.

Foley, F. W., Miller, A. H., Traugott, U., LaRocca, N. G., Scheinberg, L. C., Bedell, J. R., & Lennox, S. S. (1988), Psychoimmunological dysregulation in multiple sclerosis. *Psychosomatics*, 29:398–403.

Fox, B. H. (1992), LeShan's hypothesis is provocative, but is it plausible? *Advances*, 8:82–84.

Frankenhauser, M. (1983), The sympathetic-adrenal and pituitary-adrenal response to challenge: Comparison between the sexes. In: *Biobehavioral Bases of Coronary Heart Disease*, ed. T. M. Dembroski, T. H. Schmidt, & G. Blumchen. New York: Karger.

Fredrikson, M., Fuerst, C. J., Lekander, M., Rotstein, S., & Blomgren, H. (1993), Trait anxiety and anticipatory immune reactions in women receiving adjuvant chemotherapy for breast cancer. *Brain, Behav., & Immunity*, 7:79–90.

Gatti, G., Cavallo, R., Sartori, M. L., del Ponte, D., Masera, R., Salvadori, A., Carignola, R., & Angeli, A. (1987), Inhibition of cortisol of human natural killer (NK) cell activity. *J. Steroid Biochem.*, 26:49–58.

Glaser, R., Kiecolt-Glaser, J. K., Speicher, C. E., & Holliday, J. E. (1985), Stress loneliness, and changes in herpes virus latency. *J. Behav. Med.*, 8:249–260.

—— —— Stout, J. C., Tarr, K. L., Speicher, C. E., & Holliday, J. E. (1985), Stress-related impairments in cellular immunity. *Psychiatry Res.*, 16:233–239.

—— Pearson, G. R., Bonneau, R. H., Esterling, B. A., Atkinson, C., & Kiecolt-Glaser, J. K. (1993), Stress and the memory T-cell response to the Epstein-Barr virus in healthy medical students. *Health Psychol.*, 12:435–442.

—— —— Jones, J. F., Hillhouse, J., Kennedy, S., Mao, H., & Kiecolt-Glaser, J. K. (1991), Stress-related activation of Epstein-Barr virus. *Brain, Behav., & Immunity*, 5:219–232.

———— Rice, J., Sheridan, J., Fertel, R., Stout, J., Speicher, C., Pinsky, D., Kotur, M., Post, A., Beck, M., & Kiecolt-Glaser, J. K. (1987), Stress-related immune suppression: Health implications. *Brain, Behav., & Immunity*, 1:7–20.

———— ———— Speicher, C. E., Stout, J. C., & Kiecolt-Glaser, J. K. (1986), Stress depresses interferon production concomitant with a decrease in natural killer cell activity. *Behav. Neurosci.*, 100:675–678.

Goodkin, K., Fuchs, I., Feaster, D., Leeka, J., & Rischel, D. D. (1992), Life stressors and coping style are associated with immune measures in HIV-1 infection—A preliminary report. *Internat. J. Psychiatry in Med.*, 22:155–172.

Gorelik, E., & Herberman, R. B. (1986), Role of natural killer (NK) cells in the control of tumor growth and metastatic spread. In: *Cancer Immunology: Innovative Approaches to Therapy*, ed. R. B. Herberman. Boston: Martinus Nijhoff, pp. 151–176.

Grossman, C. J. (1985), Interactions between the gonadal steroids and the immune system. *Science*, 227:257–261.

Henry, J. P., & Stephens, P. M. (1977), *Stress, Health, and the Social Environment*. New York: Springer-Verlag.

Herbert, T. B., & Cohen, S. (1993a), Depression and immunity: A meta-analytic review. *Psycholog. Bull.*, 113:472–486.

———— ———— (1993b), Stress and immunity in humans: A meta-analytic review. *Psychosom. Med.*, 55:364–379.

Ironson, G., LaPerriere, A., Antoni, M., O'Hearn, P., Schneiderman, N., Klimas, N., & Fletcher, M. A. (1990), Changes in immune and psychological measures as a function of anticipation and reaction to news of HIV-1 antibody status. *Psychosom. Med.*, 52:247–270.

Irwin, M., Daniels, M., Smith, T. L., Bloom, E., & Weiner, H. (1987), Impaired natural killer cell activity during bereavement. *Brain, Behav., & Immunity*, 1:98–104.

Jabaaij, L., Grosheide, P. M., Heijtink, R. A., Duivenvoorden, H. J., Ballieux, R. E., & Vingerhoets, A. J. J. M. (1993), Influence of perceived psychological stress and distress on antibody response to low dose rDNA hepatitis B vaccine. *J. Psychosom. Res.*, 37:361–369.

Kay, N., Allen, J., & Morley, J. (1984), Endorphins stimulate normal human peripheral blood lymphocyte natural killer activity. *Life Sci.*, 35:53–59.

Kelley, D. D., Ed. (1986), Stress-induced analgesia. *Ann. NY Acad. Sci.*, 467:241–428.

Kemeny, M. E., Cohen, F., Zegans, L. S., & Conant, M. A. (1989), Psychological and immunological predictors of genital herpes recurrence. *Psychosom. Med.*, 51:195–208.

———— Fahey, J. L., Schneider, S., Taylor, A., Weiner, H., & Visscher, B. (1989), Psychosocial co-factors in HIV infection: Bereavement, depression, and immune status in HIV seropositive men. *Psychosom. Med.*, 51:249.

Kiecolt-Glaser, J. K., Cacioppo, J. T., Malarkey, W. B., & Glaser, R. (1992), Acute psychological stressors and short-term immune changes: What, why, for whom, and to what extent? *Psychosom. Med.*, 54:680–685.

———— Dura, J. R., Speicher, C. E., Trask, O. J., & Glaser, R. (1991), Spousal caregivers of dementia victims: Longitudinal changes in immunity and health. *Psychosom. Med.*, 53:345–362.

——— Fisher, L. D., Ogrocki, P., Stout, J. C., Speicher, C. E., & Glaser, R. (1987), Marital quality, marital disruption, and immune function. *Psychosom. Med.*, 49:13–34.

——— Garner, W., Speicher, C. E., Penn, G., & Glaser, R. (1984), Psychosocial modifiers of immunocompetence in medical students. *Psychosom. Med.*, 46:7–14.

——— Glaser, R., Shuttleworth, E. C., Dyer, C. S., Ogrocki, P., & Speicher, C. E. (1987), Chronic stress and immunity in family caregivers of Alzheimer's disease victims. *Psychosom. Med.*, 49:523–535.

——— ——— Strain, E., Stout, J., Tarr, K., Holliday, J., & Speicher, C. (1986), Modulation of cellular immunity in medical students. *J. Behav. Med.*, 9:5–21.

——— ——— Williger, D., Stout, J. C., Messick, G., Sheppard, S., Ricker, D., Romisher, S. C., Briner, W., Bonnell, G., & Donnerberg, R. (1985), Psychosocial enhancement of immunocompetence in a geriatric population. *Health Psychol.*, 4:25–41.

——— Kennedy, S., Malkoff, S., Fisher, L., Speicher, C. E., & Glaser, R. (1988), Marital discord and immunity in males. *Psychosom. Med.*, 50:213–229.

——— Malarkey, W. B., Chee, M., Newton, T., Cacioppo, J. T., Mao, H., & Glaser, R. (1993), Negative behavior during marital conflict is associated with immunological down-regulation. *Psychosom. Med.*, 55:395–409.

——— Ricker, D., George, J., Messick, G., Speicher, C. E., Garner, W., & Glaser, R. (1984), Urinary cortisol levels, cellular immunocompetency, and loneliness in psychiatric inpatients. *Psychosom. Med.*, 46:15–23.

——— Stephens, R. E., Lipetz, P. D., Speicher, C. E., & Glaser, R. (1985), Distress and DNA repair in human lymphocytes. *J. Behav. Med.*, 8:311–320.

Kimsey, S. L. (1975), The effects of extended space flight on hematologic and immunologic systems. *J. Amer. Women's Med. Assn.*, 30:218–232.

——— Johnson, P. C., Ritzman, S. E., & Mengel, C. E. (1976), Hematology and immunology studies: The second manned spacelab mission. *Aviation, Space, & Environment. Med.*, 47:383–390.

Landmann, R. M. A., Mueller, F. B., Perini, C. H., Wesp, M., Erne, P., & Buehler, F. R. (1984), Changes of immunoregulatory cells induced by psychological and physical stress: Relationship to plasma catecholamines. *Clin. & Experiment. Immunol.*, 58:127–135.

LaPerriere, A. R., Antoni, M. H., Schneiderman, N., Ironson, G., Klimas, N., Caralis, P., & Fletcher, M. A. (1990), Exercise intervention attenuates emotional distress and natural killer cell decrements following notification of positive serologic status for HIV-1. *Biofeedback & Self-Reg.*, 15:229–242.

LeShan, L. (1991), A new question in studying psychosocial interventions and cancer. *Advances*, 7:69–71.

Levy, S. M., Herberman, R. B., Whiteside, T., Sanzo, K., Lee, J., & Kirkwood, J. (1990), Perceived social support and tumor estrogen/progesterone receptor status as predictors of natural killer cell activity in breast cancer patients. *Psychosom. Med.*, 52:73–85.

——— ——— Lippman, M., & D'Angelo, T. (1987), Correlation of stress factors with sustained depression of natural killer cell activity and predicted prognosis in patients with breast cancer. *J. Clin. Oncol.*, 5:348–353.

————— ————— ————— ————— Lee, J. (1991), Immunological and psychosocial predictors of disease recurrence in patients with early-stage breast cancer. *Behav. Med.*, 13:67–75.

————— ————— Maluish, A. M., Schlien, B., & Lippman, M. (1985), Prognostic risk assessment in primary breast cancer by behavioral and immunological parameters. *Health Psychol.*, 4:99–113.

————— Lee, J., Bagley, C., & Lippman, M. (1988), Survival hazards analysis in first recurrent breast cancer patients: Seven-year follow-up. *Psychosom. Med.*, 50:520–528.

Locke, S., Kraus, L., Kutz, I., Edbril, S., Phillips, K., & Benson, H. (1984), Altered natural killer cell activity during norepinephrine infusion in humans. *Proceedings of the First International Workshop on Neuroimmunomodulation*, Bethesda, MD.

Mandler, R. N., Biddison, W. E., Mandler, R., & Serrate, S. A. (1986), Beta-endorphin augments the cytolytic activity and interferon production of natural killer cells. *J. Immunol.*, 136:934–939.

Manuck, S. B., Cohen, S., Rabin, B. S., Muldoon, M. F., & Bachen, E. A. (1991), Prediction of individual differences in cellular immune response to stress. *Psycholog. Sci.*, 2:111–115.

Mayne, T. J., O'Leary, A., McCrady, B., Contrada, R. J., & Labouvie, E. (1994), The differential effects of acute marital distress on emotional, physiological and immune functions in men and women. Typescript. Rutgers University.

McCracken, L. M. (1991), Cognitive-behavioral treatment of rheumatoid arthritis: A preliminary review of efficacy and methodology. *Ann. Behav. Med.*, 13:57–65.

McKinnon, W., Weisse, C. S., Reynolds, C. P., Bowles, C. A., & Baum, A. (1989), Chronic stress, leukocyte subpopulations, and humoral response to latent viruses. *Health Psychol.*, 8:389–402.

Meuleman, J., & Katz, P. (1985), The immunologic effects, kinetics, and use of glucocorticosteroids. *Med. Clin. N. Amer.*, 69:805–816.

Monjan, A. A., & Collector, M. I. (1977), Stress-induced modulation of the immune response. *Science*, 196:307–308.

Naliboff, B. D., Benton, D., Solomon, G. F., Morley, J. E., Fahey, J. L., Bloom, E. T., Makinodan, T., & Gilmore, S. L. (1991), Immunologic changes in young and old adults during brief laboratory stress. *Psychosom. Med.*, 53:121–132.

Neale, J. M., Cox, D. S., Valdimarsdottir, H., & Stone, A. A. (1988), On the relation between immunity and health: Comment on Pennebaker, Kiecolt-Glaser, and Glaser. *J. Consult. & Clin. Psychol.*, 56:636–637.

O'Leary, A. (1989), A two-pathway model for effects of emotional processes on cancer. Paper presented at the First Annual Block Island Conference on Psychotherapy and Affect, Block Island, RI.

————— (1990), Stress, emotion, and human immune function. *Psycholog. Bull.*, 108:363–382.

————— Miller, S. M., Mills, M., Brown, S., & Grey, M. (1994), A psychoneuroimmunologic model for cervical cancer risk. Paper presented at the American Psychological Association, "Psychosocial and Behavioral Factors in

Women's Health: Creating an Agenda for the 21st Century," Washington, DC, May.
—— Shoor, S., Lorig, K., & Holman, H. (1988), A cognitive-behavioral treatment for rheumatoid arthritis. *Health Psychol.*, 7:527–544.
Onsrud, M., & Thorsby, E. (1981), Influence of *in vivo* hydrocortisone on some human blood lymphocyte populations. I. Effect on NK cell activity. *Scand. J. Immunol.*, 13:573–579.
Palmblad, J., Bjorn, P., Wasserman, J., & Akerstedt, T. (1979), Lymphocyte and granulocyte reactions during sleep deprivation. *Psychosom. Med.*, 41:273–278.
Panksepp, J., Siviy, S. M., & Normansell, L. A. (1985), Brain opioids and social emotions. In: *The Psychobiology of Attachment and Separation*, ed. M. Reite & T. Field. San Diego, CA: Academic Press, pp. 1–49.
Parker, J. C., Smarr, K. L., Angelone, E. O., Mothersead, P. K., Lee, B. S., Walker, S. E., Bridges, A. J., & Caldwell, C. W. (1992), Psychological factors, immunologic activation, and disease activity in rheumatoid arthritis. *Arthritis Care & Res.*, 5:196–201.
—— —— Walker, S. E., Hagglund, K. J., Anderson, S. K., Hewett, A. J., & Caldwell, C. W. (1991), Biopsychosocial parameters of disease activity in rheumatoid arthritis. *Arthritis Care & Res.*, 4:73–80.
Pennebaker, J. W., Kiecolt-Glaser, J. K., & Glaser, R. (1988a), Disclosure of traumas and immune function: Health implications for psychotherapy. *J. Consult. & Clin. Psychol.*, 56:239–245.
—— —— —— (1988b), Confronting traumatic experience and immunocompetence: A reply to Neale, Cox, Valdimarsdottir, and Stone. *J. Consult. & Clin. Psychol.*, 56:638–639.
Rabkin, J. G., Williams, J. B., Remien, R. H., Goetz, R., Kertzner, R., & Gorman, J. M. (1991), Depression, distress, lymphocyte subsets, and Human Immunodeficiency Virus symptoms on two occasions in HIV-positive gay men. *Arch. Gen. Psychiatry*, 48:111–119.
Reichlin, S. (1993), Neuroendocrine-immune interactions. *New Eng. J. Med.*, 329:1246–1253.
Schleifer, S. J., Keller, S. E., Camarino, E., Thornton, J. C., & Stein, M. (1983), Suppression of lymphocyte stimulation following bereavement. *JAMA*, 250:374–377.
Sgoutas-Emch, S. A., Cacioppo, J. T., Uchino, B. N., Malarkey, W., Pearl, D., Kiecolt-Glaser, J. K., & Glaser, R. (in preparation), The effects of an acute psychological stressor on cardiovascular, endocrine, and cellular immune response: A prospective study of individuals high and low in heart rate reactivity. *Psychophysiology.*
Shavit, Y. (1991), Stress-induced immune modulation in animals: Opiates and endogenous opioid peptides. In: *Psychoneuroimmunology*, 2nd ed., ed. R. Ader, D. L. Felten, & N. Cohen. New York: Academic Press, pp. 789–806.
Sieber, W. J., Rodin, J., Larson, L., Ortega, S., & Cummings, N. (1992), Modulation of human natural killer cell activity by exposure to uncontrollable stress. *Brain, Behav., & Immunity*, 6:141–156.
Snyder, B. K., Roghmann, K. J., & Sigal, L. H. (1993), Stress and psychosocial factors: Effects on primary cellular immune response. *J. Behav. Med.*, 16:143–161.

Solomon, G. F., Kemeny, M. E., & Temoshok, L. (1991), Psychoneuroimmunologic aspects of Human Immunodeficiency Virus Infection. In: *Psychoneu-
roimmunology*, 2nd ed., ed. R. Ader, D. L. Felten, & N. Cohen. New York:
Academic Press, pp. 1081–1112.
Spiegel, D., Bloom, J. R., Kraemer, H. C., & Gottheil, E. (1989), Effect of psychosocial treatment on survival of patients with metastatic breast cancer.
Lancet, 2:888–891.
Stein, M., Miller, A. H., & Trestman, R. L. (1991), Depression, the immune
system, and health and illness: Findings in search of meaning. *Arch. Gen.
Psychiatry*, 48:171–177.
Toennesen, E., Toennesen, J., & Christensen, N. J. (1984), Augmentation of
cytotoxicity by natural killer (NK) cells after adrenaline administration in
man. *Acta Patholog. Microbiolog. Immunolog. Scand., Sect C Immunologica*,
92:81–83.
Van Rood, Y. R., Bogaards, M., Goulmy, E., & van Houwelingen, H. C. (1993),
The effects of stress and relaxation on the *in vitro* immune response in
man: A meta-analytic study. *J. Behav. Med.*, 16:163–181.
Weisse, C. S. (1992), Depression and immunocompetence: A review of the literature. *Psycholog. Bull.*, 111:475–489.
——— Pato, C. N., McAllister, C. G., Littman, R., Breier, A., Paul, S. M., &
Baum, A. (1990), Differential effects of controllable and uncontrollable
acute stress on lymphocyte proliferation and leukocyte percentages in
humans. *Brain, Behav., & Immunity*, 4:339–351.
Wiedenfeld, S., O'Leary, A., Bandura, A., Brown, S., Levine, S., & Raska, K.
(1990), Impact of perceived self-efficacy in coping with stressors on components of the immune system. *J. Personal. & Soc. Psychol.*, 59:1082–1094.
Williams, J. M., Peterson, R. G., Shea, P. A., Schmedtje, J. F., Bauer, D. C., &
Felten, D. L. (1981), Sympathetic innervation of murine thymus and
spleen: Evidence for a functional link between the nervous and immune
systems. *Brain. Res. Bull.*, 6:83–94.
Winslow, J. T., Hastings, N., Carter, C. S., Harbaugh, C., & Insel, T. R. (1993),
A role for central vasopressin in pair bonding in monogamous prairie
voles. *Nature*, 365:545.
Zakowski, S. G., McAllister, C. G., Deal, M., & Baum, A. (1992), Stress, reactivity,
and immune function in healthy men. *Health Psychol.*, 11:223–232.
Zautra, A. J., Okun, M. A., Robinson, S. E., Lee, D., Roth, S. H., & Emmanual,
J. (1989), Life stress and lymphocyte alterations among patients with rheu-
matoid arthritis. *Health Psychol.*, 8:1–14.

Chapter 10
Psychological Stress in Humans and Susceptibility to the Common Cold

SHELDON COHEN, Ph.D., DAVID A. J. TYRRELL, M.D., AND
ANDREW P. SMITH, Ph.D.

Stressful life events are commonly believed to suppress host resistance to infection. When demands imposed by events exceed a person's ability to cope, a psychological stress response composed of negative cognitive and emotional states is elicited (Lazarus and Folkman, 1984). In turn, psychological stress is thought to influence immune function through autonomic innervates of lymphoid tissue (Felten, Felten, Carlson, Olschowka, and Livnat, 1985; Felten and Olschowka, 1987) or hormone mediated alteration of immune cells (Shavit, Lewis, Terman, Gale, and Liebeskind, 1984; Rabin, Cohen, Ganguli, Lysle, and Cunnick, 1989).

This research was conducted at the Medical Research Council's Common Cold Unit in Salisbury, U.K.

Supported by National Institute of Allergies and Infectious Disease AI23072, Office of Naval Research N00014-88-K0063, a Research Scientist Development Award to SC from the National Institute of Mental Health MH00721 and by Medical Research Council's Common Cold Unit. We thank S. Bull, J. Greenhouse, M. Jarvis, H. Parry, M. Russell, M. Sargent, J. Schlarb, S. Trickett, the medical, nursing and technical staff of the CCU, and the volunteers for their contributions to the research; and J. Cunnick, R. Dawes, D. Klahr, K. Kotovsky, K. Matthews, B. Rabin, and M. Scheier for comments on an earlier draft.

Originally published in the *New England Journal of Medicine,* Vol. 325, pp. 606–612, 1991. Copyright © *New England Journal of Medicine,* 1991. Reprinted by permission.

Stress may also alter immune response through coping behaviors such as increased smoking and alcohol consumption (Kiecolt-Glaser and Glaser, 1988).

There is substantial evidence that stressful life events and self-reports of stress are associated with changes in immune function (Ader, 1981; Calabrese, Kling, and Gold, 1987; Kiecolt-Glaser and Glaser, 1991). Although effects of psychological stress on immune response are often described as immunosuppressive, the implications of stress-induced immune changes for disease susceptibility have not been documented (Laudenslager, 1987; Cohen and Williamson, 1991).

There is some direct evidence that psychological stress increases risk of verified acute respiratory infectious illness (Meyer and Haggerty, 1962; Boyce, Cassel, Collior, Jensen, Ramey, and Smith, 1977; Graham, Douglas, and Ryan, 1986). These studies, however, do not control for possible effects of stressful events on exposure to infectious agents (as opposed to effects on host resistance) or provide evidence about other behavioral and biological pathways through which stress might influence susceptibility to infection. Moreover, this literature is not entirely consistent with several studies failing to find relations between stress and respiratory disease (Alexander and Summerskill, 1956; Cluff, Cantor, and Imboden, 1966).

We present data from a prospective study of the association between psychological stress and susceptibility to the common cold. Healthy persons are assessed for stress and then experimentally exposed to one of five cold viruses. The association between stress and the development of biologically verified clinical disease is examined with controls for prechallenge serostatus, experimental virus, allergic status, weight, season, number of volunteers housed together, whether any housing mates were infected, and demographic factors. Further analyses test the possibility that a relation between stress and susceptibility to illness could be attributable to differences in health practices or differences in prechallenge enumerations of white blood cell populations or total antibody levels. A final analysis examines the possibility that differences in personality rather than exposure to environmental stressors may account for the association between stress and clinical colds.

Subjects and Methods

The subjects were 154 male and 266 female residents of Britain who volunteered to participate in trials at the Medical Research Council's Common Cold Unit (CCU) in Salisbury. All reported no chronic or acute illness or regular medication regimen on their applications and were judged in good health following clinical and laboratory examination on arrival at the unit. Pregnant women were excluded. Volunteers' ages ranged from 18 to 54 years, with a mean of 33.6 and standard deviation of 10.6. Sixty-three percent of volunteers were women. Twenty-two percent did not complete their secondary education, 51 percent completed secondary education but did not attend college and 27 percent attended at least one year of college. Volunteers were reimbursed for their traveling expenses and received free meals and accommodations. The trial was approved by the Harrow District Ethical Committee and informed consent was obtained from each volunteer after the nature and possible consequences of the study were fully explained.

Procedures

During their first 2 days at the CCU, volunteers were given a thorough medical examination, completed a series of self-reported behavioral protocols including psychological stress, personality, and health practice questionnaires, and had blood drawn for immune and cotinine assessments. Subsequently, volunteers were exposed via nasal drops to a low infectious dose of one of five respiratory viruses: rhinovirus types 2 (RV2; n = 86), 9 (RV9;

n = 122), 14 (RV14; n = 92), respiratory syncytial virus (n = 40), and coronavirus type 229E (n = 54). An additional 26 volunteers received saline. Viral doses were intended to stimulate those that occur in person-to-person transmission and result in illness rates of between 20 and 60 percent. For 2 days before and 7 days after viral challenge, volunteers were quarantined in large apartments (alone or with one or two others). Starting 2 days before viral challenge and continuing through 6 days postchallenge, each volunteer was examined daily by a clinician using a standard respiratory sign-symptom protocol (Beare and Reed, 1977). Examples of items on the protocol include sneezing, watering of eyes, nasal stuffiness, nasal obstruction, postnasal discharge, sinus pain, sore throat, hoarseness, cough, and sputum. An objective count of the number of tissues used daily by a volunteer was also part of the protocol. Approximately 28 days after challenge a second serum sample was collected by volunteers' own physicians, and shipped back to the CCU. All investigators were blind to volunteers' psychological status and to whether they received virus or saline.

PSYCHOLOGICAL STRESS INDEX

Three measures of psychological stress were used: (1) number of major stressful life events judged by the respondent as having a negative impact; (2) perception that current demands exceed capabilities to cope; and (3) current negative affect. The major stressful life events scale consisted of events that might happen in the life of the respondent (41 items) or close others (26 items). The events were from the List of Recent Experiences (Henderson, Byrne, and Duncan-Jones, 1981) and were chosen because of their potential for negative impact and the relatively high frequency of occurrence in population studies. The scale score was the number of events occurring during the previous 12 months that the respondent indicated as having a negative impact on his or her life. The 10-item Perceived Stress Scale (PSS-10; [Cohen and Williamson, 1988]) was used to assess the degree to which situations in life are perceived as stressful (reliability [Cronbach, 1951] (α) = .85). Items in the PSS-10 were designed to tap how unpredictable, uncontrollable, and overloading respondents find their lives. Finally, the negative affect scale included 15 items from Zevon and Tellegen's (1982) list of negative emotions. The items included distressed, nervous, sad, angry, dissatisfied with self, calm (reverse scored), guilty, scared, angry at yourself, upset, irritated, depressed, hostile, shaky, and content (reverse scored). A 5-point (0 to 4) Likert-type response format was used to report affect intensity during the last week (reliability [α] = .84).

All three stress scales formed a single principal component with loadings of .66, .86, and .86 respectively; providing evidence that the scales measure a common underlying concept (Afifi and Clark, 1984). Hence an index combining the three measures was used as an indicator of psychological stress. Because life events were not normally distributed, an index based on normalized scores was not appropriate. Instead, the index was created by quartiling each scale and summing quartile ranks for each volunteer (1 for lowest quartile and 4 for highest) resulting in a stress index ranging from 3 to 12. The quartiles were 0, 1–2, 3–4, and 5–14 for the life events scale; 0–10, 11–14, 15–18, and 19–33 for the PSS-10; and 0–7, 8–13, 14–20, and 21–49 for the negative affect scale. Index scores were approximately normally distributed.

ASSAYS FOR VIRAL ISOLATION AND VIRAL-SPECIFIC ANTIBODY LEVELS

Nasal wash samples for viral isolation were collected before inoculation and on days 2 through 6 after viral inoculation. They were mixed with broth and stored in aliquots at −70° C. Rhinoviruses were detected in O-Hela cells, respiratory syncytial virus in Hep2 cells, and coronavirus in C-16 strain of continuous human fibroblast cells. When a characteristic cytopathic effect was observed the tissue culture fluids were passaged into further cultures and identity tests on the virus were performed. Rhinoviruses and coronaviruses were confirmed by neutralization tests with specific rabbit immune serum, and respiratory syncytial virus by immunofluorescent staining of culture cells.

Levels of neutralizing antibodies, and of specific antiviral IgA and IgG were determined before and 28 days after challenge. Neutralizing antibodies (for RVs only) were determined by neutralizing tests with homologous virus (Al Nakib and Tyrrell, 1988). Results were recorded as the highest dilution showing neutralization, and a fourfold rise was regarded as significant. Suitable neutralizing tests were not available for respiratory syncytial virus and coronavirus.

Viral specific IgA and IgG levels for rhinoviruses (Barclay and Al Nakib, 1987), coronavirus and respiratory syncytial virus (Callow, 1985) were determined by enzyme-linked immunosorbent assays. This test detects antibody which correlates with neutralization titer, is associated with resistance to infection, and increases in response to infection (Al Nakib and Tyrrell, 1988).

INFECTIONS AND CLINICAL COLDS

A volunteer was deemed *infected* if the virus was isolated postchallenge or there was a significant rise in pre- to postchallenge viral specific serum antibody, that is, a fourfold increase in neutralizing antibody (RVs only) or an IgG or IgA increase of two standard deviations greater than the mean of nonchallenged volunteers (all viruses). Eighty-two percent (325) of the volunteers receiving the virus were infected. Five (19%) of the volunteers receiving saline were infected. We attribute infections among the saline group to volunteer transmission of virus to others housed in the same apartment. A control for person-to-person transmission is included in the data analysis.

At the end of the trial, the clinician judged the severity of each volunteer's cold on a scale ranging from nil (0) to severe (4). Ratings of mild cold (2) or greater were considered positive clinical diagnoses. Volunteers also judged the severity of their colds on the same scale. Clinician diagnosis was in agreement with self-diagnosis for 94 percent of the volunteers. Volunteers were defined as having developed clinical colds if they were both infected and diagnosed by the clinician as having a clinical cold. Of the 394 volunteers participating in the trials, 38 percent (148) developed clinical colds. *None* of the 26 saline controls developed colds.

Seven persons with positive clinical diagnosis but no indication of infection were excluded from the sample because we assumed the illness was caused by pretrial exposure to another virus. Analyses including them (by definition no clinical cold, no infection) result in identical conclusions.

STANDARD CONTROL VARIABLES

We employ a series of control variables that might provide alternative explanations for a relation between stress and illness. These include prechallenge serostatus for the experimental virus, age, gender, education, allergic status, weight, season, number of others the volunteer was housed with, whether an apartment mate was infected, and challenge virus.

Serostatus was defined as positive when a volunteer had a neutralizing prechallenge antibody titer greater than 2 for rhinoviruses and prechallenge antibody level greater than the sample median for coronavirus and respiratory syncytial virus. Forty-three percent of volunteers were seropositive before the challenge, including 55 percent for RV2, 48 percent for RV9, 20 percent for RV14, 50 percent for respiratory syncytial virus, and 50 percent for coronavirus.

Age and gender were based on self-report. Because age was not normally distributed it was scored categorically based on a median split: 18–33 or 34–54. Scores on education were based on an 8-point self-report scale ranging from no schooling (0) to doctoral degree (8). Allergic status was based on physician interview questions regarding allergies to food, drugs, or other allergens. Persons reporting any allergy were defined as allergic. A ponderal index (weight/height^3) was used to control for volunteers' weight. We used number of hours of daylight on the first day of the trial as a continuous measure of season. Number of daylight hours is correlated .80 ($p < .001$) with average temperature on the same day. A control for the possibility that person-to-person transmission rather than the virus inoculation might be responsible for infection or clinical colds was also included. Because person-to-person transmission would only be possible if an apartment mate was infected by the viral challenge, the control variable indicated whether or not any housing mate was infected. Finally, challenge virus is a categorical variable representing the experimental virus to which a volunteer was exposed.

HEALTH PRACTICE MEASURES

Health practices including smoking, drinking alcohol, exercise, quality of sleep, and dietary practices were assessed as possible pathways linking stress and susceptibility. Cotinine as assessed in serum by gas chromotography was used as a biochemical indicator of smoking rate because it provides an objective measure of nicotine intake that is not subject to self-report bias (Jarvis, Tunstall-Pedoe, Feyerabend, Vesey, and Saloojee, 1987; Feyerabend and Russell, 1990). We use the $\log_{10}$ of the average of the two (pre- and 28 days postchallenge) cotinine measures as an indicator of smoking rate. (The correlation between the two measures was .95, $p < .001$, n = 348). The correlation between $\log_{10}$ average cotinine and $\log_{10}$ self-reported number of cigarettes smoked per day was .96 ($p < .001$, n = 372).

The remaining health practices were assessed by questionnaire before viral challenge. Average number of alcoholic drinks per day was calculated using separate estimates of weekday and weekend drinking. A half pint, bottle, or can of beer, glass of wine, and shot of whiskey contain approximately equal amounts of alcohol and were each treated as a single drink. The exercise index included items on the frequency of walking, running, jogging, swimming, aerobics, and work around the house. The quality of sleep index included items on feeling rested, difficulty falling asleep, and awakening early; and the dietary habit index was made up of items designed to assess concern with a healthy diet and included frequencies of eating breakfast, fruits, and vegetables.

White Blood Cell Populations and Total Immunoglobulin Levels

White blood cell populations and total immunoglobulin levels were assessed as possible pathways linking psychological stress to susceptibility. Assays were conducted on samples collected prior to viral challenge. White blood cells were counted with an automatic cell counter and differentials (lymphocytes, monocytes, and neutrophils) calculated from 200 cells in a stained film. Total serum and nasal IgA and IgE and total nasal protein were assessed by enzyme-linked immunosorbent assays (Callow, 1985).

Personality Measures

Because psychological stress could reflect stable personality styles rather than responses to environmental stressors, self-esteem and personal control (two personality characteristics closely associated with stress) were assessed prior to viral challenge. Self-esteem was measured by self-regard and social confidence subscales of the Feelings of Inadequacy Scale (Fleming and Watts, 1980) (reliability [α] = .89); personal control by personal efficacy and interpersonal control subscales of the Spheres of Control Scale (Paulhus, 1983) (reliability [α] = .76). A third personality characteristic, introversion–extroversion, was also assessed because of an existing literature suggesting that introverts were at higher risk for infection (Totman, Kiff, Reed, and Craig, 1980; Broadbent, Broadbent, Phillpotts, and Wallace, 1984). It was assessed by the Eysenck Personality Inventory (Eysenck and Eysenck, 1964) (scale reliability [α] = .80).

Statistical Analysis

The primary analysis tests whether psychological stress is associated with greater rates of clinical colds. Secondary analyses assess the importance of the two components of the definition of a clinical cold, infection, and illness (clinical symptomatology), in accounting for an association of stress and clinical colds. Specifically, we determine whether the relation between stress and colds

is attributable to increases in infection or to increases in diagnosed colds among infected persons. The saline-control subjects
are not included in the analyses.

Logistic regression is used to predict these binary outcomes
(Hosmer and Lemeshow, 1989). We report a sequential series of
analyses. In the first stage, only the psychological stress index is
entered as a predictor. In the second, we enter the standard control variables in the initial step of the regression and then test
whether there is a significant change in log-likelihood when the
stress index is added to the equation. Education, weight, season,
and number of apartment mates are entered as continuous variables and the remainder of the standard controls as dummy (categorical) variables (Hosmer and Lemeshow, 1989). Because the
predictor (the stress index score) is a continuous variable, we
report raw regression coefficients (b) and their standard errors
(SE) (Hosmer and Lemeshow, 1989). To estimate effect sizes, we
also report odds ratios (OR) and their 95 percent confidence
intervals (CI) as derived from modified regression models where
the continuous stress index score is replaced with a contrast of
the persons in the bottom and top quartiles of the stress index.
The OR approximates how much more likely it is for the outcome
(infection or clinical colds) to be present among those with high
(top quartile) than those with low (bottom quartile) stress scores
(Hosmer and Lemeshow, 1989).

Additional analyses test possible roles of immunity, health practices, and personality variables in the relation between stress and
clinical colds. In the first analysis, the possibility that enumerations of white blood cell populations, total antibody levels, or
five different health practices operate as pathways through which
psychological stress influences risk for clinical colds, is assessed
by entering these variables along with the standard controls in
the first step of the regression equation and then testing whether
adding stress to the equation accounts for a significant change in
log-likelihood. In the second, the possibility that effects of stress
might actually reflect differences in personality rather than reactions to environmental stressors is assessed by adding two personality variables associated with stress (self-esteem and personal

control) and then another personality variable previously associated with susceptibility to infection (introversion–extroversion) to the set of control variables and testing for the additional contribution of stress. All immune measures, health practices and personality measures are entered as continuous variables.

RESULTS

Preliminary analysis indicated no statistically reliable interactions between standard control variables and stress in predicting clinical colds (highest t = 1.62, p = .11) (Hosmer and Lemeshow, 1989). Hence, reported effects are *similar across viruses, and levels of serostatus, age, gender, allergic status, education, weight, number of apartment mates, whether an apartment mate is infected, and season.* There were main effects of only three of the standard control variables, serostatus ($p < .001$), virus ($p < .001$), and whether an apartment mate was infected ($p < .02$); $p > .20$ for remaining variables. Seronegatives developed more colds (49.3%) than seropositives (22.2%). Rates of colds by virus were 61.6 percent for coronavirus, 42.4 percent for RV14, 37.5 percent for respiratory syncytial virus, 33.6 percent for RV9, and 23.3 percent for RV2. Finally, persons with an infected apartment mate developed more colds (40.9%) than those without an infected mate (26.4%). Although associated with the development of clinical colds, *none* of these three controls was reliably associated with the stress index (highest F = 1.44, p = .22).

As apparent from Figure 10.1, the rate of clinical colds increased in a dose–response manner with increases in the stress index (b = .10, SE = .04, $p < .02$, N = 394; OR for comparison of top and bottom quartile = 1.98, CI = 1.10,3.56). Moreover, entering the standard control variables into the equation (adjusted rates in figure) does not alter this association (b = .10, SE = .05, $p < .04$, N = 394; OR = 2.16, CI = 1.11,4.23).

As apparent from Figure 10.2, rates of infection also increase with increases in stress (b = .15, SE = .05, $p < .005$, N = 394;

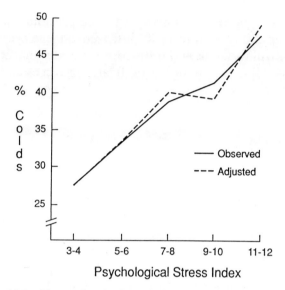

Figure 10.1. Observed and adjusted (for standard controls) association between the psychological stress index and clinical cold rates (N = 394).

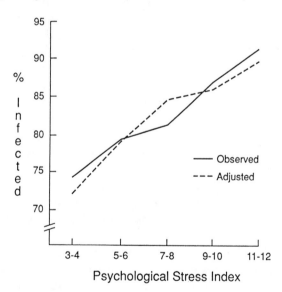

Figure 10.2. Observed and adjusted (for standard controls) association between the psychological stress index and infection rates (N = 394).

OR for comparison of top and bottom quartiles = 3.45, CI = 1.51,7.87). This relation is similarly unaltered by inclusion of standard control variables in the equation (b = .17, SE = .06, $p <$ .004; OR = 5.81, CI = 2.12,15.91). Stress is not, however, reliably associated with rates of colds *for infected persons* (b = .07, SE = .04, p = .13; with controls b = .06, SE = .05, p = .24; N = 325). Hence, the relation between stress and colds is primarily attributable to stressed persons having more infections rather than to stressed persons who are infected having more colds.

The equivalency of the effect of stress across levels of each of the standard control variables (lack of interactions between stress and each control) was noted above. Of special importance in interpreting this study is that stress had equivalent effects across viruses, infectious status of apartment mates, and prechallenge serostatus. The consistency of the effects of stress across the five viruses is illustrated in Figures 10.3 and 10.4. These figures present the adjusted (for standard controls) rates of colds and infection by virus for persons below (low stress) and above (high stress)

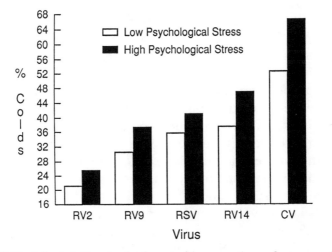

Figure 10.3. Adjusted (for standard controls) proportions of persons with low (below the median) and high (above the median) psychological stress developing colds in each virus challenge group (N = 394).

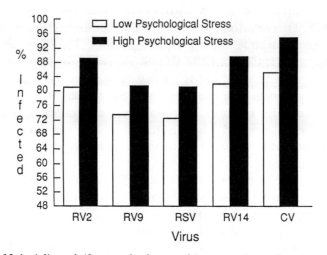

Figure 10.4. Adjusted (for standard controls) proportions of persons with low (below the median) and high (above the median) psychological stress becoming infected in each virus challenge group (N = 394).

the median of the stress index. Consistency across viruses suggests the biologic generality of the effect. Table 10.1 presents similar data for prechallenge serostatus and infectious status of apartment mates. The data on apartment mates indicate that greater person-to-person transmission among stressed persons (possible with an infected mate but not without one) cannot explain the association between stress and colds. Finally, consistency across prechallenge serostatus suggests that if an immune mechanism is the mediator of the relation between stress and colds, it is a primary not secondary (immune memory) mechanism.

Health practices and quantitative measures of prechallenge cellular and humoral immune status were assessed as possible pathways linking stress and susceptibility. Adding *all* of the enumerations of white blood cell populations, total antibody levels (specific antibody levels are already included in the equation as serostatus), and health practice measures to the equation (including standard controls) had little effect on the relation between stress and colds (b = .14, SE = .05, $p < .01$). Hence none

TABLE 10.1
Adjusted (for standard controls) Rates of Infection and of Colds by Psychological Stress and Prechallenge Serostatus, and by Psychological Stress and Infectious Status of Apartment Mates

	Infection Rates		Cold Rates	
	Stress Index		Stress Index	
	Low	High	Low	High
Prechallenge Serostatus				
Positive (N = 171)	67.2	79.8	18.7	25.5
Negative (N = 223)	86.2	92.4	43.7	55.2
Infectious Status of				
Apartment Mates				
Not Infected (N = 91)	68.7	81.4	20.8	32.6
Infected (N = 303)	81.2	88.3	37.2	44.6

Note: The categorization of low and high stress is based on a median split. Infectious status of apartment mates is coded as infected if any person housed with the volunteer was infected.

of these hypothetical pathways are responsible for the association between stress and illness in this study.

Self-esteem and personal control were assessed to control for the possibility that personality styles rather than responses to environmental stressors were responsible for the association between the stress index and susceptibility. Higher levels of stress were associated with both lower levels of personal control ($r = -.25$, $p < .001$) and self-esteem ($r = -.52$, $p < .001$). However, adding self-esteem and control to the regression equation (including standard controls, health practices and immune measures) had little effect on the relation between stress and colds ($b = .13$, SE $= .06$, $p < .03$). A measure of introversion–extroversion was also included because of previous work suggesting that introverts were more susceptible to infection. Introversion–extroversion was not associated with the stress index ($r = -.04$, $p = .46$) nor did its addition to the equation described above influence the contribution of stress to the prediction of clinical colds ($b = .13$, SE $= .06$, $p < .04$). Hence none of these personality characteristics can account for the relation between stress and colds.

Discussion

Stress is associated with increased risk for acute respiratory infectious illness in a dose–response manner and this risk is attributable to increased rates of infection. Although there was some person-to-person transmission of virus in this study, the effect of stress on colds was independent of whether such transmission was possible; that is, whether a volunteer had an infected apartment mate. Moreover, the relation between stress and colds was equivalent for those with and without infected apartment mates. In short, the stress index is associated with host resistance and not with differential viral exposure.

The relation between stress and colds also proved to be independent of a variety of health practices. If increased risk of illness for stressed persons is not due to associations between stress and viral exposure or between stress and health practices, what accounts for this relation? Evidence from both human and infrahuman studies indicates that stress modulates immunity (Ader, 1981; Calabrese et al., 1987; Kiecolt-Glaser and Glaser, 1991). Although the immune measures assessed in this study (prechallenge white blood cell counts and antibody levels) did not explain the relation between stress and colds, these are quantitative measures and qualitative (functional) measures of immunity were not assessed. Because stress effects were equivalent for both prechallenge seropositives and seronegatives, immune explanations would need to focus on primary as opposed to secondary (memory) immune response. Some examples of primary immune functions that could play a role in this association include endothelial or lymphocyte production of interferon, mucus production, and natural killer cell activity (Morahan and Murasko, 1989).

The association between stress and clinical illness is only moderate (adjusted OR = 2.16) and detection of the effect required a large sample. The relation of stress and infection, however, is more substantial (adjusted OR = 5.81). Moreover, the consistency of the stress–illness relation across three very different viruses, rhinovirus, coronavirus, and respiratory syncytial virus (as well as across rhinovirus types) was impressive. This suggests that stress is associated with a suppression of a general host resistance process leaving persons susceptible to multiple infectious agents or that stress is associated with a suppression of many different immune processes with similar result.

Although psychological stress is conceptualized here as a response to environmental events, our measures may also reflect personality characteristics that are independent of environmental stressors. Self-esteem and personal control, two personality characteristics strongly associated with stress, did not, however, account for the effect of stress in this study. Another personality characteristic previously found to predict susceptibility to infection, introversion–extroversion, similarly did not account for the effect of stress. However, because the psychological stress index assesses negative cognitive and emotional states rather than environmental stressors, it is possible that it reflects other individual dispositions not controlled for in the current study.

The research on the role of stress as a risk factor in verified infectious disease has been inconsistent (Cohen and Williamson, 1991). This inconsistency may be attributable to insensitive techniques for detecting a relatively small effect on clinical illness. Our data suggest that a relation between stress and susceptibility may be best detected in studies with controls for important demographic and biologic parameters, reliable and broadly defined stress measurement, control over exposure to the infectious agent, and relatively large sample sizes.

REFERENCES

Ader, R., Ed. (1981), *Psychoneuroimmunology*. New York: Academic Press.

Afifi, A. A., & Clark, V. (1984), *Computer-Aided Multivariate Analysis*. Belmont, CA: Lifetime Learning Publications.

Alexander, R., & Summerskill, J. (1956), Factors affecting the incidence of upper respiratory complaints among college students. *Student Med.*, 4:61–73.

Al Nakib, W., & Tyrrell, D. A. J. (1988), *Picornviridae*: rhinoviruses—common cold viruses. In: *Laboratory Diagnosis of Infectious Diseases: Principles and Practice*, Vol. 2, eds. E. M. Lennette, P. Halonen, & F. A. Murphy. New York: Springer-Verlag, pp. 723–742.

Barclay, W. S., & Al Nakib, W. (1987), An ELISA for the detection of rhinovirus specific antibody in serum and nasal secretion. *J. Virol. Meth.*, 15:53–64.

Beare, A. S., & Reed, S. E. (1977), The study of antiviral compounds in volunteers. In: *Chemoprophylaxis and Virus Infections*, Vol. 2, ed. J. S. Oxford. Cleveland, OH: CRC Press, pp. 27–55.

Boyce, W. T., Jensen, E. W., Cassel, J. C., Collior, A. M., Smith, A. H. & Ramey, C. T., (1977), Influence of life events and family routines on childhood respiratory tract illness. *Pedia*, 60:609–615.

Broadbent, D. E., Broadbent, M. H. P., Phillpotts, R. J., & Wallace, J. (1984), Some further studies on the prediction of experimental colds in volunteers by psychological factors. *J. Psychosom. Res.*, 28:511–523.

Calabrese, J. R., Kling, M. A., & Gold, P. W. (1987), Alterations in immunocompetence during stress, bereavement, and depression: Focus on neuroendocrine regulation. *Amer. J. Psychiatry*, 114:1123–1134.

Callow, K. A. (1985), Effect of specific humoral immunity and some non-specific factors on resistance of volunteers to respiratory coronavirus infection. *J. Hyg. Camb.*, 95:173–189.

Cluff, L. E., Cantor, A., & Imboden, J. B. (1966), Asian influenza: Infection, disease, and psychological factors. *Arch. Intern. Med.*, 117:159–163.

Cohen, S., & Williamson, G. (1988), Perceived stress in a probability sample of the United States. In: *The Social Psychology of Health*, eds. S. Spacapan & S. Oskamp. Newbury Park, CA: Sage, pp. 31–67.

——— ——— (1991), Stress and infectious disease in humans. *Psych. Bull.*, 109:5–24.

Cronbach, L. (1951), Coefficient alpha and the internal structure of tests. *Psychometrika*, 16:297–334.

Eysenck, H. J., & Eysenck, S. B. G. (1964), *Manual of the Eysenck Personality Inventory*. London: University of London Press.

Felten, D. L., Felten, S. Y., Carlson, S. L., Olschowka, J. A., & Livnat, S. (1985), Noradrenergic sympathetic innervation of lymphoid tissue. *J. Immunol.*, 135:755–765.

Felten, S. Y., & Olschawka, J. A. (1987), Noradrenergic sympathetic innervation of the spleen. II. Tyrosine hydroxylase (TH)-positive nerve terminals from synaptic-like contacts on lymphocytes in the splenic white pulp. *J. Neurosci. Res.*, 18:37–48.

Feyerabend, C., & Russell, M. A. H. (1990), A rapid gas-liquid chromatographic method for the determination of cotinine and nicotine in biological fluids. *J. Pharm. Pharmacol.*, 42:450–452.

Fleming, J. S., & Watts, W. A. (1980), The dimensionality of self-esteem: Some results for a college sample. *J. Pers. Soc. Psychol.*, 39:921–929.

Graham, N. M. H., Douglas, R. B., & Ryan, P. (1986), Stress and acute respiratory infection. *Amer. J. Epidem.*, 124:389–401.

Henderson, S., Byrne, D. G., & Duncan-Jones, P. (1981), *Neurosis and the Social Environment*. Sydney, Australia: Academic Press.

Hosmer, D. W., Jr., & Lemeshow, S. (1989), *Applied Logistic Regression.* New York: John Wiley.

Jarvis, M. J., Tunstall-Pedoe, H., Feyerabend, C., Vesey, C., & Saloojee, Y. (1987), Comparison of tests used to distinguish smokers from nonsmokers. *Amer. J. Pub. Health,* 77:1435–1438.

Kiecolt-Glaser, J. K., & Glaser, R. (1988), Methodological issues in behavioral immunology research with humans. *Brain Behav. Immun.,* 2:67–78.

——— ——— (1991), Psychosocial factors, stress, disease, and immunity. In: *Psychoneuroimmunology,* eds. R. Ader, D. L. Felten, & N. Cohen. New York: Academic Press, pp. 849–867.

Laudenslager, M. L. (1987), Psychosocial stress and susceptibility to infectious disease. In: *Viruses, Immunity, and Mental Disorder,* eds. E. Kurstak, A. J. Lipowski, & P. V. Morozov. New York: Plenum Medical Books, pp. 391–402.

Lazarus, R. S., & Folkman, S. (1984), *Stress, Appraisal, and Coping.* New York: Springer.

Meyer, R. J., & Haggerty, R. J. (1962), Streptococcal infections in families. *Pedia,* 29:539–549.

Morahan, P. S., & Murasko, D. M. (1989), Viral infections. In: *Natural Immunity in Disease Processes,* ed. D. S. Nelson. New York: Academic Press, pp. 557–586.

Paulhus, D. (1983), Sphere-specific measures of perceived control. *J. Pers. Soc. Psychol.,* 44:1253–1265.

Rabin, B. S., Cohen, S., Ganguli, R., Lysle, D. T., & Cunnick, J. E. (1989), Bidirectional interaction between the central nervous system and the immune system. *Crit. Rev. Immunol.,* 9:279–312.

Shavit, Y., Lewis, J. W., Terman, G. S., Gale, R. P., & Liebeskind, J. C. (1984), Opioid peptides mediate the suppressive effect of stress on natural killer cell cytotoxicity. *Science,* 223:188–190.

Totman, R., Kiff, J., Reed, S. E., & Craig, J. W. (1980), Predicting experimental colds in volunteers from different measures of recent life stress. *J. Psychosom. Res.,* 24:155–163.

Zevon, M. A., & Tellegen, A. (1982), The structure of mood change: An idiographic/nomothetic analysis. *J. Pers. Soc. Psychol.,* 43:111–122.

Chapter 11
Psychiatric Consequences of Traumatic Amputations

Peter V. Kamenchenko, M.D., V. S. Yastrebov, M.D., and A. S. Tiganov, M.D.

Considerable interest in the psychiatric consequences of traumatic amputations and the concept of psychosomatic disorder has been expressed in the recent literature on stressful life events (Krinichanskii, 1977; Grunert, Devine, and Matloub, 1988; Miller, Kraus, Kamenchenko, and Krasnianski, 1992; Miller and Başoğlu, 1992). The National Mental Health Research Center of the Academy of Medical Sciences, Moscow, Russia, has been examining the impact of stressful life events, including traumatic amputation, both in victims of natural disasters and veterans of the Afghanistan war.

Amputation of a limb is one of the most serious and widespread physical mutilations (Parkes, 1972, 1975; Miller, Kamenchenko, and Krasnianski, 1992). Frierson and Lippmann (1987) examined traumatic amputations and found that one in every 300 persons has had a major limb amputation, and at least 60,000 amputations

Acknowledgments. The authors wish to acknowledge the assistance of the National Mental Health Research Center of the Russian Academy of Medical Sciences, the National Center for Post-Traumatic Stress Disorder, and the Department of Psychiatry of the University of Kentucky. Appreciation is expressed to Deborah Kessler, Katrina Scott, Tag Heister, Virginia Lynn Morehouse, and Robin Oakley of the Department of Psychiatry, College of Medicine, University of Kentucky for their contributions to the completion of this manuscript.

take place annually. With ethnicity reported, it is reasonable to understand the psychiatric implications and consequences of such trauma. Zalkind, Wittakouer, and Parks (1987) report that the frequency of psychiatric disorders among traumatic amputees range from 65 to 95 percent, with most patients in these categories requiring psychiatric and psychotherapeutic intervention.

The purpose of this study is to examine the psychiatric consequences of traumatic amputation. Measurable environmental stress and the onset of symptoms are crucial in our understanding of psychosomatic mechanisms. The biopsychosocial model of understanding psychosomatic disorders has been the model of choice in studying the psychiatric impact of various traumatic events including traumatic amputations. Russian clinical studies by Galenko (1986) and Soloviova (1986) attest to the emergence of psychiatric disorders in amputees. These studies resulted in correlations of psychiatric disorders in amputees with psychotrauma. The emergence of Posttraumatic Stress Disorder (PTSD) in the *Diagnostic and Statistical Manual* of the American Psychiatric Association in the early 1980s led to greater understanding on the part of clinician-researchers in addressing the issues of psychiatric complications related to traumatic amputation.

METHODOLOGY

SUBJECTS

This research was conducted by the National Mental Health Research Center of the Russian Academy of Medical Sciences. Subjects were 80 amputees (42 male and 38 female) with ages ranging from 18 to 67 years of age. The research took place during their inpatient care at the Central Prosthetic Research Institute of the Academy of Medical Sciences.

Inclusion criteria for this study recognized that the amputation was caused through traumatic injury, that the patients were at least 16 years of age at the time of the trauma, and that all patients being evaluated in the study were less than 6 months from the traumatic injury. Exclusion criteria for the study included patients with a diagnosis of premorbid mental disorders or who had serious chronic somatic and neurological dysfunction.

INSTRUMENTS

A standardized protocol approved by the National Mental Health Research Center of the Russian Academy of Medical Sciences was utilized. This standardized protocol includes the Symptom Problem Checklist-90, a structured clinical interview for DSM-III-R (APA, 1987), the Mississippi Scale (civilian version), all of which were translated and back translated from English to Russian to assure the diagnostic consistency, precision, validity, and reliability of the instruments utilized in this study.

The SCL-90 is a multidimensional self-report symptom inventory designed to assess symptomatic psychological distress. A prototypical version of the scale was developed in 1983 (Derogatis, Lipman, and Covi, 1973), and the final version of the instrument was written by Derogatis (1975). The SCL-90 reflects psychological distress in terms of nine primary symptom dimensions and three global indices of distress (Som); obsessive-compulsive (Obs); interpersonal sensitivity (Int); depression (Dep); hostility (Hos); anxiety (Anx); phobic anxiety (Phob); psychosis (Psy); and paranoid ideation (Par). The primary symptom constructs are utilized in the SCL-90. Three global indices represent summary measures of psychological disorders that, although correlated, have been shown to display distinct aspects of psychopathology. These are the General Sensitivity Index (GSI), and its combination or interface with information on numbers of symptoms and intensity of distress. A second index is the Positive Symptom Total (PST), which is a reflection only of the number of symptoms reported, and finally the Positive Symptom Distress Index (PSDI), which is a pure intensity measure adjusted for numbers of symptoms present.

The SCL-90 has demonstrated high levels of both test–retest and internal consistency reliability (Derogatis, 1977). In the more than two decades since its introduction, the SCL-90 has become somewhat of a standard in the multidimensional measurement of psychological distress. It is therefore seen as a very appropriate measure within this model.

The Mississippi Scale (civilian; Keane, 1988) is a 39-item inventory based on the Mississippi Scale for conduct-related PTSD but adapted to civilian experiences of combat or war. Its applicability and utilization include natural disasters and other types of traumatizing experience. The factor structure for this instrument attempts to measure symptomatology consistent with traumatic stress, including sleep disturbance, memory and concentration difficulties, interpersonal problems, depression, and reexperiencing of traumatic events.

The Structured Clinical Interview for DSM-III-R (SCID) (Spitzer and Williams, 1987) for PTSD was utilized in this study. It is an instrument that provides operational criteria for assessing the 17 symptoms of PTSD within the categories of experiencing, numbing avoidance, and physiological arousal. The SCID instructs the clinician to ask specific questions, the answers to which determine whether a patient satisfies the diagnostic criteria for PTSD. The number of symptoms positively endorsed is totaled to arrive at an index of PTSD symptom severity.

RESULTS

The results of this study show that the character of psychopathology symptomatology is dependent upon the period of disturbance; that is, the time between the traumatic event and the first evaluation for treatment of the traumatic injury.

In the acute period at the time of the trauma, when psychopathological symptoms developed, the most prominent symptomatology was consistent with acute traumatic stress disorder and subsequent depression. The seriousness of the psychopathological disorders noted during the acute period clearly reflect the trauma accommodation syndrome noted by Miller (1989) and stress response syndromes noted by Horowitz, Field, and Classen (1993). The psychic reactions of patients in the acute period of trauma included hyperalertness, poor concentration, sleep disturbance, and startle, as noted by Weitbrecht (1983). Most notable among the symptomatology was the presence of delayed traumatic stress with the following symptoms: (1) increased physiological arousal; (2) reexperiencing of the trauma; (3) avoidant types of behaviors; (4) depression; (5) some emergence of personality disorder. Patients were noted to be easily irritated, labile in mood, showing some level of poor concentration and memory, with outbursts of anger as prevailing symptoms. Some patients were noted also to be fatigued and have difficulty with concentration and memory.

DISCUSSION

Clearly evident in this population was reexperiencing of the trauma related to the traumatic amputation. Recurrent, intrusive, and distressing recollections were noted, as were dreams related to the events, and intense psychological distress when exposed to either internal or external cues that symbolized or resembled any aspect of the trauma. Among this patient group, persistent avoidance of stimuli associated with the trauma and numbing of general responsiveness were noted. Most specifically, there was inability to recall important aspects of the traumatic amputation, diminished interest in participation in some of life's significant activities, and some feeling of detachment and avoidance with respect to activities, people, or places related to the recollection of the trauma.

In examining personality change as a result of traumatic amputation, two types of personality were identified as related to the posttrauma experience of the individuals in the study. The two types were identified as the asthenic and sthenic. Patients identified in the first group (asthenic personality disorders) were characterized by subdepressive and psychosomatic symptoms. They also had symptoms which could be related to the chronic form of PTSD, such as persistent avoidance of events or people associated with the trauma, nightmares associated with the trauma, and flashbacks. The vegetative component of asthenia was also noted in these patients. It was displayed through symptoms such as hyperhydrosis, lability of blood pressure and pulse, vertigo, sense of "pounding heart," a burning sensation, and numbness in the stomach. Conversion disorders were related to a hysteroasthenic cluster of symptoms including crying spells with elements of hysteria and depression. In everyday life these patients often showed reticence, avoidance of contact with others, loss of interest in everyday activities, and self-imposed restrictions and indifference to various activities.

Patients in the second group (sthenic) were characterized by increased activity, excitability, and a combination of hostile and aggressive behaviors. These patients were significantly more active, craved for different forms of activity, and desired to overcome all challenges. In some cases, these behaviors promoted the achievement of successful results in adapting to prosthetic appliances. There were improved levels of concentration noted, and greater compliance with management and care of their traumatic experience. Other characteristics noted among this more sthenic group were individuals who were more litigious and compensation seeking.

Results obtained on the SCL-90 are summarized in Table 11.1 and are compared for the two subtypes of personality disorders noted, that is, asthenic and sthenic. There was a control group drawn from a normal (i.e., nonamputee) population. Note that the results suggest that the asthenic group shows greater somatization, obsessive–compulsive disorder, interpersonal sensitivity, depression, anxiety, and phobic anxiety, than does the sthenic group. The sthenic group, or type 2, had higher scores on psychosis, paranoid ideation, and hostility.

TREATMENT AND REHABILITATION PROCEDURES

In addressing treatment and rehabilitation of traumatic amputation patients, a combination of psychotherapy and psychopharmacology were offered. The use of individual psychotherapy for

TABLE 11.1

SCL-90 Classified Diagnosis for Asthenic, Sthenic, and Normal Control Groups for Traumatic Amputees

Scale	I Type Asthenic	II Type Sthenic	III Type Control Group
Somatization	2.32	0.90	0.72
Ob.-Comp.	2.79	1.51	0.96
Interp. Sens.	3.08	2.45	0.96
Depression	2.95	1.65	1.12
Anxiety	2.86	2.33	0.83
Hostility	0.74	3.38	0.68
Phobic Anxiety	3.00	2.43	0.48
Paranoid Id.	1.07	2.43	0.73
Psychoticism	0.71	0.97	0.43

these patients to help them adapt to the traumatic experience was found to be useful, as were the use of pharmacological agents such as low-dose neuroleptics, antidepressants, and tranquilizers. Where there was a delay in treating patients in either group, greater psychopathology seemed to be present.

Horowitz (1974) has noted that traumatizing events often destroy an individual's perception of reality. Survivors of trauma, such as traumatic amputees, experience symptoms in an identifiable series of stages. Miller, Kraus, Kamenchenko, and Krasnianski (1993) discuss the Trauma Accommodation Syndrome wherein individuals such as traumatic amputees have extreme difficulty in discussing various aspects of their traumatizing experience. The initial stage involves the traumatic amputation itself. This is followed by a stage which addresses both physical impact as well as the emotional or psychological components to readjustment. The next phase is one of cognitive disorganization and confusion. In this stage, there is marked vagueness and uncertainty, possibly denial, withdrawal, and isolation. Many of these symptoms were to be found in the asthenic group in this study. Usually through some triggering event there is a therapeutic reevaluation and reconsideration. In this stage, the individual reexperiences both the physical trauma and the emotional difficulties

in adjustment. The final phase is one of accommodation or resolution, wherein the patient has been able through supportive psychotherapy to deal with the issues related to the traumatic
amputation, and the realization and understanding of the impact
of this stressor on life adjustment.

FUTURE DIRECTIONS

Clinical research on a cross-cultural level needs to address both
the diagnostic and therapeutic aspects of traumatic amputation.
It is recommended that cross-cultural clinical research address
personality components, neurobiological markers in adaptation,
and cultural and environment differences, and the processing
and accommodating of stressful life experiences realized in traumatic amputation.

REFERENCES

American Psychiatric Association (1987), *Diagnostic and Statistical Manual of Men-
    tal Disorders*, 3rd ed. rev. (DSM-III-R). Washington, DC: American Psychiat-
    ric Press.
Derogatis, L. R. (1975), *The SCL-90-R.* Baltimore: Clinical Psychometric Re-
    search.
——— (1977), *SCL-90-R Administration, Scoring and Procedures Manual*, Vol. 1.
    Baltimore: Clinical Psychometric Research.
——— Lipman, R. S., & Covi, L. (1973), SCL-90: An outpatient psychiatric
    rating scale—Preliminary report. *Psychopharmacol. Bull.*, 9:13–25.
Frierson, R. L., & Lippmann, S. B. (1987), Psychiatric consultation for acute
    amputees. *Psychosomatics*, 28(4):183–189.
Galenko, V. E. (1986), Psychosomatic disorders in patients with amputations.
    *Issues of the Academy of Medical Sciences of USSR. References of Scientific Research-
    ers*, 4:77–78.
Grunert, B. K., Devine, C. A., & Matloub, H. S. (1988), Flashbacks after traumatic
    hand injuries: Prognostic indicators. *J. Hand Surgery*, 13a(1):125–127.
Horowitz, M. J. (1974), Stress response syndromes. *Arch. Gen. Psychiatry*,
    31:768–781.

—— Field, N. P., & Classen, C. C. (1993), Stress response syndromes and their treatment. In: *Handbook of Stress*, ed. L. Goldberger & S. Breznitz. New York: Macmillan, pp. 757–775.

Keane, T. M. (1988), Development of the Mississippi Scale for PTSD. *J. Consult. & Clin. Psychol.*, 56:85–90.

—— Malloy, P. F., & Fairbank, J. A. (1984), Empirical development of an MMPI subscale for the assessment of combat-related posttraumatic stress disorder. *J. Consult. & Clin. Psychol.*, 52:881–891.

Krinichanskii, A. V. (1977), Psychological adaptation and a system of psychotherapy in the rehabilitation of patients with limb amputations. Dissertation work, Kharkov.

Miller, T. W., Ed. (1989), *Stressful Life Events: Clinical Readings in Health Care Delivery*. Madison, CT: International Universities Press.

—— Başoğlu, M. (1992), Post-traumatic stress disorder: The impact of life stress events on adjustment. *Integrat. Psychiatry*, 8:209–217.

—— Kamenchenko, A., & Krasnianski, A. (1992), Assessment of life stress events: The etiology and measurement of traumatic stress disorder. *Internat. J. Soc. Psychiatry*, 38:672–676.

—— Kraus, R. J., Kamenchenko, P., & Krasnianski, A. (1992), Assessment of PTSD in Soviet and American Veterans. Paper presented at 25th International Congress of Psychology, Brussels, Belgium, July 19–24.

—— —— Krasnianski, A., & Kamenchenko, P. (1993), Post-traumatic stress disorder in U.S. and Russian veterans. *Hosp. & Commun. Psychiatry*, 44(6):585–589.

Parkes, C. M. (1972), Components to the reaction of loss of a limb. *J. Psychosom. Res.*, 16:343–349.

—— (1975), Psychosocial transition: Comparison between reactions of loss of a limb and loss of a spouse. *Brit. J. Psychiatry*, 127:204–210.

Soloviova, M. V. (1986), Psychological symptoms of veterans of the Patriotic War with traumatic amputations. *Psihosomaticheskie Pastroistva* (Moscow), pp. 93–101.

Spitzer, R. L., & Williams, J. B. (1987), *Structured Clinical Interview for DSM-III (SCID)*. New York: Biometrics Research Department, New York State Psychiatric Institute.

Weitbrecht, K. (1963), *Psychiatrie im Gundriss* (Psychiatric Aspects of Amputation). Berlin, pp. 95–126.

Zalkind, E. M., Wittakouer, E., & Parks, J. (1987), Clinical structure of psychopathological syndromes in traumatically injured patients. Trends of the Central Institute of Psychiatry, Russian Ministry of Health, Moscow, pp. 271–279.

Chapter 12
The Relationship Between Alcohol and Life Stress

BRYAN M. JOHNSTONE, Ph.D., THOMAS F. GARRITY, Ph.D., AND ROBERT STRAUS, Ph.D.

The primary purpose of this chapter is to examine perceptions and evidence regarding relationships between the uses and abuses of alcohol and the experience of emotions such as stress, tension, and anxiety and of situations that are considered stressful life events.

The assumption that alcohol is an effective, frequently used, and expected response to stress is well ingrained in the folk beliefs of our society. It is implied in many aspects of work culture, including the martini lunch, the after work beer, the cocktail on reaching home. It is perceived as expected in association with activities such as diplomacy, jobs away from a home base, particularly dangerous occupations, politics, and sudden loss of a job. It has long been supported and reinforced by portrayals in novels, plays, movies, and television that relate reaching for a drink, offering a drink, or getting drunk as usual or appropriate responses to a wide variety of stressful situations.

Basic questions that we will address include: To what extent do people intentionally use alcohol as an antianxiety, tension-reduction, stress-response substance, or as a way of responding to stressful life events? Do people who use alcohol for these reasons achieve satisfaction? Does the use of alcohol in response to stress constitute a particular risk for either intoxication or the development of alcohol dependence? Is the relation between alcohol use and stress a two-way street? To what extent and under what circumstances may drinking cause or exacerbate tension, anxiety, or stress? To what extent are drunkenness and alcohol dependence stressful life events? Does the stress–alcohol relationship vary according to historical and cultural context, sociodemographic status, and position in the life course?

Beliefs and practices that relate alcohol use to stress reduction appear to be as old as the uses of alcohol itself, and these can be traced to before the beginnings of recorded history and to many diverse cultures. The Bible, a source of many references to alcohol, both positive and negative, includes the following advice: "Give strong drink to the desperate and wine to the embittered; such men will drink and forget their poverty and remember their trouble no longer" (Proverbs 31:6–7). In the 1940s, when the modern scientific study of both alcohol and the concept of stress were gaining momentum, there was a prevalent, unquestioned assumption that a major reason why people used alcohol was in order to relieve or reduce anxiety, tension, and stress. This assumption was supported by available historical documents, by then current perceptions about alcohol's pharmacological properties, and by the then available evidence in anthropological, psychological, and sociological writings.

An assumption that people often use alcohol in response to particularly stressful situations or life events was succinctly stated in 1978 by Ewing and Rouse: "People in general who find themselves in stressful situations may be at high risk of becoming heavy drinkers regardless of their age, ethnic group or sex. Such circumstances include divorce, separation, adverse job changes, or the death of a loved one. In addition, drinkers who find themselves relocated to unfamiliar places without friends tend to increase their drinking. Those moving from small towns or rural areas into large cities are especially vulnerable" (p. 360). During the past 50 years, a substantial empirical literature has emerged that has enhanced our understanding of alcohol use and alcohol problems and has extended and refined our conceptualization of stress.

Versatility of Alcohol

Alcohol is a remarkably versatile substance. Unlike all other psychoactive drugs, it is also very high in caloric value, and, as such, it has been a significant source of food and human energy. As a drug, alcohol has a long list of properties. It is both an analgesic and anesthetic and, used externally, an antiseptic. Its use for these purposes made possible the beginnings of modern surgery. Alcohol has long been perceived as producing effects that are similar to what we now call tranquilizers or antianxiety drugs. For some people it appears to have a disinhibiting effect. Although it is generally classified as a sedative–depressant drug, the immediate effects of small amounts appear to provide a stimulating effect for some users. Alcohol is also a very toxic substance. Even small amounts can produce irritation of the tissues of the gastrointestinal tract and destroy cells of the organs involved in its metabolic process. Its most obvious toxic effects occur in the brain where, as an intoxicant, it can compromise such vital functions as perception, judgment, motor control, and memory. As a food, because of its high caloric value, alcohol has been widely used to quickly replenish the human energy expended in heavy physical labor. Relative to many other kinds of food, the calories of alcohol are cheap to transport and are not subject to spoilage. Thus, historically, alcohol was often used to reduce the stresses of both hunger and thirst. It was especially significant for military, maritime, and exploration activities which often involved both great effort and the need to transport food over long distances requiring long periods of time.

Paradoxes of Alcohol

In addition to its considerable versatility, alcohol is a paradoxical substance, a fact that is particularly relevant to a consideration of alcohol and stress, because it may help explain some of the inconsistencies that have been found by those who have attempted to study this relationship.

As a food, although high in caloric value and functional for quenching hunger and thirst, alcohol contains virtually none of the other nutrients that are required by the human body. For this reason, people who have relied too much on alcohol at the expense of other foods have been particularly vulnerable to the stresses and diseases of malnutrition. Only 50 years ago, prevailing scientific thought assumed that the only impacts of alcohol abuse on health were diseases caused by alcohol induced malnutrition and some relatively minor consequences of unhygienic living (Haggard and Jellinek, 1942).

As noted above, in small amounts shortly after ingestion, alcohol can provide a sensation of stimulation; yet, its ultimate effect is sedation and depression. As a sedative, alcohol can help induce sleep; yet, such sleep is often restless and unsatisfying. Although alcohol is an effective analgesic drug, its toxic properties can irritate or injure human tissues causing such problems as gastritis, pancreatitis, and other sources of human pain and discomfort.

In many contemporary societies, alcohol's mood modifying functions are perceived as its most sustaining virtue. By relaxing inhibitions, for some drinkers it facilitates their engaging in and enhances their perceived enjoyment of social functions; yet, in some drinkers and in amounts that for them are excessive, it can help release aggression, indiscretion, and other violations of social amenity, propriety, or law. As a tranquilizing or antianxiety drug, alcohol can provide a sense of well-being and enable some users to face situations they perceive as threatening; yet, in some drinkers, in amounts that for them are excessive, it can produce a sense of unwellness, tension, and acute psychic distress. By suppressing inhibitions and anxiety, alcohol can help enhance sexual desire and capacity; yet, as many have noted, too much alcohol can deflate sexual performance or destroy sexual enjoyment. Alcohol can help people face and undertake tasks that they perceive as difficult or dangerous. It can also seriously impair their capacity to fulfill such tasks successfully.

These paradoxes of alcohol involve a complex interaction of pharmacological, biological, psychological, cultural, and social factors. They rest in part on the fact that, for the individual user, different doses of alcohol produce quite different effects. Contrary to the hopes of many users, if two drinks are good, four drinks are not necessarily better. In part, the paradoxes are complicated by varying customs or circumstances that prescribe different kinds of behavior associated with alcohol. The effects produced by alcohol that may be acceptable or reasonably harmless in some situations may be clearly unacceptable or dangerous in other circumstances. In part, they reflect the considerable variability among individual human beings in their capacities to use alcohol safely. Amounts of alcohol that may be considered "small" for some individuals are clearly "too much" for others. There are also widely varying cultural norms with respect to how much would be considered "smaller" or "larger."

The paradoxes of alcohol are also a reflection of changes that have been occurring for many years in the relative functions and liabilities of alcohol that are a result of the changing nature of human societies and human activities and the changing chemical environment in which alcohol is used. Prior to the industrial revolution, a majority of human beings spent much of their waking time in activities that consumed a large amount of energy but were relatively routine. Under such conditions, the value of alcohol as a source of energy was much greater and the liabilities of alcohol intoxication were much less than they are today. For more than a century, however, with increasing acceleration, the activities of human beings have become more sedentary while the tasks that people perform have become ever more demanding of such brain functions as judgment, motor control, perception, memory, and rapid decision making, all of which can be severely compromised by alcohol.

Just 50 years ago, when people spoke of intoxication they meant alcohol intoxication. Although many other psychoactive drugs were in use, such practices were neither widespread or widely recognized while the toxic effects of industrial chemicals were not paramount in the public conscience. The past half-century has witnessed substantial changes in the chemical environment in which alcohol is used, and in the liabilities of alcohol when it interacts with other chemicals which drinkers may be consuming, medicinally or nonmedicinally, or to which they may be exposed from industrial sources. Of special significance medicinally are the antianxiety, antihistamine, and other mood modifying and/or sedative medicines which are now used by millions of persons and have the potential for synergistic interactions with alcohol. Nonmedicinally, the drug culture that has emerged since the 1960s has involved waves of powerful illegal substances that have been used in epidemic proportions with a confusing and ever changing relationship to alcohol use.

VARIABILITY OF HUMAN RESPONSES TO ALCOHOL

An additional characteristic of alcohol that has complicated our efforts to study the relationship between alcohol and stress, is the evidence of wide variability in the ways in which different people respond to alcohol. Some of these differences appear to be biologically determined and of a genetic nature; some involve body weight and the distribution of body fat and water; others reflect differences in exposure to alcohol and the cumulative experiences of drinking; still others involve the beliefs and expectations of the alcohol users. There are also sexual differences that reflect a number of biological and sociocultural variables. Clearly, there are some people for whom even small amounts of alcohol produce such unpleasant effects on their body and mind that alcohol is a producer rather than a reducer of stress. All drinkers have their limits where the paradoxical characteristics of alcohol set in and pleasant effects give way to distressing or dangerous ones. Of special relevance is the fact that people vary widely in terms of how much alcohol they can comfortably consume and how much is too much. Variability in responses to given amounts of alcohol is not limited to differences between drinkers, but there are also significant variations of response experienced by individual drinkers according to such factors as age, time of day, health status, levels of fatigue, the concentration of alcohol in the beverages they are consuming, how rapidly they drink, the presence when drinking of foods, medicines, or other psychoactive substances, the social and physical environment in which they are drinking, their expectations for a particular drinking situation, and their cumulative experience with drinking. Factors of individual variability in response to alcohol are particularly relevant to a consideration of studies of alcohol and stress reduction for they may help account for inconsistent or inconclusive findings.

INITIAL SCIENTIFIC ASSUMPTIONS—ALCOHOL STUDIES

As we have noted above, most of the scientific study of alcohol use and alcohol problems has taken place within the past 50 years. Because many contemporary beliefs about alcohol are influenced by assumptions that prevailed in the 1940s, it is important to identify these beliefs.

In 1942, in a critical review of the then available scientific literature on alcohol's effects on the individual, E. M. Jellinek identified alcohol use to reduce anxiety as a common motive for what he called normal drinking (p. 11). He also identified heightened anxiety as a common concomitant of what he called pathological intoxication, including delirium tremens and acute alcohol hallucinosis (pp. 93, 98–99, 138). Also in 1942, the medical historian Howard W. Haggard together with Jellinek published a book for the lay reader entitled *Alcohol Explored* in which they suggested that the anxiety and stress associated with the widespread technologically induced unemployability brought about by the industrial revolution led to excessive drinking and alcohol addiction on a major scale. Along with feelings of frustration, humiliation, and hopelessness "these men and women were dominated by their anxieties and they drowned their anxieties in alcoholic intoxication" (p. 161). They noted that anxiety to some degree is present in all excessive drinkers and that "many modern psychiatrists, psychologists and sociologists have been inclined to view addiction, and indeed all excessive drinking, as a manifestation of anxiety" (p. 161).

This commonly held view of "experts" in the 1940s was further demonstrated in Jellinek's 1945 volume that included 29 lectures that had been presented at the Yale Summer School of Alcohol Studies the year before. In this volume, Jellinek introduced what others later labeled the "tension reduction theory" of drinking. After referring to the many normal experiences of life in society that tend to produce tensions and anxiety, and the socially recognized need for relief from tension, he noted, "through the use of alcohol this desired relaxation of tension is achieved" (p. 17). In a chapter on the functions of alcohol in primitive societies, anthropologist Donald Horton (1945) summarized: "alcohol appears to have the very important function throughout the world, in all kinds and levels of human social activity, of reducing the inevitable anxieties of human life . . . alcohol solves the problem of anxiety-reduction" (pp. 161–162). In his discussion of alcohol use in complex contemporary societies, sociologist Selden D. Bacon (1945) suggested that the many problems of living in complex societies are even more difficult, anxiety-provoking, and exhausting than in simpler societies, and that "since alcohol can reduce the impact, can allow escape from the tensions, fears, sensitivities, feelings of frustration, which constitute this insecurity, its role will be even more highly valued" (p. 192).

Additional references in this volume assumed that alcohol use is related to stresses experienced in marriage and the family and those associated with poverty. (Drinking by women, African Americans, and other minorities and special populations was not much studied at this time, although a 1937 paper by Wall had suggested that stressful life events were significant in the development of alcoholism in women.) The overall impression for the reader of these lectures is a general assumption, supported by scientific thinking of the day, that a significant function of alcohol consumption in human societies is the reduction of feelings of tension and anxiety, and a response to stressful events that cause these feelings.

A year later, sociologist Robert Freed Bales (1946) published a now classic article on "Cultural Differences in Rates of Alcoholism" in which he suggested that high rates of heavy drinking and alcohol-related problems among males of Irish descent can be traced to the culturally condoned use of alcohol in response to the stresses imposed by a unique combination of economic, religious, and family norms that prevailed in nineteenth century rural Irish society. Of interest is the extent to which strong feelings of ambivalence may have served as a significant stressor. Relatively low rates of alcohol problems among traditional Jewish and Italian cultures were ascribed in part to the fact that prevailing beliefs, norms, and customs for alcohol use either rejected or did not accord importance to alcohol use for tension or stress reduction.

Animal model experiments of the 1940s supported the thesis that alcohol has significant tension-reduction properties and also suggested that alcohol used in this way could reinforce the development of addiction. In 1946, Masserman and Yum reported an experimental study with cats demonstrating that paralyzing anxiety induced by an imposed conflict situation could be overcome by the use of alcohol. Oversimplified and popularized, this thesis was frequently cited in the late 1940s to support the alcohol–stress reduction assumption. Further support was provided by John Conger (1951) through experiments with albino rats that demonstrated the effect of alcohol in the resolution of approach–avoidance conflicts.

PUBLIC PERCEPTIONS

Through much of the 1940s, American society was rebounding from the years of Prohibition and for half of the decade the country was at war. Most people did not want to think about alcohol

problems, and there were certainly more pressing issues competing for attention. As noted earlier, the media repeatedly depicted
alcohol use, and often drunkenness, as normal and usually haz-
ard-free responses to stressful situations. This was also a period,
when, perhaps in justification for repeal of the eighteenth amend-
ment, there was widespread denial of alcohol problems. It was
popularly assumed that alcoholism was a problem pretty well con-
fined to chronically arrested public inebriates, to the homeless
men who frequented skid row districts, and to those who popu-
lated the large institutions that were used for the incarceration
of persons diagnosed as "mentally ill." This popular stereotype
was reinforced by the fact that the few available descriptions of the
characteristics of "alcoholics" had been made with the captive
populations of skid row shelters, mental hospitals, and jails. Another common stereotype was that the road to alcoholism, and
hence to "hitting bottom," was paved with misfortunes such as
loss of a job, death of a dear one, dissolution of a family, or onset
of a disability. These events, it was assumed, had "driven" the
alcoholic to "drink." Such events, which tended to absolve the
alcoholic from blame for his drinking, were often the first explanations or excuses they offered when discussing their own
problems.

The stereotype that drinking precipitated by stressful events
had been the "downfall" of conspicuously heavy drinkers of skid
row was tested in studies conducted in the mid-1940s in New
Haven and New York City (Straus, 1946; Straus and McCarthy,
1951). There, based on interviews with about 650 men, it was
found that the vast majority had not experienced dramatically
significant stressful life events unless these were their social status
at birth and their poverty and life deprivations ever since. A majority of these men had been deprived of the opportunity of growing
up in a stable two-parent family. Many had experienced institutional living in their childhood and/or adolescence. Relatively
few had sustained educational experiences. A majority were un-
dersocialized and dependent, unskilled in making decisions, exerting initiative, and adapting to family or community living.
Their drinking was not in response to a particularly stressful

event, but more a way of dealing with the pains, anxieties, and tensions of their daily living. For many, when relieved of such stresses by incarceration in a jail or other institution, the desire or need for alcohol temporarily abated.

The stereotype of alcoholism as a problem primarily of social and mental misfits was exploded in the 1940s by the emergence of Alcoholics Anonymous (AA) and of specialized alcoholism treatment programs. It was quickly apparent that a majority of persons who sought help through these resources were neither destitute or deranged (although for many years the AA approach continued to assume that many candidates had to "hit bottom" before they would be ready to begin recovery). In 1951, Straus and Bacon published a study of the first 2023 male patients who had been seen in the first nine specialized alcoholism treatment clinics that had been established in the United States. Contrary to the stereotypes, "this study revealed a significant and hitherto unrecognized segment of alcoholics who display a relatively high degree of social and occupational integration" (p. 28). Half of these men were married and living with their wives; three-fourths were living in established households; 9 out of 10 had lived in their present towns of residence for at least 2 years; nearly two-thirds were gainfully employed; 56 percent had held steady jobs for at least 3 years and 25 percent for at least 10 years. For 7 out of 10, their jobs involved significant skills or responsibilities. Because the study identified a segment of alcoholics who had maintained, despite their alcoholism, a high degree of family, community, and occupational integration, it helped initiate a modification of the way in which alcoholics were perceived. Of particular significance was that alcoholism and its complications, not precipitating factors, were often the most significant stressful events in the lives of many of these men. In 1958, Selden Bacon emphasized that there are fundamental differences between the phenomenon of drinking and that of alcohol use by those who become dependent on alcohol. By 1960, Jellinek was emphasizing that alcohol, as consumed by alcoholics, was in fact precipitating rather than relieving strong anxiety (pp. 61–62, 145–146).

THE PARADOX OF ALCOHOL AND INDIVIDUAL VARIABILITY

At this point, the purpose of our earlier discussions of the paradoxical effects of alcohol and of individual variability should be clear. Because alcohol is a "two-edged sword" it can both alleviate and contribute to feelings of tension, stress, and anxiety. It may be used as a response to some stressful life event, but when used to produce incidental intoxication or addiction, its use can cause or constitute a stressful event. Because of variability both between individuals and for given individuals in their responses to given amounts of alcohol, generalizations regarding how much alcohol is "good" and "safe" can be misleading or dangerous. The issue is confounded by the fact that the variable responses of individuals are influenced not only by biological differences, but by psychological factors such as expectations, prior experience and mood, by sociocultural norms governing a particular drinking situation, and by the protections or liabilities for drinking in a particular environment or social setting. The relevance of these factors to questions of stress and alcohol will become even more apparent as we proceed to an overview of research that has addressed this relationship in recent decades.

RECENT DIRECTIONS

Research on the relationship between stress and alcohol has developed in an enormous variety of directions since the 1950s. Many of the confident assertions of early studies have received fundamental challenges. Today, we have a much greater appreciation of the multidimensionality of both sides of the stress–alcohol paradigm and the complexity of connections between these phenomena. The contingent character of alcohol's effects on the individual is now fully recognized. High levels of variability between persons in their sensitivity to alcohol, including "stress dampening" effects, have been repeatedly observed in experimental studies. The biological, psychological, and social sources of such diversity are still poorly understood in many cases. However, there is increasing awareness of the influence of multiple factors on the response to alcohol, including dose, physiological state of the organism, prior drinking history, exposure to other drugs, and family history of alcohol dependence. Recently, we have also begun to understand how cultural and individual beliefs or expectancies about the effects of alcohol shape our experiences when we drink. Basic assumptions about the impact of chronic stressors or stressful life events on alcohol use and the risk of dependence have also come under increasing scrutiny. Finally, we have begun to ask how social context affects the association between stress and reliance upon alcohol.

The accumulation of evidence during recent decades has resulted in a progressive narrowing of "tension reduction theory" as the fundamental explanation for drinking and the primary pathway to alcohol addiction. Cappell and Greeley (1987) have observed that it is now obvious that stress reduction is only one of multiple motives for alcohol use (p. 46). It is also clear that alcohol consumption can *increase* as well as reduce tension, especially at high doses during single drinking occasions or as a consequence of chronic heavy consumption. Experimental studies of the pharmacologic effects of alcohol additionally highlight the importance of "individual differences" in sensitivity to alcohol. For example, it has been argued that the tension-reducing properties of alcohol are most effective at moderate dosage levels (Cappell and Greeley, 1987). As we have emphasized, however, what qualifies as a moderate dose can vary greatly between persons, or even for the same individual under different circumstances or at different points in the life course. Recent experimental research on self-administration also emphasizes that differences between individuals in coping styles and expectations have a crucial influence on the likelihood of reliance on drinking as a response to stress. At the group level, the results of survey and other observational research also reinforce the notion of diversity in the relationship between tension and the use of alcohol. Studies have evaluated the differential effects of a variety of social and demographic factors on the tendency to turn to alcohol under stressful life circumstances. Variability is also the keynote in the results of studies of the effects of stressful social contexts on alcohol consumption and problems. Diverse findings have been obtained in research on alcohol use when individuals encounter stress in the workplace, in the family or social conditions of economic adversity or disaster. Recent research in each of these domains underscores the difficulties involved in making generalizations about the relationship between alcohol and stress.

The following sections briefly review contemporary directions in this research domain, with special reference to the influence of stressful life events on drinking. The growth of research on stress and alcohol has been explosive, so the coverage is necessarily highly selective. Discussion is broadly divided according to the following categories: (1) experimental studies on the tension-reducing properties of alcohol and alcohol self-administration under stress; (2) observational studies of sociodemographic variation in the relationship between stress and alcohol use; (3) studies of the influence of stressful life events on individuals' alcohol consumption and problems; (4) studies of the impact of societal stress on aggregate levels of alcohol consumption and problems; (5) clinical studies of stressful life events among alcohol dependent individuals.

Experimental Studies

Experimental research has continued on the twin questions of whether alcohol in fact reduces tension, and whether animals or humans drink alcohol to obtain these effects. There is a growing consensus that the anxiolytic effect of alcohol is in general "neither robust nor reliable" (Cooper, Russell, Skinner, Frone, and

Mudar, 1992, p. 139). Cappell and Greeley (1987) contend that this observation is probably a consequence of the diversity of alcohol's pharmacologic actions: "The simple conclusion is that even if alcohol is a tension reducing agent, it is a relatively ineffective one, primarily because it has other actions which negate its ability to reduce tension, especially at higher doses" (p. 48). Again, it is also crucial to recognize that the potency of alcohol's stress-reducing effects can vary dramatically between individuals. In part, this heterogeneity may be the result of biogenetic differences in sensitivity to alcohol's stress dampening effects (Sher and Levenson, 1982). A variety of other factors can also influence variability in response to alcohol. In addition to dose, the age, sex, and extent of physiological arousal of the organism may be important, as well as the history of exposure to alcohol and other drugs, the timing of the drinking event, and whether or not alcohol use is accompanied by the ingestion of food. Individual response to alcohol may also vary depending on the type of stressor applied and the outcome measures selected for evaluation. Experiments have applied a variety of strains, including conflict situations, noxious stimuli such as electric shocks, and social stressors such as verbal harassment or the requirement for self-disclosure. The evidence for a tension-reduction effect of alcohol varies substantially depending upon which stressor is under evaluation. Outcome variables selected to measure stress reduction in the subject have variously included self-reported anxiety, psychophysiological measures such as heart rate, blood pressure, and electrodermal activity, and biochemical outcomes such as alterations in plasma catecholamines. However, it is a common result that alternative outcomes within the same study may not be highly correlated with each other (Pohorecky, 1991).

Individuals also differ in the tendency to resort to alcohol under stressful circumstances. Recent attention has focused especially on the concept of expectancy. In the experimental context, expectancy generally refers to the instructional set given to individuals about whether they are receiving alcohol or a placebo. The instructions may or may not be valid. However, expectancies also refer to the beliefs about the effects of alcohol that individuals bring to the drinking occasion. These notions often develop at an early age and without personal experience of alcohol. Although results have not always been consistent, it is clear that the belief that alcohol relieves stress is an important concomitant of the decision to drink under stressful conditions (Goldman, Brown, and Christiansen, 1987). Differences in beliefs about the effects of alcohol may of course also help to explain why alcohol reduces tension for one individual but not another. Experimental studies have also illuminated other aspects of the "vulnerability" of individuals to use alcohol under stress. For example, some laboratory research suggests that alcohol use, as a general coping response, is invoked only when other effective coping mechanisms are unavailable to the subject (Sher, 1987). This suggests that persons who have limited adaptive coping responses and hold positive expectancies for alcohol's effects, may be especially vulnerable to excessive use of alcohol under stress (Cooper et al., 1992). In general, therefore, the results of laboratory research underscore that the effectiveness of alcohol as a tension reducer, and the decision to use alcohol to relieve tension are the products of a complex interaction of biological, psychological, and social factors.

OBSERVATIONAL STUDIES

Nonexperimental research on the general population provides another perspective on the relationship between stress and alcohol consumption and problems. The scope of this literature is imposing, encompassing both retrospective and prospective survey, epidemiologic, ethnographic, and historical studies. Efforts to examine the salience of tension reduction theory within particular social and demographic categories of persons have been especially important. Early tension reduction theory largely ignored the effects of social distinctions. As Pearlin (1989) has pointed out, however, sociodemographic status structures the likelihood of experiencing a stressor, the type of stressor encountered, the interpretation given to the experience, and the selection of a coping response. A growing literature has examined these questions in the alcohol field. Studies have asked whether drinking under stressful life circumstances differs as a consequence of gender, age, minority racial or ethnic status, sexual orientation, urbanicity, and religion. The results of this research suggest additional complexities in the relationship between stress and the use of alcohol.

The study of gender differences in the association between stressful life events and problem drinking provides one example. The idea that men and women differ in the precipitants of heavy drinking and alcohol dependence has a long history. Early small-scale studies of treatment populations, beginning with Wall (1937), suggested that women were especially vulnerable to develop alcohol problems as a consequence of the experience of stressful life events. This view was succinctly stated by Beckman in 1975: "Alcoholism and heavy drinking in women appear more likely to be linked to psychological stress and a specific precipitating circumstance or situation than is alcoholism or heavy drinking in men" (cited in Allan and Cooke, 1985, p. 147). Potential explanations for this difference have centered especially on stressful events unique to women or others presumed to affect them more deeply, including premenstrual tension, menopause, infertility, miscarriage or abortion, sexual dysfunction, marital conflict, and the "empty nest syndrome" accompanying the departure of children from the home. Allan and Cooke (1985) have criticized both the theoretical assumptions underlying this literature and the methodological limitations of early studies. While recognizing the limitations of prior studies, including her own, Gomberg's (1986) report on a study of psychosocial issues in alcoholism among women noted: "it is our contention that a very large proportion of the alcoholic women we studied carried into adult life habitual patterns of behavior that impaired their capacity to cope with the universal stresses of living . . . Life events and experienced distress appear to be relevant as triggers to female problem drinking. The high percentages of women who describe pre-onset painful life events suggest that we should not yet set aside stressors as precipitants of alcohol abuse" (p. 83). She concludes: "Triggering events appear to be no more or less than the stressors experienced by most people: loss, displacement, divorce, and the like. But the alcoholic woman was high risk before the events occurred and experiences such stresses with more distress than is true for others" (p. 89).

In general, however, recent research using larger samples and rigorous methodology has questioned many of the conclusions from early studies. For example, Cooke and Allan (1984) found no association between the experience of stressful life events and high intake of alcohol in a general population sample of Scottish women. Wilsnack, Klassen, Schur, and Wilsnack (1991), reporting results of a 5-year follow-up of a national sample of women in the United States, did confirm that the experience of sexual dysfunction was significantly associated with persistent problem drinking. However, marital dissolution and the departure of children from the home did not predict either the onset or the chronicity of problem drinking among women. Both of these events were more likely to follow than to precede alcohol problems. Even more surprising, divorce or separation during the interval of measurement actually *lowered* the risk that women who were problem drinkers at the initial measurement would continue to be alcohol dependent at the follow-up. Cooper et al. (1992), using a "stress vulnerability" model that explicitly controlled for differences between individuals in alcohol expectancies and coping styles, compared men and women directly with respect to the relationship between negative life events and alcohol use and problems. Stressful events were highly predictive of both alcohol consumption and drinking problems among men who held positive expectancies for alcohol's effects and were characterized by avoidant coping styles. Stressors were unrelated to drinking among women regardless of their expectancies or style of coping behavior. In fact, the direction of evidence from recent studies has shifted so much that Pohorecky (1991, p. 454) questions whether stress has any influence on alcohol consumption by women in her recent review of the literature.

It is of course premature to draw firm conclusions from this developing body of research; however, the naiveté of early assumptions is clear. The hypothesis that gender influences the relationship between alcohol and stress poses many methodological challenges, especially including identification of the direction and temporal priority of effects, control for individual differences in expectancies and coping behavior, and the possibility that men and women will differ in the way they attribute responsibility for drinking problems. Saunders (1980) has even suggested that historical confounds may be present in the literature. Recent decades have been characterized by significant increases in women's drinking. It is possible that under earlier conditions of restricted access to alcohol, stressful life events played a particularly important role in precipitating drinking problems among women. As women's drinking became increasingly normative, however, the determinants of alcohol problems among them may have changed. Future research must address these and other potential sources of variability in the relationship.

STUDIES OF STRESSFUL LIFE EVENTS AND ALCOHOL USE

Intensive study has also been directed toward the question of whether the stress associated with major life activities is related to alcohol consumption or problems. Both prospective and retrospective research has evaluated the influence of major normative "events" of the life course on drinking, including the transition from adolescence to adulthood, marriage and family, career, retirement, and the death of significant others. Survey research on the general population has indicated with relative consistency that marrying, having children, and becoming employed exert a moderating influence on heavy drinking and alcohol problems, although these relationships may vary by sex, age, or other factors

(Temple, Fillmore, Hartka, Johnstone, Leino, and Motoyoshi, 1991). Stress plays a significant role in the theoretical assumptions underlying this literature. It is presumed that the adoption of nonnormative developmental trajectories, the failure to achieve normative statuses, or the loss of these statuses is associated with significant levels of anxiety and may promote alcohol use. Thus, "negative" events such as remaining single, the loss of a job, or divorce, separation, and widowhood have received substantial study. Less attention has been directed to chronic stressors associated with "positive" events. For example, McLanahan and Adams (1987) have reviewed studies indicating that the responsibilities of parenthood are frequently associated with significant declines in happiness, life satisfaction, and other indices of psychological well-being. However, studies of stress and alcohol largely ignore this potential direction of influence.

The literature on drinking and employment is an exception. Research has separately evaluated the effects of stress on drinking behavior associated with the assumption of job responsibilities, stress on the job, and the loss of work through layoff, firing, or retirement (e.g., Trice, 1992). Although the belief that work stress and unemployment promote elevated alcohol consumption and problems is widespread both among scientists and the general public, the results of formal research on these questions are surprisingly problematic. In their review of the literature, for example, Cooper, Russell, and Frone (1990) conclude that no convincing empirical support exists for the hypothesis that work stress is associated with problem drinking. Recent research by these authors, which was explicitly designed to overcome the methodological limitations of prior studies, also failed to demonstrate substantial support for an association between stress on the job and increase in alcohol consumption or problems. The literature on the effects of unemployment on drinking behavior is also notoriously inconsistent. Crawford, Plant, Kreitman, and Latcham (1987) conclude that the body of studies on this topic can support each of the following conclusions: (1) unemployment increases alcohol use and abuse; (2) unemployment decreases alcohol use and abuse; (3) unemployment does not alter drinking behavior; and (4) some people drink more, some drink less, and some do not alter their consumption when they become unemployed.

The inconsistency of results on the association between the stresses of working and unemployment and drinking may be a consequence of analysts' pursuit of a general relationship between these factors that is valid across social groups, occupations, persons, and alcohol consumption outcomes. Research has frequently failed to adjust for potential confounds of the relationship at any of these levels. For example, studies of unemployment and drinking have evaluated a haphazard collection of populations which differ broadly in nationality, age, sex, social class, occupational characteristics, and cultural attitudes about drinking. Moreover, research on this topic has rarely taken note of the caution that drinking is associated with many motivations in addition to stress. An exception is Ames and Janes (1987) who examined the change in drinking in a sample of American blue-collar workers laid off from a manufacturing plant. Ethnographic interviews with these individuals revealed that their drinking had indeed changed, but the stresses of unemployment had little to do with the shift:

We believed we would find more heavy drinkers than in an employed group . . . however, we immediately discovered that the exact opposite was the case here; men reported reducing their consumption substantially, often from heavy to moderate levels, subsequent to the layoff. Due to the availability of substantial company, union, and state unemployment benefits, which kept workers' income levels near what they were prior to the layoff, reduction in consumption was not related to economic issues. Instead, our in-depth interviews revealed that the workplace environment and work-related social networks played a central role in the development and maintenance of heavy drinking practices. After forced departure from this environment, heavy drinking practices decreased. A picture of the workplace emerged from these interviews that suggested that heavy drinking had become a symbolically important and normative behavior for a significant proportion of the workers [p. 952].

These and other recent findings in this research domain confirm again that it is extremely difficult to generalize about the relationship between stressful life circumstances and alcohol consumption or problems. Consistency between the results of studies cannot be reasonably expected until investigators begin to adjust for variability at multiple levels of analysis.

AGGREGATE LEVEL STUDIES

A small set of studies has recently revived the question of whether stressful societal conditions are related to levels of alcohol consumption or problems. Such research asks whether economic depression or recession, rapid industrialization, cultural change, disasters, or other "stressful events" at the societal level are reflected in elevated levels of alcohol problems or other social pathologies. This literature is attended by many serious methodological difficulties, and considerable debate continues as to the interpretation of results. For example, Horton's (1943) pioneering cross-cultural comparison of drinking behavior in primitive societies reported significant correlations between alternative indices of stress and the frequency of intoxication. However, contemporary anthropological and historical research has cast doubt on many of the primary sources Horton relied upon. As Hill (1984) has noted, "Ethnohistorical studies . . . indicate that the conventional view that sees heavy drinking in native societies as exclusively or predominately produced, singularly or in combination, by sociocultural disorganization, economic deprivation, or psychological maladjustment is often overdrawn, if not flatly inaccurate" (p. 328).

Brenner (1973, 1975) initiated a major debate about the effects of national economic trends on levels of alcohol consumption and associated problems. Utilizing times series of aggregate level indicators, he argued that stress associated with economic downturns (indexed by unemployment) was associated with significant increases in alcohol consumption, particularly distilled spirits, and concomitant expansion in rates for a variety of alcohol problems including cirrhosis, arrest for intoxication, and hospital admissions for alcoholism. In a series of state level analyses, Linsky and associates (Linsky, Straus, and Colby, 1985; Linsky, Colby, and Straus, 1987) also reported significant correlations between stressful economic and other circumstances and levels of alcohol consumption and problems. Brenner's work and related aggregate level research on economic stress and alcohol use has come under intense methodological scrutiny, and the final interpretation of this question has not been resolved. From the standpoint of this discussion, however, the key point is that such research suggests that another level of analysis, that of the general societal context, may also influence variability in the relationship between stress and alcohol use.

CLINICAL STUDIES OF STRESS AND ALCOHOL DEPENDENCE

Studies of the significance of stressful life events in the onset and persistence of alcohol dependence require separate consideration. Stress continues to play an integral, if less prominent, role in contemporary popular and scientific understanding of alcohol dependence. There is no question that the incidence of stressful life events and alcohol addiction is strongly correlated. As a group, "alcoholics" experience more frequent, more severe, and more prolonged stress than nonalcoholics (Pohorecky, 1991). There is also relatively consistent evidence for an association between posttreatment stressful events and relapse to the use of alcohol among dependent individuals (O'Doherty and Davies, 1987). However, the attribution of cause and effect is especially difficult in this context. Several basic methodological issues can confound the interpretation of results. Most studies of the role of life events in alcohol addiction are retrospective in design.

Unfortunately, the validity of recalled information can be especially problematic among alcoholics. Of course, prolonged heavy intake of alcohol can result in serious disruption of memory and cognitive distortions in the interpretation of events. Perhaps more important is the general human tendency for "effort after meaning" to account for severe difficulties in life. Allan and Cooke (1985) note that the interpretation of experience involves an active reorganization of memory that can introduce significant distortions in autobiographical accounts. This makes it very difficult to evaluate the validity of retrospective statements attributing the onset of alcohol dependence to stressful life events.

Even if recalled information is valid, questions of the direction of causal influence and the temporal contiguity of events must still be resolved. The fact that alcohol is itself a stressor that can precipitate negative events is still insufficiently accounted for in many studies of the relationship between life events and alcohol addiction. For example, Dudley, Mules, Roszell, Glickford, and Hague (1977) reported a high incidence of stressful events prior to hospitalization in a sample of alcohol dependent individuals. O'Doherty and Davies (1987) point out that at least four of the seven major categories of events experienced by this group might as easily occur as a result of rather than being a cause of excessive alcohol use: serious personal illness, arrest and imprisonment, change in financial status, and marital dissolution. Tatossian, Charpy, Remay, Prinquey, and Poinso (1983) attempted to resolve the question of causal direction by asking subjects separately about events in the year prior to the onset of alcohol abuse, during the first year of abuse and during the subsequent 5 years. As a group, subjects reported a dramatic increase in stressful events during the year prior to the onset of excessive alcohol intake; their reported incidence of stressful events also remained "abnormally" high throughout the subsequent period of measurement. However, the retrospective design of this study does not address the other methodological issues already discussed. Additionally, few studies of alcoholics have controlled for temporal order and contiguity between stressful events and drinking outcomes. Studies of the impact of life events in other domains have indicated that their impact on other behavior decays as a function of time, and decline in influence may accelerate after 12 months have elapsed (Allan and Cooke, 1985). Research on stressful events and alcohol dependence has employed a chaotic miscellany of temporal frames, a circumstance that has probably contributed significantly to the inconsistency in results.

A final illustration of the potential paradoxes of the relationship between the experience of stressful events and alcohol dependence is given by the phenomenon of "spontaneous remission," that is, stopping alcohol dependence without the assistance of Alcoholics Anonymous or formal treatment. A logical question is whether individuals who spontaneously remit are aided by the cessation of some stressful factor in their lives. To the contrary, in several studies of such individuals, it has been found that the overwhelmingly most significant motivating factor was not the reduction or elimination of some stressor that had caused their drinking, but rather the fact that the stresses in their lives associated with or resulting from their alcoholism had become more than they could tolerate (Stall, 1979; Tuchfeld, 1981; Ludwig, 1985).

Research in areas previously discussed also raises other questions that have not been systematically addressed in studies of the role of stressful events in the development and maintenance of alcohol dependence. Are individuals at high risk for alcohol dependence either more or less sensitive to the tension-reducing properties of alcohol? Do positive expectancies for a tension reduction effect of alcohol contribute to the risk of developing dependence on alcohol? Do alcoholics differ from nonalcoholics with respect to the experience or interpretation of stressors or the coping styles with which they attempt to mediate stress? Does the causal significance of stressful events for the development of dependence vary between males and females, or as a function of other social factors? None of these questions has been fully addressed in studies to date.

In general, recent research on stress and alcohol has advanced our understanding in a number of key areas. The impact of differences between individuals along many dimensions of influence from the biological to the macrosocial on variability between the results of studies has become increasingly recognized. At present, we have a much greater appreciation for and comprehension of the complexity of the relationships between alcohol and stress. Knowledge in many areas is still highly incomplete, however.

Thus far, we have considered the relationship between stress and alcohol primarily from the perpective of the field of alcohol studies. We will now turn to a review of this topic from the perspective of stress-related research and the significance or usefulness of such a perspective to a better understanding of research that has addressed questions of alcohol and stress.

OVERVIEW COMMENTS

Even this highly selective review of the stress-alcohol literature should convey that the scope of research is unusually broad with substantial historical depth. Recent reviews already mentioned indicate that research activity on the stress–alcohol relationship includes variables at the biological, psychological, social, and cultural levels. In stress research, it is difficult to think of a health problem area other than alcohol consumption in which the full range of the biopsychosocial perspective is represented. Historically, we were also able to indicate that notions about connections between stress and alcohol can be found as early as biblical times, and that systematic research on the stress–alcohol connection was already ongoing in the 1940s.

Currently, the volume of publications on stress–alcohol connections is quite large. One reason for this is that several levels of analysis—biological, psychological, social, cultural—invite research attention. There are also several types of research design available to investigators, from the laboratory experiment to the population survey. Another explanation for the volume of research reports on the stress–alcohol connection is the variety of operationalizations of these two key variables. These are described next.

Stress is predominantly measured in this literature as major aversive life events and as ongoing negative life conditions. The former are significant happenings that require personal effort at readjustment after their occurrence; the latter are continuing situations that call for ongoing adaptation. Life events include undesirable happenings such as deaths, relationship breakups, natural disasters, and loss of employment. The chronic conditions would be represented by enduring situations such as job stress, relationship strain, and the like. There is an additional measure of stress that receives some attention: personal emotional distress, such as anxiety, depression, low sense of well-being, and various measures of negative mood. A fourth operationalization of stress that has not yet received much attention as a measure in alcohol research is the minor daily irritation or hassle.

Several approaches to measuring alcohol-relevant variables are also found. There are several indicators of extent of alcohol consumption. These are usually represented by quantity of beverage or absolute alcohol consumed per unit of time and frequency of drinking measured as counts of drinking occasions over time. Both quantity and frequency are sometimes represented as categories—abstainer through heavy consumer. There are also indicators of the presence of problem drinking, such as alcohol-related accidents, arrests, and referrals to dependency treatment centers, and there are indicators of alcohol dependency, such as fulfillment of DSM-IV-R criteria of alcohol addiction (APA, 1994). The number of possible combinations of bivariate relationships of these stress and alcohol use indicators may explain how the literature can be so large and still contradictory and inconclusive.

The inconclusiveness of the literature on the stress–alcohol connection is not absolute. The predominance of research reported in the past two decades finds significant relationships between indicators of stress and indicators of alcohol consumption or problems under at least some circumstances. These relationships are not yet so well replicated that the essential nature and direction of causal influence can be specified. Moreover, recent correlational research, the dominant analytic approach, consistently finds that conditional or moderating factors influence the strength of the stress–alcohol relationship.

Of all populations examined, studies of alcoholics have most consistently reported the relevance of stressful events and emotions to alcohol consumption behavior. It is especially clear that throughout the process of addictive drinking, problem drinking behavior, and stress are cooccurrent. So intertwined are the two that the direction of causal influence and the causal mechanisms have not yet been fully clarified.

As stated in the foregoing discussion, the vast majority of research designs have been correlational with the intent of demonstrating a potentially causal connection between stress and alcohol drinking variables. Moreover, most of these studies are highly dependent on retrospective self-reports of the major variables of interest. Consequently, the literature is not very far along in defining particular mechanisms that link stress and alcohol variables.

Progress toward understanding mechanisms will require the testing of more detailed causal models of the stress–alcohol process. Unfortunately, most available models linking stress and alcohol describe only segments of what stress researchers now generally understand to be a multistage, multidimensional process. The general model of Lazarus and his colleagues is a representation of such a model that permits the articulation of biological, individual, social, and cultural factors in the context of stress and coping (Lazarus, 1966; Lazarus and Folkman, 1984). As such, it provides a heuristically valuable road map for conceptualizing the interplay between stress and alcohol behaviors.

This general model describes a process that begins with the presentation of an event that may be "appraised" as either threatening or not based on a variety of factors that influence the judgment of the evaluator. If appraised as threatening, emotional arousal results with its cognitive and physiological elements. A secondary appraisal follows with a more or less conscious weighing of strategies suitable for dealing with both presenting threat and resultant arousal. To the extent that a selected coping strategy works, the threat of arousal is diminished.

The general model just described has rarely been used in the context of stress–alcohol research (for exceptions see Folkman,

Bernstein, and Lazarus, 1987; Huffine, Folkman, and Lazarus, 1989). Use of such a general model could provide several advantages. First, it could provide a common conceptual framework and vocabulary around which to integrate the variety of phases and levels of analysis represented in the literature. How, for example, do we include the influence of an abstract cultural assumption about the effects of alcohol, and the unique, individual, physical sensitivity of a person to alcohol into the same explanation of the stress–alcohol relationship? The general model, with its concept of secondary appraisal, might suggest that they come together as the individual weighs options for coping with a threatening and upsetting event.

A common conceptual framework would facilitate understanding of the relationship of various existing stress–alcohol models to one another. Currently available models of the stress–alcohol connection may be understood as representing parts of the general model. For example, a model described by Hull (1981) postulates that alcohol ingestion may dull self-awareness such that self-relevant, negative information is not appraised as threatening. In a related manner, Steele and Josephs (1988) describe an attention–allocation model of alcohol's effects on stress. They argue that ingested alcohol affects appraisal in a way that makes more likely the diversion of attention from potentially threatening stimuli to competing, nonthreatening ones. Both of these models deal with mechanisms affecting initial threat appraisal. Several representations of stress reduction models (Conger, 1956; Marlatt, 1976; Sher, 1987) describe a learned response springing from secondary appraisal in which alcohol ingestion is judged to reduce arousal. The work of Cooper and colleagues (Cooper, Russell, and George, 1988) also relates to the general model's secondary appraisal and coping segments: expectations about the powers of alcohol ingestion to meet certain external threats influence appraisals about appropriate coping strategies.

There are other related advantages to the use of a common general model of stress as a framework for stress–alcohol research. The model identifies an explicit junction at which biological and behavioral studies connect, namely, at the phenomenon of psychophysiological arousal. This would enable those who study stress, defined as subjective psychophysiological distress, to acknowledge the existence of another, antecedent type of stressor that generated the arousal state being studied. It would also help to keep producers and consumers of this research mindful of the heterogeneity of arousal with its species of psychological distress (e.g., anxiety, depression, anger) and physiological reactivity (e.g., cardiovascular, immunologic, hormonal).

Use of a general model would promote conceptualization of mechanistic studies that would take the literature beyond sheer correlational studies of associations of stress and alcohol-related phenomena. For example, use of a general model would promote questions such as: Why do men and women, adolescents and elderly, rural and urban residents appraise the threat potential of particular events differently? Why do these groups view alcohol consumption differently in terms of its usefulness as an anxiolytic? What beliefs about the usefulness of alcohol as a coping means affect the secondary appraisals of the unemployed? Distinctions about primary and secondary appraisals, and identification of arousal and coping in the same overarching model, promote clarifications of how and in what sequence factors come into play in the relationships of stress and alcohol.

REFERENCES

Allan, C. A., & Cooke, D. J. (1985), Stressful life events and alcohol misuse in women: A critical review. *J. Studies on Alcohol,* 46:147–152.

American Psychiatric Association (1994), *Diagnostic and Statistical Manual of Mental Disorders,* 4th ed. (DSM-IV). Washington, DC: American Psychiatric Press.

Ames, G. M., & Janes, C. R. (1987), Heavy and problem drinking in an American blue-collar population: Implications for prevention. *Soc. Sci. & Med.,* 25:949–960.

Bacon, S. D. (1945), Alcohol and complex society. In: *Alcohol, Science and Society.* New Haven, CT: Quarterly Journal of Studies on Alcohol, Inc., pp. 179–200.

——— (1958), Alcoholics do not drink. *Ann. Amer. Acad. Pol. & Soc. Sci.,* 315:55–64.

Bales, R. F. (1946), Cultural differences in rates of alcoholism. *Quart. J. Studies on Alcohol,* 6:480–499.

Beckman, L. J. (1975), Women alcoholics: A review of social and psychological studies. *J. Stud. Alch.,* 36:747–824.

Brenner, M. H. (1973), *Mental Illness and the Economy.* Cambridge, MA: Harvard University Press.

———— (1975), Trends in alcohol consumption and associated illnesses: Some effects of economic changes. *Amer. J. Pub. Health,* 65:1279–1292.

Cappell, H., & Greeley, J. (1987), Alcohol and tension reduction: An update on research and theory. In: *Psychological Theories of Drinking and Alcoholism,* ed. H. T. Blane & K. E. Leonard. New York: Guilford Press, pp. 15–54.

Conger, J. J. (1951), The effects of alcohol on conflict behavior in the albino rat. *Quart. J. Studies on Alcohol,* 12:1–29.

———— (1956), Reinforcement theory and the dynamics of alcoholism. *Quart. J. Studies on Alcohol,* 17:296–305.

Cooke, D. J., & Allan, C. A. (1984), Stressful life events and alcohol abuse in women: A general population study. *Brit. J. Addict.,* 79:425–430.

Cooper, M. L., Russell, M., & Frone, M. R. (1990), Work stress and alcohol effects: A test of stress-induced drinking. *J. Health & Soc. Behav.,* 31:260–276.

———— ———— George, W. H. (1988), Coping, expectancies, and alcohol abuse: A test for social learning formulations. *J. Abnorm. Psychol.,* 97:218–230.

———— ———— Skinner, J. B., Frone, M. R., & Mudar, P. (1992), Stress and alcohol use: Moderating effects of gender, coping, and alcohol expectancies. *J. Abnorm. Psychol.,* 101:139–152.

Crawford, A., Plant, M. A., Kreitman, N., & Latcham, R. W. (1987), Unemployment and drinking behaviour: Some data from a general population survey of alcohol use. *Brit. J. Addict.,* 82:1007–1016.

Dudley, D. L., Mules, J. E., Roszell, P. K., Glickford, G., & Hague, W. H. (1976), Frequency and magnitude distribution of life changes in heroin and alcohol addicts. *Internat. J. Addict.,* 11:977–987.

Ewing, J. A., & Rouse, B. A. (1978), An overview of drinking behaviors and social policies. In: *Drinking: Alcohol in American Society—Issues and Current Research,* ed. J. A. Ewing & B. A. Rouse. Chicago: Nelson-Hall, pp. 339–381.

Folkman, S., Bernstein, L., & Lazarus, R. S. (1987), Stress processes and the misuse of drugs in older adults. *Psychol. & Aging,* 2:366–374.

Goldman, M. S., Brown, S. A., & Christiansen, B. A. (1987), Expectancy theory: Thinking about drinking. In: *Psychological Theories of Drinking and Alcoholism,* ed. H. T. Blane & K. E. Leonard. New York: Guilford Press, pp. 181–226.

Gomberg, E. S. (1986), Women and alcoholism: Psychosocial issues. In: *Women and Alcohol: Health-Related Issues.* National Institute on Alcohol Abuse and Alcoholism Research Monograph No. 16, DHHS Publication No. (ADM) 86-1139. Washington, DC: Government Printing Office, pp. 78–120.

Haggard, H. W., & Jellinek, E. M. (1942), *Alcohol Explored.* New York: Doubleday, Doran.

Hill, T. W. (1984), Ethnohistory and alcohol studies. *Rec. Develop. in Alcohol.,* 4:313–337.

Horton, D. (1943), The functions of alcohol in primitive societies: A cross-cultural study. *Quart. J. Studies on Alcohol*, 4:199–320.

——— (1945), The functions of alcohol in primitive societies. In: *Alcohol, Science and Society*. New Haven, CT: Quarterly Journal of Studies on Alcohol, Inc., pp. 153–157.

Huffine, C. L., Folkman, S., & Lazarus, R. S. (1989), Psychoactive drugs, alcohol, and stress and coping processes in older adults. *Amer. J. Drug & Alcohol Abuse*, 15:101–113.

Hull, J. G. (1981), A self-awareness model of the causes and effects of alcohol consumption. *J. Abnorm. Psychol.*, 90:586–600.

Jellinek, E. M. (1942), *Alcohol Addiction and Chronic Alcoholism. Effects of Alcohol on the Individual*, Vol. 1. New Haven, CT: Yale University Press.

——— (1945), The problems of alcohol. In: *Alcohol, Science and Society*. New Haven, CT: Quarterly Journal of Studies on Alcohol, Inc., pp. 13–29.

——— (1960), *The Disease Concept of Alcoholism*. New Haven, CT: Hillhouse Press.

Lazarus, R. S. (1966), *Psychological Stress and the Coping Process*. New York: McGraw-Hill.

——— Folkman, S. (1984), *Stress, Appraisal, and Coping*. New York: Springer-Verlag.

Linsky, A. S., Colby, Jr., J. P., & Straus, M. A. (1987), Social stress, normative constraints and alcohol problems in American states. *Soc. Sci. & Med.*, 24:875–883.

——— Straus, M. A., & Colby, Jr., J. P. (1985), Stressful events, stressful conditions and alcohol problems in the United States: A partial test of Bales' theory. *J. Studies on Alcohol*, 46:72–80.

Ludwig, A. M. (1985), Cognitive processes associated with "spontaneous recovery from alcoholism." *J. Studies on Alcohol*, 46:53–58.

Marlatt, G. A. (1976), Alcohol, stress and cognitive control. *Stress & Anxiety*, 3:271–296.

Masserman, J. H., & Yum, K. S. (1946), An analysis of the influence of alcohol on experimental neurosis in cats. *Psychosom. Med.*, 8:36–52.

McLanahan, S. S., & Adams, J. (1987), Parenthood and psychological well-being. *Ann. Rev. Immunol.*, 5:237–257.

O'Doherty, F., & Davies, J. B. (1987), Life events and addiction: A critical review. *Brit. J. Addict.*, 82:127–137.

Pearlin, L. I. (1989), The sociological study of stress. *J. Health & Soc. Behav.*, 30:241–256.

Pohorecky, L. A. (1991), Stress and alcohol interaction: An update of human research. *Alcohol.: Clin. & Experiment. Res.*, 15:438–459.

Saunders, W. M. (1980), Psychological aspects of women and alcohol. In: *Women and Alcohol*, ed. Camberwell Council on Alcoholism. New York: Tavistock Publications, pp. 67–100.

Sher, K. J. (1987), Stress response dampening. In: *Psychological Theories of Drinking and Alcoholism*, ed. H. T. Blane & K. E. Leonard. New York: Guilford Press, pp. 227–271.

——— Levenson, R. W. (1982), Risk for alcoholism and individual differences in the stress-response-dampening effect of alcohol. *J. Abnorm. Psychol.*, 91:350–367.

Stall, R. D. (1979), *An Examination of Spontaneous Remission from Problem Drinking in the Bluegrass Area of Kentucky.* Unpublished master's thesis. University of Kentucky, Lexington, Kentucky.

Steele, C. M. & Josephs, R. A. (1988), Drinking your troubles away II: An attention-allocation model of alcohol's effect on psychological stress. *J. Abnorm. Psychol.,* 97:196–205.

Straus, R. (1946), Alcohol and the homeless man. *Quart. J. Studies on Alcohol,* 7:360–404.

———— Bacon, S. D. (1951), *Alcoholism and Social Stability.* New Haven, CT: Hillhouse Press.

———— McCarthy, R. G. (1951), Nonaddictive pathological drinking patterns of homeless men. *Quart. J. Studies on Alcohol,* 12:601–611.

Tatossian, A., Charpy, J. P., Remay, M., Prinquey, P., & Poinso, Y. (1983), Étude des événements dans la vie de 120 éthyliques chroniques étude preliminaire. *Annalés Medico-Psychologiques,* 141:824–841.

Temple, M. T., Fillmore, K. M., Hartka, E., Johnstone, B., Leino, E. V., & Motoyoshi, M. (1991), A meta-analysis of change in marital and employment status as predictors of alcohol consumption on a typical occasion. *Brit. J. Addict.,* 86:1269–1281.

Trice, H. M. (1992), Work-related risk factors associated with alcohol abuse. *Alcohol Health & Res. World,* 16:106–111.

Tuchfeld, B. S. (1981), Spontaneous remission in alcoholics: Empirical observations and theoretical implications. *J. Studies on Alcohol,* 42:626–641.

Wall, J. H. (1937), A study of alcoholism in women. *Amer. J. Psychiatry,* 93:943–952.

Wilsnack, S. C., Klassen, A. D., Schur, B. E., & Wilsnack, R. W. (1991), Predicting onset and chronicity of women's problem drinking: A five-year longitudinal analysis. *Amer. J. Pub. Health,* 81:305–318.

Part IV

Stressful Life Events and the Life Span

Chapter 13
Traumatic Events Over the Life Span: Survivors of the Buffalo Creek Disaster

BONNIE L. GREEN, Ph.D., TERESA L. KRAMER, Ph.D., MARY C. GRACE, M.S., GOLDINE C. GLESER, Ph.D., ANTHONY C. LEONARD, B.A., MARSHALL G. VARY, M.D., AND JACOB D. LINDY, M.D.

The present chapter focuses on a series of studies of survivors of the Buffalo Creek dam collapse and flood which our research group had the opportunity to conduct over nearly two decades. Survivors of all age groups were assessed 2 years after the disaster, and followed up in the second decade to assess any continuing impact of that event. While some of the separate information on subsamples of these survivors is available in other reports, here we attempt to synthesize them, focusing on how the impact of such an event may change over time, as well as how the particular life stage of the person, both at exposure to the disaster, and at follow-up, may affect their adaptation to the event. We are guided by theories of adult development, and especially by theorists who have conceptualized the impact of trauma across the life span rather than at a single point in time. We are fortunate to have

This work was supported by NIMH grants RO1 MH 26321 to Dr. Gleser, and grants RO1 MH 40401 and RO1 MH 42644 to Dr. Green.

both cross-sectional and longitudinal data to address these questions.

BACKGROUND

Laufer (1988) has written specifically about the impact of war trauma on the soldier over the life span. While some aspects of his conceptualization are quite specific to war stress, other aspects may be generalizable to survivors of other traumatic events. In his notion of the "serial self," Laufer (1988) argued that the young soldier develops an identity as a warrior for purposes of participating in combat. The warrior mentality, which accepts and promotes violent behavior in order to serve the society at large, is at odds with the individual's civilian identity. Society promotes the schism between these two identities. It strips him of the warrior identity upon his return, but he continues to have the war experience as part of his psyche on a permanent basis. Society is not interested in hearing what occurred during the war. Further, it cannot acknowledge the psychological cost of sending its young men to war if it would continue to do so. Thus, Laufer's hypothesis is that the core experience of the war exists in a vacuum and cannot be used to validate subsequent stages of the life course. Rather, it retains an autonomous existence and can disrupt the lifeline. The war self, then, is arrested developmentally at a point where it had a premature death encounter, and it stays, at some level, preoccupied with death and survival.

The warrior must then struggle to integrate these two selves (the warrior self and the civilian self). Laufer hypothesizes that this is a lifelong task. While some of the work may be done upon the warrior's return, it needs to be revisited each time he faces a major life transition and reassesses his values, goals, and so on. The adaptive (civilian) self is thus episodically vulnerable to the "pathology of the war self" and adaptation throughout the life course is structurally unstable. The interaction between the two "selves" at transitional periods is labeled by Laufer the "serial" self because the adaptive self is serially vulnerable to the war self.

While the clash between the self systems of the warrior and the civilian may not be totally applicable to disaster survivors, it is likely that disaster survivors, especially those who were extremely traumatized by the event via death encounters, retain an aspect of their personality that is connected with the earlier traumatic experience. Indeed, a number of trauma researchers and theoreticians have posited that the traumatic experience imposes a break in continuity from the earlier self, and that part of the task of recovery is to reestablish the continuity with the earlier self (e.g., Hendin and Haas, 1984; Danieli, 1985; Horowitz, 1986; Lifton, 1988). Other therapists view trauma as an event which shatters aspects of an individual's prior self—such as their assumptions about the world (Janoff-Bulman, 1992) or central organizing fantasies of the self or selfobject (Ulman and Brothers, 1988)—which must be reorganized or restored for healthy adaptation to occur. Some empirical work (Elder, 1986) also suggests that trauma may disrupt certain aspects of the psychological self so that the relationship between earlier and later functioning is less continuous in individuals exposed to military service. Not all changes in individuals in Elder's study were negative, however, a finding that may in part be explained by the function of the service for men in the lower socioeconomic levels.

Side by side with these notions of trauma recovery are those from both child and adult developmental psychology which suggest that certain life stages bring with them particular issues which must be negotiated (e.g., Erikson, 1950; Mahler, Pine, and Bergman, 1975; Levinson, Darrow, Klein, Levinson, and McKee, 1978). Individuals would be expected to be vulnerable to different events or aspects of events at these times. Such formulations suggest that individuals have the opportunity to rework issues and grow at each stage, or, conversely, to be less successful in negotiating a stage, resulting in negative consequences. No particular age, therefore, is universally vulnerable to all types of stresses. Actually, little research presently exists to support these developmental stages and their unique vulnerabilities, their sequences, and their specific ties with age (Strauss and Harding, 1990). There is some suggestion, however, that life stage may indeed influence the course of posttraumatic stress disorder (PTSD) symptoms. Van der Kolk and Ducey (1984) reported examples of World War II veterans of retirement age. Although these individuals had been free of nightmares and other trauma-related symptoms for years, their symptoms recurred when they no longer had the structure of a job.

The longitudinal course of symptoms following disaster has been studied in the relatively short term only. Most studies of adults have shown a decrease in symptoms over the first several years following disaster exposure. For natural disasters, this decrease often means a return to "normal" within this time period (e.g., Shore, Tatum, and Vollmer, 1986; Krause, 1987; Norris, Phifer and Kaniasty, 1994), while for technological disasters, residual symptoms may remain for longer periods. For example, Holen (1991) found persistent symptoms over an 8-year period in survivors of an oil rig collapse in the North Sea, where many coworkers were killed.

Longitudinal studies of children are less clear-cut. Some studies show improvement over time (e.g., Dollinger, 1985; Milgram, Toubiana, Klingman, Raviv, and Goldstein, 1988), while others show no improvement, or actually show symptoms worsening over time (e.g., Galante and Foa, 1986; McFarlane, 1987). Again, these follow-ups tend to be only for the first year or so following the event.

Longer follow-ups have been done on war-related events, and indicate that the emotional impact of a traumatic event may last for many years after the occurrence of the event. For example, Harel, Kahana, and Kahana (1988) showed that Holocaust survivors in Israel, compared to individuals who immigrated to Israel before the war, rated their health to be poorer, and reported greater severity of illness decades later, when survivors were in their sixties. Elder and Clipp (1988) showed persistent differences, after age 55, between World War II veterans exposed to heavy combat and those exposed to light or no combat with regard to stress symptoms and painful thoughts about military service. It has also been shown that PTSD in Vietnam veterans remained in about 15 percent of those who had served in that theater 15 to 20 years earlier (Kulka, Schlenger, Fairbank, Hough, Jordon, Marmar, Weiss, and Grady, 1988).

Cross-sectional studies have not allowed the examination of whether effects are associated with age at exposure, or with current age, since the two covary perfectly in these studies. However, a number of studies of adult disaster survivors have examined age as a risk factor for disaster-related negative psychological outcomes. These findings have tended to be mixed, with some studies showing no differences by age (e.g., Lima, Pai, Santacruz, Lozano, and Luna, 1987; Freedy, Shaw, Jarrell, and Masters, 1992), some showing younger individuals to be at higher risk (e.g., Huerta and Horton, 1978), and a few showing older people to be at higher risk (e.g., Wilkenson, 1983). These studies have used very different age groups to represent "older" and "younger" subjects, and many examined only linear relationships between age and outcome. Putting these findings together and taking into account the actual age groups used in the various studies, a plausible synthesis of the findings is that the relationship between age group and outcome is curvilinear, with "middle-aged" groups doing the worst.

Age-related findings for children show a somewhat consistent pattern. Regressive behaviors typically associated with younger children (e.g., bed-wetting, general phobias) tend to decrease with age (e.g., Milne, 1977; Blom, 1986), while anxiety and depression symptoms, and more global ratings of dysfunction, tend to increase with age (e.g., Seroka, Knapp, Knight, Siemon, and Starbuck, 1986). In an earlier review of these findings (Green, Korol, Grace, Vary, Leonard, Gleser, and Smitson-Cohen, 1991), we suggested that stress responses show a developmental progression in which younger children manifest a relatively disorganized traumatic state, where the disaster is not well-understood and responses are primarily mediated through parents. Older children display a more "adultlike" response, with increased understanding of the event (and associated losses) and more traditional PTSD symptoms.

THE PRESENT STUDY

In February 1972, the collapse of a slag dam built by a mining company was followed by the unleashing of a huge wall of water into a small mining community in Logan County, West Virginia. The disaster killed 125 people, making it one of the deadliest human-caused disasters of the decade in the United States. Families tended to be together, since it was a Saturday morning, and thus to die together, so few survivors lost nuclear family members. However, nearly everyone lost a friend or relative, and the landscape was devastated. The coal company which built the dam was sued for wrongful death, property damage, and "psychic impairment," brought about by its substandard construction of the dam. The University of Cincinnati Department of Psychiatry and the original research team became involved in the case when UC was asked to examine all of the 588 plaintiffs for the prosecution. A psychiatrist from West Virginia also examined all of the plaintiffs for the defense. The research findings were based upon *both* sets of reports, and on postlawsuit data collected on plaintiffs (adults and children) and nonplaintiffs (adults) at follow-up. The focus of the studies has been upon risk factors (extent of exposure, demographic variables, family relationships) as they relate to outcome within the samples, and change over time, rather than on absolute levels of impairment.

The methods of the studies will be briefly described below and the overall findings summarized. Then the findings of most relevance to this discussion will be presented in somewhat more detail. Finally, the various aspects will be synthesized to draw some conclusions about the impacts of the event on different age groups at different points in time, attempting to place our findings in the developmental context introduced earlier.

METHODS

Original Data Collection. Data were originally gathered, as noted, on 381 adults and 207 children in the context of a lawsuit (Gleser,

Green, and Winget, 1981). The suit included claims of "psychic injury" and all plaintiffs were interviewed by psychiatrists and other mental health professionals on both sides of the lawsuit approximately 2 years after the dam collapse. Families were originally seen together in their homes by the UC diagnosticians, then each individual was interviewed privately and a report dictated. The psychiatrist for the defense saw all plaintiffs in his office, which was about $1^1/_2$ hours from Buffalo Creek. Parents provided information on their children to both sides of the suit, and children were also seen separately, except for the very youngest. For the UC reports, children were seen by child psychiatrists, and parents were interviewed about their children by psychiatric social workers. Psychologists, adult psychiatrists, and psychiatric social workers interviewed the adults. In addition to general functioning, the University of Cincinnati interviewers were examining for symptoms of "traumatic neurosis," and the psychiatrist for the defense was examining for symptoms of "gross stress reaction," so that many symptoms of PTSD were identified. However, at the time of the original study (1974), PTSD was not an official diagnosis.

After obtaining the reports from both sides of the lawsuit, the research team rated both sets of reports using the Psychiatric Evaluation Form (PEF; Spitzer, Endicott, Mesnikoff, and Cohen 1968; Endicott and Spitzer, 1972). This instrument allows ratings of 19 symptom dimensions (e.g., suicide, depression, anxiety, alcohol abuse) from the written reports, as well as overall severity. Scales that were not utilized frequently were deleted and the remaining scales clustered into three areas based on the interrelationships among the scales in this and a prior study. These clusters were Depression (from depression, suicide / self-mutilation, social isolation, daily routine impairment, and retardation / lack of emotion); Anxiety (from agitation-excitement, anxiety, and somatic concerns); and Belligerence (from suspicion–persecution, belligerence, and antisocial attitudes and acts). Overall Severity and Alcohol Abuse were used separately. The scales showed good interrater generalizability and scores for the two sides of the lawsuit were significantly correlated, although attributions for the cause of the symptoms usually varied by side of the suit (Gleser et al., 1981). Since the reports from the two sides were related, the average of the two scores was used in all analyses as the best estimate of the person's functioning, reducing the bias in perspective of the two sides of the suit.

The extent of exposure to the disaster was rated from the reports by the research team along the dimensions of bereavement (loss by death in the disaster), life threat (e.g., proximity to flood waters, extent of warning) at the time of the dam collapse, extended trauma in the form of exposure to the elements and other experiences, and displacement from original home site. Family atmosphere (violent, irritable, depressed, and/or supportive) in the home was also rated from the children's reports (Gleser et al., 1981).

A subsample of adults (ages 16 and up at the time of the disaster) also filled out a modified 47-item version of the Hopkins Symptom Checklist (Lipman, Rickles, Covi, Derogatis, and Uhlenhuth, 1969).

Follow-Up Data Collection. The suit having been settled in the summer of 1974, follow-up data on several small subsamples were collected between 1975 and 1977 (Gleser et al., 1981). The major follow-up data were collected 14 years postdisaster on the adults, and 17 years postdisaster on the "children" (who were, at that point, adults). One hundred and twenty of the original 381 adult plaintiffs were located and reinterviewed; that is, 39 percent of the living survivors, since 52 individuals (14%) were known to have died. Of the remainder not interviewed, some individuals had moved out of state (33%), some could not be contacted or scheduled (32%) and some refused (36%) (Green and Grace, 1988). Based on the 1974 reports, survivors who participated in the follow-up had suffered significantly *less* personal loss through death in the disaster than those who refused. However, there were no differences between these two groups in 1974 pathology on any of the measures (Green and Grace, 1988). At the time of the follow-up, 80 individuals who were in the dam collapse disaster but not the lawsuit were also interviewed, as well as a comparison sample from a culturally and demographically similar area who had not been exposed to the event.

Of the original 207 children, 99 were located and followed up. We were able to obtain information on the whereabouts of 91 percent of the sample. A few subjects had died and we were not able to locate others. Of those we approached to participate (n = 132), 100 (76%) agreed. One completed only self-report data and was not included in the study (Green, Grace, Vary, Kramer, Gleser, and Leonard, in press). The longitudinal sample, compared to those not followed-up, were rated as significantly *less impaired* in 1974 on overall severity, belligerence, alcohol abuse, and suspicion. Since most of the children in the area eventually sued the coal company, only a non-exposed comparison sample was obtained (Green, Grace, Vary, et al., 1994).

Data collected at follow-up for both the adult and child samples included slightly different versions of the Structured Clinical Interview for DSM-III-R (SCID; Spitzer and Williams, 1986; Spitzer, Williams, Gibbon, and First, 1989) a full diagnostic interview for past and present psychiatric diagnoses. The nonpatient version, with a PTSD module added, was used. At the end of the interview, subjects were rated on the PEF, described above. All subjects filled out the Symptom Checklist 90R (SCL-90; Derogatis, 1983), as well as the Impact of Event Scale (Horowitz, Wilner, and Alvarez, 1979; Zilberg, Weiss, and Horowitz, 1982) as it pertained to their disaster experience. Flood experiences had been previously quantified; however, we had subjects recount their experiences (since some had been incomplete) and based our later findings on the synthesis of the two reports. Data on a number of other instruments were also collected, but will not be reported upon here.

OVERVIEW OF FINDINGS

An overview of the study findings with the adults at 2 years showed relatively high levels of impairment in the sample, although levels of symptoms should be interpreted with caution since the sample was not necessarily representative of the community at large. In reports by the psychiatrist for the defense, 29 percent of men and 42 percent of women displayed symptoms that led to a rating of moderate to severe on Overall Severity. The comparable figures for the UC reports were 66 and 70 percent, the differences being primarily a function of the defense examiner eliciting fewer depression symptoms. The combined figures were similar to outpatient norms on the PEF. A sample of 40 exposed *nonlitigants* from the area showed nearly identical scores on the symptom checklist (Gleser et al., 1981).

Generally speaking, the most prominent type of impairment differed by gender. Women were significantly higher than men on depression, anxiety, and overall severity of symptoms, while men were significantly higher on belligerence and alcohol abuse. Outcome was related to the extent of exposure to aspects of the disaster. Those who lost close friends and relatives and those who nearly lost their own lives were the most severely affected. Hardships following the flood also contributed to poorer functioning at 2 years. Women were additionally negatively affected by being displaced to temporary housing in a new neighborhood, and men did better if they could clean up and restore their houses. The most severe pathology was shown by individuals, especially couples, between the ages of 25 and 55, with older and younger adults less affected (see below for additional findings regarding age). Spouses were found to be quite similar in the degree and nature of their problems, over and above what would be expected from their background and common disaster experience. These stressors, demographic and family factors together accounted for about 30 to 40 percent of the variance in the outcome measures that we studied (see Gleser et al., 1981, for more details).

The children at 2 years postdisaster were between the ages of 4 and 17. Their symptoms (depression, anxiety, belligerence), rated from the clinical reports, increased with age (Gleser et al., 1981). With regard to PTSD symptoms, rated retrospectively, the differences were primarily between the youngest group (2–7 years old at the time of the disaster) and the two older groups (8 to

15 years old) (Green et al., 1991), with the older children showing more symptoms. Gender differences were found similar to those for the adults: girls were higher on anxiety, depression, and PTSD, while boys were higher on belligerence. The outcomes for the children were predicted by their levels of exposure (loss, life threat), by how impaired their parents were at the time, and by the overall rated atmosphere in the home. The effects of a specific parent (mother or father) or specific atmosphere (e.g., irritable, supportive) depended on the age and gender of the child. Again, about 30 percent of the variance in overall severity and PTSD was accounted for by these variables (Gleser et al., 1981; Green et al., 1991).

In the adult follow-up at 14 years, we located, as noted earlier, 120 of the original sample. The earlier 3- to 5-year follow-up on a small sample showed decreases in pathology after the settlement of the lawsuit. At 14 years, scores on the PEF and the SCL had continued to decline; significant decreases were noted for both men and women for all symptom types except alcohol abuse, which was relatively low to begin with. Also, the reports from 1974 were retrospectively rated for "probable" PTSD diagnoses. The proportion of PTSD went down from 44 to 28 percent for the men and women combined, a significant change for the women (52 to 31%) but not the men (32 to 23%) (Green, Lindy, Grace, Gleser, Leonard, Korol, and Winget, 1990). While the decrease was clear-cut, subjects continued to show significant impairment in the areas of anxiety and depression symptoms, relative to a nonexposed sample in a similar area. However, they were no different than a comparison group of 80 exposed nonlitigants who had been in the valley at the time of the disaster and did not differ with regard to exposure from our follow-up subjects (Green, Grace, Lindy, Gleser, Leonard, and Kramer, 1990).

In the 17-year follow-up of the children, 99 of the original 207 survivors participated (Green, Grace, Vary, et al., 1994). At the time of the follow-up, subjects were between the ages of 19 and 33. Over this time period, ratings on the PEF generally declined. Anxiety, belligerence, somatic concerns, and agitation decreased significantly. At the same time, symptoms of substance abuse and suicidal ideation, not present at all in the original sample, increased significantly. Postdisaster rates of PTSD and Major Depression (32 and 33%, respectively) were down to current rates of 7 and 13 percent. While these latter rates are higher than norms, they were quite similar to those found in the comparison community (as were SCL-90 and PEF scores), suggesting that the specific impact of the disaster was no longer detectable in these subjects (Green, Grace, Vary, et al., 1994). Older children continued to show the highest levels of symptoms but most comparisons were not significant. The PTSD rate in the oldest group was 14 percent compared to 3 to 4 percent in the younger groups, and the number of PTSD symptoms was marginally higher in this group ($p < .06$). On the other hand, gender differences were striking (although circumscribed), with women showing significantly higher ratings on anxiety, social isolation, and self-reported PTSD symptoms on the Impact of Event Scale. Their PTSD and depression rates were marginally higher ($p < .06$) (Green, Grace, Vary, et al., 1994).

To summarize then, both adults and children showed clear-cut improvement from the first to the second decade following the disaster. There were some differences between the samples over time, however. The adults continued to be more impaired than their nonexposed neighbors, while the children were similar to their nonexposed counterparts with regard to symptom levels. Further, while gender differences by type of symptom were found in both samples at 2 years, the gender differences were no longer evident in the adult sample by 14 years, but continued in the child sample at 17 years.

FINDINGS RELATED TO AGE

One of the most interesting aspects of the study was the opportunity to examine both longitudinal findings and cross-sectional findings with regard to vulnerability associated with age differences. With cross-sectional data, particularly that collected near the time of an important negative life event, differential risk associated with age is usually interpreted as being due to the age of the subject at the time of experiencing the event. With a longitudinal study, one can compare early and late cross-sectional age trends to determine whether the age at exposure or the age at the time of follow-up (current age) is relatively more important as a risk factor.

Our original study revealed significant curvilinear trends relating age and psychopathology in the adult sample (Gleser et al., 1981). The middle-aged survivors were doing the worst. Subjects in the age range of 40 to 54 displayed the most anxiety symptoms on the Psychiatric Evaluation Form, while the group aged 25 to 39 showed the most belligerence symptoms. Women aged 25 to 39 were particularly at risk for depression. With regard to overall severity, the women were most at risk between ages 25 and 39, while the men were more at risk between 40 and 54.

At follow-up, the age groups used were slightly different since many of the oldest group had died, and we needed to have the groups more equivalent for data analysis purposes (total N with complete data = 117). Since men and women differed with regard to symptomatology in 1974, we retained the sexes separately for purposes of analysis. Analyses of covariance on the PEF ratings (controlling for disaster-related loss, living arrangements, and education, all of which differed somewhat by age group) were conducted with gender and age as between-subject factors and occasion (first vs. second decade) as the within-subject factor. Differences between men and women were significant, as expected, for the cluster scores of anxiety, depression, and overall severity, with women having higher scores. Decreases in symptoms over time were also significant, but there were no significant main effects for age or age-by-time interactions, indicating that change in status over time did not differ by age. There were some complicated three-way interactions suggesting that women aged 16 to 23 at the time of the disaster (30 to 37 at follow-up), and men aged 24 to 38 (38 to 52 at follow-up), recovered more slowly than their opposite sex counterparts, with similar curves for men and women in the other age groups (Green, Gleser, Lindy, Grace, and Leonard, in press).

The follow-up cross-sectional data included nonlitigant survivors as well. The findings from this analysis showed that the groups most at risk for self-reported and clinically rated symptoms (PTSD differences were not significant) were those individuals who were 22 to 31 at the time of the disaster (36 to 45 at follow-up when these assessments were done). The two oldest groups were doing the best, although they contained some of the individuals in the age groups at highest risk earlier (Green, Gleser, Lindy, et al., in press). Although the findings are a bit difficult to follow given the need to adjust age groups, they suggest that at each point in time, subjects of "middle-age" were at highest risk for impairment, and that there were not different general patterns of recovery by age group.

For the present chapter, in order to reconcile the earlier to the later analyses, we went back to the original data. The original analyses broke the age groups at 25 to 39 and 40 to 54; that is, splitting subjects at the age 40 mark, rather than analyzing a category encompassing 40, as we did with the follow-up data. This breakdown showed that it was indeed the group aged 36 to 45 (at the early follow-up) which scored the highest on the PEF, with the second highest group being those between 46 to 55. The findings with the symptom checklist showed similar trends but were not as clear-cut. These self-report data, obtained on a subsample, were not analyzed by age in the original study, but showed that the groups endorsing the most symptoms were somewhat older on the average, with the most symptoms endorsed by individuals between the ages of 36 and 65. These findings, especially those on the PEF, are in line with other studies showing that the elderly are not at particular risk following disaster, and that those in the middle ranges of age evidently have a higher risk. Our data suggest, then, that for adults, the age-related risk may be relatively less associated with the age of exposure, and relatively more associated with the age at the time of the assessment; that is, individuals may be more at risk for symptoms when they reach a certain age (see below for further discussion of this point).

Breaking the groups down by gender, the findings remained essentially the same. PEF Overall severity ratings were highest for the women between the ages of 36 and 45 at the early follow-up, and for the men between the ages of 36 and 55.

When the children were originally studied, the youngest children were doing the best. This is consistent with other disaster studies, which have shown the same trends except for regressive behaviors (certain fears, bed-wetting, clinging, etc.) found only in very young children. In the follow-up of the children, who were now 19 to 33, fewer age differences were obtained, with only a trend for the oldest group to have more PTSD symptoms. Thus, clear-cut prior differences had disappeared. The oldest group of subjects had not yet reached the age at which the adult samples were most vulnerable at both follow-up points (i.e., around 40). However, the age-related increases (up to middle age) are consistent with the age trends in the child follow-up, particularly among the women (5 of the 7 cases of PTSD were in the oldest group of women).

STABILITY OF SYMPTOMS OVER TIME

A final set of findings related to the overall perspective of this chapter is the stability of PTSD and other symtoms over time. That is, are the people who had PTSD, or relatively high symptom levels at 2 years, the same ones who had high levels of symptoms in the second decade?

A general answer to the question posed above is *no*. Scores in 1974 for the adults and children were not highly predictive of later functioning. For the adults, the highest relationship was for the Symptom Checklist total score ($r = .43$). Overall Severity at the two points in time was correlated only .17, and PTSD was correlated .18 at the two points. While these figures were all significant, they are relatively low, and imply that pathology at one point in time is not a good predictor of later pathology. Specific subscale scores were not correlated between 1974 and 1986, and women's scores were more stable than men's (Green, Lindy, Grace, et al., 1990).

With regard to PTSD per se, 61 percent of the adult sample had the same diagnosis at both points (17%, PTSD; 44%, no PTSD). Twenty-eight percent of the sample changed from having the diagnosis in 1974 to not having it in 1986, while 11 percent showed delayed symptoms (Green, Lindy, Grace, et al., 1990). Part of the low correlation is clearly related to the overall decrease in symptoms and the reduction in variability/range at follow-up. However, other factors than 1974 pathology predicted 1986 outcome at a higher level (prior diagnosis, marital status, stressors).

Findings for the children were similar. Although there was an overall decline in levels of impairment, correlations between the same scales on the PEF in 1974 and in 1989 were nonsignificant (Green, Grace, Vary, et al., 1994), suggesting no prediction between the two time periods. The number of past PTSD symptoms *measured in 1974* was correlated .21 ($p < .05$) with the number of current PTSD symptoms in 1989. However, if one compares the current number of PTSD symptoms with the number of past symptoms *remembered in 1989* on the SCID, the correlation is .68. Thus, the retrospective data provide a more stable picture than do the longitudinal data.

Discussion

The findings presented in this chapter are derived from studies extending over a 19-year period, with disaster-related follow-up extending out to 17 years following the event. This is the longest follow-up of a disaster of which we are aware, and one of the longest longitudinal studies of any traumatic event. The data are not necessarily representative of all of the survivors of this event. Those who participated in the earlier phase of the study were all plaintiffs in a lawsuit, and as such, may be different in a number of ways from those who did not participate. However, there is no reason to believe that the longitudinal stability or instability of symptoms should be particularly different in this subset of individuals, especially noting their similarity at two points with groups of nonplaintiffs exposed to the same event (Gleser et al., 1981; Green, Grace, Lindy, et al., 1990).

It should also be noted that this trauma was prolonged. Individuals lost friends, loved ones, and belongings, but they also lost their community as they knew it, and most were not resettled for years following the event. So the Buffalo Creek disaster represents both an acute, life-threatening trauma, as well as an ongoing stressful situation affecting work, economic viability, living arrangements, and so forth. The trauma, specifically a technological disaster, is one that originates in the environment and is not interpersonal in nature (one-on-one with a victim and a perpetrator). Thus, the findings with regard to long-term effects and vulnerability by age may apply only to similar types of events.

The overall findings of this study are compatible with the hypothesis that individuals may be more vulnerable to the impacts of earlier traumatic events at certain points in their lives than at other points, regardless of their age at the time of exposure, suggesting that psychopathology is not necessarily continuous. Further, the particular nature of the response may vary as a function of current age as well.

The age-related findings were not completely clear-cut, but in the adults, individuals in the middle age ranges appeared to be more at risk for increased psychopathology at both study points. Our prior understanding of this information related to the likelihood that at this age, individuals may have responsibility both for aging parents and for developing children, or those who have more recently left home. Several theoreticians have focused on the middle-age transition as a time of particular stress and reassessment of one's values, goals, etc. (Jung, 1933), as well as a time to confront polarities in one's life. Levinson et al. (1978) suggested that these polarities include those of young/old, destruction/creation, masculine/feminine, and attachment/separateness. For Erikson (1950) this would likely be the point in time when individuals would be addressing the life crisis of generativity versus stagnation and focusing on the generations to come. While all of these conceptualizations were based on studies of men, there is growing evidence that women may also be vulnerable to "mid-life crises" (Lewittes, 1982). The notion that this is a particularly difficult time for both men *and* women is also bolstered by findings from the Epidemiologic Catchment Area (ECA) studies. These studies found that with regard to current mental disorders, although there were clearly some exceptions, the patterns showed middle-aged individuals to be, on the average, at higher risk for a number of disorders, particularly anxiety and depression (Myers, Weissman, Tischler, Holzer, Leaf, Orvaschel, Anthony, Boyd, Burke, Kramer, and Stoltzman, 1984). A primary exception is substance abuse, for which younger (than 25) individuals were more at risk.

However, some of the differences between men and women (women having more symptoms, especially depression, before age 40, and the somewhat slower recovery of women in their thirties [longitudinal data], compared to men being at higher risk up to age 56, and a slower recovery in their forties) may actually be due to somewhat different developmental trajectories. While the work of Levinson and colleagues indicated a major transition for men around the age of 40, studies of women suggest that transitional upheaval may be more common, or at least as common, in the period between 27 and 30 years of age (Reinke, Holmes, and Harris, 1985). Jung (1933) also noted that midlife transitions may occur earlier in women. This means that interpreting findings related to age might be more appropriately done by gender, if enough subjects are available, since the genders may have somewhat different periods of vulnerability.

The apparent finding of noncontinuity of risk is supported in both the adult and the child samples by the relationships between the pathology measures at the two time periods, which were relatively low. While there was some prediction, overall, those individuals with relatively high symptom levels at one point were not the same individuals as those with high levels later on, again supporting the notion of time periods in the life cycle that are more problematic rather than risk associated with age at the time of the traumatic event.

The children's data indicated that the form that the symptoms take at the earlier developmental stages may reflect primarily the developmental competencies and issues that the child is dealing with at the time and, by themselves, are not predictive of later functioning. That is, younger children are more likely to wet the bed and older children to "act out" because of their *current* developmental stage. Depending upon age, their distress may be expressed in very different ways. We do not tend to make these types of distinctions within adulthood, and it is not clear whether they are relevant. But the children, *as adults*, did not differ greatly by age, either for global or specific symptoms. We had hypothesized that the older children would experience the disaster with more comprehension than the younger children, and therefore would tend to have more (adultlike) PTSD symptoms, while the younger children would have more global problems, and problems more mediated by their parents' reactions. These predictions turned out to be supported by the data. The oldest group had the most PTSD symptoms as children, and tended to have the most PTSD symptoms as adults as well (Green et al., 1991; Green, Grace, Vary, 1994).

We were quite interested in the findings with regard to gender differences. These were quite strong at 2 years postdisaster for both the adults and the children. When the gender differences disappeared for the adults, we interpreted this to be a social phenomenon, related to societal changes in sex roles rather than to the aging of the sample. The differences were primarily in the improvement of the women, rather than the worsening of the men. However, the children's follow-up data did not show the same findings. In that data set, the women continued to have significantly more psychopathology, although this was primarily in the realm of PTSD symptoms. This incongruence forces us to rethink our original findings, since a social forces interpretation would suggest fewer differences in the "younger generation." While we continue to be somewhat puzzled at these findings, we may need to put them in a more developmental framework as well, and wonder why younger adults would be more likely to show sex differences in pathology than older adults, on average. A possible understanding at this point is that sex differences are less salient as adults age, as men and women are more in touch with a larger variety of aspects of their personalities and find being more like the opposite sex to be less threatening. Again, these studies do not provide definitive answers, but raise interesting questions for future research.

In summary, the overall findings indicate a noncontinuity of psychopathology over time, likely associated with the developmental stage of the individual, whether child or adult. This suggests that, at least for disaster (i.e., nonfamilial events), high-risk groups might be better defined by their current age rather than by the age at which they experienced the traumatic event. When one is intervening immediately after an event, these are the same. However, for purposes of later follow-up, and when working with individuals in psychotherapy, it might be helpful to keep in mind current issues in the developmental stage of the individual which may make the prior trauma more salient, in addition to the focus on the situation at the time of the trauma.

These findings also suggest that Laufer's notion of the "serial self" in the combat veteran may be useful in conceptualizing survivors of other traumatic events as well, although the divisions may be less severe. Thus, integrating the "trauma self" with the "nontrauma self" may be a challenge that continues throughout the lifetime. It may need to be revisited during major life transitions, and leave the individual more vulnerable at these times. Clearly, more longitudinal data on traumatized children and young adults are needed in order to answer these questions empirically.

REFERENCES

Blom, G. (1986), A school disaster—Intervention and research aspects. *J. Amer. Acad. Child Psychiatry*, 25:336–345.

Danieli, Y. (1985), The treatment and prevention of long-term effects and inter-generational transmission of victimization: A lesson from Holocaust survivors and their children. In: *Trauma and Its Wake*, ed. C. R. Figley. New York: Brunner/Mazel.

Derogatis, L. R. (1983), *SCL-90 R version: Manual I*. Baltimore: Johns Hopkins University.

Dollinger, S. (1985), Lightning-strike disaster among children. *Brit. J. Med. Psychology*, 58:375–383.

Elder, G. H. (1986), Military times and turning points in men's lives. *Development. Psychol.*, 22:233–245.

Elder, G. H., Jr., & Clipp, E. C. (1988), Wartime losses and social bonding: Influences across 40 years in men's lives. *Psychiatry*, 51:177–197.

Endicott, J., & Spitzer, R. (1972), What! Another rating scale? The Psychiatric Evaluation Form. *J. Nerv. Ment. Dis.*, 154:88–104.

Erikson, E. H. (1950), *Childhood and Society*, 2nd ed. New York: W. W. Norton, 1963.

Freedy, J., Shaw, D., Jarrell, M., & Masters, C. (1992), Towards an understanding of the psychological impact of natural disasters: An application of the conservation resources stress model. *J. Traum. Stress*, 5:441–454.

Galante, R., & Foa, E. B. (1986), An epidemiological study of psychic trauma and treatment effectiveness for children after a natural disaster. *J. Amer. Acad. Child Psychol.*, 25:357–363.

Gleser, G., Green, B., & Winget, C. (1981), *Prolonged Psychosocial Effects of Disaster*. New York: Academic Press.

Green, B. L., Gleser, G. C., Lindy, J. L., Grace, M. C., & Leonard, A. C. (1996), Age related reactions to the Buffalo Creek Dam Collapse: Second decade effects. In: *Aging and Posttraumatic Stress Disorder*, ed. P. Ruskin & J. Talbott. Washington, DC: American Psychiatric Press.

—— Grace, M. C. (1988), Conceptual issues in research with survivors and illustrations from a followup study. In: *Human Adaptation to Extreme Stress: From the Holocaust to Vietnam*, ed. J. P. Wilson, Z. Harel, & B. Kahana. New York: Plenum Press.

—— —— Lindy, J., Gleser, G., Leonard, A., & Kramer, T. (1990), Buffalo Creek survivors in the second decade: Comparison with unexposed and nonlitigant groups. *J. Applied Soc. Psychol.*, 20:1033–1050.

—— —— —— Titchener, J., & Lindy, J. (1983), Levels of functional impairment following a civilian disaster: The Beverly Hills Supper Club fire. *J. Consult. Clin. Psychol.*, 51:573–580.

—— —— Vary, M. G., Kramer, T. L., Gleser, G. C., & Leonard, A. C. (1994), Children of disaster in the second decade: A 17-year follow up of Buffalo Creek survivors. *J. Amer. Acad. Child Adol. Psychiat.*, 33:71–79.

—— Korol, M., Grace, M., Vary, M., Leonard, A., Gleser, G., & Smitson-Cohen, S. (1991), Children and disaster: Age, gender, and parental effects on PTSD symptoms. *J. Amer. Acad. Child Adol. Psychiatry*, 30:945–951.

—— Lindy, J., Grace, M., Gleser, G., Leonard, A., Korol, M., & Winget, C. (1990), Buffalo Creek survivors in the second decade: Stability of stress symptoms. *Amer. J. Orthopsychiatry*, 60:43–54.

Harel, Z., Kahana, B., & Kahana, E. (1988). Psychological well-being amongst Holocaust survivors and immigrants in Israel. *J. Traum. Stress*, 1:413–429.

Hendin, H., & Haas, A. P. (1984), *The Wounds of War*. New York: Basic Books.

Holen, A. (1991), A longitudinal study of the occurrence and persistence of post-traumatic health problems in disaster survivors. *Stress Med.*, 7:11–17.

Horowitz, M. J. (1986), *Stress Response Syndromes*, 2nd ed. Northvale, NJ: Jason Aronson.

—————— Wilner, N., & Alvarez, W. (1979), Impact of Event Scale: A measure of subjective stress. *Psychosom. Med.*, 41:209–218.

Huerta, F., & Horton, D. (1978), Coping behavior of elderly flood victims. *Gerontologist*, 18:541–546.

Janoff-Bulman, R. (1992), *Shattered Assumptions*. New York: Free Press.

Jung, C. G. (1933), The stages of life. In: *The Portable Jung*, ed. J. Campbell, tr. R. F. C. Hull. New York: Viking Press.

Kalter, N., Riemer, B., Brickman, A., & Chen, J. W. (1985), Implications of parental divorce for female development. *J. Amer. Acad. Child Psychiatry*, 24:538–544.

Krause, N. (1987), Exploring the impact of a natural disaster on the health and psychological well-being of older adults. *J. Hum. Stress*, 14:61–69.

Kulka, R. A., Schlenger, W. E., Fairbank, J. A., Hough, R. L., Jordan, B. K., Marmar, C. R., Weiss, D. S., & Grady, D. A. (1990), *Trauma and the Vietnam War Generation*. New York: Brunner/Mazel.

Laufer, R. S. (1988), The serial self: War trauma, identity, and adult development. In: *Human Adaptation to Extreme Stress*, ed. J. P. Wilson, Z. Harel, & B. Kahana. New York: Plenum Press.

Levinson, D. J., Darrow, C. N., Klein, E. B., Levinson, M. H., & McKee, B. (1978), *The Seasons of a Man's Life*. New York: Ballantine Books.

Lewittes, H. (1982), Women's development in adulthood and old age: A review and critique. *Internat. J. Ment. Health*, 11:115–134.

Lifton, R. J. (1988), Understanding the traumatized self: Imagery, symbolization, and transformation. In: *Human Adaptation to Extreme Stress*, ed. J. P. Wilson, Z. Harel, & B. Kahana. New York: Plenum Press.

Lima, B., Pai, S., Santacruz, H., Lozano, J., & Luna, J. (1987), Screening for the psychological consequences of a major disaster in a developing country: Armero, Columbia. *Acta Psychiat. Scand.*, 76:561–567.

Lipman, R. S., Rickles, K., Covi, L., Derogatis, L. R., & Uhlenhuth, E. H. (1969), Factors of symptom distress. *Arch. Gen. Psychiatry*, 21:328–338.

Mahler, M. S., Pine, F., & Bergman, A. (1975), *The Psychological Birth of the Human Infant: Symbiosis and Individuation*. New York: Basic Books.

McFarlane, A. (1987), Posttraumatic phenomena in a longitudinal study of children following a natural disaster. *J. Amer. Acad. Child Adol. Psychiatry*, 26:764–769.

Milgram, N., Toubiana, Y., Klingman, A., Raviv, A., & Goldstein, I. (1988), Situational exposure and personal loss in children's acute and chronic stress reactions to a school bus disaster. *J. Traum. Stress*, 1:339–352.

Milne, G. (1977), Cyclone Tracy: II. The effects on Darwin children. *Austral. Psychologist*, 12:55–62.

Myers, J. K., Weissman, M. W., Tischler, G. L., Holzer, C. E., Leaf, P. J., Orvaschel, H., Anthony, J. C., Boyd, J. H., Burke, J. D., Kramer, M., & Stoltzman, R. (1984), Six-month prevalence of psychiatric disorders in three communities. *Arch. Gen. Psychiatry*, 41:959–967.

Norris, F., Phifer, J., & Kaniasty, K. (1994), Individual and community reactions to the Kentucky floods: Findings from a longitudinal study of older adults. In: *Individual and Community Responses to Trauma and Disaster*, ed. R. Ursano, B. McCaughey, & C. Fullerton. Cambridge, U.K.: Cambridge University Press.

Reinke, B. J., Holmes, D. S., & Harris, R. L. (1985), The timing of psychosocial changes in women's lives: The years 25 to 45. *J. Personal. & Soc. Psychol.*, 48:1353–1364.

Seroka, C., Knapp, C., Knight, S., Siemon, C., & Starbuck, S. (1986), A comprehensive program for postdisaster counseling. *J. Contemp. Soc. Work*, 67:37–44.

Shore, J., Tatum, E., & Vollmer, W. (1986), Psychiatric reactions to disaster: The Mount St. Helens experience. *Amer. J. Psychiatry*, 143:590–595.

Speed, N., Engdahl, B., Schwartz, J., & Eberly, R. (1989), Posttraumatic stress disorder as a consequence of the POW experience. *J. Nerv. Ment. Dis.*, 177:147–153.

Spitzer, R. L., Endicott, J., Mesnikoff, A. M., & Cohen, M. S. (1968), *The Psychiatric Evaluation Form*. New York: Biometrics Research Department, New York State Psychiatric Institute.

——— Williams, J. W. (1986), *Structured Clinical Interview for DSM-III: Non-patient Version (SCID-NP-11-1-86)*. New York: Biometrics Research Department, New York State Psychiatric Institute.

——— ——— Gibbon, M., & First, M. B. (1989), *Structured Clinical Interview for DSM III-R: Non-patient version (5/1/89)*. New York: Biometrics Research Department, New York State Psychiatric Institute.

Strauss, J. S., & Harding, C. M. (1990), Relationships between adult development and the course of the mental disorder. In: *Risk and Protective Factors in the Development of Psychopathology*, ed. J. Rolf, A. S. Masten, D. Cicchetti, K. H. Nuechterlein, & S. Weintraub. Cambridge, U.K.: Cambridge University Press.

Ulman, R. B., & Brothers, D. (1988), *The Shattered Self*. Hillsdale, NJ: Analytic Press.

van der Kolk, B. A., & Ducey, C. (1984), Clinical implications of the Rorschach in post-traumatic stress disorder. In: *Post-Traumatic Stress Disorder: Psychological and Biological Sequelae*, ed. B. A. van der Kolk. Washington, DC: American Psychiatric Press.

Wilkenson, C. (1983), Aftermath of a disaster: The collapse of the Hyatt Regency Hotel skywalk. *Amer. J. Psychiatry*, 140:1134–1139.

Zilberg, N. J., Weiss, D. S., & Horowitz, M. J. (1982), Impact of Event Scale: A cross-validation study and some empirical evidence supporting a conceptual model of stress response syndromes. *J. Consult. Clin. Psychol.*, 50:407–414.

Chapter 14
Stress and Eating Disorders

Laurie L. Humphries, M.D.

The field of stress research and eating disorders will make significant advances over the next decade. This advance will come in part from a change of classification in the *Diagnostic and Statistical Manual of Mental Disorders*, 4th edition (DSM-IV; APA, 1994). With the publication of DSM-IV, the eating disorders anorexia nervosa and bulimia nervosa will become independent clinical syndromes, parallel with the mood disorders. This change reflects our understanding that anorexia and bulimia are not only disorders of children and adolescents. Although starting in adolescence, the eating disorders are found throughout the life cycle. Anorexia nervosa and bulimia nervosa will no longer be subsumed under the class of disorders in childhood and adolescence. Also a new syndrome, Binge Eating Disorder, will be added to the appendix as a syndrome requiring further study.

This new classification system will enhance research. Researchers, who have studied adult eating-disorder patients (Sohlberg and Norring, 1992), have noted little correlation between stressful life events and the patient's course. This finding is not surprising since anorexia nervosa and bulimia nervosa start in adolescence. A significant number of patients continue to suffer from their disorders in adulthood. Therefore, if stressful life events play a role in the etiology of these disorders, researchers must look at adolescent populations.

"NORMATIVE" STRESSFUL EVENTS

Because eating disorders develop in adolescent girls, instruments that are sensitive to adolescent *female* stress and resilience need to be developed. Adolescent females suffer higher levels of stress than male peers. Girls act out stress in an inner directed manner (Harris, Blum, and Resnick, 1991). Is this one factor that predisposes females to the illness? Resilience in adolescent females was associated with connectedness with parents and family. In contrast, hardiness components of commitment, control, and challenge relate to stress and psychological symptoms in males, but not in females (Sheppard and Kashani, 1991).

In a study of normal, 13- to 19-year-old adolescents from 10 countries, adolescent girls showed more vulnerabilities, compared to boys (Offer, Ostrov, and Howard, 1988). Girls described themselves a sadder, lonelier, more easily hurt, and more other directed. They were more upset by criticism, and they had less faith in their coping abilities.

CULTURAL PRESSURE AS A STRESSOR

Women in the Western industrialized world face constant pressure to maintain a thin body (Garner, Garfinkel, Schartz, and Thompson, 1980). There is a strong prejudice against obesity (Wadden and Stunkard, 1985). Women know that the way to get spontaneous compliments and support is to lose weight. If a woman has low self-esteem and an external locus of control, then weight loss provides a mechanism to attain approval and feel better about yourself. Weight loss is the one action that inevitably leads to positive feedback and affirmation. Women are sold the perfect image, in part, through the visual media. How many models or actresses have a body mass index (BMI) between 20 and 25? This range is considered to be nutritionally healthy, but the

BMI of most models is 18 or lower. Most models who are 65 inches tall are expected to model at 100 pounds. Although a causal relationship between culture and the syndromes is hard to prove, these syndromes are referred to as "culture bound." In a genetic epidemiology study of bulimia nervosa, being born after 1960 was identified as a risk factor (Kendler, MacLean, Neale, Kesler, Heath, and Evans, 1991). This finding raises the question of the impact of television on the birth cohort of women.

DEVELOPMENTAL ISSUES, EATING DISORDERS, AND STRESS

The interface between developmental issues and the stress process is an important area of enquiry. The developmental spectrum includes prenatal and perinatal stress. Animal models may help clarify some of these complex issues. In an animal model, females born to mildly stressed, pregnant rats have fewer benzodiazepine receptors in their hippocampus (Fride, Dan, Gavish, and Weinstock, 1985). Chatoor, Conley, and Dickson (1988) point out that food refusal represents a symptom of separation and individuation for the infant.

DISORDERED EATING AND STRESS IN ADOLESCENT POPULATIONS

Studies of large nonclinical adolescent populations show that disordered eating is prevalent. While only 2 percent of these teenagers endorse items reflecting a full eating disorder syndrome, as many as 12 percent of females fall into the emotional eating category. Kagan and Squires (1984) found stress precipitated emotional eating in this population, with the most frequently cited stressor being a failure to meet the expectations of others. Not unexpectedly, a significant positive correlation is found between scores on a social conformity scale and a screening test for bulimia (McCormack and Carman, 1989).

Normative eating behaviors in adolescent females reflect wide variations. Although dieting and bingeing occur in a cycle in clinical populations, dieting and bingeing are not cyclic in these normal groups. Daily energy intake fluctuates markedly in normal populations (Lacey, Chadbund, Crisp, Whitehead, and Stordy, 1978).

While eating large amounts of food is common, purging behavior occurs in a small number of females. Purging is associated with more pathological conditions. Females who purge with diuretics, laxatives, or vomiting are more likely to get drunk and to drink during the day. The use of laxatives is correlated with a history of abuse (Hibbard, Brack, Rauch, and Orr, 1988). The alcohol and purging is used to reduce stress (Killen, Taylor, Telch, Saylor, Maron, and Robinson, 1987).

Studying noneating disordered university students, Cattanach, Malley, and Rodin (1988) found that the group of students who exhibited attitudes similar to eating disorder patients did not exhibit increased cardiovascular reactivity to stress. This group did experience an increased desire to binge with stress, more global distress, and lower self-esteem. Also, they found interpersonal conflict to be very stressful as compared to their peers with the eating disordered attitudes.

Using a causal modeling analysis, Shatford and Evans (1986) found that environmental stress did not lead to bulimia. Instead, they found that depression was the stress that resulted in ineffective coping mechanisms, thereby leading to bulimia. In a pilot study, Willenbring, Levine, and Morley (1986) showed that a complex relationship exists between age, stress level, stress-induced eating, caloric density preference, and sweet preference.

Dieting in adolescent females happens so frequently in Western industrial countries that it represents the norm. In a longitudinal study, Roesen, Tracy, and Howell (1990) followed a cohort for a

4-month period. During this short time, dieting predicted stress, but dieting did not predict eating disorder symptoms. In a prospective study with a 12-month follow-up, dieting increased the risk of having an eating disorder eightfold (Patton, Johnson-Sabine, Wood, Mann, and Wakeling, 1991). These authors concluded that dieting was necessary for the development of an eating disorder, but dieting alone was not sufficient to instigate a full-blown syndrome.

Certain factors are associated with an increased risk of developing eating disorders. Engaging in any activity that puts an emphasis on body weight and shape increases the risk. Modeling, gymnastics, cheerleading, track, and ballet represent a few of the many activities that fall in this category. The more the teenager places an emphasis on their weight or body image, then the more they will practice dietary restraint. Female university athletes contending with weight control exhibited their depression, anger, and anxiety through binge eating. Binge eating was a symptom of frustration in 29 percent of the females, but only 2 percent of the males studied (Selby, Weinstein, and Bird, 1990). The distribution of body fat represents a risk factor. Females with greater lower body fat, compared to abdominal fat, were more eating disordered and saw the right weight as central to their self-esteem (Sharpe-Radke, Whitney-Saltiel, and Rodin, 1990).

In medical students, 17 percent appeared at risk for an eating disorder. When asked the motivation for their disordered eating patterns, the students stated that these behaviors helped them cope with loneliness, depression, and to relieve tension (Herzog, Borus, Hamburg, Ott, and Concus, 1987).

Knowing the relationship between the level of the acute and chronic stressors and disordered eating in a normal population is essential prior to drawing conclusions about the role of stress in a clinical population. The research in this area has focused on discrete life events, but knowledge of the level of ongoing adversity is required (Jensen, Richters, Ussery, Bloedan, and Davis, 1991).

COPING STYLE

The process of stress is complex. Negative life events are only one component of the interaction. Coping styles are another facet. Personal coping styles may either accentuate the stressful experience or diminish its impact. The stressful encounter does not occur in a vacuum. Cognitive appraisal of the event and coping strategies may modify the outcome (Folkman, Lazarus, Dunkel-Schietter, De Longis, and Gruen, 1986). Coping mechanisms in hospitalized patients and outpatients with anorexia nervosa and bulimia have been studied. Moreover, specific eating attitudes and behaviors in nonclinical populations have been linked to coping styles.

Little is known about the neuropathological impairment that malnutrition causes. Cognitive appraisal may be impaired by malnutrition. A complex interplay exists between psychological issues, cognitive performance, and the physiologic changes that are precipitated by dieting in young females. Mild malnutrition causes affective changes in males (Keyes, Brozek, Henshel, Micholson, and Taylor, 1950). Jones, Duncan, Browers, and Mirsky (1991) compared normal weight bulimics and underweight anorexia nervosa patients, and found that both patient groups showed poorer performance in focusing as compared to controls. Comparing bulimic patients to exercising women, Neckowitz and Morrison (1991) found that the groups did not differ on appraisal, but that the bulimics used escape-avoidance as a means of coping in both intimate and nonintimate contexts and sensed greater threat in situations. Bulimics, more than drug abusers or normal controls, rely on the approval of others, denigrate themselves, exert self-imposed pressure, and experience chronic tension (Butterfield and Leclair, 1988).

If appraisal appears intact in bulimics, internal scanning is altered in anorexic patients. Internal scanning appears impaired in anorexia nervosa patients when compared to bulimics (Heilbrun and Bloomfield, 1986). The prolonged course of anorexia nervosa has been linked to inadequate coping skills. When attempting a stress-inducing speech task, weight-restored anorexic patients continue to have increased salivary cortisol at a 2-year follow-up (Steiner and Levine, 1988). When ill, anorexic patients failed to lower their systolic blood pressure when faced with a stressful task. Yet when they are weight restored, they show less physiologic response to stress even though they obtained high Type A personality scores (Brunner, Maloney, Daniels, Mays, and Farrell, 1989).

Although hospitalized bulimics scored higher on a measure of negative life experiences than either anorexic or control individuals, anorexia nervosa patients did not differ from controls on this measure. Both anorexic and bulimic patients are reluctant to share personal problems and feelings and use avoidance to cope (Beiler and Terrell, 1990).

As Billings and Moos (1981) suggest the reliance on avoidance as a primary coping mechanism over an extended period of time seriously impairs the ability to make an effective response to a stressful experience.

Families of anorexia nervosa patients exhibit rigid, inflexible, and concrete ways of coping (Kalucy, Crisp, Harding, and Britta, 1977).

The use of dissociation as a coping strategy occurs in a subgroup of eating disorder patients. Dissociative symptoms were reported in 37 percent of bulimics, 25 percent of anorexia nervosa patients with bulimia, and 12.1 percent of restricting anorexics. The traumatic events associated with dissociative symptoms were incest, sexual abuse, and the loss of a family member (Vanderlinden, Vandereycken, van Dyck, and Vertommen, 1993).

Given their difficulty in coping, helping these patients develop more adaptive coping styles would be one facet of treatment. Laessle, Beumount, Batow, Lenner, O'Connor, Pirke, Touyz, and Waadt (1991) compared nutrition management to stress management over a 3-month intervention. Both proved effective, but on different aspects of bulimia nervosa. While the nutritional management helped to decrease the eating behaviors, the stress management intervention improved the patients' psychological symptoms of ineffectiveness, interpersonal distrust, and anxiety. They concluded that both strategies should be used in treatment with the nutritional intervention proceeding the stress management.

PERSONALITY AND EATING DISORDERS

The personality of the patient affects their response to stress. In the seminal article on bulimia nervosa, Russell (1979) noted that of his 30 patients only 8 appeared to have a normal personality. Levine and Hyler (1986) found that two-thirds of their bulimic patients met criteria for either borderline or histrionic personality disorder with the remaining third diagnosed as compulsive or avoidant. The most frequent personality disorder associated with anorexia nervosa is obsessive–compulsive disorder.

THE ROLE OF SUPPORT

The availability and use of support acts as a mediator of the stress process. Using bulimic's subjective appraisal of their recovery process, Rorty, Yager, and Rosotto (1993) found that friends' and parents' support and the experience of empathy and understanding were very important to recovery. These bulimic women judged their families' support as insufficient. Furthermore, they saw their parents, particularly their mothers, as hindering their recovery. This negative influence consisted of blaming the bulimic and buying foods that were known to trigger binge eating. Using a structural analysis approach, Humphrey (1986) showed that the bulimic's family was more rejecting and belittling and less understanding and empathetic. In a genetic epidemiologic study, low paternal care was found to be a risk factor for bulimia (Kendler et al., 1991). There is no typical anorexia nervosa family, but the mothers show an overly strict attitude toward discipline (Rastam and Gillberg, 1991).

Studying a large number of patients with bulimia nervosa, Mitchell, Hatsukami, Eckert, and Pyle (1985) found that the syndrome itself interfered with interpersonal relationships and impaired work. Indeed, if the bulimic fears eating a normal meal on a date or eating pizza with a group of friends, they avoid these encounters and become isolated from peer support. Using a social adjustment scale at evaluation and at follow-up one year later, the bulimic patient exhibited poorer adjustment than schizophrenic and alcoholic patients (Norman and Herzog, 1984). Whether these patients showed poor adjustment prior to the onset of the illness is unclear since a prospective study of an adolescent patient is lacking.

STRESSFUL LIFE EVENTS IN ANOREXIA NERVOSA AND BULIMIA NERVOSA

Negative encounters may interact on eating disorders in many ways. A single event or a series of negative events over time may precipitate an eating disorder syndrome. Stressful events may initiate altered eating attitudes or behaviors that develop over time into full-blown syndromes. Beyond playing a role in the etiology of these disorders, stressful events may affect the severity of anorexia nervosa and bulimia. For example, multiple negative events may produce greater severity of symptoms. On the other side, the lack of stressful events may cause a diminution of symptoms. Adverse events may be correlated with outcome. Since these are chronic illnesses, stressful encounters must be assessed, not only at intake, but throughout the course of the illness.

Many patients with anorexia nervosa and bulimia nervosa are young women who are still living with their families or who are financially dependent upon them. The stressful events impingeing on the family unit must be assessed since this social network may support or undermine the patient. One caveat applies to this issue. The patient may be unaware of certain negative events, and informants other than the patient need to be interviewed. Events involving parental psychiatric disorders, finances, parental illegal activities, and marital infidelity are underreported by the young patient. For example, a 16-year-old girl presenting with bulimia nervosa may be unaware that her father has had to file for bankruptcy. The patient may only be aware that her previously supportive father is irritable and emotionally unavailable to her.

The Diagnostic and Statistical Manual of Mental Disorders (DSM-III-R) (1987) lists stressful life events as a predisposing factor in some people with anorexia nervosa. In a study of bulimia nervosa, Lacey, Coker, and Birtchnell (1986) found that major life stresses occurred in the 6 months prior to the onset of illness. The most frequently cited stressors were sexual conflict endorsed by 72 percent of the bulimics and a major life change, such as a move or job change, endorsed by 70 percent. The authors point out that these events occurred while the women were dieting. In the same study, perpetuating factors for bulimia were doubts about femininity and attractiveness, poor relations with parents, academic striving, parental marital conflict, and poor peer group relations. Johnson, Stuckey, Lewis, and Schwartz (1982) found that bulimics identified their difficulty in handling emotions, such as boredom, loneliness, and anger, as the precipitating event that initiated their bingeing. Thirty-four percent of this sample were involved in restrictive dieting.

With a retrospective study of adolescents with their first episode of anorexia nervosa, Strober (1983) found that a bulimic subgroup of anorexia nervosa patients had twice as many life change events as the restrictor subgroup.

In the area of body image, adolescent girls felt ashamed of their bodies, ugly, and unattractive (Offer et al., 1988).

Sexual Abuse in Eating Disorder Patients

The issue of sexual abuse as a stressful event has drawn significant interest. High rates of sexual abuse in eating disorder patients have been reported. Solurshi, Bissett, and Fournier (1990) hypothesize that the bulimic subtype of anorexia patients have suffered childhood sexual trauma. They point to the intrusive food thoughts, avoidance of intimate relationships, and marked startle response as indicators of the trauma. In a study of anorexic and bulimic inpatients, 50 percent reported histories of sexual abuse. Of the abusive experiences, only rape had been reported to others. The most frequent form of sexual abuse was incest, and the perpetrator was most frequently the father (Hall, Tice, Beresford, Wooley, and Hall, 1989). Most eating disorder patients are treated on an outpatient basis, no study has looked at the prevalence of sexual trauma in eating disorder subtypes compared to other psychiatric outpatients and controls. A treatment intervention that addresses the abuse may be more effective for this subgroup, and may produce a better outcome.

Folsom, Krahn, Nairn, Gold, Demitrack, and Silk (1993) reported high rates of sexual abuse for eating disorder patients, but found that this rate was not significantly higher than the rate of sexual abuse in other hospitalized psychiatric patients. They found no relationship between the severity of symptoms and sexual abuse. But the sexually abused eating disorder patients were more severely disturbed psychiatrically. Phobic and obsessive symptoms were particularly prominent in the abused group.

ZINC DEFICIENCY AND EATING DISORDERS

The combination of increased utilization with the growth spurt of puberty, decreased intake from cultural pressure, and possible increased loss all make the adolescent girl at risk for low zinc status. These physiological factors combined with individual pathology and family stresses may establish the groundwork for anorexia nervosa and bulimia nervosa.

In conceptualizing the development of these disorders, stress from cultural, psychological, and biological components must be considered. Cases of posttraumatic anorexia nervosa (Damlouji and Ferguson, 1985) have been reported. The onset of the syndrome is associated with a physical injury or illness. This group of cases well may represent an interaction of these three components of stress and the medical condition of zinc deficiency. The stress from any chronic or acute infection or any tissue injury lowers serum zinc. The signs and symptoms of zinc deficiency and anorexia nervosa and bulimia are remarkably similar.

Zinc is necessary for every phase of cell division, normal immune function, and appetite regulation. It is contained in over 200 coenzymes necessary for brain function. Recently it has been found to be a transcription factor and is essential for the adequate function of nerve growth factor.

The syndrome of zinc deficiency (ZD) was defined by Prasad, Halsted, and Nadini (1961). Zinc deficiency in humans is comprised of:

Loss of appetite (anorexia);
Loss of menses in females and impotence in males;
Skin lesions;
Abnormal immune function;
Lack of growth; and
Lack of maturation of sexual function if it occurs in a juvenile.

The normal dietary requirement for zinc is 12 mg/day for females 12 and over and 15 mg/day for males (National Research Council, 1989). Sources of zinc in the Western diet come primarily from red meat, but other sources are nuts and beans. For example, a 3-oz steak will contain 6 mg of zinc. The richest known dietary source of zinc comes from Atlantic oysters at 76 mg/3 oz serving. Many foods contain zinc, but in low levels; only about 40 percent of dietary zinc is absorbed. Vegetarian diets are often lacking in adequate zinc, and knowledgeable vegetarians will often use zinc supplements.

Cultures that do not eat meat for religious reasons or have a limited meat supply have strongly adhered to dietary customs that facilitate the absorption of zinc. In India it is common wisdom that "good" mothers always follow children's meals with yogurt.

Our group has shown that fermented products like yogurt facilitate the absorption of zinc to as much as 80 percent of dietary zinc consumed.

Zinc is a regulator of appetite. Besides anorexia, a cyclic eating pattern occurs if the diet of a zinc-deficient animal contains 20 percent protein. Animals fed a zinc deficient diet with 20 percent protein show a regular cycle of eating then abstaining from eating (Chesters and Quarterman, 1970). It is important to add that most American diets contain 20 percent protein.

In addition to the cyclic eating pattern, zinc deficient animals "play" with their food. They will knock it out of their bowls, or spill food out of their mouths while eating. This is such a hallmark of the zinc deficit rat that cage floors littered with food indicate which rats are zinc deficient.

Adolescent females in Western cultures are bombarded with messages about body shape and at any given time a significant proportion of this population is dieting. The diets vary in content and extent, but most of them involve the avoidance of meat, particularly red meat. Zinc deficiency may develop from zinc loss.

Besides low intake, there are several known factors which result in zinc loss. Growth uses zinc stores; any type of tissue injury results in significant zinc loss; a well-known phenomenon is the decrease of serum zinc levels in pregnancy. The placenta actively transports zinc to the fetus. Alcohol ingestion causes the loss of zinc with urinary excretion. Vomiting results in zinc loss because gastric enzymes contained in the vomitus are rich in zinc. Rising estrogen levels are correlated with low serum zinc.

In a study of patients attending an eating disorder service, 40 percent of the patients with bulimia nervosa and 54 percent of the patients with anorexia nervosa were defined as zinc deficient (Humphries, Vivian, Stuart, and McClain, 1989). Zinc deficiency was defined as a serum zinc below 70 mg/dL or a 24-hour urinary zinc below 200 mg. The normal range for serum zinc is 70 to 120 mg/dL and the normal range for a 24-hour urinary collection is 200 to 700 mg/24 hr. The interaction between stress and dieting in teenage girls may lead to a physiologic condition, zinc deficiency, that causes anorexia or bulimia.

CONCLUDING REMARKS

The complex interplay between stress and eating behaviors provides a fertile area of inquiry. Western culture, developmental issues, nutrition, physiologic status all interact, and the study of this area invites multidisciplinary inquiry.

REFERENCES

American Psychiatric Association (1987), *Diagnostic and Statistical Manual of Mental Disorders*, 3rd ed. rev. (DSM-III-R). Washington, DC: American Psychiatric Press.
——— (1994), *Diagnostic and Statistical Manual of Mental Disorders*, 4th ed. (DSM-IV). Washington, DC: American Psychiatric Press.
Beiler, E. M., & Terrell, F. (1990), Stress, coping style, and problem solving ability among eating-disordered inpatients. *J. Clin. Psychol.*, 46:592–599.
Billings, A. G., & Moos, R. H. (1981), The role of coping measures and social resources in attenuating the stress of life events. *J. Behav. Med.*, 6:139–157.
Brunner, R. L., Maloney, M. J., Daniels, S., Mays, W., & Farrell, W. (1989), A controlled study of type A behavior and psychophysiologic responses to stress in anorexia nervosa. *Psychiat. Res.*, 30:223–230.
Butterfield, P. S., & Leclair, S. (1988), Cognitive characteristics of bulimic and drug abusing women. *Addict. Behav.*, 13:131–138.
Cattanach, L., Malley, R., & Rodin, J. (1988), Psychologic & physiologic reactivity to stressors in eating disordered individuals. *Psychosom. Med.*, 50(6):591–599.
Chatoor, I., Conley, C., & Dickson, L. (1988), Food refusal after an incident of choking: A post traumatic eating disorder. *J. Amer. Acad. Child Psychiatry*, 27:105–110.
Chesters, J. K., & Quarterman, J. (1970), Effects of zinc deficiency on food intake and feeding patterns in rats. *Brit. J. Nutr.*, 24:1061–1069.
Damlouji, N. F., & Ferguson, J. M. (1985), Trazodone-induced delirium in bulimic patients. *Amer. J. Psychiatry*, 141(3):434–435.
Folkman, S., Lazarus, R. S., Dunkel-Schietter, C., De Longis, A., & Gruen, R. J. (1986), The dynamic of stressful encounter: Cognitive appraisal, coping, and encounter outcome. *J. Person. & Soc. Psychol.*, 50:992–1003.
Folsom, V., Krahn, D., Nairn, K., Gold, L., Demitrack, M. A., & Silk, K. R. (1993), The impact of sexual and physical abuse on eating disordered and psychiatric symptoms: A comparison of eating disordered and psychiatric inpatients. *Internat. J. Eat. Disord.*, 13:249–257.

Fride, E., Dan, Y., Gavish, M., & Weinstock, M. (1985), Prenatal stress impairs maternal behavior in a conflict situation and reduces hippocampal benzodiazepine receptors. *Life Sci.*, 36:2103–2109.

Garner, D. M., Garfinkel, P. E. Schartz, D. M., & Thompson, M. (1980), Cultural expectations of thinness in women. *Psychol. Rep.*, 47(2):483–491.

Hall, R. C. W., Tice, L., Beresford, T. P., Wooley, B., & Hall, A. K. (1989), Sexual abuse in patients with anorexia nervosa and bulimia. *Psychosom.*, 39:73–79.

Harris, E. L., Blum, R., & Resnick, M. (1991), Teen females in Minnesota: A potrait of quiet disturbances. *Women & Therapy*, 11:119–135.

Heilbrun, A. B., Jr., & Bloomfield, D. L. (1986), Cognitive differences between bulimic and anorexic females: Self-control deficits in bulimia. *Internat. J. Eat. Disorder*, 5:209–222.

Herzog, D. B., Borus, J. F., Hamburg, P., Ott, I. L., & Concus, A. (1987), Substance use, eating behaviors, and social impairment. *J. Med. Ed.*, 62:651–657.

Hibbard, R. A., Brack, C. J., Rauch, S., & Orr, D. P. (1988), Abuse, feelings, and health behaviors in a student population. *Amer. J. Dis. Child.*, 142:326–330.

Humphrey, L. L. (1986), Structural analysis of parent-child relationships in eating disorders. *J. Abnorm. Psychol.*, 95:395–402.

Humphries, L., Vivian, B., Stuart, M., & McClain, C. (1989), Zinc deficiency and eating disorders. *J. Clin. Psychiatry*, 50(12):456–459.

Jensen, P. S., Richters, J., Ussery, T., Bloedan, L., & Davis, H. (1991), Child psychopathology and environmental influences: Discrete life events versus ongoing adversity. *J. Amer. Acad. Child Adolesc. Psychiatry*, 30:303–309.

Johnson, C. L., Stuckey, M. L., Lewis, D. L., & Schwartz, D. M. (1982), Bulimia: A descriptive survey of 316 cases. *Internat. J. Eat. Disord.*, 2:3–16.

Jones, B. P., Duncan, C. C., Browers, P., & Mirsky, A. F. (1991), Cognition in eating disorders. *J. Clin. Experim. Neuropsychol.*, 13:711–728.

Kagan, D. M., & Squires, R. L. (1984), Eating disorders among adolescents: Patterns and prevalence. *Adolescence*, 19:15–29.

Kalucy, R. S., Crisp, A. H., Harding, B., & Britta, C. (1977), A study of 56 families with anorexia nervosa. *Brit. J. Med. Psychol.*, 50:381–395.

Kendler, K. S., MacLean, C., Neale, M., Kessler, R., Heath, A., & Evans, L. (1991), The genetic epidemiology of bulimia nervosa. *Amer. J. Psychiatry*, 148:1627–1636.

Keyes, A., Brozek, J., Henshel, A., Micholson, O., & Taylor, H. L. (1950), *Biology of Human Starvation*. Minneapolis: University of Minnesota Press.

Killen, J. D., Taylor, C. B. Telch, M. J., Saylor, K. E., Maron, D. J., & Robinson, T. N. (1987), Evidence for alcohol-stress link among normal weight adolescents reporting purging behavior. *Internat. J. Eat. Disord.*, 3:349–356.

Lacey, J. H., Chadbund, C., Crisp, A. H., Whitehead, J., & Stordy, J. (1978), Variations in energy intake of adolescent school girls. *J. Hum. Nutrit.*, 32:419–429.

———— Coker, S., & Birtchnell, S. A. (1986), Bulimia: Factors associated with its etiology and maintenance. *Internat. J. Eat. Disord.*, 5:475–478.

Laessle, R. G., Beumount, P. J., Batow, P., Lenner, W., O'Connor, M., Pirke, K. M., Touyz, S. W., & Waadt, S. (1991), A comparison of nutritional management with stress management in the treatment of bulimia nervosa. *Brit. J. Psychiatry*, 159:250–261.

Levine, A. P., & Hyler, S. E. (1986), DSM-III personality diagnosis in bulimia. *Comp. Psychiatry*, 27:47–53.

McCormack, S., & Carman, R. S. (1989), Eating motivations and bulimic behavior among college women. *Psychol. Rep.*, 64:1163–1166.

Mitchell, J. E., Hatsukami, D., Eckert, E. D., & Pyle, R. L. (1985), Characteristics of 275 patients with bulimia. *Amer. J. Psychiatry*, 142:482–485.

National Research Council (1989), *Recommended Daily Allowances/Subcommittee on the Tenth Edition of the RDA's*. Washington, DC: National Academy Press.

Neckowitz, R., & Morrison, J. L. (1991), Interactional coping strategies of normal-weight bulimic women in intimate and nonintimate stressful situations. *Psychol. Rep.*, 69:1167–1175.

Norman, D. K., & Herzog, D. B. (1984), Persistent social maladjustment in bulimia: A one year follow-up. *Amer. J. Psychiatry*, 141:444–446.

Offer, P., Ostrov, E., & Howard, K. I. (1988), *The Teenage World: Adolescents' Self-Image in Ten Countries*. New York: Plenum Press.

Patton, G. C., Johnson-Sabine, E., Wood, K., Mann, A. H., & Wakeling, A. (1991), Abnormal eating attitudes in London schoolgirls—a prospective epidemiological study: Outcome at twelve-month follow-up. *Psychol. Med.*, 20:383–394.

Prasad, A., Halsted, J., & Nadini, M. (1961), Syndrome of iron deficiency: Anemia, hepatosplenomegaly, hypogonadism, dwarfism and geophagia. *Amer. J. Med.*, 31:532.

Rastam, M., & Gillberg, C. (1991), The family background in anorexia nervosa: A population-based study. *J. Amer. Acad. Child Adolesc. Psychiatry*, 30(2): 283–289.

Roesen, J. C., Tracy, B., & Howell, D. (1990), Life stress, psychological symptoms and weight reducing behavior in adolescent girls: A prospective analysis. *Internat. J. Eat. Disord.*, 9:17–26.

Rorty, M., Yager, J., & Rosotto, E. (1993), Why and how women recover from bulimia nervosa. The subjective appraisals of forty women recovered for a year or more. *Internat. J. Eat. Disord.*, 14:249–260.

Russell, G. (1979), Bulimia nervosa: An ominous variant of anorexia nervosa. *Psychol. Med.*, 9:429–448.

Selby, R., Weinstein, H. M., & Bird, T. S. (1990), The health of university athletes: Attitudes, behaviors, and stressors. *J. Amer. Coll. Health*, 39:11–18.

Sharpe-Radke, N., Whitney-Saltiel, D., & Rodin, J. (1990), Fat distribution as a risk factor for weight and eating concerns. *Internat. J. Eat. Disord.*, 9:27–36.

Shatford, L. A., & Evans, D. R. (1986), Bulimia as a manifestation of the stress process: A LISREL causal modeling analysis. *Internat. J. Eat. Disord.*, 5:451–473.

Sheppard, J. A., & Kashani, J. H. (1991), The relationship of hardiness, gender, and stress to health outcomes in adolescents. *J. Personality*, 59:747–768.

Sohlberg, S., & Norring, C. (1992), A three-year prospective study of life events and course for adults with anorexia nervosa/bulimia nervosa. *Psychosom. Med.*, 54:59–69.

Solurshi, L. P., Bissett, A. D., & Fournier, J. A. A. (1990), Bulimia associated with sexual trauma (Letter to the editor). *Amer. J. Psychiatry*, 147(3):373.

Steiner, H., & Levine, S. (1988), Acute stress response in anorexia nervosa. *Child Psychiat. Hum. Dev.*, 18:208–218.

Strober, M. (1983), Stressful life events associated with bulimia in anorexia nervosa. *Internat. J. Eating Dis.*, 3:3–16.

Vanderlinden, J., Vandereycken, W., van Dyck, R., & Vertommen, H. (1993), Dissociative experiences and trauma in eating disorders. *Internat. J. Eat. Disord.*, 13:187–193.

Wadden, T. A., & Stunkard, A. J. (1985), Social and psychological consequences of obesity. *Ann. Intern. Med.*, 103(6 Part 2):1062–1067.

Willenbring, M. L., Levine, A. P., & Morley, J. E. (1986), Stress induced eating and food preference in humans: A pilot study. In: *Pharmacology of Eating Disorders*, 5, ed. M. O. Carrula & J. E. Blundell. New York: Raven Press, pp. 855–864.

Chapter 15
Retirement as a Stressful Life Event

Raymond Bossé, Ph.D., Avron Spiro III, Ph.D., and Michael R. Levenson, Ph.D.

Most humans spend a major portion of their adult lives working. Our own self-concept and the view we have of others is very much influenced by what we and they do for a living. In the United States, when people meet, very early in their conversation, one or all of the following questions tend to be asked: "What do you do for a living?" "What does your wife or husband do?" "What does your mother or father do?" Occupation, like race, ethnicity, or religion, has served as a marker by which we define ourselves, maintain our self-identity, and relate to others.

As retirement became a more frequent occurrence earlier in this century, it was natural for social scientists to hypothesize that the loss of the work role would cause distress. (For a historical perspective on the projected deleterious consequences of retirement see Barron, Streib, and Suchman [1952]; MacBride [1976]). The medical profession also enunciated a "retirement impact theory" based on the assumption that retirement is a stressful experience resulting in physical disorders and sometimes death (McMahan and Ford, 1955; Tyhurst, Salk, and Kennedy, 1957). The stress of retirement has been attributed invariably to the losses it entails in such areas as income, companionship, activity, prestige, and self-identity (Streib and Schneider, 1971; Crawford, 1972, 1973).

Adding to the negative view of retirement is the fact that some workers retire because of an illness which may lead to an early death after retirement. Almost everyone knows someone who retired and died soon after; thus it is easy to conclude post hoc ergo propter hoc.

It is therefore not surprising that retirement found its way into and continues to be included in stressful life events inventories (Holmes and Rahe, 1967; Murrell, Norris, and Hutchins, 1984; Aldwin, 1990). The inclusion of retirement in such inventories initially had validity because it is a major event which interrupts or modifies 30 to 50 years of previous participation in the labor force. Its inclusion did not seem to require any more justification than did the inclusion of the death of a loved one. It seemed natural that the loss of a major aspect of one's self-definition should be stressful.

Nevertheless, the issue of retirement as a stressful experience remained an open question in gerontology and in the stress literature in general. One reason for this is that much of the "evidence" was indirect or the stressfulness was inferred or implied.

STRESS IMPLIED

For instance, the experience of retirement as a stressful event has been implicated in matters as serious as the higher rates of suicide among white males beginning at age 65 (Miller, 1979) and also in the higher mortality rates among retirees compared to workers (Myers, 1954; Powers and Bultena, 1972; Palmore and Stone, 1973; Haynes, McMichael, and Tyroler, 1978; Adams and Lefebvre, 1981).

It should be noted that not all studies of retirement and death have found a significant positive relationship. Rowland (1977), who found relocation and death of a loved one, but *not* retirement, to be fairly accurate predictors of death, suggested that studies relating retirement to increased death rates have had a number of weaknesses. In particular, many of these studies failed to take account of health status which may have precipitated the retirement.

More moderate consequences of retirement stress have also been suggested, such as retirees having a poorer sense of morale compared to workers (Thompson, 1973). Additionally, there are reports that retirees miss the income received from working (Harris and Associates, 1981) as well as reports of substantial reductions in income after retirement (Parnes, 1981). It has been suggested that marital relations become strained following retirement (Keating and Cole, 1980; Szinovacz, 1980; Hill and Dorfman, 1982).

Another view is that the apparent stress of retirement is indirect, that is, not due to retirement itself but to the circumstances surrounding the event or to the retiree's personal characteristics. For instance, Blau, Oser, and Stephens (1982) found only 17.3 percent of male and 11.1 percent of female retirees dissatisfied with retirement, and reported that, compared to the satisfied retirees, the dissatisfied retirees had less education, less adequate income, saw friends less often, and reported poorer physical and mental health. Thus, Blau et al. suggest that even for those people who may be dissatisfied with retirement and who therefore find it stressful, the stress may be due to factors other than the retirement itself. Similarly, Palmore, Burchett, Fillenbaum, George, and Wallman (1985) suggested that "negative consequences" of retirement will depend on the type of outcome measured such as loss of income, the timing of the retirement event, or on "the type of workers."

An entirely new perspective has begun to appear in the literature, concomitant with the focus on posttraumatic stress disorder (PTSD) in American war veterans. Convincing anecdotal and case report evidence now suggest that World War II and Korean War veterans who had never been diagnosed as suffering from PTSD, begin to manifest symptoms of PTSD following retirement (e.g., Van Dyke, Zilberg, and McKinnon, 1985; Pary, Turns, and Tobias, 1986; Pomerantz, 1991).

More recent research has attempted more direct investigations of the two fundamental questions related to retirement stress: Is retirement stressful? and if so, for whom is retirement stressful?

IS RETIREMENT STRESSFUL?

Early on, a number of studies reported at least a percentage of retirees to be unhappy, dissatisfied, or in one way or another experiencing difficulty with retirement. For instance Atchley (1975) reported that 30 percent of the retired teachers and telephone company employees he studied felt they would never get used to retirement. A report in 1965 noted that 33 percent of the retirees studied were less than satisfied with retirement, while Streib and Schneider (1971) found 10 percent of their sample scoring high on a job deprivation scale and rejecting retirement by taking another job. Braithwaite, Gibson, and Bosly-Craft (1986) reported that 32 percent of the males and females in their study found retirement adjustment either difficult or somewhat difficult. Although these studies and others did not measure stress specifically, they nevertheless suggest that retirement is stressful for at least some retirees.

A study by Matthews, Brown, Davis, and Denton (1982) is probably the first published report which specifically asked retirees about the stressfulness of their retiring. Retirees were asked to rate on a scale of 1 to 5 the stressfulness of 34 life events which they had personally experienced at some point in their lifetime. The authors reported that the event of retirement ranked 28th among the 34 stressful life events listed. The events that were more stressful than retirement included: 29, the end of a romance; 30, leaving home for the first time; 31, when you or spouse stopped smoking; 32, a change in religion; 33, when you or spouse stopped drinking; 34, when you left school. The first and second most stressful events were: death of a spouse and the birth of a child or children.

A prospective study in Turku, Finland, concluded that "retirement is not a stressor of crucial importance or a life crisis" (Mattila, Joukamaa, and Salokangas, 1989), thus supporting the general findings of Matthews and her associates. It should be noted, however, that the Matthews et al. (1982) findings should be viewed with caution because they are based on lifelong recollection. It may not be valid to compare the stress of a recent event like retirement with that of the death of a spouse, which could have occurred at any time in the past, or with the even more remote adolescent experience of leaving home for the first time.

Retirement Transition Stress vs. State Stress

With retirement as with other major life events we routinely anticipate a short-term "acute" effect in addition to long-term delayed effects. The importance of differentiating the short-term from the long-term consequences of retirement was suggested some time ago. Atchley (1976), for instance, stressed this point in describing phases of retirement adaptation. Cherry, Zarit, and Krauss (1984) underscored the importance of length of time retired after observing significantly different postretirement adaptation patterns between relatively short-term retirees (3–6 years) compared to longer-term retirees (7+ years). The relatively recent retirees scored higher on satisfaction with retirement but lower on self-esteem and happiness, while the pattern for longer-term retirees was the reverse.

Although the retirees in the Matthews et al. (1982) study population had been retired from 1 to 5 years, the authors did not attempt to examine systematically the effect of length of time retired on stress. The only report of a differential effect of stress due to the experience of retiring (*retirement transition stress*) compared to the stress of "being in retirement" (*retirement state stress*) was a weak .09 zero-order correlation coefficient ($p < .05$) "between the recency of retirement and the perception of it as a critical event." Thus Matthews et al. (1982) suggest that, overall, retirement transition is more stressful than the retirement state.

The research of Bossé, Aldwin, Levenson, and Ekerdt (1987) showed that cross-sectionally, even controlling for physical health, retirees reported significantly more emotional health problems as assessed by the SCL-90-R (Derogatis, 1983) than workers. Subsequent longitudinal data revealed that it was the long-term retirees, men retired for 3 or more years, who reported more emotional symptoms. The recent retirees (less than 3 years) did not report more symptoms than the workers. This finding suggested that it is "being in retirement" that is stressful rather than experiencing the event of retirement (Bossé, Aldwin, Levenson, Workman-Daniels, 1989).

Inspired by this finding, Bossé Aldwin, Levenson, and Workman-Daniels (1991) and Bossé, Levenson, Spiro, Aldwin, and Mroczek (1992) differentiated retirement transition from retirement state in their study of retirement stress.

Bossé et al. (1991) investigated the stressfulness of retirement among the participants in the Normative Aging Study (NAS) of the Veterans Administration Outpatient Clinic, Boston. Among the respondents to a 1985 questionnaire, 676 (45%) were retired. Of these, 200 had retired during the previous year and constituted the subsample used for the study of retirement *transition* stress while the entire group of retirees was included in analyses of retirement *state* stress. To be considered a retiree one had to be either retired and not employed at all or retired but still employed part-time.

TRANSITION STRESS

The stressfulness of retirement as a life event was measured by the Elders Life Stress Inventory (ELSI: Aldwin, 1990). The ELSI is composed of a list of 31 stressful life events. Men were asked to identify those events which they had experienced in the last year and to score the stressfulness of the event on a scale of 1 "not at all stressful" to 5 "extremely stressful."

Of the men who had retired the previous year, 69.6 percent said they found retirement "not at all" or "a little" stressful, and 30.4 percent found it "somewhat," "very," or "extremely" stressful. Furthermore, of the 31 life events listed, a respondent's own retirement scored thirtieth with the second lowest mean stressfulness rating (1.95). The only life event that received a lower mean stress rating (1.63) was "spouse's retirement." These retirement stress ratings contrasted with the stress rating of other events experienced in the past year such as death of spouse (4.42), death of son or daughter (4.20), institutionalization of spouse (4.07), and worsening relations with a child (3.98).

STATE STRESS

To examine retirement state stress the respondents to the NAS survey were asked to identify the most troubling work or retirement hassle they had experienced in the last 3 months and to rate their stressfulness on a scale from 1 ("Not troubled at all") to 7 ("The most troubled I've ever been").

Of the 676 retirees who responded to this question, 466 (68.9%) reported no retirement-related problems during the previous 3 months, while 210 (31.1%) reported a variety of problems. The most frequent problems reported by retirees were boredom (6.2%) and finances (6.1%).

By contrast, 545 of the 840 workers (64.9%) reported a work problem, most of which dealt with organizational problems (19.9%), interpersonal relations (13.1%), or planning for retirement (9.4%). Thus, twice as many workers reported having a work problem as retirees who reported a retirement problem.

As for the stressfulness of work-related problems compared to the stress of retirement, the 4.49 mean stress rating for workers was significantly greater than that of retirees at 4.07. Because of the significant mean age difference between workers (54.63) and retirees (64.87), age was controlled in the preceding analysis.

Hence, although retirement has tended to be ranked as less stressful than other life events and declared not to be stressful by a great majority of retirees, Matthews et al. (1982) and Bossé et al. (1991) both reported retirement to be stressful for approximately 30 percent of the retirees they surveyed.

The U.S. census for 1990 lists over 10 million people between the ages of 62 and 65, who are thus eligible for retirement with Social Security benefits. If two-thirds of these people are retired, as workforce participation statistics suggest, 30 percent implies that some 2 million people may find retirement stressful at any one time.

For Whom Is Retirement Stressful?

Though the findings reviewed above suggest that retirement may not be stressful for all, they do not help us identify those who might regard retirement as stressful. The evidence indicates that research should no longer address general questions such as, Is retirement stressful? or How stressful is retirement? but rather pose more specific questions such as, For whom is retirement stressful? and What are the predictors of retirement stress? In other words, among those who find retirement to be stressful, What are the circumstances of the retirement event or the personal characteristics of these retirees? To answer these questions one should examine in particular the social, demographic, motivational, and other psychological and health factors related to retirement.

In addition, because of important differences suggested between the experience of the retirement as an event and that of retirement as a state, we should also be sensitive to asking: (1) for whom is the event or the process of retiring stressful? and (2) for whom is the state of being retired stressful?

Predictors of Retirement State Stress

Unfortunately, most research on the consequences of retirement does not differentiate the stress experienced as a result of retiring (transition stress) from the stress of being in retirement (state stress). Consequently the data reviewed in this section invariably refer to retirement consequences in general without differentiating transition from state. That is, these studies have tended to lump retirees together irrespective of time since the event.

The question of who finds retirement stressful is a particularly difficult issue because of the diversity of predictor variables used in different studies. The issue is further complicated by the fact that few studies assess specifically the stressfulness of retirement. Instead, the literature is replete with studies of retirement adjustment, retirement satisfaction, morale, physical, or emotional health. If we take these as proxies for retirement stress, then a picture (if not a caricature) of the "stressed-out" retiree begins to emerge.

Socioeconomic Status. Overall, the importance of socioeconomic status tends to be different for men and women retirees. Matthews and Brown (1987), using regression analysis, found higher socioeconomic status a significant predictor of retirement stress for men, while for women, socioeconomic status was unrelated to retirement stress. Bossé et al. (1991) found that while white collar occupation in males was correlated with state stress on a bivariate level, that relationship disappeared in analyses with multivariate controls.

In contrast to Matthews and Brown, Blau et al. (1982) found that women who were dissatisfied with retirement (presumably experiencing stress), reported less *education* and less *income* in retirement than satisfied retirees. Loss of income in particular has been found to be a significant predictor of poor morale (Richardson and Kilty, 1991), or of poor adjustment (Palmore et al., 1985) following retirement.

Circumstances of the Event. Several circumstances related to the event of retiring have been found to be related to state stress.

Timing. Men who retired early, defined as prior to age 62 (i.e., before eligibility for Social Security benefits) have been reported to have lower income, to have more likely retired for health reasons, and to report less happiness and life satisfaction in retirement (Palmore, Fillenbaum, and George, 1984). In addition,

Palmore et al. (1985) reported significant negative relationships between early retirement and income and health. Although the preceding studies focused on retirement satisfaction rather than on retirement stress, the findings reported coincide with those of Bossé et al. (1987) who found early retirees to report higher levels of emotional distress as assessed by the SCL-90-R (Derogatis, 1983) than workers of similar age. This latter finding also supports the notion that early retirees are more likely to be stressed, although there is no evidence that the stress is caused by retirement itself. Stress could well be caused by a third factor, such a declining health, which may have prompted the early retirement, or by loss of income due to retirement.

The Reason for Retirement. Men whose retirement was unexpected or involuntary have been shown to find retirement stressful (Matthews and Brown, 1987). In a similar fashion Bossé et al. (1992) found men who retired for negative reasons, including unexpected or involuntary retirement, saw retirement as stressful.

Men retired for 2 to 3 years whose retirement was involuntary scored significantly lower than voluntarily retired men on emotional satisfaction, sense of usefulness, self-image, emotional stability, and interpersonal relations (Peretti and Wilson, 1975). Such findings lend credence to the notion that an unplanned, unexpected, or involuntary retirement is a significant predictor of retirement stress. Comparable findings were reported by Floyd, Haynes, Doll, Winemiller, Lemsky, Burgy, Werle, and Heilman (1992). (For a thorough evaluation of the impact of the reason for retiring on retirement adjustment see Crowley [1985].)

Health. Health is probably the most commonly studied variable relative to retirement in general, but it is most often considered as an outcome or consequence of retirement. That approach has generally not been fruitful because retirement has been shown to have deleterious health consequences only for a minority of retirees. In studies where poor health has been examined as a precipitator of retirement, the focus has tended to be on outcomes such as the poor adaptation, satisfaction, or morale of retirees rather than on retirement stress per se. That literature generally reports that retirees who were forced to retire because of health are less well adapted, less satisfied with retirement, or have lower morale than retirees who did not retire for health reasons. Retiring for reasons of health is therefore analogous to other unplanned retirements as described above.

Nevertheless, in the two major retirement stress studies, retiring for health reasons was *not* found to predict retirement state stress (Matthews and Brown, 1987; Bossé et al., 1992). In addition, Matthews and Brown also showed that although poor health *during* retirement was reported to predict low morale for both men and women, it did not predict their viewing retirement as a critical life event. It should be noted, however, that in the Bossé et al. (1992) study, health was not used as a single predictor of retirement but was combined with three other variables to define a measure of hassles as described below.

Other Life Events. Research on role transitions and role loss in later life has suggested that there is a cumulative impact of life events, both positive and negative (George, 1980; Elwell and Maltbie-Crannell, 1981). This evidence prompted investigations into the cumulative effect of other life events on retirement. Matthews and Brown (1987) found that for male retirees, the greater the number of critical or stressful life events in their lifetime the more *negative* the impact of retirement. For women, on the other hand, the greater the number of critical life events experienced, the more *positive* the impact of retirement. Bossé et al. (1991) similarly found that male retirees who found retirement stressful experienced more stressful life events in the year before they retired.

Hassles. Bossé et al. (1991) assessed daily stressors or "hassles" experienced in five life domains: health, marital (which could include marital problems and/or their spouse's own difficulties), social relations, household finances, and work or retirement. The respondents indicated whether they had experienced a problem in any of these areas *during the previous 3 months*, and indicated how much they were troubled by that problem on a scale from 1 ("Not troubled at all") to 7 ("The most troubled I've been"). Ratings for four of the domains (health, marital, social relations, and household finances) were summed and divided by the number of valid items. The investigators felt justified in generating an overall hassles measure, rather than examining the four domains singly, because the purpose of the research was to examine the global effect of hassles on coping with retirement. The resulting measure thus provided an indicator of the stressfulness of hassles during the past 3 months. This measure proved to be strongly associated with retirement state stress at the bivariate level as well as in multivariate regressions including other social and personality variables. It should be noted that this seemingly powerful predictor of retirement stress is in fact multidimensional, including health and income which, as noted above, are significant predictors in their own right.

Social Support. There is evidence from a study by Sagy and Antonovsky (1992) that family sense of coherence (SOC) correlates with adaptation to retirement. Unfortunately, the family SOC construct is not uniformly conceptualized. In various contexts it refers to "family personality," a cognitive map, a family perception, a family worldview, or shared constructs. The assumption of researchers who have used the concept is that the adaptation of a family to stressors is shaped by the family's view of the world it lives in and not just by the views of the individual family members.

In some of their analyses, Sagy and Antonovsky found that the family sense of coherence was a more important predictor of the retiree's adaptation to retirement than the retiree's own sense of coherence. The authors suggest that the process of overcoming a stress such as that of retirement may be better understood by viewing it in its social context, presumably because of the importance of social support. Mattila, Joukamaa, and Salokangas (1988), like Sagy and Antonovsky, found that well-adjusted retirees reported significantly more social support than did poorly adjusted retirees.

On the other hand, Matthews and Brown (1987) examined a number of indices of social support such as marital status, presence of children, changes in social activities, and change in contact with friends. They failed to find a relationship between these indices of social support and retirement stress.

Somewhat more sophisticated concepts of quantitative and qualitative social support were examined by Bossé et al. (1992) as possible predictors of retirement stress, but no significant relations were found. Perhaps the failure to relate loss of social support following retirement to stress was due to the fact that quantitative and qualitative support were differentiated from one another. Consistently, Bossé, Aldwin, Levenson, Workman-Daniels, and Ekerdt (1990) and Bossé, Aldwin, Levenson, Spiro, and Mroczek (1993), have found losses in quantitative social support but continuity of qualitative support following retirement. Their findings coincide with convoy theory (Kahn and Antonucci, 1980; Antonucci and Akiyama, 1987) and with selectivity theory (Carstensen, 1987; Fredrickson and Carstensen, 1990), both of which propose that well-being among the elderly is relatively unaffected by losses in quantitative social support.

If these theories are correct, loss of quantitative support after retirement may not be stressful because of the continuity of qualitative supports. Also, if these theories are correct, it may be erroneous to think of the Sagy and Antonovsky (1992) findings relative to family SOC, or a family's "cognitive map," as referring to social support. The fact that Mattila et al. (1988) found social support related to retirement adaptation which is seen as a proxy for stress appears to leave as an open question the effect of social support on retirement stress.

Work Saliency. The extent to which retirees miss the intrinsic satisfactions of the job has been hypothesized to predict adaptation to retirement. As in other instances it is assumed that those who are adapted are less stressed. There is much speculation as to gender differences in work saliency, because women have been presumed to have lower work saliency and therefore to be less stressed by retirement or to have less difficulty in adapting to it (see Matthews and Brown, 1987).

Although we found no studies that related work saliency to retirement stress specifically, there is evidence that male retirees who scored high on work saliency were less well adapted to retirement (George and Maddox, 1977) or reported lower morale (Matthews and Brown, 1987). In similar fashion, male and female retirees who scored high on work ethics (Protestant Ethic scale) were less likely to be satisfied with retirement as measured by the Retirement Description Index and the Life Satisfaction Index (Hooker and Ventis, 1984). But, in the Matthews and Brown study, work saliency was not related to morale for women, nor was it related to the perception of retirement as a critical life event by men or by women.

Prior Work Stress. Wheaton (1990) studied 120 full-time workers aged 55 and over in 1977. By 1981, 95 had retired. Wheaton reported a three-way interaction between retirement, work problems, and gender indicating a strong effect of work problems on the impact of retirement among men, but little effect among women. Specifically, for men, retirement after a job with low stress resulted in an increase in psychological symptoms, while retirement after a job with high stress resulted in fewer symptoms, compared to nonretirees. Wheaton concludes that this pattern among men suggests a cathartic effect manifested in increased symptomatology for the low work–stress group and a decrease for the high work–stress retirees. His findings further suggest that retirement itself is less a loss and more a relief from prior work stressors.

Salokangas and Joukamaa (1991) also reported that both male and female retirees who were stressed at work had positive changes in mental health following retirement. They did not report, however, whether retirees who were not stressed at work subsequently found retirement stressful.

Personality. For some time it has been suggested that personality is related to retirement adjustment. Among the first to propose this relation were Reichard, Livson, and Peterson (1962) who took a continuity perspective by suggesting that male retirees tend to resolve the problem of adjusting to retirement in a manner similar to the way they resolved earlier "vicissitudes" of life. Others have suggested that persons with such traits as flexibility and farsightedness were more likely to adjust well to retirement (Darnley, 1975). Though other suggestions have been made (see review in Friedmann and Orbach, 1974), there has been little systematic investigation into the relationship of personality to retirement adjustment and, in particular, to retirement transition or state stress.

In their research Bossé et al. (1991) attempted to relate neuroticism and extroversion as assessed by the EPI-Q (Eysenck and Eysenck, 1968; Floderus, 1974) to retirement stress, but failed to establish a significant relationship. Subsequently, Bossé et al. (1992) examined personality predictors of retirement stress using the MMPI-2 (Butcher, Dahlstrom, Graham, Tellegen, and Kramer, 1989; Butcher, Aldwin, Levenson, Ben Porath, Spiro, and Bossé, 1991). Correlations were examined between retirement state stress and the MMPI-2 clinical and validity scales. The three validity scales (L, F, and K) assess evasive responding and are used to determine overall response validity. At levels below those defined as indicating an invalid questionnaire, however, elevations on L, F, or K suggest psychopathology (Graham, 1990). The ten standard clinical scales are Hypochondriasis (Hs), Depression (D), Hysteria (Hy), Psychopathic Deviate (Pd), Masculinity-Femininity (Mf), Paranoia (Pa), Psychasthenia (Pt), Schizophrenia (Sc), Hypomania (Ma), and Social Introversion (Si). L and K were significantly negatively correlated with state stress while six of the clinical scales (Hs, Pd, Mf, Pt, Sc, and Ma) were positively correlated with state stress. In a multiple regression procedure with stepwise elimination, the validity scales were no longer significant while four of the clinical scales remained significant. However, the relationship of Sc to state stress became negative. In a regression analysis which included social circumstance variables along with the MMPI-2 scales, the only personality scale which remained a significant predictor of state stress was Ma. In a final regression analysis which included other variables such as other life events, hassles, and reason for retiring, along with the MMPI-2 scales, the only MMPI-2 scale which remained as a predictor of state stress was Ma.

PREDICTORS OF RETIREMENT TRANSITION STRESS

The predictors of retirement stress just described refer to retirees in general. Because most studies do not differentiate retirement transition from state, many of the preceding findings may also be applicable to transition retirees. In fact, several of the same variables have been identified as predictors of retirement transition stress, that is, stress occurring within 3 years or less of the retirement event. Specifically these are:

Circumstances of the Event. As was the case with state stress, an unplanned retirement was found to significantly correlate with transition stress. However, in multivariate analysis including other social and psychological variables such as other life events, hassles, and personality, no single reason for retirement was identified as a predictor of retirement transition stress (Bossé et al., 1992).

Other Life Events. Of the predictors of retirement transition stress, having experienced more stressful life events during the year preceding retirement proved to be one of the most statistically significant and most consistent (Bossé et al., 1992). The relationship persisted from correlation analysis to multivariate procedures, including variables from various domains such as personality, hassles, and reason for retiring.

Hassles. Like number of life events, hassles, or daily stressors also proved to be a strong and consistent predictor of transition stress for the men studied by Bossé and associates (1992).

Personality. Whereas two of the three MMPI-2 validity scales were found to be correlates of state stress (L and K), none of them was correlated with retirement transition stress. Among the clinical scales, a slightly different pattern of traits was correlated with transition stress at the bivariate level. Pd, Pt, Sc, and Ma continued to be correlates of transition stress as they were of state stress. However, Hs and Mf, although correlated with state stress, were not found to be significant correlates of transition stress. Scale D, which had not correlated with state stress, now became a significant correlate of transition stress (Bossé et al., 1992).

At the multivariate level Bossé and associates (1992) present a somewhat different picture. Whereas five clinical scales were found to predict state stress, only two clinical scales (D and Si) and one validity scale (K) were significantly related to transition stress in the regression equation including only the MMPI-2 scales. K and Si were negatively related to transition stress while only D was positively related to it. When the social, demographic, and circumstance variables were entered along with the MMPI-2 scales, the D scale remained a significant positive predictor while the Si scale approached significance ($p < .10$) as a negative predictor.

Conclusion

This chapter began by reviewing the literature on retirement stress. It is safe to say that historically retirement was hypothesized to be stressful, based on a theory of losses incurred by retirement. This view also influenced the notion that retirement leads to health decline and death which in turn prompted the inclusion of retirement in stressful life events inventories.

Much of the evidence provided in support of retirement stress was indirect, based on the study of retirees alone without comparing them with working age peers or, if working age peers were included, proper controls (e.g., for prior health) were not introduced. When direct testimony as to the stressfulness of retirement was obtained, retirement was found to be stressful for a minority of retirees only, usually about 30 percent (Matthews et al., 1982; Braithwaite et al., 1986; Bossé et al., 1991).

The fact that so much evidence contradicts the presumed stress-fulness of retirement leads us to suspect that at least one of the initial assumptions to be false, that is, either the meaning and nature of work, or the nature of retirement itself.

THE MEANING OR NATURE OF WORK

It may have been false to assume that work is the only or the primary source of self-identity, self-conception, or fulfillment. Except for some stimulating jobs that demand high skill, creativity, autonomy, or self-determination, many occupations offer little intrinsic satisfaction and are endured only because the need for income and financial security provides no other option. It may be that most work does not provide conceptual or emotional meaning. On the contrary many jobs are boring, physically demanding, and carried out under oppressive or antagonistic management. Accordingly, people retire without regret or stress and as early a possible.

THE NATURE OF RETIREMENT

Retirement is now normative in most industrial countries (Ekerdt, 1989; Neugarten, 1990). The establishment of Social Security in 1936 was the first step toward making retirement in the United States the norm rather than the exception. For over 50 years workers have come to accept and expect to spend the last years of their lives in retirement. Many workers begin to plan for retirement years before the actual event. In fact from the time people begin to work, pay stubs specify the amount of money deducted for the company's retirement plan and for Social Security. This is a very different situation from that of the 1920s and 1930s, and certainly before then, when few people lived long enough to retire. Those who did could certainly have found it stressful. Few people retired, there was little planning, and no pensions, and those who retired likely did so because of illness or disability. Under those circumstances retirement could legitimately have found its way into stressful life events inventories.

It is noteworthy that in the 1950s no one believed that American workers would ever want to retire and in fact 70 percent said they would never retire (Atchley, 1991). By the 1990s 80 percent of workers looked forward to retirement. This new attitude is reflected in the 73.9 percent of males aged 62 who were in the labor force in 1970 compared to 53.5 percent who remained in the labor force for that age in 1986. For 65-year-old males the numbers were 49.9 percent in 1970 and 30.8 percent in 1986. The corresponding percentages for females were 36.1 percent and 31.9 percent for age 62, 22.1 percent and 18.6 percent for age 65 respectively in 1970 and 1986.

The fact that retirement has not been found to be stressful for the vast majority of retirees does not mean that it is not stressful for some. The 30 percent of retirees who find retirement stressful translates into millions of people.

Among those who find retirement stressful, there are a number of fairly consistent predictors. One of these is an involuntary retirement. Poor health is another consistent predictor of retirement stress and may frequently be the reason why the retirement was involuntary. Loss of income is a third consistent predictor of retirement stress and is frequently linked to early retirement which in turn may have been involuntary. These predictors hold true for both retirement state and transition stress.

Another important predictor from our own research of both retirement state and transition stress is hassles. It should be noted, however, that our hassles variable (Bossé et al., 1992) included health and income as well as marital and social relations problems as described earlier.

While health, income, and involuntary retirement are commonly recognized as predictors of retirement state stress, other predictors include: number of other life events experienced, work saliency, and the absence of prior work stress. The loss of social support following retirement seems to be somewhat controversial. The evidence at this time does not suggest that the loss of social support is a predictor of retirement stress. This may be due to the continuity of qualitative social support after retirement and beyond.

Interestingly, a number of variables in the social and circumstances domains, found to be predictors of retirement state stress, were unrelated to transition stress. It should be noted, however, that little research has differentiated the consequences of the retirement transition from those of retirement state.

Dimensions of personality were related to retirement stress but some differences were found in the traits which were related to retirement state and transition stress. Social and personality variables were independently related to both retirement state and transition stress with social variables about twice as predictive of stress as personality. The effective social variables (other life events and hassles) were consistent across state and transition stress while the personality variables were not (Bossé et al., 1992). From a clinical viewpoint, the relationship of depression to transition stress is probably most interesting since it confirms that retirement transition is a "trouble zone" for some people. Special attention may be advisable for prospective retirees who have had depressive episodes in the past. Clearly more research needs to be done in the domain of personality to better understand its role in the prediction of who finds retirement stressful.

It may also be appropriate to recall the reports of PTSD among World War II and Korean War veterans following their retirement (Van Dyke et al., 1985). Such occurrences appear to result from retirement transition stress and may warrant further investigation into the personality traits or other personal characteristics of veterans who experience PTSD following retirement.

One possible point of departure for such research is the intriguing observation that some degree of difficulty in retirement is experienced by around 30 percent of the sample in six of the studies reviewed above (Atchley, 1975; Blau et al., 1982; Matthews et al., 1982; Braithwaite et al., 1986; Bossé et al., 1991). This suggests that person variables may be involved in retirement stress. Personality definitely affects the perception of stress (Smith and Frohm, 1985; Aldwin, Levenson, Spiro, and Bossé, 1989). Although personality did not play a large role in the final regression model, the pattern of correlations suggests that it is likely that personality has indirect effects on adaptation in retirement via its influence on health status, stress appraisals and the process of coping with the inevitable losses of late life (Aldwin, 1994). The correlation of MMPI-2 scales Pt (Psychasthenia) and Sc (Schizophrenia) with both transition and state stress is of special interest. These constitute a well-known two-point code type which reflects psychological turmoil (Graham, 1990). Future research should seek to discover if, indeed, those who experience the greatest retirement stress are, *ceteris paribus*, distinguished by greatest elevations on these two scales. Interestingly, Pt, Sc, and Pd were three of four MMPI-2 clinical scales which best classified chronic problem drinkers in the Normative Aging Study population (Levenson, Aldwin, Spiro, and Bossé, 1992). Obviously, much more research is needed before any conclusions can be drawn about generally "problematic" personalities and retirement stress.

Some important gender differences have been presumed to exist with regards to retirement stress because female workforce participation has been quite different from that of men. A thorough review of the literature by Gratton and Haug (1983), however, concluded that the adaptation of women to retirement has not been dramatically different from that of men. In this chapter we have attempted to identify gender differences in retirement stress whenever such differences were specified. But future research needs to concentrate much more thoroughly on specifying the precise differences in the experience of retiring for women compared to men. As the present generation of working women reaches retirement age it is hoped that researchers will focus their attention on gender differences in retirement transition and state stress.

Future research needs to pay more attention to the length of time retired and to differentiating retirement transition from retirement state. There also is a need to be more specific about the length of time identified as the retirement transition. In our own research on retirement stress (Bossé et al., 1991, 1992) we defined transition as the first year. In earlier publications, however, inspired by the concept of retirement phases (Atchley, 1976; Ekerdt, Bossé, and Levkoff, 1985) we referred to men retired for up to 18 months as constituting the cohort of recent retirees and compared them to long-term retirees, men retired more than 3 years (Bossé et al., 1990). Though it is clear that transition needs to be differentiated from state, the upper boundary of the transition period remains to be defined. The boundary may be a range of up to 18 months or more based on individual differences related to the retirement event or any of the other predictors of retirement stress described above.

A final observation is that retirees constitute a very heterogeneous group. Just as there is no single definition of retirement itself, there also is no single type of retiree. Any number of factors or combinations thereof could lead to retirement transition or state stress. We have identified some of those factors in the aggregate, to do so in individual cases is a much more subtle task requiring great sensitivity. We see this as a major future challenge for retirement researchers, counselors, and therapists.

REFERENCES

Adams, O., & Lefebvre, L. (1981), Retirement and mortality. *Aging & Work,* 4:115–120.

Aldwin, C. M. (1990), The Elders Life Stress Inventory (ELSI): Egocentric and nonegocentric stress. In: *Stress and Coping in Late Life Families,* ed. M. A. P. Stephens, S. E. Hobfoll, J. H. Crowther, & D. L. Tennenbaum. New York: Hemisphere, pp. 49–69.

———— (1994), *Stress, Coping, and Development: An Integrative Approach.* New York: Guilford Press.

———— Levenson, M. R., Spiro, A., & Bossé, R. (1989), Does emotionality predict stress? Findings from the Normative Aging Study. *J. Pers. Soc. Psychol.,* 56:618–624.

Antonucci, T. C., & Akiyama, H. (1987), Social networks in adult life and a preliminary examination of the convoy model. *J. Gerontol.,* 42:519–527.

Atchley, R. C. (1975), Adjustment to loss of job at retirement. *Internat. J. Aging & Hum. Dev.,* 6:17–27.

———— (1976), *The Sociology of Retirement.* New York: Halsted Press.

———— (1991), *Social Forces and Aging.* Belmont, CA: Wadsworth.

Barron, M. L., Streib, G., & Suchman, E. A. (1952), Research on the social disorganization of retirement. *Amer. Soc. Rev.,* 17:479–482.

Blau, Z. S., Oser, S. T., & Stephens, R. C. (1982), Patterns of adaptation in retirement: A comparative analysis. In: *Coping With Medical Issues: Aging,* ed. A. Kolker & P. E. Ahmed. New York: Elsevier Biomedical, pp. 119–138.

Bossé, R., Aldwin, C. M., Levenson, M. R., & Ekerdt, D. J. (1987), Mental health differences among retirees and workers: Findings from the Normative Aging Study. *Psychol. Aging*, 2:383–389.

——— ——— Spiro, A., III, & Mroczek, D. K. (1993), Change in social support after retirement: Longitudinal findings from the Normative Aging Study. *J. Gerontol.*, 48:210–217.

——— ——— ——— Workman-Daniels, K. (1991), How stressful is retirement? Findings from the Normative Aging Study. *J. Gerontol.*, 46:9–14.

——— ——— ——— ——— (1989), Psychological symptoms and retirement. *The Gerontologist*, 29:43A. Abstract presented at Annual Scientific Meeting of the Gerontological Society of America, Minneapolis, Minnesota, November.

——— ——— ——— ——— Ekerdt, D. J. (1990), Differences in social support among retirees and workers: Findings from the Normative Aging Study. *Psychol. Aging*, 5:41–47.

——— Levenson, M. R. Spiro, A., III, Aldwin, C. M., & Mroczek, D. K. (1992), For whom is retirement stressful? Findings from the Normative Aging Study. *L'Anneé Gérontologique* (Facts and Research in Gerontology), Canadian Ministry of Health, pp. 393–408.

Braithwaite, V. A., Gibson, D. M., & Bosly-Craft, R. (1986), An exploratory study of poor adjustment styles among retirees. *Soc. Sci. Med.*, 23:493–499.

Butcher, J. N., Aldwin, C. M., Levenson, M. R., Ben Porath, Y., Spiro, A. III, & Bossé, R. (1991), Personality and aging: A study of the MMPI-2 in older men. *Psychol. Aging*, 6:361–370.

——— Dahlstrom, W. G., Graham, J. R., Tellegen, A., & Kaemer, B. (1989), *Minnesota Multiphasic Personality Inventory (MMPI-2): Manual for Administration and Scoring*. Minneapolis: University of Minnesota Press.

Carstensen, L. L. (1987), Age-related changes in social activity. In: *Handbook of Clinical Gerontology*, ed. L. L. Carstensen & B. A. Edelstein. New York: Pergamon Press, pp. 222–237.

Cherry, D. L., Zarit, S. H., & Krauss, I. K. (1984), The structure of post-retirement adaptation for recent and longer-term women retirees. *Exp. Aging Res.*, 10:231–236.

Crawford, M. (1972), Retirement as a psycho-social crisis. *J. Psychosom. Res.*, 16:375–380.

——— (1973), Retirement: A rite de passage. *Soc. Rev.*, 21:447–461.

Crowley, J. E. (1985), Longitudinal effects of retirement on men's psychological and physical well being. In: *Retirement Among American Men*, ed. H. S. Parnes, J. E. Crowley, R. J. Haurin, L. J. Less, W. R. Morgan, F. L. Mott, & G. Nestel. Lexington, MA: Lexington Books, pp. 147–173.

Darnley, F., Jr. (1975), Adjustment to retirement: Integrity or despair? *Fam. Coord.*, 24:217–221.

Derogatis, L. R. (1983), *SCL-90-R Revised Manual*. Baltimore, MD: Johns Hopkins University School of Medicine.

Ekerdt, D. J. (1989), Retirement preparation. In: *Annual Review of Gerontology and Geriatrics*, ed. M. P. Lawton, Vol. 9. New York: Springer, pp. 321–356.

——— Bossé, R., & Levkoff, S. (1985), An empirical test for phases of retirement: Findings from the Normative Aging Study. *J. Gerontol.*, 40:95–101.

Elwell, F., & Maltbie-Crannell, A. B. (1981), The impact of role loss upon coping resources and life satisfaction of the elderly. *J. Gerontol.*, 36:223–232.

Eysenck, H. J., & Eysenck, S. B. (1968), *Manual of the Eysenck Personality Inventory.* San Diego, CA: Educational & Industrial Testing Service.

Floderus, B. (1974), Psycho-social factors in relation to coronary heart disease and associated risk factors (Special issue). *Nordisk Hygienisk Tid Skrift Supplementum,* 6.

Floyd, F. J., Haynes, S. G., Doll, E. R., Winemiller, D., Lemsky, C., Burgy, T. M., Werle, M., & Heilman, N. (1992), Assessing retirement satisfaction and perceptions of retirement experiences. *Psychol. Aging,* 7:609–621.

Frederickson, B. L., & Carstensen, L. L. (1990), Choosing social partners: How old age and anticipated endings make people more selective. *Psychol. Aging,* 5:335–347.

Friedmann, E. A., & Orbach, H. L. (1974), Adjustment to retirement. In: *American Handbook of Psychiatry,* ed. S. Arieti. New York: Basic Books, pp. 610–645.

George, L. K. (1980), *Role Transitions in Later Life.* Monterey, CA: Brooks/Cole.
————— Maddox, G. (1977), Subjective adaptation to loss of work role: A longitudinal study. *J. Gerontol.,* 32:456–462.

Graham, J. R. (1990), *MMPI-2: Assessing Personality and Psychopathology.* New York: Oxford University Press.

Gratton, B., & Haug, M. R. (1983), Decision and adaptation: Research on female retirement. *Res. Aging,* 5:59–76.

Harris, L., & Associates (1981), *Aging in the Eighties: America in Transition.* Washington, DC: National Council on Aging.

Haynes, S. G., McMichael, A. J., & Tyroler, H. A. (1978), Survival after early and normal retirement. *J. Gerontol.,* 33:269–278.

Hill, E. A., & Dorfman, L. T. (1982), Reaction of housewives to the retirement of their husbands. *Fam. Rel.,* 31:195–200.

Holmes, T. H., & Rahe, R. H. (1967), The social readjustment rating scale. *J. Psychosom. Res.,* 11:213–218.

Hooker, K., & Ventis, D. G. (1984), Work ethic, daily activities, and retirement satisfaction. *J. Gerontol.,* 39:478–484.

Kahn, R. L., & Antonucci, T. C. (1980), Convoys over the life course: Attachment, roles, and social support. In: *Life Span Development and Behavior,* Vol. 3, ed. P. B. Baltes & O. G. Brim, Jr. New York: Academic Press, pp. 253–286.

Keating, N. C., & Cole, P. (1980), What do I do with him 24 hours a day? Changes in the housewife role after retirement. *Gerontologist,* 20:84–89.

Levenson, M. R., Aldwin, C. M., Spiro, A., & Bossé, R. (1992), Personality, alcohol problems and heavy drinking in older men. *The Gerontologist,* 32:259. Abstract presented at Annual Scientific Meeting of the Gerontological Society of America, Washington, DC, November.

MacBride, A. (1976), Retirement as a life crisis: Myth or reality? *Can. Psychiat. Assn. J.,* 21:547–556.

Matthews, A. M., & Brown, K. H. (1987), Retirement as a critical life event. *Res. Aging,* 9:548–571.

———— ———— Davis, C. K., & Denton, M. A. (1982), A crisis assessment technique for the evaluation of life events: Transition to retirement as an example. *Can. J. Aging,* 1:28–39.

Mattila, V. J., Joukamaa, M. I., & Salokangas, R. K. R. (1988), Retirement, ageing and adaptation (The Turva Project) Part II: Design of the project and some preliminary findings. *Eur. J. Psychiatry,* 2:46–58.

———— ———— ———— (1989), Retirement, aging, psychosocial adaptation and mental health. *Acta Psychiat. Scand.,* 80:356–367.

McMahan, C. A., & Ford, T. R. (1955), Surviving the first five years of retirement. *J. Gerontol.,* 10:212–215.

Miller, M. (1979), *Suicide After Sixty: The Final Alternative.* New York: Springer.

Murrell, S., Norris, F. H., & Hutchins, G. L. (1984), Distribution and desirability of life events in older adults: Population and policy implications. *J. Commun. Psychol.,* 12:301–311.

Myers, R. J. (1954), Factors in interpreting mortality after retirement. *J. Amer. Stat. Assn.,* 49:499–509.

Neugarten, B. L. (1990), Retirement in the life course. *Triangle,* 29:119–125.

Palmore, E. B., Burchett, B. M., Fillenbaum, G. G., George, L. K., & Wallman, L. M. (1985), *Retirement Causes and Consequences.* New York: Springer.

———— Fillenbaum, G. G., & George, L. K. (1984), Consequences of retirement. *J. Gerontol.,* 39:109–116.

———— Stone, J. (1973), Predictors of longevity: A follow-up of the aged in Chapel Hill. *Gerontologist,* 13:88–90.

Parnes, H. (1981), *Work and Retirement.* Cambridge, MA: Massachusetts Institute of Technology Press.

Pary, R., Turns, D. M., & Tobias, C. R. (1986), A case of delayed recognition of posttraumatic stress disorder (Letter to the Editor). *Amer. J. Psychiatry,* 143:941.

Peretti, P. O., & Wilson, C. (1975), Voluntary and involuntary retirement of aged males and their effect on emotional satisfaction, usefulness, self-image, emotional stability, and interpersonal relationships. *Internat. J. Aging Hum. Dev.,* 6:131–138.

Pomerantz, A. S. (1991), Delayed onset of PTSD: Delayed recognition or later disorder? (Letter to the Editor). *Amer. J. Psychiatry,* 148:1609.

Powers, E. A., & Bultena, G. L. (1972), Characteristics of decreased dropouts in longitudinal research. *J. Gerontol.,* 27:530–535.

Reichard, S., Livson, F., & Peterson, P. (1962), *Aging and Personality: A Study of Eighty-Seven Older Men.* New York: John Wiley.

Richardson, V., & Kilty, K. M. (1991), Adjustment to retirement: Continuity vs. discontinuity. *Internat. J. Aging Hum. Dev.,* 33:151–169.

Rowland, K. F. (1977), Environmental events predicting death for the elderly. *Psychol. Bull.,* 84:349–372.

Sagy, S., & Antonovsky, A. (1992), The family sense of coherence and the retirement transition. *J. Marr. Fam.,* 54:983–993.

Salokangas, R. K. R., & Joukamaa, M. (1991), Physical and mental health changes in retirement age. *Psychother. Psychosom.,* 55:100–107.

Smith, T. W., & Frohm, K. B. (1985), What's so unhealthy about hostility? Construct validity and psychosocial correlates of the Cook and Medley Ho Scale. *Health Psychol.,* 4:503–520.

Streib, G., & Schneider, C. J. (1971), *Retirement in American Society: Impact and Process.* Ithaca, NY: Cornell University Press.

Szinovacz, M. E. (1980), Female retirement: Effects on spousal roles and marital adjustment. *J. Fam. Issues,* 1:423–440.

Thompson, G. B. (1973), Work versus leisure roles: An investigation of morale among employed and retired men. *J. Gerontol.,* 28:339–344.

Tyhurst, J. S., Salk, L., & Kennedy, M. (1957), Mortality, morbidity and retirement. *Amer. J. Pub. Health,* 47:1134–1144.

Van Dyke, C., Zilberg, N. J., & McKinnon, J. A. (1985), Posttraumatic stress disorder: A thirty-year delay in a World War II veteran. *Amer. J. Psychiatry,* 142:1070–1073.

Wheaton, B. (1990), Life transitions, role histories, and mental health. *Amer. Soc. Rev.,* 55:209–223.

Part V

Treatment and Future Considerations

Chapter 16
Lessons Learned in the Treatment of Chronic, Complicated Posttraumatic Stress Disorder

Patrick A. Boudewyns, Ph.D., Leon A. Hyer, Ed.D., A.B.P.P., Darlene S. Klein, Ph.D., Charles W. Nichols, Ph.D., and Edwin V. Sperr, Ph.D.

Although people respond differently to traumatic stressors, it is clear that under the right conditions stressful events can lead to a chronic form of posttraumatic stress disorder (PTSD) that seriously disrupts work, social functioning, intimate relationships, emotional self-control, and mental coherence. Over time, the trauma victim shifts into a fully defensive mode of existence in

Most of our research data and clinical insights are based on work with Vietnam veteran patients who have been treated through our Special Inpatient Treatment Program for Post-Traumatic Stress Disorders at the Department of Veterans Affairs Medical Center in Augusta, Georgia. We are also grateful to those many veterans who have unselfishly volunteered as subjects in studies carried out through the Augusta War Trauma Project over the past 10 years.

Acknowledgments. The writing of this chapter was supported in part by resources from the Department of Veterans Affairs Research Service. We also wish to thank Ms. Kimberly White, Ms. Verneida Pinkston, and Ms. Doris Megginson for their highly skilled technical assistance in helping to prepare the manuscript.

which fear, anger, confusion, and impulsiveness predominate. The disturbance of life-style and personality becomes so pervasive and toxic that even those intimately connected to the victim become dysfunctional and can themselves be traumatized by their interactions with the victim (Matsakis, 1988).

This chronic form of PTSD has been identified by several researchers with such labels as "complicated reactivated trauma" (Solomon, Garb, Bleich, and Grupper, 1987; Catherall, 1989; Keane, 1989; Hiley-Young, 1992), "Traumatic Personality" (Hyer, Woods, and Boudewyns, 1991), and "Type-II PTSD" (Terr, 1991).

The psychological and behavioral consequences of this complicated, chronic PTSD have much in common with current trauma-based reconceptualizations of borderline personality disorder. Indeed, personality scale profiles among Vietnam combat veterans with chronic PTSD reflect borderline personality styles in 52 percent of the cases (Hyer et al., 1991). The basic difference between chronic PTSD and borderline personality disorder may be the nature and timing of the trauma (White, 1948). Severe or chronic trauma in childhood leads to borderline personality if not adequately resolved. Severe war trauma in late adolescence and the early twenties leads to chronic PTSD if not treated and resolved. Those veterans with unresolved trauma reactions from childhood *and* Vietnam appear to have a mix of PTSD and borderline personality disorder along with other Axis I diagnoses (primarily substance abuse and dependence) which is extremely difficult to treat. These multiply traumatized and disordered veterans are the type of patient we are seeing in our special inpatient PTSD treatment program today (Boudewyns, Albrecht, Hyer, and Talbert, 1991; Boudewyns, Woods, Hyer, and Albrecht, 1991; Hyer et al., 1991).

Military combatants in Vietnam are a group with a high incidence of chronic PTSD. The largest and most sophisticated epidemiological study ever conducted on veterans (Kulka, Schlenger, Fairbank, Hough, Jordan, Marmar, and Weiss, 1990) demonstrated that even the most dire predictions concerning long-term effects of combat trauma were underestimates. Over 30 percent of male veterans suffered from PTSD at some time after Vietnam, and over 15 percent still suffered from PTSD at the time of the study—approximately 10 to 20 years after their service in Vietnam.

Sufferers of chronic PTSD report a long list of trauma-related problems. Their psychological lives have become so disorganized and intense that many endorse most items on symptom checklist measures (Derogatis, 1983) to some degree, and usually at very distressing levels of intensity. These symptoms cluster around themes of dysthymia, depression, suicidal rumination, anxiety, anger, hypervigilance, paranoia, bizarre mental experiences, depersonalization, derealization, dissociation, substance abuse, avoidant and schizoid themes, physical complaints, alienation from self, amotivational syndromes, guilt, and incompetence, in addition to endorsing most DSM-III-R (APA, 1987) symptoms of PTSD. On the Minnesota Multiphasic Personality Inventory—2 (Hathaway and McKinley, 1989) and the Millon Clinical Multiaxial Inventory—II (Millon, 1987) they endorse a high percentage of deviant responses relative to normal populations, and significantly more than individuals diagnosed with one or two discrete Axis I or Axis II disorders (Hyer, 1993). As an illustration of the power and longevity of chronic PTSD, Table 16.1 lists the average degree of symptom frequency and intensity of the core symptoms of PTSD reported by a sample of 80 Vietnam veterans with chronic PTSD, using the Clinician-Administered PTSD Scale (Blake, Weathers, Nagy, Kaloupek, Klauminzer, Charney, and Keane, 1990). Results show substantial turmoil. Core PTSD symptoms, as well as associated symptoms, tend to be experienced at least weekly at a level described as distressing.

Two decades of clinical work with traumatized combat veterans at the Augusta VA have convinced us that chronic PTSD can eventually destroy functioning beyond the point where psychotherapy and education can fully repair the damage. It takes years of intensive therapy to rebuild these individuals. Even with this effort, many achieve only a marginal psychological stability. They continue to feel vulnerable and to have a limited capacity to independently manage the stresses and hassles of normal living, relating

TABLE 16.1
Mean Frequency and Intensity Ratings of PTSD Symptoms, Based on the Clinician-Administered PTSD Scale (CAPS-1), for Vietnam Veterans Diagnosed with Chronic Combat-Related PTSD (N = 80)

PTSD Symptoms	Frequency[a]	Intensity[a]
DSM-III-R Criterion B:		
Intrusive Recollections	3.21	2.96
Distress when Exposed to Events	2.49	2.66
Acting as if Event Is Recurring	1.23	2.01
Recurrent Dreams	2.76	2.94
DSM-III-R Criterion C:		
Efforts to Avoid Trauma Thoughts	3.12	2.53
Efforts to Avoid Trauma Activities	2.81	2.44
Inability to Recall Trauma	1.81	1.81
Diminished Interest in Activities	2.69	2.78
Feelings of Detachment/Estrangement	3.32	2.49
Restricted Range of Affect	2.63	2.54
Sense of Foreshortened Future	2.35	2.19
DSM-III-R Criterion D:		
Difficulty Falling or Staying Asleep	3.51	3.32
Irritability or Outbursts of Anger	2.72	2.95
Difficulty Concentrating	3.15	2.70
Hypervigilance	3.46	2.85
Startle Response	2.47	2.47
Physiologic Overreactivity	1.96	2.05
Associated Symptoms		
Feelings of Guilt	2.48	2.55
Survivor Guilt	2.20	2.22
Homicidal Ideation	1.24	1.44
Disillusionment with Authority	2.85	2.59
Hopelessness	2.66	2.42
Memory Impairment	2.80	2.65
Sadness	3.06	2.94
Feeling Overwhelmed	2.04	2.30

[a]A frequency rating of one (1) or greater *and* an intensity rating of two (2) or greater reflect significant problems with a particular symptom, and should be considered a symptom endorsement. The maximum rating on both scales is four (4).

to others, and working. The damage done to family systems and to the individuals within these systems can be extensive and lasting.

GUIDELINES FOR THE TREATMENT OF CHRONIC PTSD

Although individuals suffering with chronic PTSD resist change, meaningful gains do occur through treatment. Productive therapy, however, requires a clear understanding of basic treatment issues specific to chronic, complicated PTSD. Inappropriate interventions, or good interventions poorly timed, may even have a destructive result.

These patients are frightened by therapy. They want to change, but have extreme difficulty trusting anyone with power over them. They maintain a defensive, suspicious orientation in which they expect the worst and prepare for it. This attitude is expressed through hypersensitivity, cognitive distortions, and powerful overreaction to threatening aspects of therapy. If treatment causes an accumulation of incompletely processed defensive reactions, and these can accumulate rapidly, the patient will begin to disconnect from therapy. At best, progress will become more difficult. At worst, this overreaction can lead to termination of therapy, to physical assault of a therapist, or to patient suicide.

During the therapeutic process, patients typically pass through three or four developmental states (Herman, 1992). The first is a highly disorganized state in which the patient is overwhelmed by symptoms and feelings of extreme vulnerability. The second is a state in which threats and symptoms are sufficiently controlled and the patient is able to thoughtfully process information. In the third state, the patient has learned enough about his or her condition, and has developed enough skill in therapy, to tolerate and benefit from deep emotional work and direct trauma work. In the fourth state, the individual has attained a modest control over emotions and behaviors. The patients are beginning to change fundamental aspects of their character, and are committed to continuing that process. The person is then ready to move on to planning for the achievement of personal goals, family therapy, and community reconnection work.

Therapy must be state appropriate. For example, although family therapy is very important, initiating it while the veteran is in the first state would be damaging to the patient and the family. Therapy goals are matched to the therapeutic state of the patient. Structuring therapy is complex and must be a flexible process. A patient can shift to different states very quickly during therapy sessions, depending on current level of stress tolerance and the ability to focus. Therapists must constantly track and respond to the patient's changing state.

Within this state framework, we work on four superordinate therapeutic objectives: (1) shifting the locus of personal control inward so the patient feels less vulnerable to external forces; (2) rehabilitating core psychological processes damaged by chronic PTSD in order to restore capacities for stable, competent, self-directed functioning; (3) dealing directly with trauma memories; and (4) facilitating reconnections to others.

Each of these are long-term treatment objectives; therapy with these individuals may take years. Repeated hospitalizations may be required for continued rehabilitation, and are not necessarily a sign of relapse. Therapy progresses slowly, often beginning with education or other preparatory work, then shifting to more advanced skill development and cognitive restructuring. We work simultaneously on these objectives, often at different paces, interweaving basic work in one area with more advanced work in another.

In our population, some patients are able to advance fairly quickly. Others are so limited by extensive psychological disorganization, that they progress slowly toward stability and improved levels of functioning. Using the DSM-III-R Global Assessment of Functioning Scale (GAF) (APA, 1987) as a reference point for change, most of our population enters therapy with a GAF of 25 to 40. A GAF in the 50's after 2 years of therapy is good progress by our standards. Few of our Vietnam chronic PTSD patients progress much beyond a GAF of 70.

ESTABLISHING PERSONAL CONTROL IN A SAFE ENVIRONMENT

The chronic PTSD patient's history of victimization has led to strong, generalized feelings of vulnerability. For the initial phase of treatment, it is essential that the patient be treated in a safe, controlled environment. The normal self-regulation of behavior and emotion has deteriorated through years of dysfunction, so that external controls are needed for them to feel safe enough to concentrate on therapy. When patients begin therapy, they typically feel little or no sense of control over their thoughts, feelings, or events in their lives. They function in a fully defensive mode, fighting against perceived threats to their stability from the outside world, and from their inner world (e.g., frightening intrusive thoughts and emotions).

Thinking is distorted and rigid. Emotionality is intense and often expressed in extreme overreaction to seemingly minor events. They feel unable to master life skills, cope with routine stress, or accomplish desired goals. They are essentially controlled by circumstances, not by internal goal-directed plans. They have few internal psychological defenses to cope with stress in a competent manner. They feel safe only in the absence of these threatening events. Avoidance is their typical solution, and it takes many forms, including self-medication with drugs or alcohol, living in isolation, rejecting social contact, avoiding situations in which the outcomes are uncertain, and suicide.

It may be difficult to establish safety on an outpatient basis, because veterans with chronic PTSD often live in chaotic and stressful environments. In our inpatient program we create a "safe haven" devoted to the treatment of chronic PTSD.

Safety is created by structuring the milieu to minimize or eliminate stressors and external events that either retraumatize the patient or activate trauma memories and related emotional responses. The treatment team must exert tight controls to accomplish this. However, patients' awareness that powerful others are exerting control over them often triggers trauma-based fear and resistance. To counter this fear, administrative processes are open and shared with the unit community. Whenever possible, we inform patients in advance of the methods by which administrative and clinical power will be exercised. Predictability reduces the fear that power will be abused. It also allows patients to experience the benevolent use of power.

Victim-based transference to staff are minimized by providing rules which specify counter-therapeutic behaviors and their consequences. Patients sign written contracts to acknowledge their acceptance of these rules. For example, we spell out policies regarding substance abuse and assaultive behavior before admission, and make clear that a violation will result in an automatic discharge. The staff is given no power to intervene if a violation occurs. We even speak of the patient "discharging himself" to reinforce that the sole responsibility for discharge rests with the patient. This policy promotes personal responsibility and self-control. It also eliminates perceptions that the staff "punishes" patients for violating rules, a perception that can reactivate trauma memories.

Patient–patient interactions must be structured to maximize the exercise of personal power over self and minimize the exercise of manipulative power over others. The structure must also promote the therapeutic goals of the unit and the individual. We accomplish this through a community government empowered with considerable responsibility, by promoting the exercise of free will within carefully defined limits, and by continually demanding respectful behavior toward others while modeling this ourselves.

Safety and trust evolve slowly. Patients test and closely observe the staff for signs of inconsistency or unfairness. When external controls have been accepted as reasonable, fair, and benevolent, patients begin to internalize the decision-making processes we model for them. This promotes the shift from external controls to the development of internal controls. The patient then has less need for defensive hypervigilance. When the cognitive burden of defensiveness and hypervigilance is lifted, attention and the capacity for learning and introspection increase. We can then work more intensively and productively on the rehabilitation objectives.

REHABILITATING CORE PSYCHOLOGICAL PROCESSES

Vietnam veterans with unresolved trauma have lived with PTSD for over 20 years. By the time they come to our program, every major psychological system has been damaged and is dysfunctional. The rebuilding process is intensely challenging. We must use all we know about human functioning and behavior to untangle and repair the many aspects of pathology in the system.

The chronic PTSD veteran requires extensive rebuilding. Attention, concentration, and perceptual processes are impaired. The meaning assigned to many events is distorted by rigid, defensive schemas and by trauma-related affect. Information processing strategies do not support reasoned thought and flexible problem solving, creative planning, or accurate appraisal of outcomes. Self-perception can be quite distorted.

Social skills and the capacity for intimacy and interpersonal engagement are seriously limited. The normal maturation through life stages has been blocked. The usual accumulation of vocational–life knowledge is limited due to the absorption of attention toward coping with PTSD. Years of vulnerability and disorganization may have attracted "bad luck" and negative influences. Family systems have developed pathological patterns in response to the stress of chronic PTSD. Coping resources are limited, immature, or ineffective. Positive, goal-directed functioning has been replaced by impulsivity and protective reactions.

Poorly controlled anger responses may have led to incarceration and further trauma. Drugs and alcohol used to self-medicate PTSD symptoms are problems in their own right. The person is in a constant state of hypervigilance, fear, and arousal. This often leads to various physical symptoms and diseases, either through stress-related mechanisms or denial mechanisms.

How do we rebuild such a person? In our program, first we educate our patients about chronic PTSD. We teach them about anxiety and anger processes and how to manage arousal states. We teach assertiveness, rational thinking, decision-making, interpersonal communication, and stress management. We consider spiritual issues. We have a class on intimacy and sexuality problems in chronic PTSD. We balance this with leisure activities and independent journal work. We pull it all together in an intense process therapy group.

Most of the content of these courses is focused on dealing with problems: negative emotions, interpersonal conflict, and coping with stressors. In this population, years of dysfunction and the constant experience of threat have caused most to abandon the pursuit of meaningful personal goals. Their motivational focus has become survival and defense. For many chronic PTSD sufferers, a good day is just a day where nothing too painful happens. In treating these individuals we must not only repair the damage, we must recharge their motivational batteries and help them reestablish connection to meaningful goals.

Perhaps more important than the desirability of adding this dimension to treatment, is the therapeutic power of this component. When life's focus shifts from survival to the positive energy of pursuing valued goals, the person has a reason to live—a reason to get up in the morning, a reason to continue the struggle against PTSD, and a reason to fight for life. Treatment of this severe disorder is a fight for life. It can only be sustained for the necessary period of years if skills are developed and activities targeted that begin to lead to desired outcomes.

In structuring our rehabilitation of motivational processes, we follow Martin Ford's (1992) Motivational Systems Theory conceptualization that identifies three basic processes of motivation: personal goals, personal agency beliefs, and emotional arousal processes. In the program, we identify and define core personal goals (Nichols, 1991); teach the advantages, necessities, and risks of goal pursuit; integrate lessons in emotional regulation and competency training; and begin formulating strategies that will lead to the achievement of positive outcomes with minimal risk. As competence and confidence increase, goal pursuit expands, positive emotion is generated, and increased stress can be tolerated.

Core psychological components are considered rehabilitated when the person develops a degree of intrapersonal competence that allows them to manage arousal, control perception, organize thought, problem solve, and maintain goal-directed functioning in the face of obstacles. These are the essential skills of living a productive, self-directed life (Ford, 1987).

We have found that having patients participate in this intense education–therapy process, free of psychotropic medication, greatly facilitates our therapeutic objectives. Although we are not opposed to psychotropic medications, we find that being free of psychotropics at least during the treatment phase has important advantages, perhaps the most important of these being an increased capacity for learning. Also, many patients have a long history of medication use. Taking a drug holiday disrupts a state of equilibrium and acts as a catalyst for change by forcing them to deal with their pain from a different perspective. Emotions are more available and more accurately perceived. When patients experience success without medications, either in coping with a difficult or frightening emotion, or mastering a new skill, they cannot attribute the success to medications, and this builds a sense of competence and self-esteem.

TRAUMA WORK

Reliving or "telling the trauma story" (Herman, 1992) to promote resolution, and/or using therapeutic exposure to reduce or extinguish the conditioned emotional response (Boudewyns and Shipley, 1983; Keane, Fairbank, Caddell, and Zimering, 1989; Boudewyns and Hyer, 1990) should probably not be carried out early in the therapeutic process with complicated, chronic PTSD patients. These patients may not have the emotional control or energy to profit from these techniques. The capacity for meaningful integration and extinction of the trauma experience into existing functional schemas may be limited by widespread defensive blocks and resistance to the trauma material. Exposure type therapy may be more successfully carried out early in therapy with nonchronic sufferers of PTSD (Foa, Rothbaum, Riggs, and Murdock, 1991).

In our program we try to help the patient set a pace toward resolution that is commensurate with their capacity to handle this difficult work. Nevertheless, when the patient is ready, trauma work involving reexperiencing and/or reprocessing the memory of the trauma can be very valuable and should be encouraged by the therapist.

PSYCHOSOCIAL IMPACT OF CHRONIC PTSD AND RECONNECTION WORK

Herman (1992) coined the term *reconnection* to refer to the phase of therapy in which the trauma victim begins to reestablish healthy interpersonal contacts with family, community, and co-workers. Over time, PTSD-driven behavior seems to contaminate others and to spawn pathology in the social systems of which the veteran has been a member. Most chronic PTSD survivors have used avoidance to manage threat and symptom intensity, and this increases isolation from family and friends, while work environments may become intolerable. The disconnection fosters a loss of identity and frightening feelings of self-alienation. This alienation and dissociation from the self can lead to temporary psychotic states.

MARITAL AND FAMILY DYSFUNCTION

Because of the compelling nature of traumatic experiences, it is common for trauma victims with PTSD to be more focused on the past trauma than the immediate present (Lansky and Karger, 1989). They may not even be aware of the tremendous impact their PTSD symptoms have on those closest to them.

The Vietnam veteran with PTSD tends to be preoccupied not only with intrusive reexperiencing phenomena, but also with the significance the Vietnam experience has for him. He is unable to concentrate on and commit himself to his current interpersonal responsibilities, and tends to rely on withdrawal to control his unpredictable moods and behavior, and to provide the freedom to focus on himself. The chronic PTSD veteran continues to engage in the distancing tactics which allowed him to engage in acts of aggression during war which are completely unacceptable during peacetime (Janoff-Bulman, 1992). He seems to be more seduced by the memories, the PTSD symptoms, and his identity struggle than by his female partner.

All of this is justifiably confusing to the wives and girl friends of these veterans. The veterans' instability and unpredictability chip away at the foundation of intimate relationships, which require trust and sharing. The women often feel shut out, isolated, and can find no validation for their feelings within or outside their relationship. Interestingly, these women are often not dealing with the disillusionment of a changed postcombat husband, because they had married him some time after combat. Yet, they often seem surprised by the severity of his disability.

Numbing and withdrawal are the PTSD symptoms most often cited by female partners as the most damaging to the relationship (DeFazio and Pascucci, 1984; Rabin and Nardi, 1991). Emotional numbing and interpersonal detachment create a wall around the veteran that precludes intimacy. Numerous studies of Vietnam veterans have found that these couples lack genuine closeness, in terms of self-disclosure, affectional expression, and sexual behavior (Roberts, Penk, Gearing, Robinowitz, Dolan, and Patterson, 1982; DeFazio and Pascucci, 1984; Rosenheck and Thomson, 1986). Williams and Williams (1987) note that veterans with PTSD are often unable to empathize with others' pain, and tend to become more distant when family members need support.

Support (especially from families) has been shown to moderate veterans' PTSD symptoms (Solomon, Waysman, and Mikulincer, 1990). Social support and PTSD appear to be incompatible, however, in that PTSD veterans tend to reject sources of potential support and wives may lose the capacity to offer it, due to the stress of the relationship (Shehan, 1987). One group of Vietnam

veterans' wives complained of isolation due to the veterans' paranoia, intolerance of crowds, and reactivity to noises (Maloney,
1988). The couples seemed to be caught up in mutual hypervigilance: he of the family and the outside world, and she of his
unpredictable (and at times violent) behavior and symptoms. Williams and Williams (1987) note that veterans' jealousy and tendency to frequently relocate can isolate the entire family.

Many studies of Vietnam veterans' relationships have reported
a lack of cohesion, or sense of emotional bonding (e.g., Silver
and Iacono, 1986; Kulka et al., 1990). However, Brown (1984)
describes veterans' family systems as enmeshed (i.e., interperson-
ally intrusive) and as having undifferentiated role boundaries.
She notes that family members "define themselves only in relation to the veteran and his problems" (p. 375). Coughlan and
Parkin (1987) compare PTSD veteran families to single-parent
families in terms of the role overload of the women. Female partners often describe themselves as caretakers of the home, family,
and the veteran, with no reciprocity from the veteran. It is likely
that these families do lack emotional closeness, but that members
are overly dependent upon one another, and thereby appear enmeshed relative to their isolation from the larger society.

The veteran's reluctance to communicate Vietnam experiences
to his partner may foster a communication style that involves with-
holding of information. Williams and Williams (1987) suggest
that veterans often either feel the family will not understand or
should be protected from the information. Shehan (1987) also
notes the lack of self-disclosure in veterans with PTSD, and adds
the observation that these veterans and their partners tend to use
defensive styles of communication which do not allow positive
feedback to be exchanged.

In the face of such poor communication, it is not surprising
that these couples have difficulty resolving conflict. Verbosky and
Ryan (1988) note that partners of Vietnam veterans may rely on
either passivity or aggression to resolve conflict. Carroll, Rueger,
Foy, and Donahoe (1985) report that veterans with PTSD exhibit
more general hostility and physical aggression toward their partners than do veterans without PTSD. In a national study, Kulka

et al. (1990) found that more acts of domestic violence were reported by veterans with PTSD than those without diagnosable PTSD. Solomon, Waysman, Avitzur, and Enoch (1991) found Israeli veterans' PTSD to be associated with wives' suffering a variety of psychiatric symptoms (e.g., depression, phobic anxiety, obsessive compulsive symptoms, paranoid ideation, interpersonal sensitivity, and hostility). Female partners of Vietnam veterans with PTSD have been described as lacking self-esteem and feeling hopeless (Brown, 1984; Williams, 1987). Partners may develop symptoms associated with PTSD, such as anger, withdrawal, poor concentration, insomnia, and self-destructive behaviors (Grueter, 1981; Coughlan and Parkin, 1987; Maloney, 1988). However, reexperiencing and avoidance symptoms are probably most common in relationships that involve direct traumatization of the female partner (e.g., battering) or some intervening family or individual psychopathology.

Seventy-six Vietnam veteran couples participated in a study of the impact of PTSD on their relationships (Klein, 1993). All of the veterans had been exposed to combat and most of the couples were married (six were in long-term cohabiting relationships). Both partners completed self-report measures of various aspects of their relationships, as well as interpersonal skills and psychiatric symptoms; PTSD was assessed by means of a clinical interview. The results indicate that veterans with PTSD reported significantly more problems in the areas of conflict resolution, communication, problem solving, closeness, intimacy, social alienation, relationship satisfaction, and psychiatric symptoms than did veterans who did not meet the diagnostic criteria for PTSD. Female partners of PTSD veterans reported significantly more problems in some areas of conflict resolution, closeness, intimacy, relationship satisfaction, and psychiatric symptoms than did partners of veterans without PTSD. Interestingly, female partners of veterans with PTSD tended to describe their relationships, themselves, and their veteran partners in more positive terms than did the veterans.

PARENTAL INADEQUACY

Traumas destroy basic assumptions, such as invulnerability, the justness and comprehensibility of the world, and positive self-evaluations (Janoff-Bulman, 1992). Both victims and their families' beliefs are shattered, and families may experience the trauma vicariously (Rosenthal, Sadler, and Edwards, 1987). Family members may develop PTSD symptoms, and families struggle with issues of closeness, role clarity, access to support, guilt, control, and difficulty coping with stress (Rosenthal et al., 1987).

Children are caught up in an even more tenuous relationship with their PTSD veteran fathers than are wives. Withdrawal, unpredictability, and poorly controlled emotion and behavior are terribly disconcerting to children. Not only are they deprived of parental nurturing, they are in danger of succumbing to the lessons of their role model fathers. Additionally, children are rarely given an explanation for their fathers' problems, which leaves them at risk for blaming themselves (Matsakis, 1988).

In her survey of counselors at 100 Vet Centers in the United States, Matsakis (1988) describes the following problematic family dynamics: mothers who act essentially as single parents (often trying to compensate for unavailable fathers); alliances between overly stressed mothers and their children; overidentification of children with fathers (secondary traumatization); fathers being overly protective of children; physical and/or emotional abuse; and substance abuse. Problems commonly observed in children of veterans with PTSD include low self-esteem, developmental difficulties in school, aggressiveness, impaired social relationships, PTSD symptoms, and feeling responsible for their fathers' emotional well-being (p. 353).

Rosenheck and Nathan (1985) note that children are greatly affected by the family dysfunction and exposure to the trauma of PTSD symptoms. They may develop symptoms of PTSD, including fears and fantasies containing elements of the father's memories and flashbacks, as well as violent behavior, initial insomnia, and anxiety.

Haley (1984) observes that Vietnam veterans may exhibit increased PTSD symptoms in response to issues of commitment to a female partner and to becoming parents. The roles of husband and father cause anxiety in veterans who previously killed or were placed in dangerous situations involving Vietnamese woman and children. Normal childhood forms of aggressive behavior (especially war games) may trigger memories or the need for control in veteran fathers. The veteran may misinterpret and feel responsible for his child's aggression.

Rosenheck (1985) also notes that as children of World War II combat veterans, some Vietnam veterans struggle with a particularly destructive form of PTSD driven by self-hatred, disillusionment, and social rejection. These veterans suffer from a loss of idealization of war and of their "war hero" fathers. Following the brutal lessons of his Vietnam experience, the veteran son feels betrayed by his country and his own father. This type of PTSD veteran may have been exposed to his father's PTSD, and is typically not the recipient of postcombat fatherly support. The child of the Vietnam veteran, in contrast, is unlikely to harbor any illusions about war, and his or her struggles have yet to be fully discovered.

SOCIAL ROLE IMPAIRMENT

The symptoms of PTSD are often frequent and dramatic, which interferes with the functioning of the veteran in many roles considered typical in our society. Kulka et al. (1990) found that Vietnam veterans with PTSD tended to report greater job instability (e.g., unemployment or frequent job changes), less formal education, briefer relationships (and proportionately more cohabiting rather than marrying), more homelessness or vagrancy, and more arrests than veterans without PTSD. In her longitudinal study Card (1987) also noted that absence from work was more common for veterans with more severe PTSD. Wives tend to be overly responsible for meeting the needs and responsibilities of the family (Coughlan and Parkin, 1987; Williams, 1987; Maloney, 1988; Solomon, 1988; Rabin and Nardi, 1991). Vietnam veterans with

PTSD utilize more federal, state, and private physical and mental health services than those without PTSD (Kulka et al., 1990).

Alcohol abuse, and to a lesser extent drug abuse, is a very frequent problem among Vietnam veterans with chronic PTSD (Boudewyns, Albrecht, Hyer, and Talbert, 1991; Boudewyns, Woods, Hyer, and Albrecht, 1991). Alcohol is often used to suppress or control PTSD symptoms, but may disinhibit aggressive behavior or dissociative experiences (Jelinek and Williams, 1987). Kulka et al. (1990) found substance abuse to be associated with greater job instability, homelessness, and arrests.

Wilson and Zigelbaum (1986) suggest that combat veterans who have not resolved their traumatic experiences are at risk for developing destructive behavior patterns. Due to their combat training and experience, they may slip into "survivor modes" of functioning (p. 309). Common patterns include violent behavior in response to dissociative stimuli, sensation-seeking behavior to maintain high levels of arousal, and creating dangerous situations to satisfy suicidal feelings. Blank (1985) suggests that episodes of sudden, explosive behavior due to flashback experiences are rare, but can result in life-threatening situations for the veteran or others. He notes that there have been hundreds of legal cases in which criminal behavior was believed to be caused by flashback episodes.

The social functioning of the Vietnam veteran with PTSD might most accurately be conceptualized as an interaction between aspects of society, characteristics of the war, and the veteran's coping reactions. The American social climate at the time of the war fostered rejection of institutional control and negative attitudes toward the war and those fighting in it. Government management of the war contributed to confusion and loss of trust. Soldiers were isolated in a foreign environment, camaraderie was not fostered, and substance abuse was common. The young age of the soldiers left them vulnerable to this rejection and confusion, and disrupted normal developmental processes such as job training and family commitment (Cross, 1990). The result was a veteran unprepared to function in society, and a society that was unwilling to nurture his functioning.

Often, veterans shy away from treatment for PTSD because they fear rejection or negative consequences from female partners, clinicians, and other veterans (Brende and Parson, 1985). Those who accept treatment may fear the responsibility that comes with improvement, or may not sustain progress because of the lack of a stable, nurturing environment (Brende and Parson, 1985). Having a supportive spouse and having veteran friends who do not reinforce problems may be more helpful in alleviating symptoms than is professional treatment (Kadushin, 1985).

THERAPEUTIC FOUNDATIONS FOR RECONNECTION

In our program, we are continuously aware of the need to guide therapy toward the reconnection with others and toward solutions to the many social problems they face outside the hospital, even as we work on intrapersonal rehabilitation. As we work to repair dysfunctional processes within the person, we model healthy relationships, and establish trust and therapeutic closeness. Both in therapy and in the unit milieu, we foster communication skills, assertiveness, listening skills, respect for others, and respect for conflicting viewpoints. We are encouraging healthy relationship dynamics and patterns at every turn. We explicitly deal with issues of sexuality and intimacy. Patients are practicing emotional control and developing increased social confidence. They are developing a restored sense of community with fellow veterans. All this is transferable to family interactions and other social settings.

The controlled, therapeutic milieu of the unit is essential for reconnection work. Those patients who develop social competence on the unit are much more likely to succeed in resolving the social problems they face outside the hospital. Although this reconnection work is critically important, for practical reasons most of the direct work is done outside our facility under the guidance of outpatient therapists.

THERAPEUTIC PACE AND INTERWEAVE

Each of the four basic treatment objectives can be pursued through an overlapping interweave of technique and therapeutic focus. The pace at which this occurs and the nature of the inter-weave are critical for therapeutic progress. The pace must be negotiated with the patient, and the patient must be taught to slow the pace if it becomes frightening. The therapist provides opportunities, encourages, and sometimes pushes, but the patient must feel in control or the therapy itself will become traumatizing.

The therapist is initially guiding the patient to repair damage to the fabric of their personality and sense of self. Later, the fabric of relationships is repaired. A strong repair requires tracing many threads of thought and feeling to insure that the strands are intact and the ends are tied securely. New strands must be introduced to strengthen the weave. Each strand touches many others. The foci of therapy alternate across levels of sophistication and depth, and among the four basic objectives. If therapy is progressing, the weave and pace are good. If therapy is deteriorating, or resistance is frequent, the weave and pace must be adjusted.

In therapy with more intact individuals, the worst consequence of therapeutic technique that misses the mark is slowed progress or wasted time. In treating individuals with chronic PTSD, the same minor errors can cause therapeutic regression or dangerous acting out. Chronic PTSD veterans feel so vulnerable and easily overwhelmed that they anticipate threat in every situation that is not clear, and they react accordingly.

Even good technique that is well timed can be misperceived by the patient and become counterproductive. Therapy in which technique is good, but knowledge of the dynamics of the disorder is lacking, can be just as dangerous to the patient. The therapist must be knowledgeable about PTSD and clear about what he or she is trying to accomplish with an intervention, so that unexpected responses or deviations can be shaped to accomplish the original therapeutic goal.

The course of therapy and improvement for patients with chronic PTSD is not a linear progression. Especially in the early phases of treatment, the patient's level of functioning can deteriorate significantly as the existing dysfunctional organization is challenged in preparation for rebuilding. The period of deterioration can last a few months to a year or more, depending on the patient and the conditions of therapy.

As therapy progresses and the rebuilding process leads to more controlled, organized, purposeful, and productive functioning, therapy shifts to an emphasis on teaching the person to become their own therapist. Autonomy and the capacity to continue self-directed therapy and growth toward increasingly competent levels of functioning are the ultimate objectives.

CHALLENGE FOR THE FUTURE: HAVE WE LEARNED OUR LESSON YET?

This chapter has focused on what we have learned about the treatment and rehabilitation of the patient who suffers from complicated, chronic, combat-related PTSD. Recognition of this devastating disorder is the result of a long process of discovering the impact of combat experiences on the young men we send off to war.

"War neurosis" has been observed by military physicians for over a century. The long-term emotional response to combat has gone through many name changes: early in its discovery it was called "shell shock" or "battle neurosis," and somewhat later "soldier's heart," "battle fatigue," or "combat exhaustion."

Over the years there has been discussion in the psychoanalytic literature as to whether war neurosis should be considered as distinct from peace time psychoneurosis, or as a subtype of traumatic neurosis. However, by 1918 Freud saw repression and its effect on the dynamic relationship between the ego, id, and super-ego as the basis of *all* neuroses, and as the unifying theoretical construct that would explain the similarities among all neurotic conflicts (White, 1948). During the first half of this century, this dynamic theory of psychoneurosis strongly influenced abnormal psychology and psychiatry with regard to the long-term psychological sequelae of trauma. Indeed, by the time the American Psychiatric Association published its first Diagnostic and Statistical

Manual (APA, 1952) Freud's influence (along with the influence of Adolph Myer's psychobiological model of mental disorders) was so strong that the section on psychoneurosis specifically discouraged the use of terms such as *traumatic neurosis* or *traumatic reaction.*

The two world wars and the Korean conflict offered ideal laboratories for the collection of data on both the long-term and short-term effects of trauma (e.g., Kardiner, 1941; Grinker and Spiegel, 1945; Dobbs and Wilson, 1960). But these early lessons of war did not seem to change our theorizing or our clinical practice. In the years between the Korean and Vietnam Wars, the notion that traumatic neurosis should be differentiated as a separate diagnostic entity was also not accepted by the authors of the DSM-II (APA, 1968).

The long Vietnam experience again focused our attention on these issues. Fortunately, by this time, experimentally oriented behaviorists, with backgrounds in learning theory, information processing, and epidemiology, uninfluenced by psychoanalytic theory, began to study posttraumatic behavior. Pressure to recognize the psychological effects of combat trauma was also driven by political and social motivations (Williams, 1980). This combination of intellectual openness and political fervor is what finally led to the "elevation" of PTSD from a "syndrome" to a full diagnostic entity in the neurosis-free DSM-III (APA, 1980).

We are now beginning to understand how traumatic events can have devastating and long-term effects, not only on the individual who experiences the trauma, but on all significant others with whom that person interacts. The traumatic experience appears almost to reach across generations. But what about the future; and is prevention possible?

In sum, after every major war, even though we recognized the phenomenon, little was done to prevent such problems in the next conflict. Were we so short-sighted as a society that we really did not care if we were damaging our young soldiers, so long as they fought the good fight? Surely now, after the lessons learned in Vietnam we will not be so short-sighted again.

Will we now also apply those lessons to civilian tragedies? For example, when our children are victimized, will we recognize the potential for disability, and come to their aid with treatment, education, and concern? Will we at last encourage women who experience abuse and sexual violence not to hide their experience in shame, so that we can help them to avoid the long-term effects that this trauma can have on them and their significant others? Have we, as a society, finally learned these lessons? If we have, then we can at least have some hope that researchers and clinicians will find ways to prevent the chronic, treatment-resistant symptoms that we see in our patients today, symptoms that resist change and persist even 20 to 30 years after the trauma has ended.

REFERENCES

American Psychiatric Association (1952), *Diagnostic and Statistical Manual of Mental Disorders*. Washington, DC: American Psychiatric Press.
———— (1968), *Diagnostic and Statistical Manual of Mental Disorders*, 2nd ed. (DSM-II). Washington, DC: American Psychiatric Press.
———— (1980), *Diagnostic and Statistical Manual of Mental Disorders*, 3rd ed. (DSM-III). Washington, DC: American Psychiatric Press.
———— (1987), *Diagnostic and Statistical Manual of Mental Disorders*, 3rd ed., rev. (DSM-III-R). Washington, DC: American Psychiatric Press.
Blake, D., Weathers, F., Nagy, L., Kaloupek, D., Klauminzer, G., Charney, D., & Keane, T. (1990), A clinical rating scale for assessing current and lifetime PTSD: The CAPS-1. *Behav. Assess. Rev.*, 13:187–188.
Blank, A. S. (1985), The unconscious flashback to the war in Viet Nam veterans: Clinical mystery, legal defense, and community problem. In: *The Trauma of War: Stress and Recovery in Viet Nam Veterans*, ed. S. M. Sonnenberg, A. S. Blank, & J. A. Talbott. Washington, DC: American Psychiatric Press, pp. 294–308.
Boudewyns, P. A., Albrecht, J. W., Hyer, L., & Talbert, F. S. (1991), Comorbidity and treatment outcome in inpatients with chronic combat-related PTSD. *Hosp. & Commun. Psychiatry*, 42:847–849.
———— Hyer, L. (1990), Physiological response to combat memories and preliminary treatment outcome in Vietnam veteran PTSD patients treated with direct therapeutic exposure. *Behav. Ther.*, 21:63–87.
———— Shipley, R. H. (1983), *Flooding and Implosive Therapy: Direct Therapeutic Exposure in Clinical Practice*. New York: Plenum Press.

———— Woods, M. G., Hyer, L., & Albrecht, J. W. (1991), Chronic combat-related PTSD and concurrent substance abuse: Implications for treatment of this frequent "dual diagnosis." *J. Traum. Stress*, 4:549–560.

Brende, J. O., & Parson, E. R. (1985), *Vietnam Veterans: The Road to Recovery.* New York: Plenum Press.

Brown, P. C. (1984), Legacies of war: Treatment considerations with Vietnam veterans and their families. *Soc. Work*, 29:372–379.

Card, J. J. (1987), Epidemiology of PTSD in a national cohort of Vietnam veterans. *Clin. Psychol.*, 43:6–17.

Carroll, E. M., Rueger, D. B., Foy, D. W., & Donahoe, C. P. (1985), Vietnam combat veterans with posttraumatic stress disorder: Analysis of marital and cohabitating adjustment. *J. Abnorm. Psychol.*, 94:329–337.

Catherall, D. R. (1989), Differentiating intervention strategies for primary and secondary trauma in post-traumatic stress disorder: The example of Vietnam veterans. *J. Traum. Stress*, 2:289–304.

Coughlan, K., & Parkin, C. (1987), Women partners of Vietnam vets. *J. Psychosoc. Nursing*, 25:25–27.

Cross, H. J. (1990), Social factors associated with post-traumatic stress disorder in Vietnam veterans. In: *Post-traumatic Stress Disorder: Assessment, Differential Diagnosis, and Forensic Evaluation*, ed. C. L. Meek. Sarasota, FL: Professional Resource Exchange, pp. 73–89.

DeFazio, V. J., & Pascucci, N. J. (1984), Return to Ithaca: A perspective on marriage and love in post traumatic stress disorder. *J. Contemp. Psychother.*, 14:76–89.

Derogatis, L. R. (1983), *SCL-90-R: Administration, Scoring, and Procedures Manual*, Vol. 2. Towson, MD: Clinical Psychometric Research.

Dobbs, D., & Wilson, W. P. (1960), Observations on persistence of war neurosis. *Dis. Nerv. Syst.*, 21:686–691.

Foa, E. B., Rothbaum, B. O., Riggs, D. S., & Murdock, T. B. (1991), Treatment of posttraumatic stress disorder in rape victims: A comparison between cognitive-behavioral procedures and counseling. *J. Consult. & Clin. Psychol.*, 59:715–723.

Ford, D. H. (1987), *Humans as Self-Constructing Living Systems: A Developmental Perspective on Behavior and Personality.* Hillsdale, NJ: Lawrence Erlbaum.

Ford, M. E. (1992), *Motivating Humans: Goals, Emotions and Personal Agency Beliefs.* Newbury Park, CA: Sage Publications.

Grinker, R. R., & Spiegel, J. P. (1945), *Men under Stress.* Philadelphia: Blackiston.

Grueter, L. (1981), Families of post-Vietnam stress syndrome. *Fam. Therapist*, 2:16–17.

Haley, S. A. (1984), The Vietnam veteran and his preschool child: Child rearing as a delayed stress in combat veterans. *J. Contemp. Psychother.*, 14:114–121.

Hathaway, S. R., & McKinley, J. C. (1989), *Minnesota Multiphasic Personality Inventory—2: Manual for Administration and Scoring.* Minneapolis: University of Minnesota Press.

Herman, J. L. (1992), *Trauma and Recovery: The Aftermath of Violence—From Domestic Abuse to Political Terror.* New York: Basic Books.

Hiley-Young, B. (1992), Trauma reactivation assessment and treatment: Integrative case examples. *J. Traum. Stress*, 5:545–555.

Hyer, L. (1993), *The Person of the Trauma Victim: Theoretical Issues and Practical Suggestions.* Muncie, IN: Accelerated Development.
—— Woods, G., & Boudewyns, P. A. (1991), A three tier evaluation of post traumatic stress disorder. *J. Traum. Stress,* 4:169–194.
Janoff-Bulman, R. (1992), *Shattered Assumptions: Towards a New Psychology of Trauma.* New York: Free Press.
Jelinek, J. M., & Williams, T. (1987), Post-traumatic stress disorder and substance abuse: Treatment problems, strategies and recommendations. In: *Post-traumatic Stress Disorders: A Handbook for Clinicians,* ed. T. Williams. Cincinnati, OH: Disabled American Veterans, pp. 103–117.
Kadushin, C. (1985), Social networks, helping networks, and Viet Nam veterans. In: *The Trauma of War: Stress and Recovery in Viet Nam veterans,* ed. S. M. Sonnenberg, A. S. Blank, & J. A. Talbott. Washington, DC: American Psychiatric Press, pp. 59–68.
Kardiner, A. (1941), *The Traumatic Neuroses of War.* New York: Hoeber.
Keane, T. M. (1989), Post-traumatic stress disorder: Current status and future directions. *Behav. Ther.,* 20:149–153.
—— Fairbank, J. A., Caddell, J. M., & Zimering, R. T. (1989), Implosive (flooding) therapy reduces symptoms of PTSD in Vietnam combat veterans. *Behav. Ther.,* 20:245–260.
Klein, D. S. (1993), Impact of combat-related PTSD on intimate relationships. Paper presented at the 101st annual convention of the American Psychological Association, Toronto, Ontario, Canada.
Kulka, R. A., Schlenger, W. E., Fairbank, J. A., Hough, R. L., Jordan, B. K., Marmar, C. R., & Weiss, D. S. (1990), *Trauma and the Vietnam War Generation: Report of Findings from the National Vietnam Veterans Readjustment Study.* New York: Brunner/Mazel.
Lansky, M. R., & Karger, J. E. (1989), Post-traumatic nightmares and the family. *Hillside J. Clin. Psychiatry,* 11:169–183.
Maloney, L. J. (1988), Post traumatic stresses on women partners of Vietnam veterans. *Smith Coll. Stud. Soc. Work,* 58:122–143.
Matsakis, A. (1988), *Vietnam Wives.* Kensington, MD: Woodbine House.
Millon, T. (1987), *Manual for the MCMI-II,* 2nd ed. Minneapolis, MN: National Computer Systems.
Nichols, C. W. (1991), *Manual for the Assessment of Core Goals.* Palo Alto, CA: Consulting Psychologists Press.
O'Donahue, W., & Elliott, A. (1992), The current status of post traumatic stress disorder as a diagnostic category: Problems in proposals. *J. Traum. Stress,* 5:421–440.
Rabin, C., & Nardi, C. (1991), Treating post traumatic stress disorder couples: A psychoeducational program. *Commun. Ment. Health J.,* 27:209–224.
Roberts, W. R., Penk, W. E., Gearing, M. L., Robinowitz, R., Dolan, M. P., & Patterson, E. T. (1982), Interpersonal problems of Vietnam combat veterans with symptoms of posttraumatic stress disorder. *J. Abnorm. Psychol.,* 91:444–450.
Rosenheck, R. (1985), Father-son relationships in malignant post-Vietnam stress syndrome. *Amer. J. Soc. Psychiatry,* 1:19–23.

—— Nathan, P. (1985), Secondary traumatization in children of Vietnam veterans. *Hosp. & Commun. Psychiatry*, 36:538–539.

—— Thomson, J. (1986), "Detoxification" of Vietnam war trauma: A combined family-individual approach. *Fam. Process*, 25:559–570.

Rosenthal, D., Sadler, A., & Edwards, W. (1987), Families and post-traumatic stress disorder. *Fam. Therapy Collections*, 22:81–95.

Shehan, C. L. (1987), Spouse support and Vietnam veterans' adjustment to post-traumatic stress disorder. *Family Relat.*, 36:55–60.

Silver, S. M., & Iacono, C. (1986), Symptom groups and family patterns of Vietnam veterans with post-traumatic stress disorders. In: *Trauma and Its Wake*, Vol. 2, ed. C. R. Figley. New York: Brunner/Mazel, pp. 78–96.

Solomon, Z. (1988), The effect of combat-related posttraumatic stress disorder on the family. *Psychiatry*, 51:323–329.

—— Garb, R., Bleich, A., & Grupper, D. (1987), Reactivation of combat-related posttraumatic stress disorder. *Amer. J. Psychiatry*, 144:51–55.

—— Waysman, M., Avitzur, E., & Enoch, D. (1991), Psychiatric symptomatology among wives of soldiers following combat stress reaction: The role of the social network and marital relations. *Anxiety Res.*, 4:213–223.

—— —— Mikulincer, M. (1990), Family functioning, perceived societal support, and combat-related psychopathology: The moderating role of loneliness. *J. Soc. & Clin. Psychol.*, 9:456–472.

Terr, L. C. (1991), Childhood traumas: An outline and overview. *Amer. J. Psychiatry*, 148:10–20.

Verbosky, S. J., & Ryan, D. A. (1988), Female partners of Vietnam veterans: Stress by proximity. *Issues in Mental Health Nurs.*, 9:95–104.

White, R. W. (1948), *The Abnormal Personality*. New York: Roland, 1956.

Williams, C. M. (1987), The veteran system with a focus on women partners. In: *Post-Traumatic Stress Disorders: A Handbook for Clinicians*, ed. T. Williams. Cincinnati, OH: Disabled American Veterans, pp. 169–192.

—— Williams, T. (1987), Family therapy for Vietnam veterans. In: *Post-Traumatic Stress Disorders: A Handbook for Clinicians*, ed. T. Williams. Cincinnati, OH: Disabled American Veterans, pp. 221–231.

Williams, T., Ed. (1980), *Post-Traumatic Stress Disorders of the Vietnam Veteran*. Cincinnati, OH: Disabled American Veterans.

Wilson, J. P., & Zigelbaum, S. D. (1986), Post-traumatic stress disorder and the disposition to criminal behavior. In: *Trauma and Its Wake*, ed. C. R. Figley. New York: Brunner/Mazel, pp. 305–321.

Name Index

Subject Index

About the Author

Thomas W. Miller, Ph.D., A.B.P.P. is Professor at Murray State University in the Departments of Leadership and Counseling and Psychology, Murray, Kentucky, and in the Department of Psychiatry, College of Medicine, University of Kentucky. He received his doctorate from the State University of New York at Buffalo and is a Diplomate of the American Board of Professional Psychology in Clinical Psychology and a Fellow of the American Psychological Association and the American Psychological Society.

Dr. Miller's interest in stressful life events can be traced to his doctoral dissertation, which addressed stress-related aspects of parent-child interaction. Since the late 1960s, Dr. Miller has published more than 100 articles in professional refereed journals and given presentations at a number of national and international symposia and conferences. He has received grant support for several clinical and research projects that focus on the impact of stressful life events in various populations, including children.

More recently, he has served on the task force for interdisciplinary clinical treatment of abusive families, supervised the psychology component of the Domestic Violence Clinic at the University of Kentucky, and along with his colleague, Lane Veltkamp, M.S.W., has overseen the grant support for the study of interdisciplinary treatment of abused families in Kentucky. In 1992, he was recognized with a Special Achievement Award by the American Psychological Association for his contributions to education and prevention and clinical services to children, adolescents, adults, and the elderly, who are victims of abuse in our society.

In 1994, Dr. Miller was awarded the Master Teacher Award at the University of Kentucky. He was the 1996 recipient of the prestigious RHR International Award for Excellence in Consulting Psychology from the American Psychological Association.